COMMUTE

COMMUTE

ERIN WILLIAMS

AN ILLUSTRATED MEMOIR OF FEMALE SHAME

ABRAMS COMICARTS • NEW YORK

Editor: Samantha Weiner
Art Director: Pamela Notarantonio
Managing Editor: Amy Vreeland
Production Manager: Erin Vanderveer

Library of Congress Control Number 2019933068

ISBN 978-1-4197-3674-2

Printed and bound in China
10 9 8 7 6 5 4 3 2 1

Abrams ComicArts books are available at special discounts when purchased in quantity for premiums and promotions as well as fundraising or educational use. Special editions can also be created to specification. For details, contact specialsales@abramsbooks.com or the address below.

Abrams ComicArts® is a registered trademark of Harry N. Abrams, Inc.

ABRAMS The Art of Books
195 Broadway, New York, NY 10007
abramsbooks.com

FOR KATE NOVOTNY
AND CAIT WEISS-ORCUTT

"DESIRE IS NO LIGHT THING."
                    -ANNE CARSON

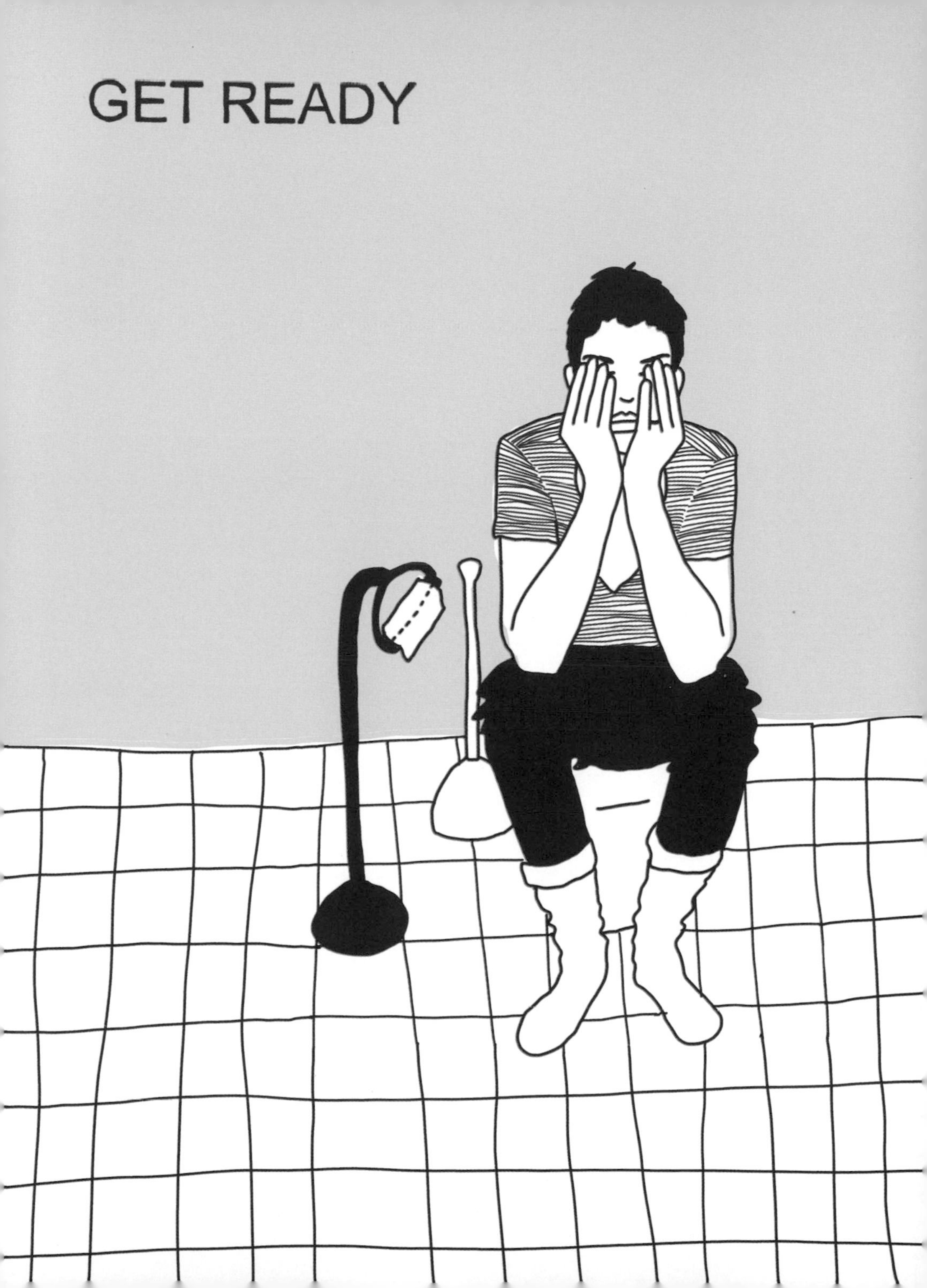
GET READY

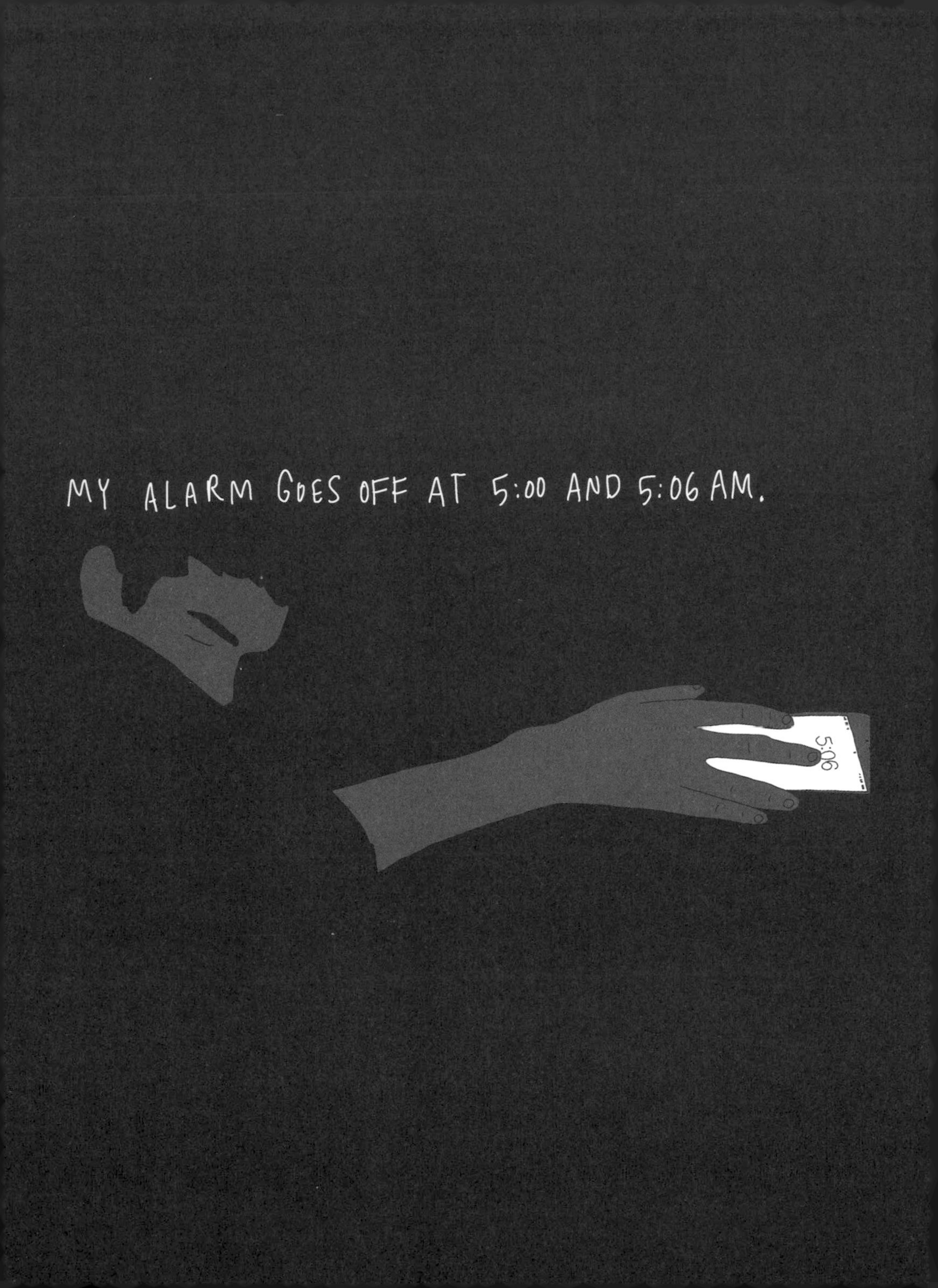
MY ALARM GOES OFF AT 5:00 AND 5:06 AM.
5:06

OUTSIDE, IT'S STILL DARK.

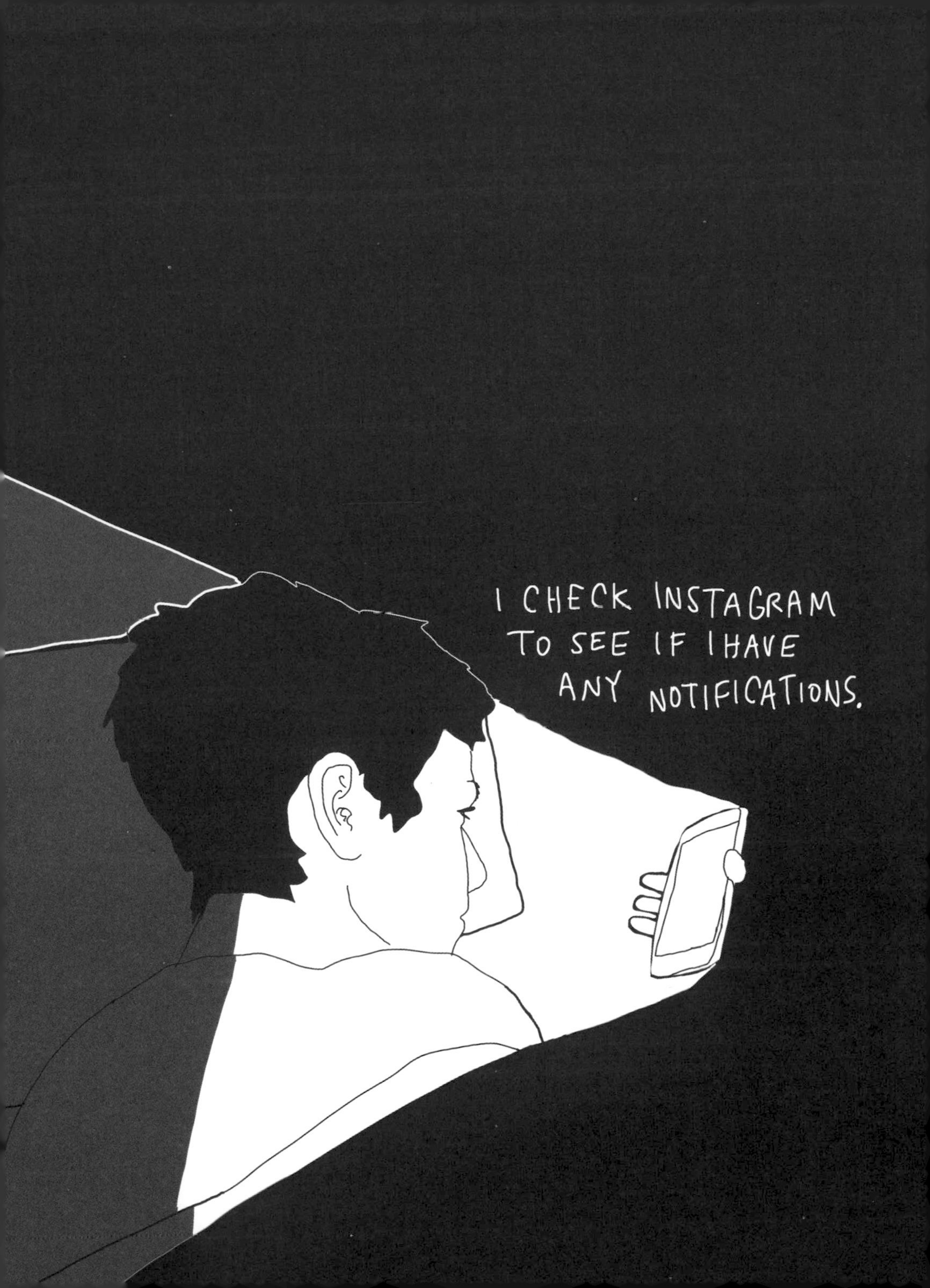
I CHECK INSTAGRAM TO SEE IF I HAVE ANY NOTIFICATIONS.

10 THINGS I SEE ON INSTAGRAM

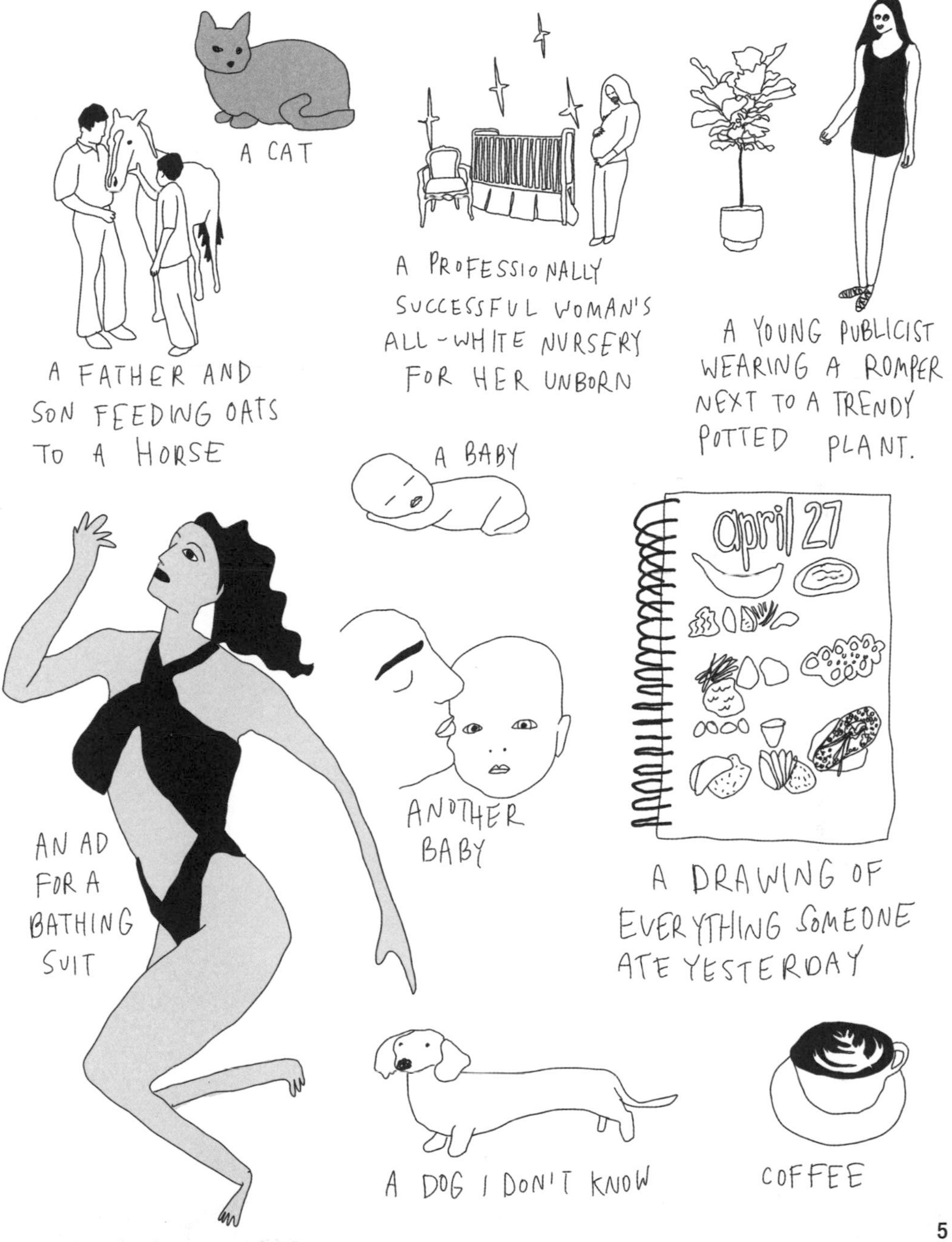
A CAT
A FATHER AND SON FEEDING OATS TO A HORSE
A PROFESSIONALLY SUCCESSFUL WOMAN'S ALL-WHITE NURSERY FOR HER UNBORN
A YOUNG PUBLICIST WEARING A ROMPER NEXT TO A TRENDY POTTED PLANT.
A BABY
april 27
AN AD FOR A BATHING SUIT
ANOTHER BABY
A DRAWING OF EVERYTHING SOMEONE ATE YESTERDAY
A DOG I DON'T KNOW
COFFEE

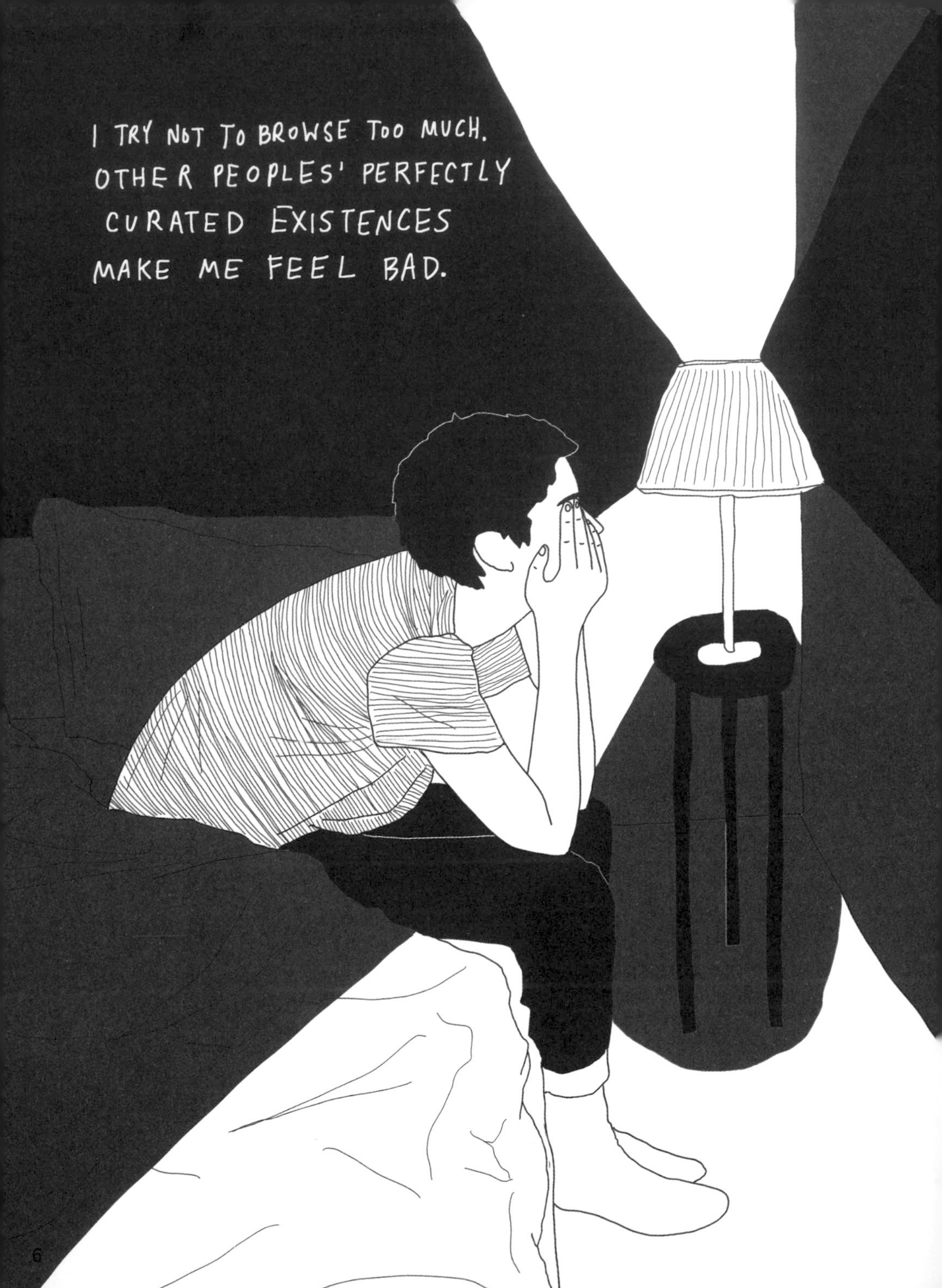
I TRY NOT TO BROWSE TOO MUCH. OTHER PEOPLES' PERFECTLY CURATED EXISTENCES MAKE ME FEEL BAD.

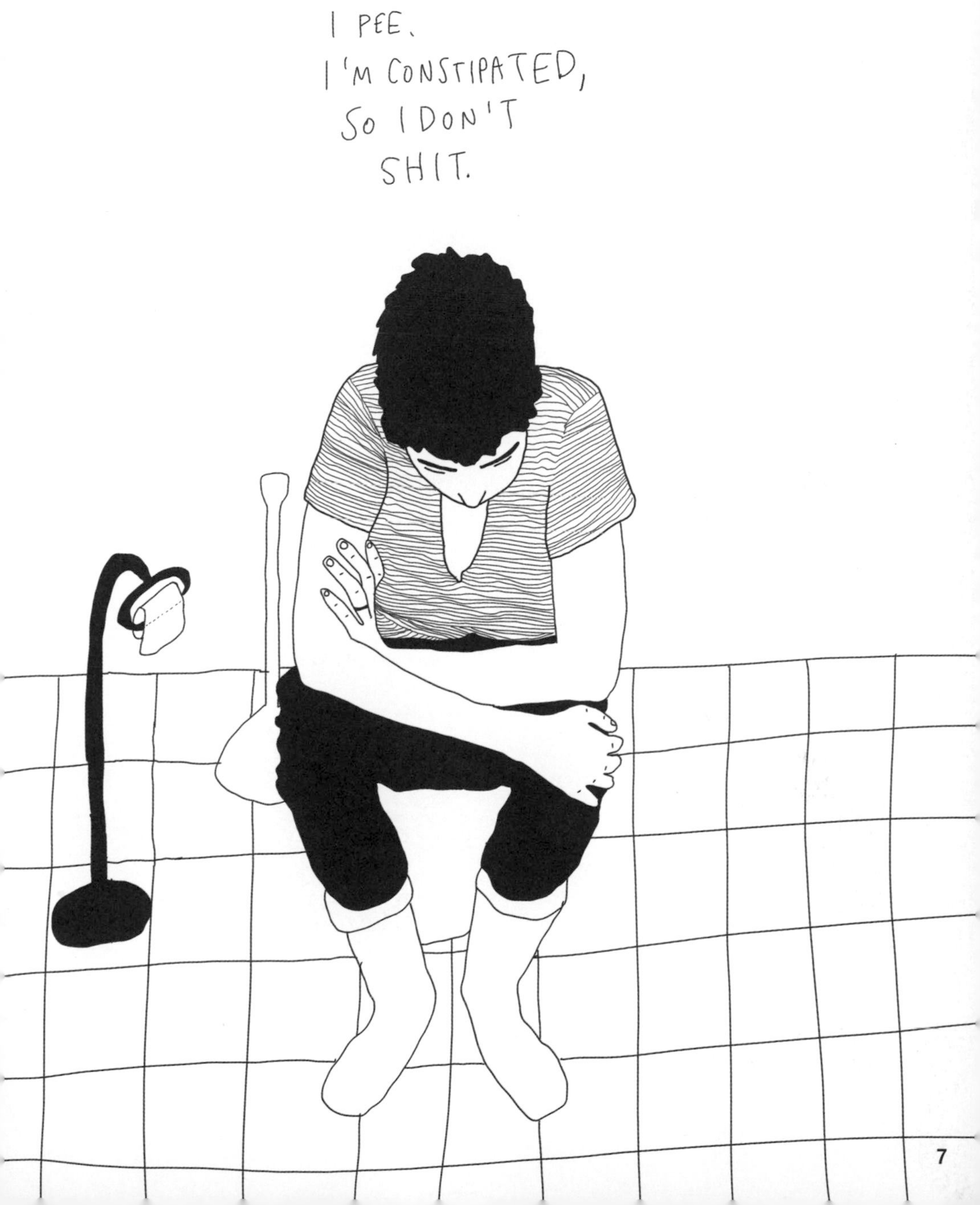
I PEE.
I'M CONSTIPATED,
SO I DON'T
SHIT.

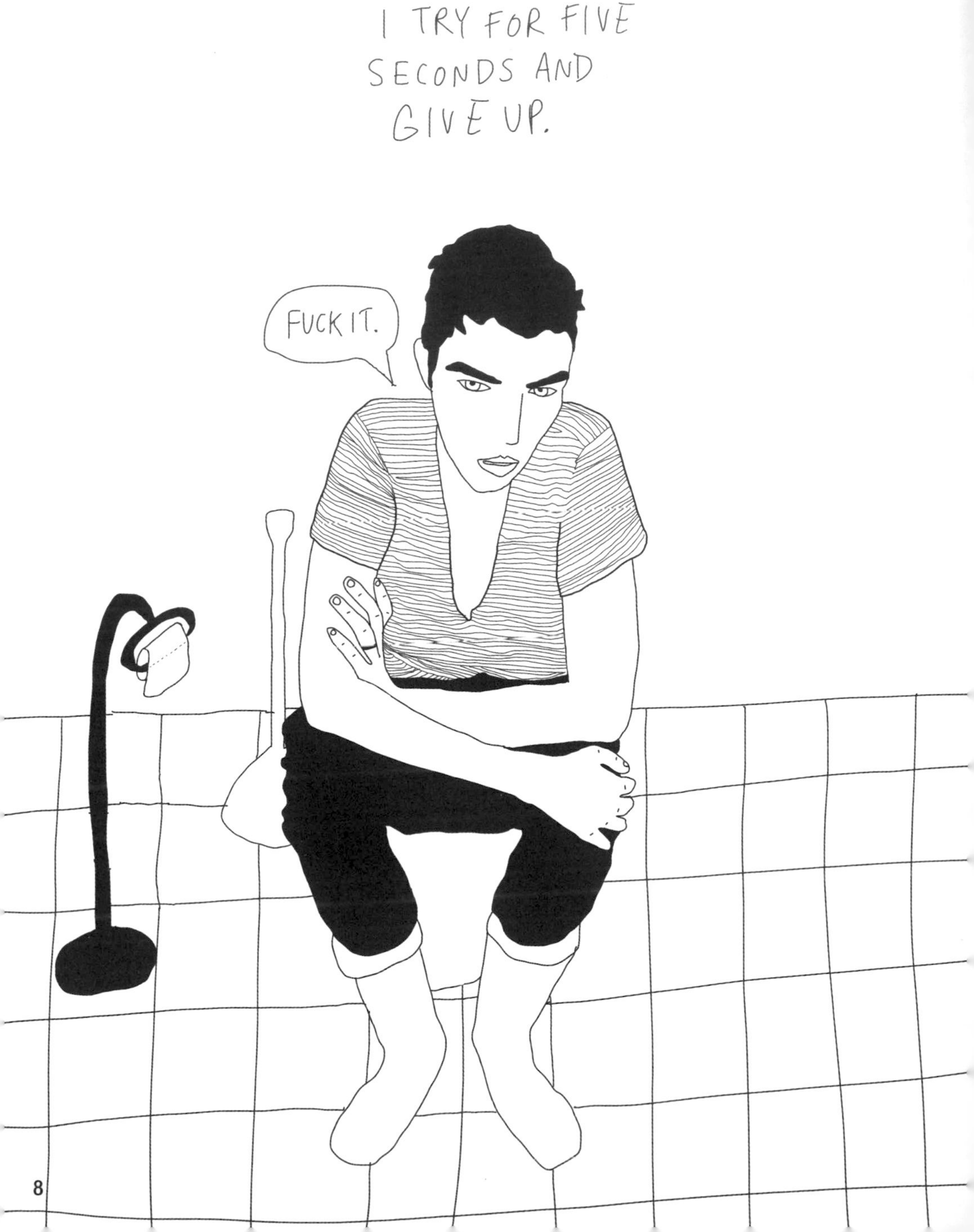
I TRY FOR FIVE SECONDS AND GIVE UP.
FUCK IT.

I MAKE TWO CUPS OF TEA.

TOOT
FWERP

ONE IS FOR HOME.

ONE'S FOR THE ROAD.

STANLEY
SINCE 1913

I DRINK IT IN A TRAVEL MUG ON THE TRAIN WHILE I READ.

(LATER—RIGHT NOW I'M STILL AT HOME.)

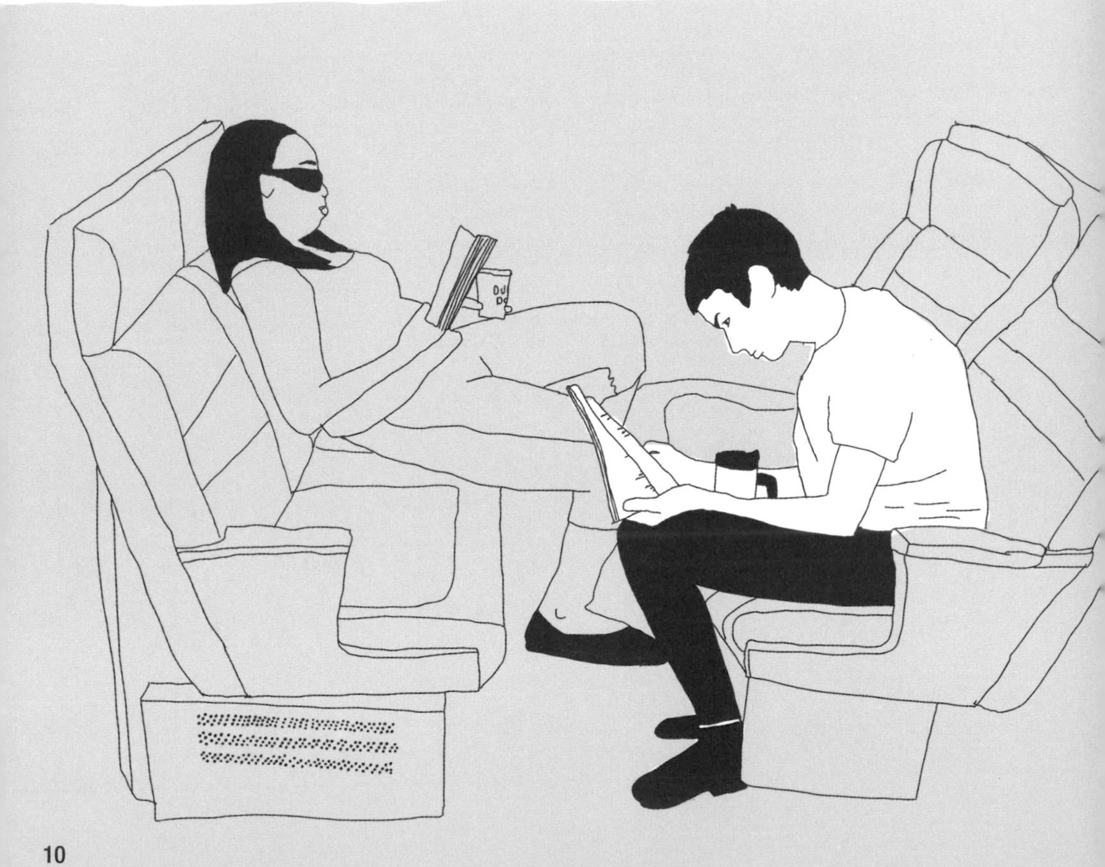

I STOPPED DRINKING COFFEE AFTER I GOT AN ULCER.

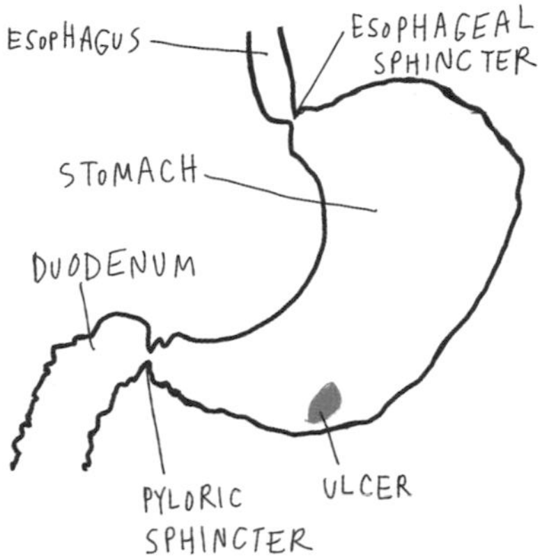
ESOPHAGUS
ESOPHAGEAL SPHINCTER
STOMACH
DUODENUM
PYLORIC SPHINCTER
ULCER

I STOPPED DRINKING ALCOHOL BECAUSE I'M AN ALCOHOLIC.

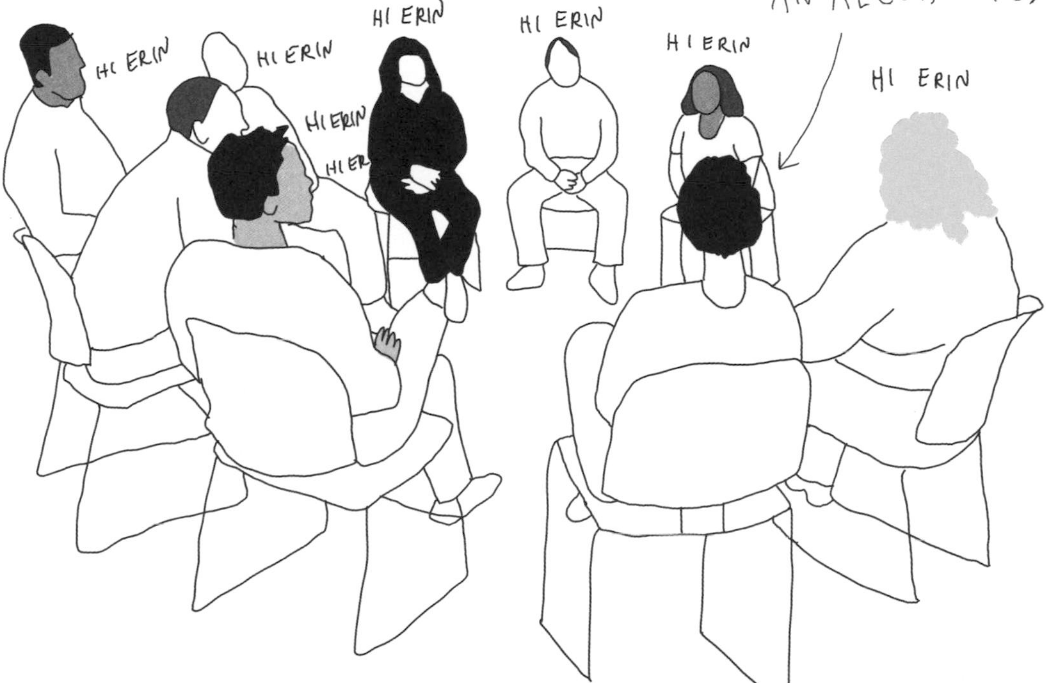
HI ERIN
HI ERIN
HI ERIN
HI ERIN
HI ERIN
HI ERIN
HI ERIN
HI ER

A LOT OF MY IDENTITY IS DEFINED BY DRINKING OR NOT DRINKING CERTAIN LIQUIDS.

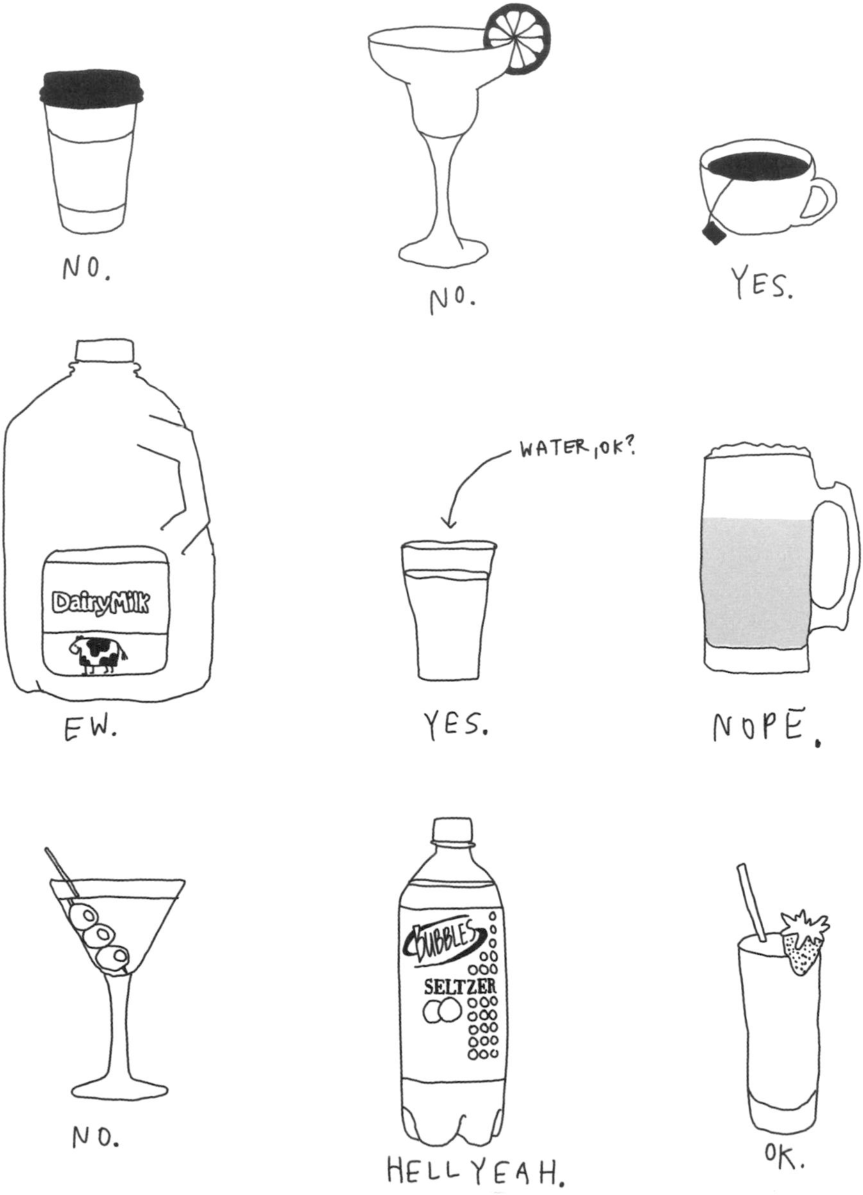
NO.
NO.
YES.
DairyMilk
EW.
WATER, OK?
YES.
NOPE.
NO.
BUBBLES
SELTZER
HELL YEAH.
OK.

I SPEND A LOT OF TIME GETTING READY FOR WORK.

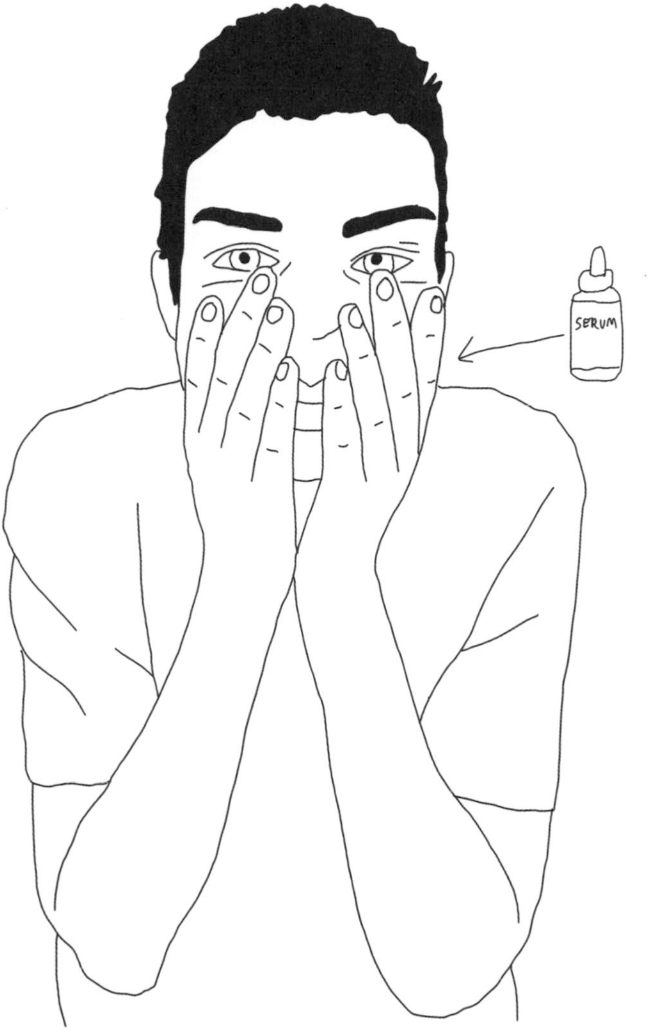
SERUM

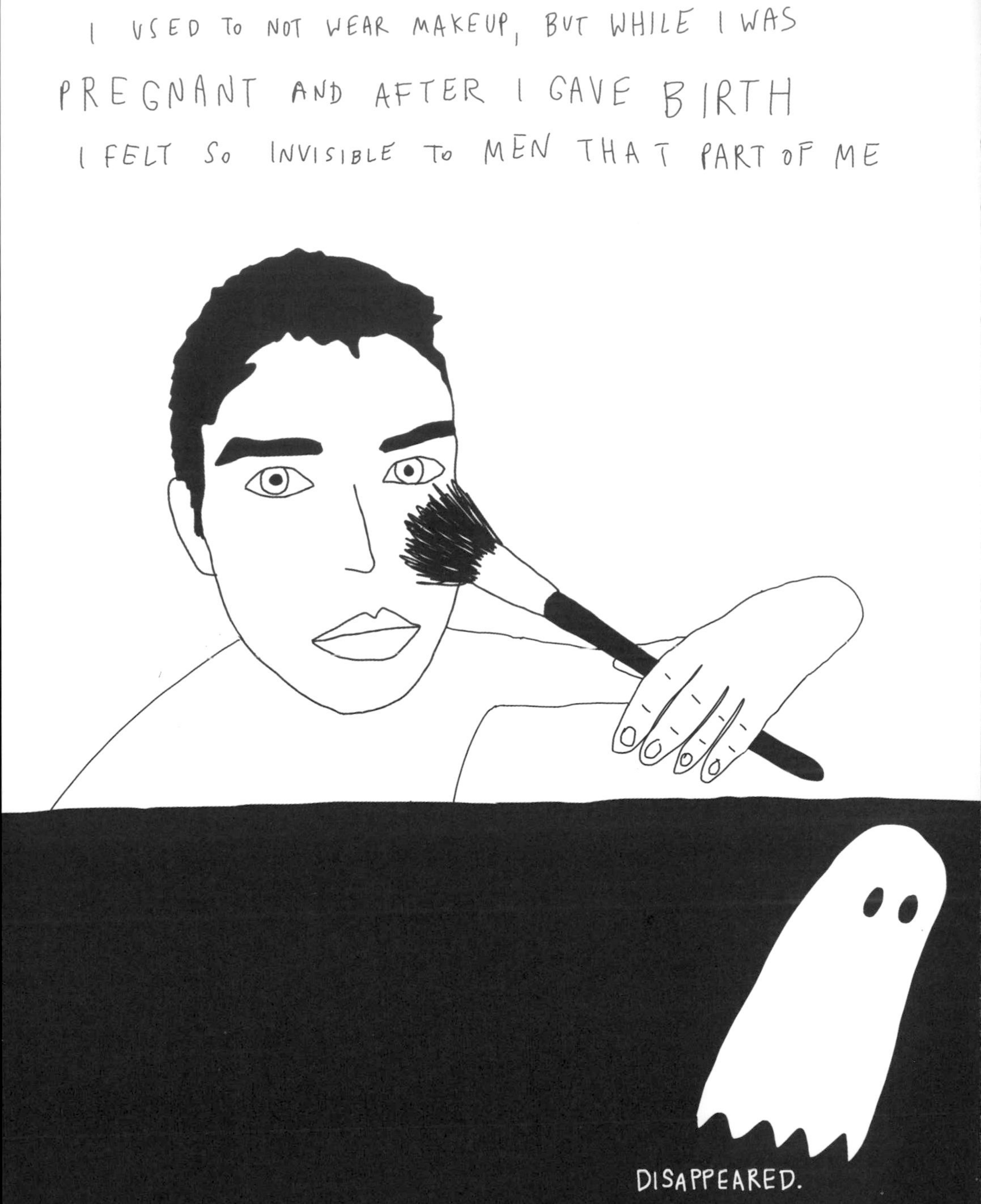
I USED TO NOT WEAR MAKEUP, BUT WHILE I WAS PREGNANT AND AFTER I GAVE BIRTH I FELT SO INVISIBLE TO MEN THAT PART OF ME
DISAPPEARED.

NOW MY ROUTINE HAS 16 STEPS

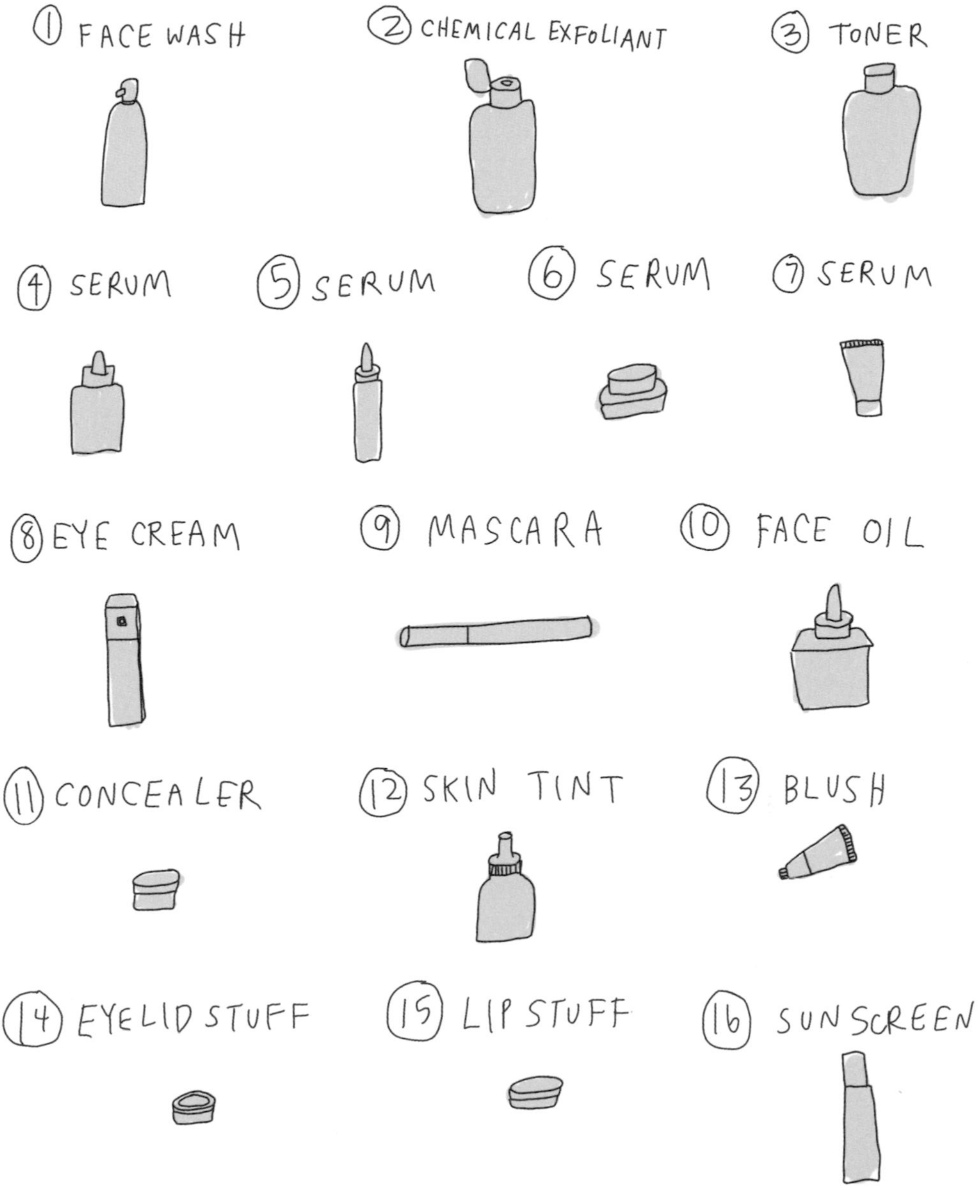

① FACE WASH
② CHEMICAL EXFOLIANT
③ TONER
④ SERUM
⑤ SERUM
⑥ SERUM
⑦ SERUM
⑧ EYE CREAM
⑨ MASCARA
⑩ FACE OIL
⑪ CONCEALER
⑫ SKIN TINT
⑬ BLUSH
⑭ EYELID STUFF
⑮ LIP STUFF
⑯ SUNSCREEN

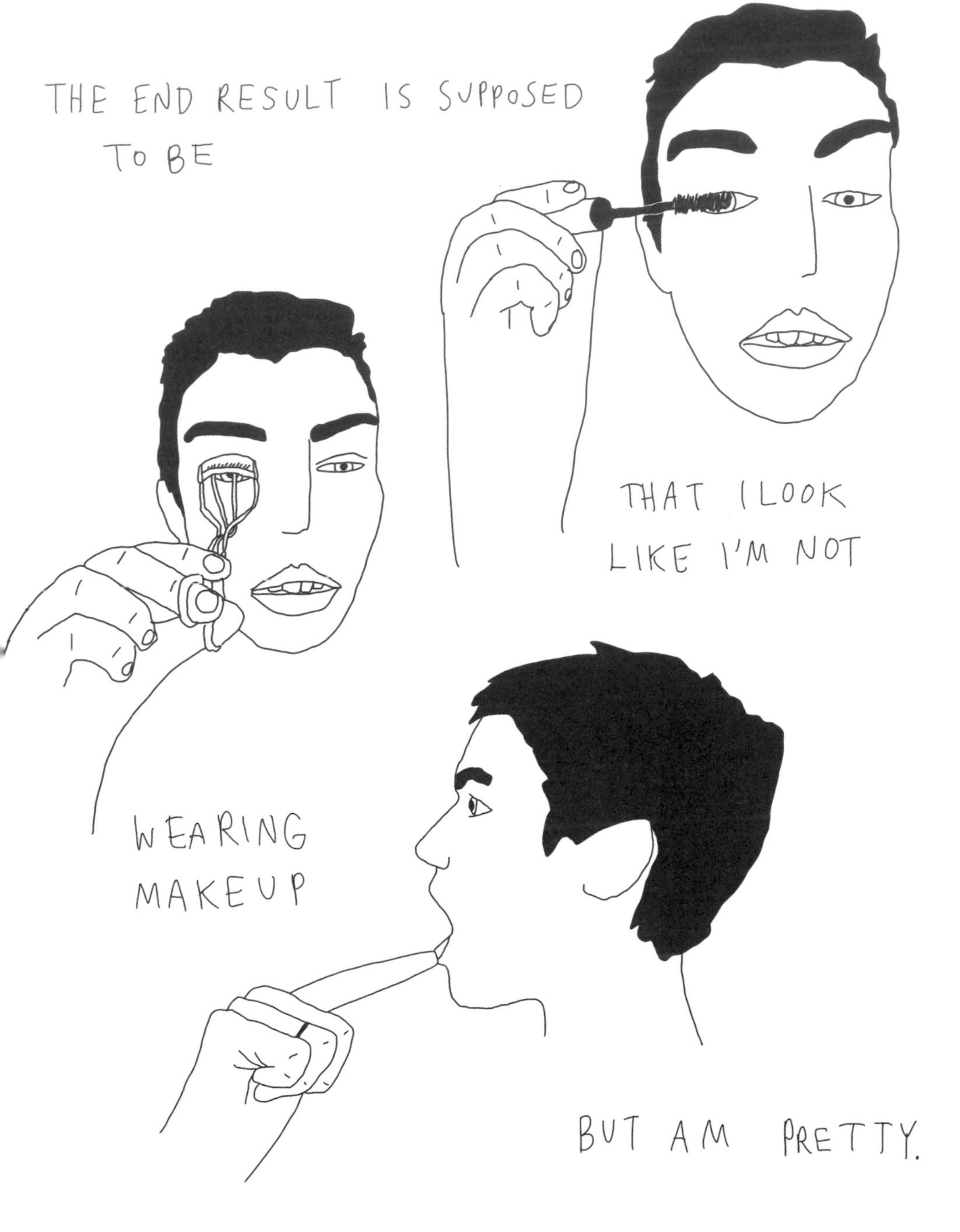
THE END RESULT IS SUPPOSED TO BE
THAT I LOOK LIKE I'M NOT
WEARING MAKEUP
BUT AM PRETTY.

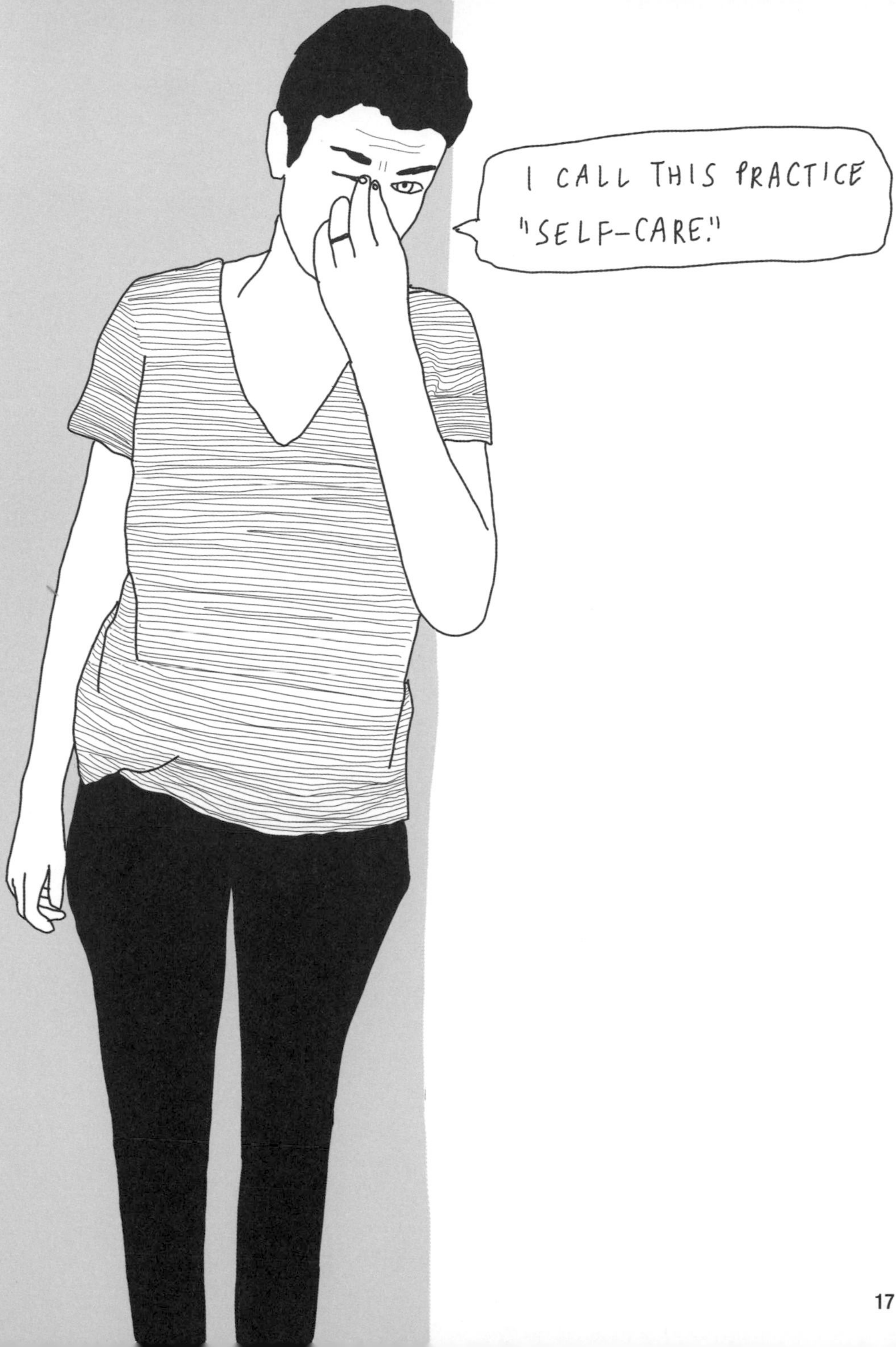
I CALL THIS PRACTICE "SELF-CARE."

WALK THE DOG

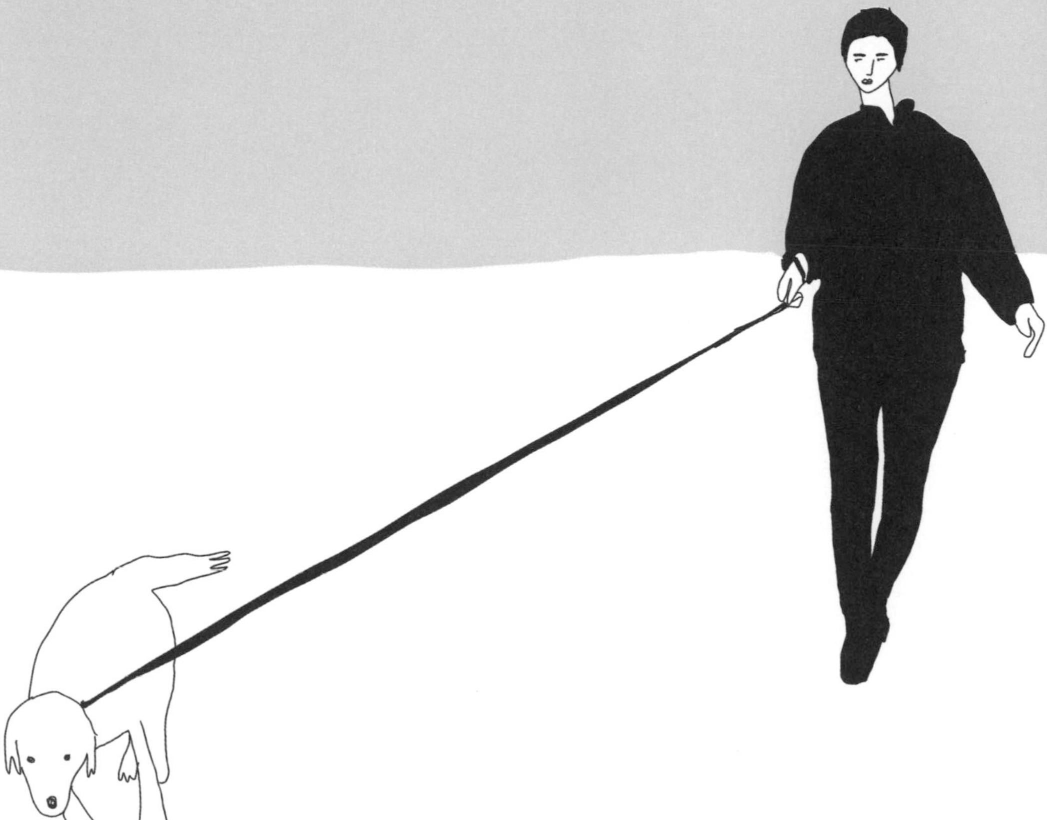

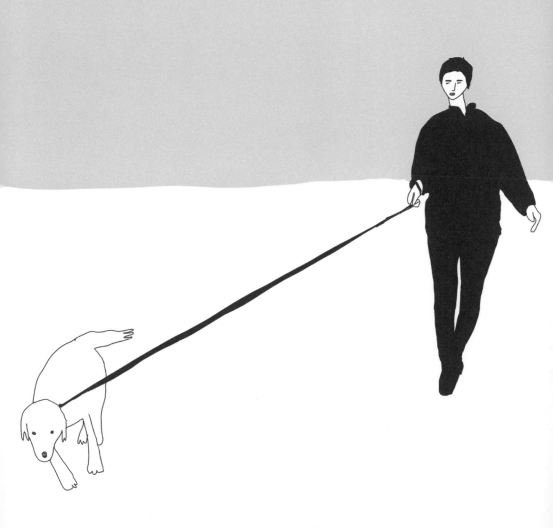

I CURVE MY BODY OVER HIS WHEN I PUT THE LEASH ON SO HIS FUR DOESN'T MAKE MY PANTS LOOK MESSY.

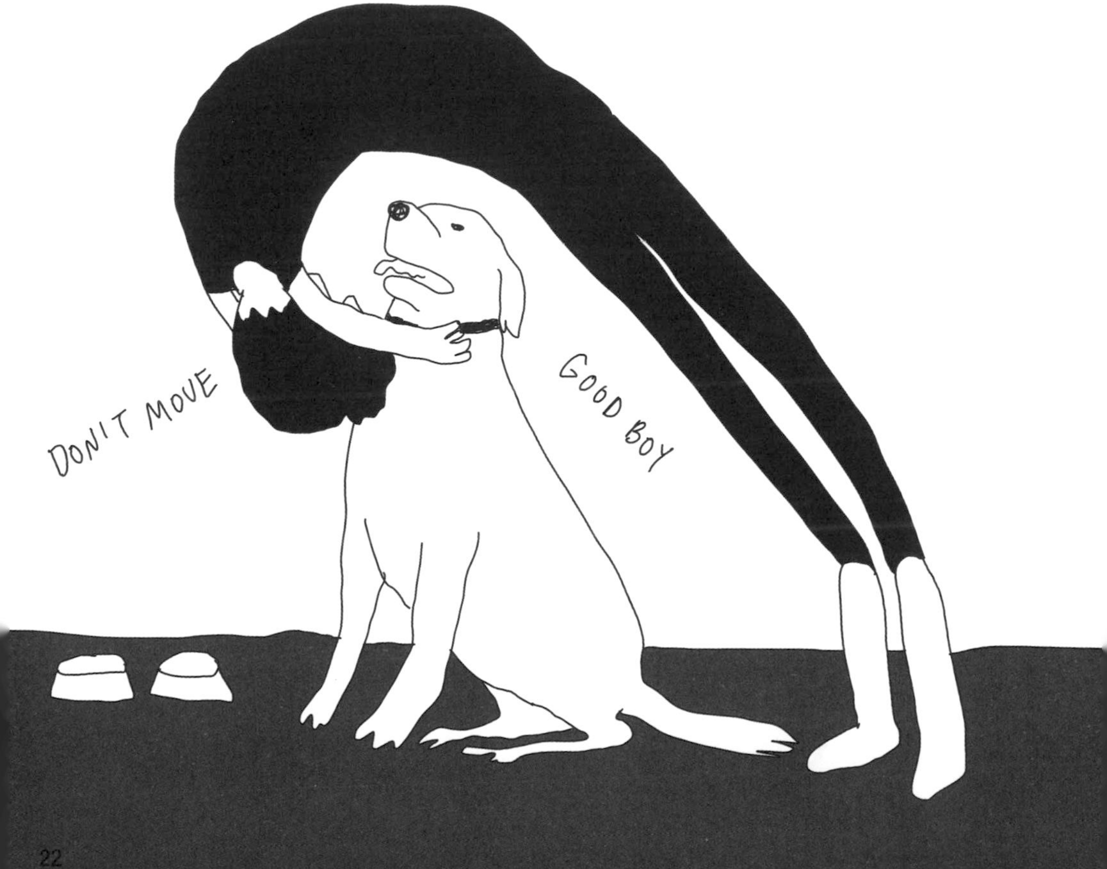
DON'T MOVE
GOOD BOY

HE SHEDS A RIDICULOUS AMOUNT.

IF I'M NOT CAREFUL, I GO TO WORK LOOKING
LIKE A HAIRBALL.

WE GO OUTSIDE, AND HE SHOOTS
URINE AT INTERESTING SMELLS.

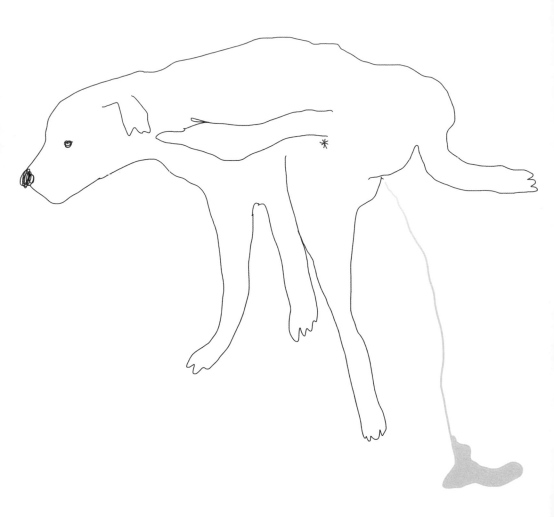

THE SUN IS UP, AND THE AIR IS LIGHT BLUE AND HEAVY WITH HONEYSUCKLE.

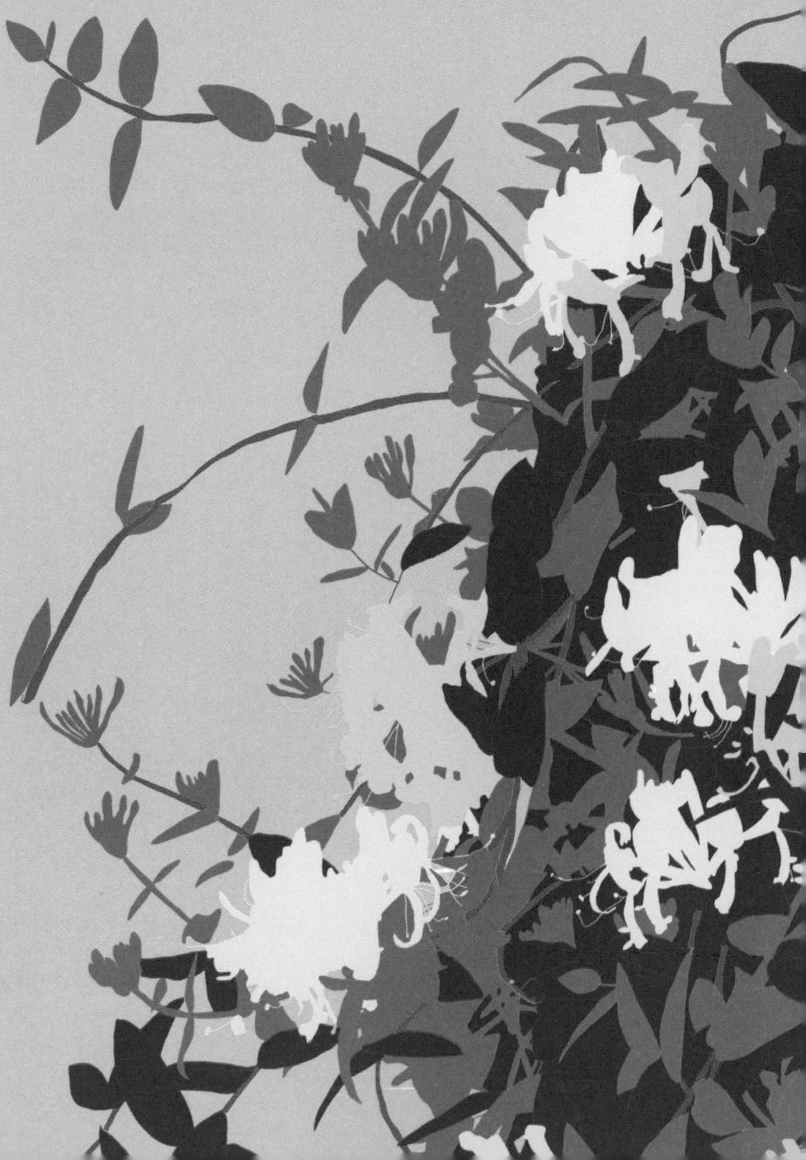

I PUT THESE WORDS TOGETHER IN MY HEAD...

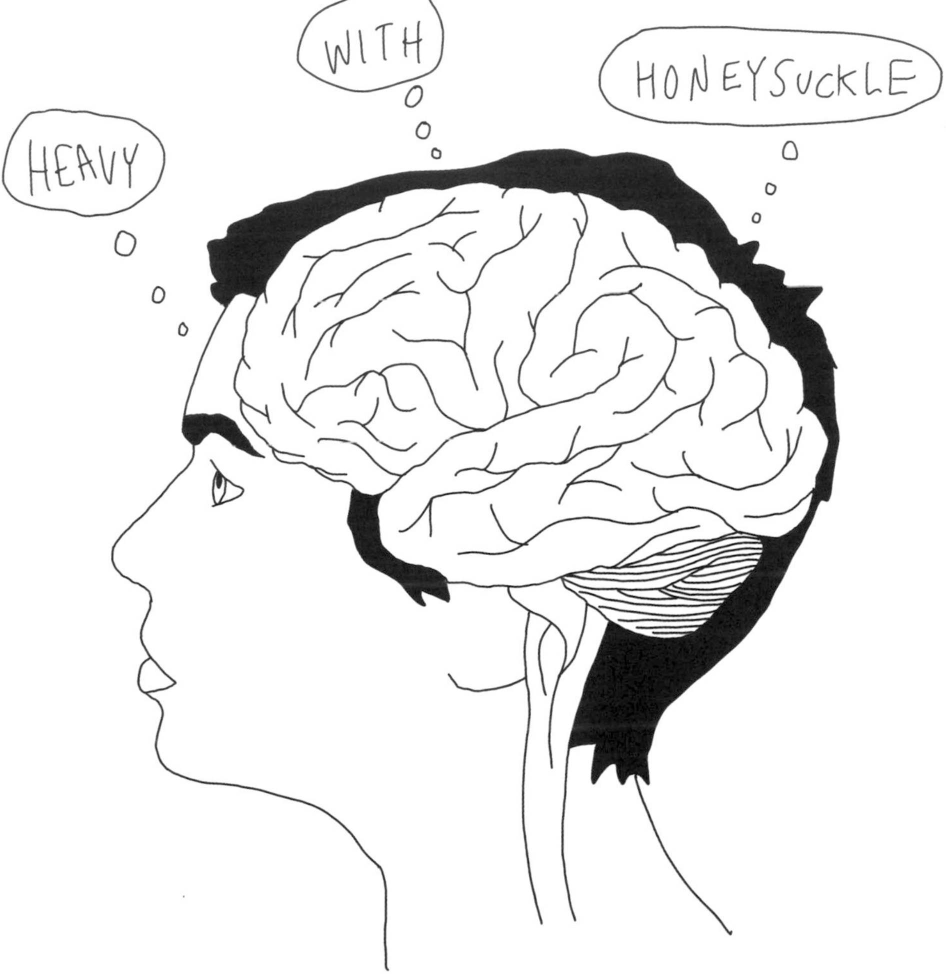
HEAVY
WITH
HONEYSUCKLE

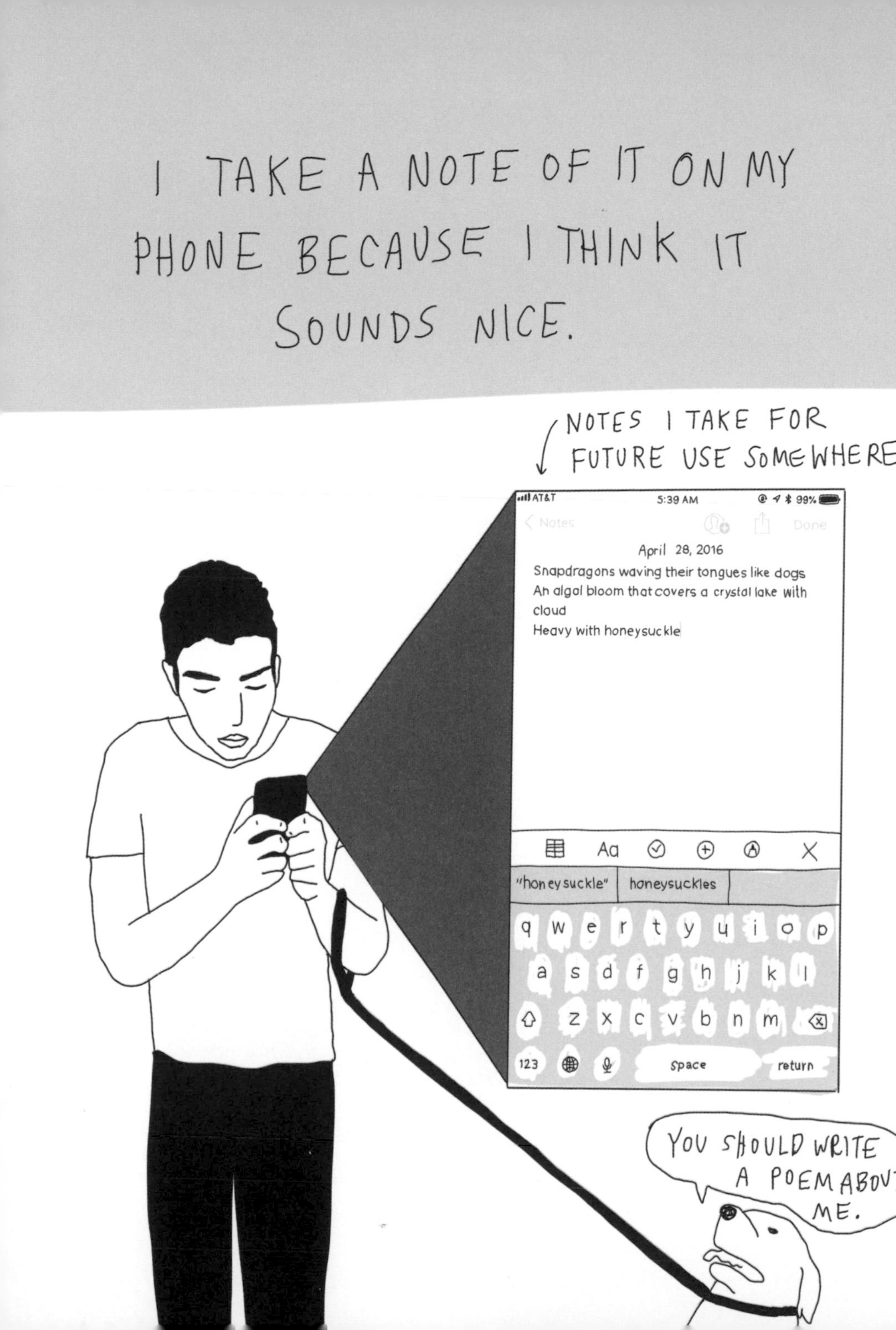
I TAKE A NOTE OF IT ON MY PHONE BECAUSE I THINK IT SOUNDS NICE.
NOTES I TAKE FOR FUTURE USE SOMEWHERE
AT&T
5:39 AM
99%
Notes
Done
April 28, 2016
Snapdragons waving their tongues like dogs
An algal bloom that covers a crystal lake with cloud
Heavy with honeysuckle
"honeysuckle"
honeysuckles
123
space
return
YOU SHOULD WRITE A POEM ABOUT ME.

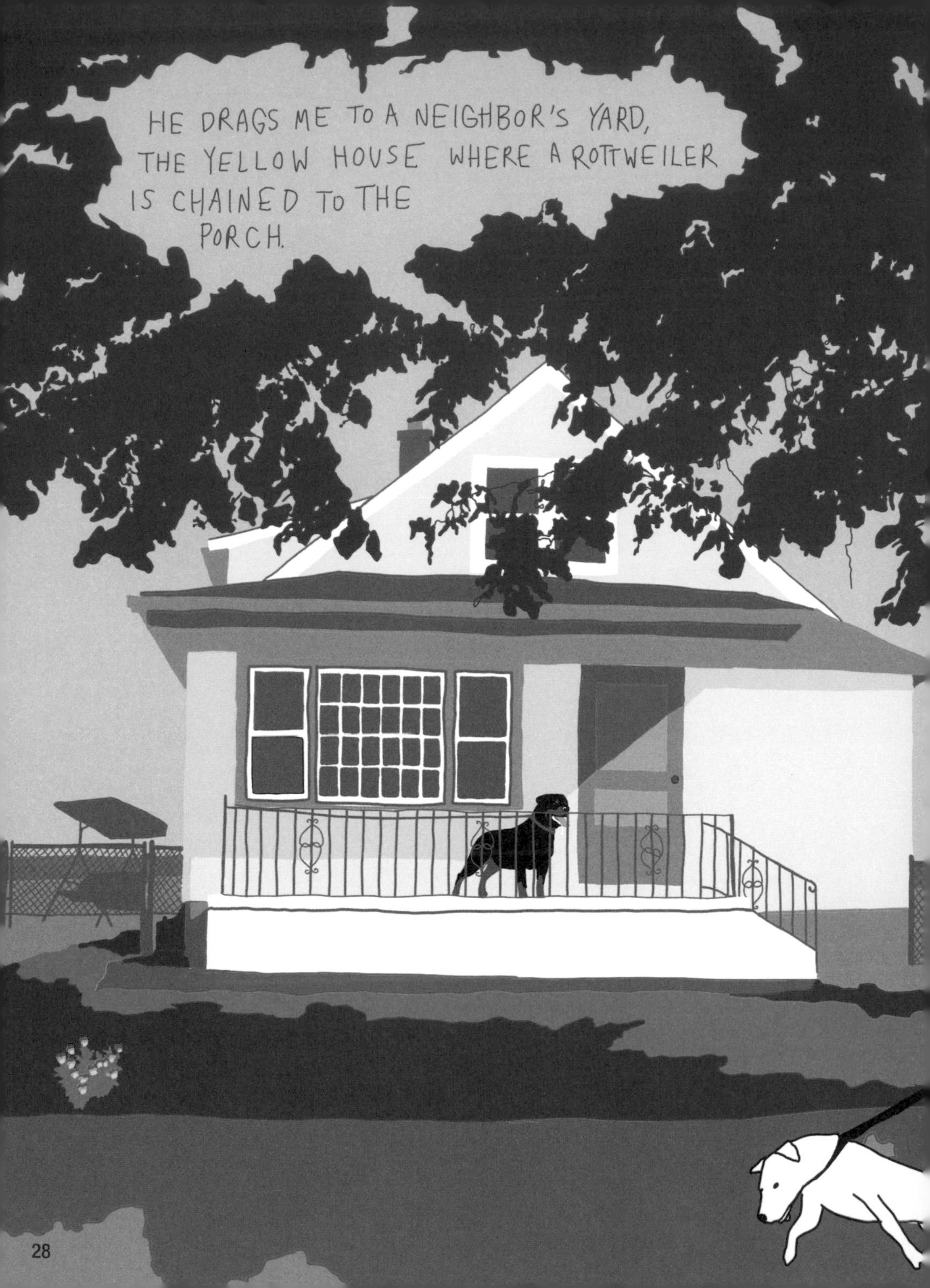
HE DRAGS ME TO A NEIGHBOR'S YARD, THE YELLOW HOUSE WHERE A ROTTWEILER IS CHAINED TO THE PORCH.

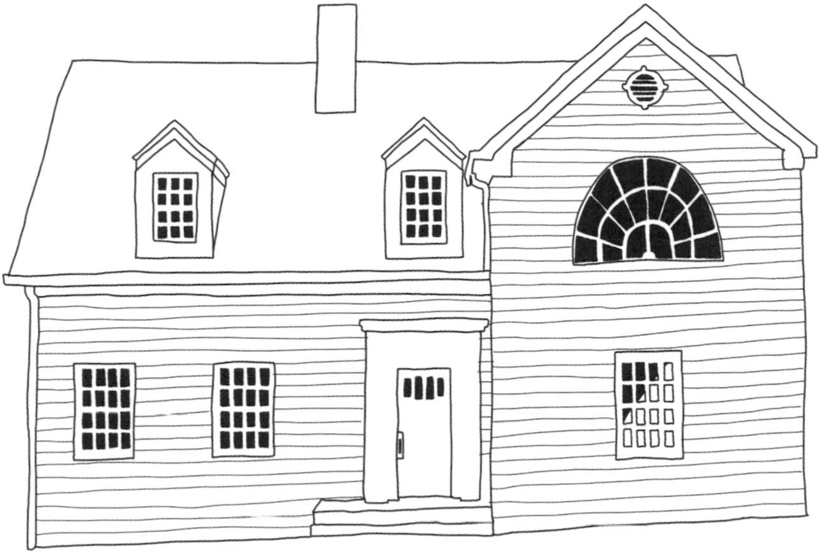

THERE'S A BIG HOUSE WHERE A WOMAN WATCHES TV EARLY IN THE MORNING BEFORE HER FAMILY WAKES UP. I ASSUME IT'S A WOMAN. I ALSO ASSUME THE BIG HALF-CIRCLE WINDOW ON THE SECOND FLOOR IS THE MASTER BEDROOM. THERE ARE PICTURE FRAMES BALANCED ON THE WINDOWSILL. I ASSUME THESE ARE FAMILY PHOTOS, THEIR KIDS AT DIFFERENT AGES DOING DIFFERENT SEMINAL ACTIVITIES. THEY HAVE A POOL THAT SEEMS OPULENT FOR THE NEIGHBORHOOD.

DONALD PEES ON THEIR FLOWERS, TOO.

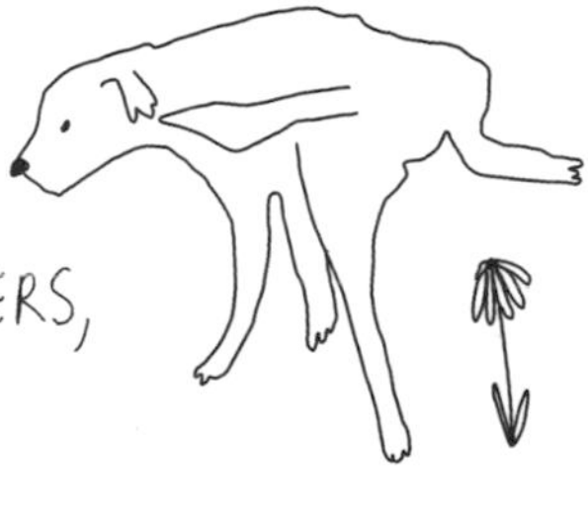

THE HOUSE OPPOSITE THE BRICK ONE IS EMPTY
BUT EERILY WELL-MAINTAINED. A VAN DRIVES UP
EVERY MORNING AND SITS OUT FRONT. MAYBE
THE DRIVER GETS THE MAIL OR MAYBE
HE JUST PRETENDS TO.
THE LAWN IS PERFECT IN A CREEPY WAY.

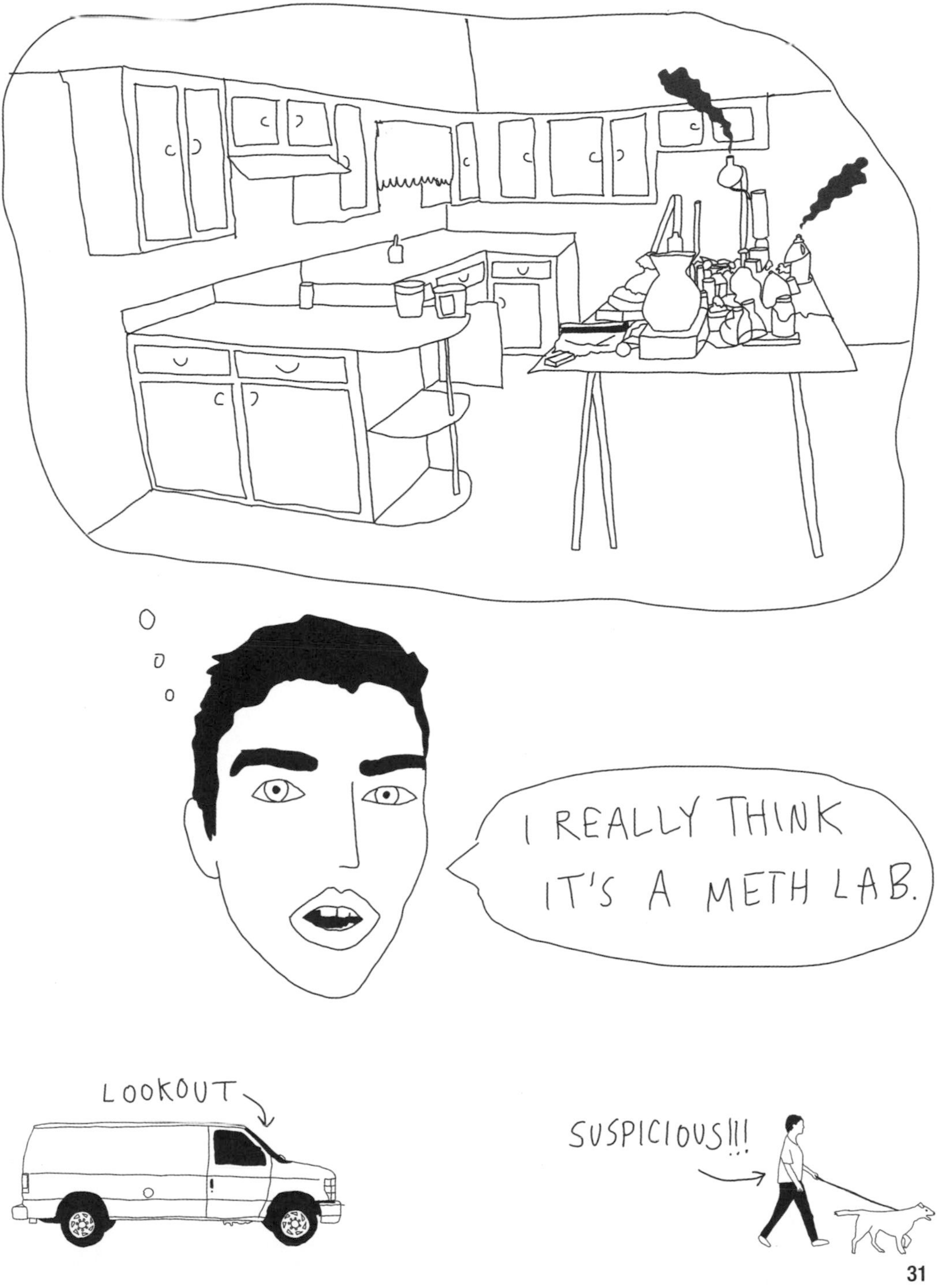
I REALLY THINK IT'S A METH LAB.
LOOKOUT
SUSPICIOUS!!!

I'M AFRAID THE GUY IN THE VAN WILL PULL A HANDGUN OUT OF HIS BEVERAGE HOLDER AND SHOOT ME AND DONNIE BECAUSE WE'RE ON TO HIS METH LAB AND HAVE HIS LICENSE PLATE MEMORIZED.

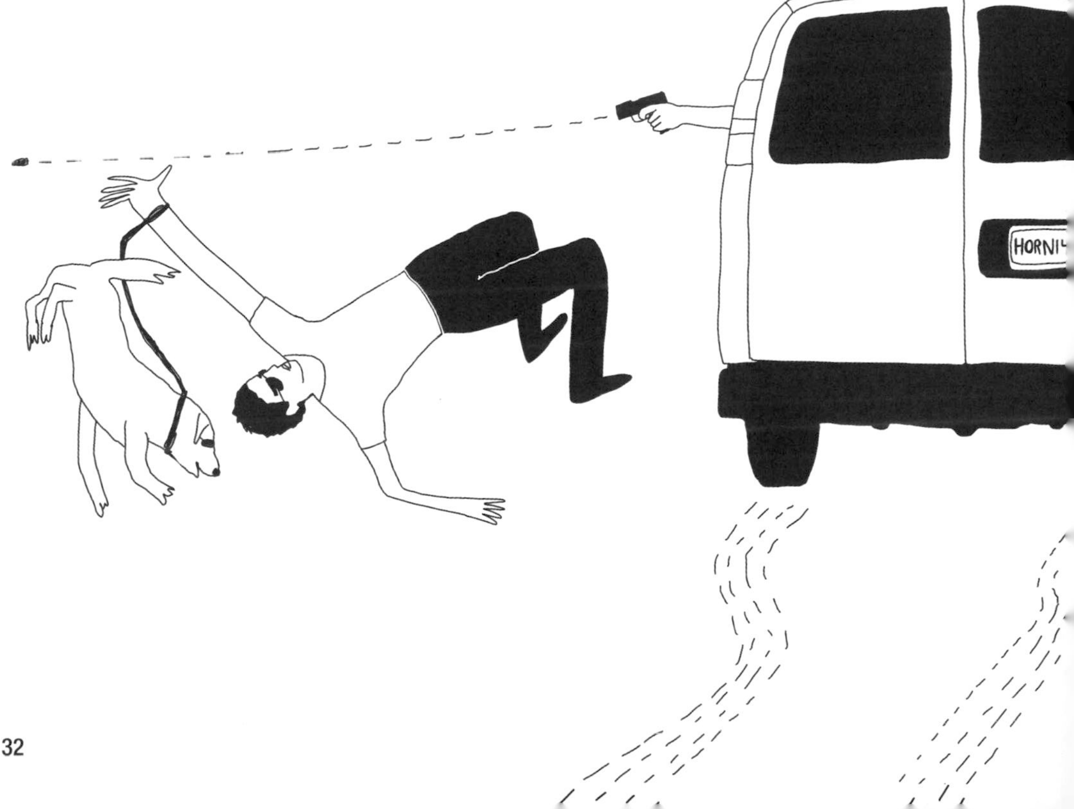
HORNI4

OR MAYBE HE'S JUST THINKING ABOUT HIS DEAD MOTHER.

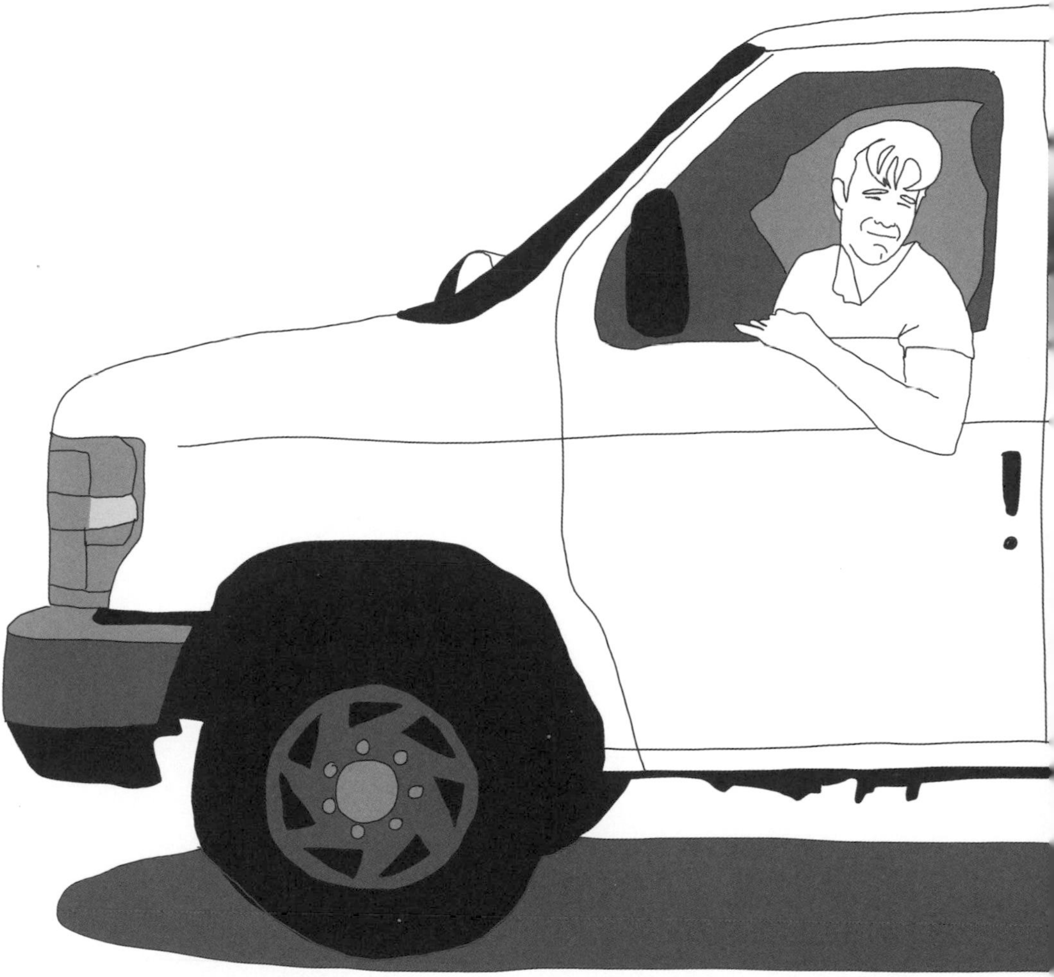

SOMETIMES HE PULLS HIS VAN VERY CLOSE TO WHERE I'M WALKING, ONTO THE WRONG SIDE OF THE STREET, AND WHISPERS

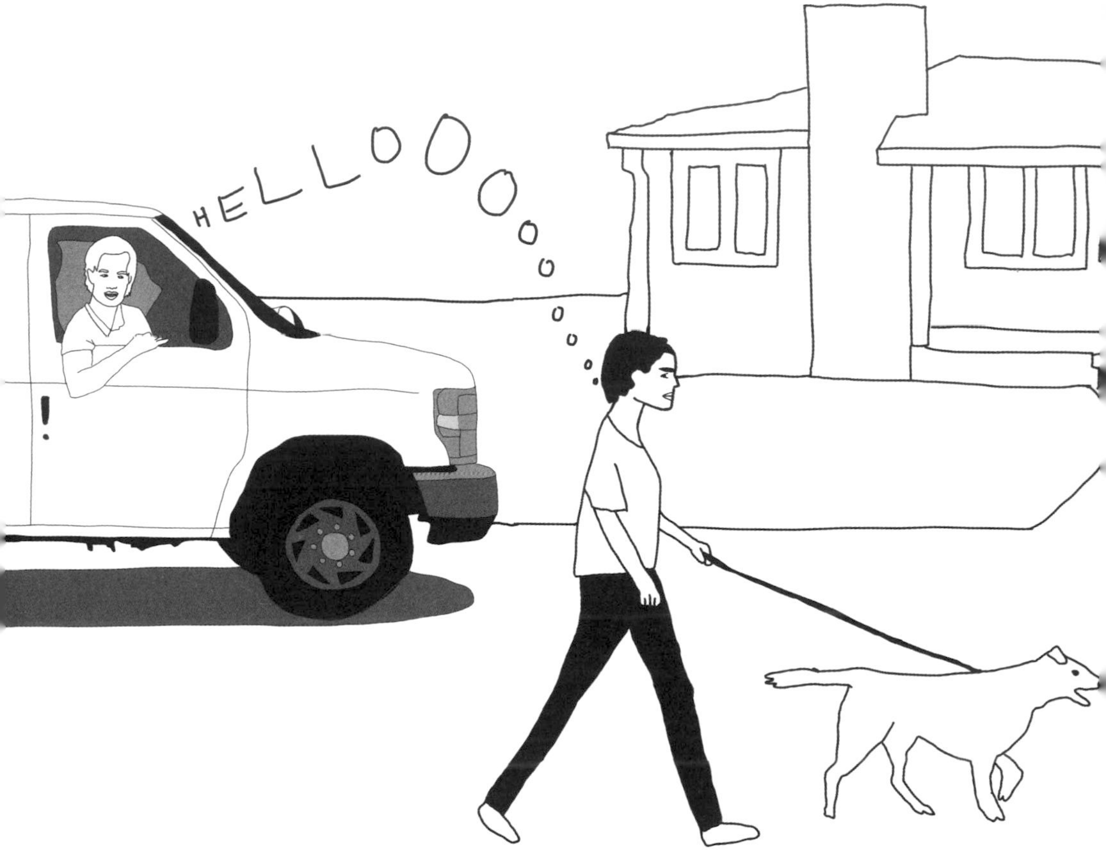
HELLOOOOooooo

THE SNAPDRAGONS OUT FRONT WAG
THEIR LITTLE TONGUES LIKE DOGS.

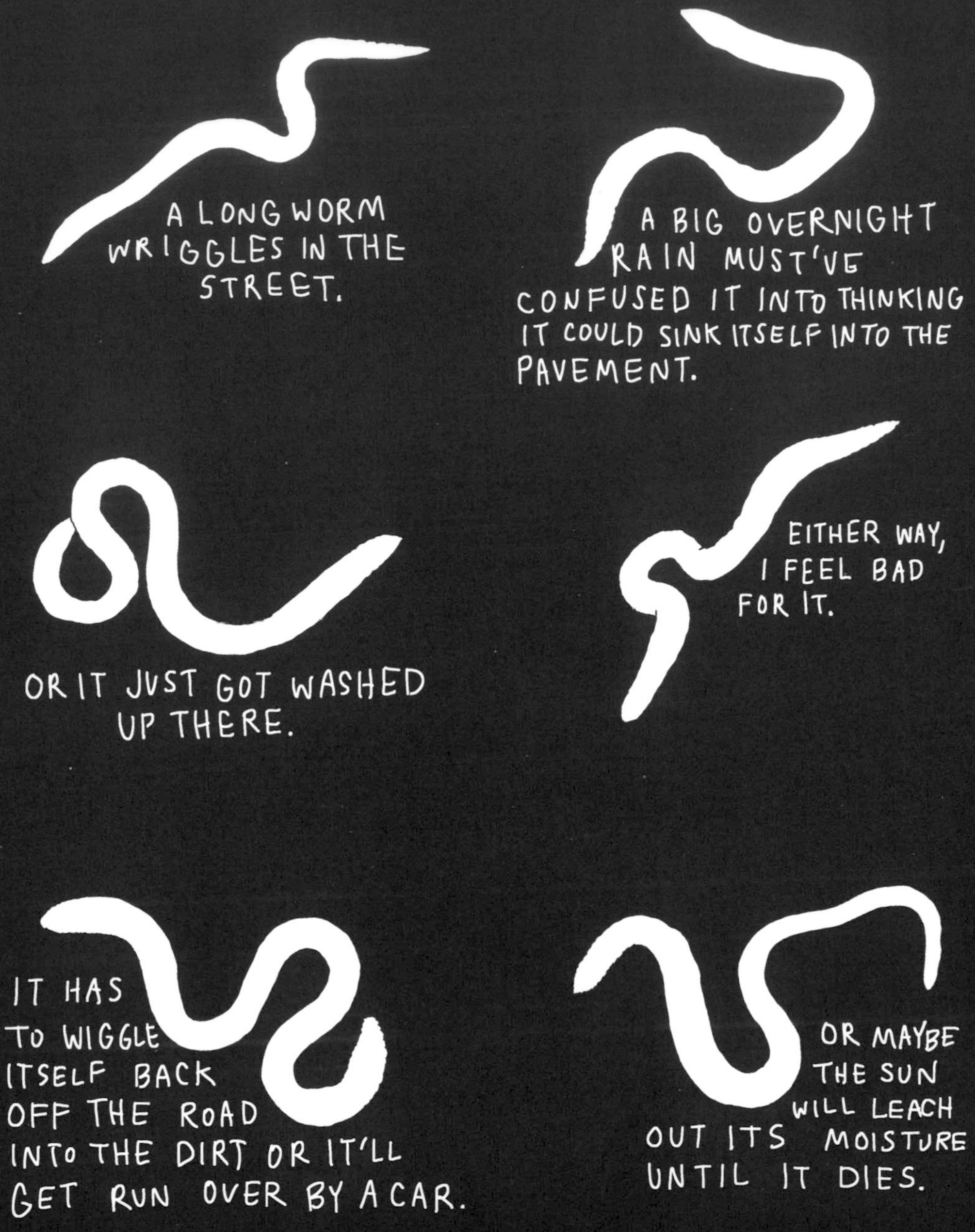
A LONG WORM WRIGGLES IN THE STREET.
A BIG OVERNIGHT RAIN MUST'VE CONFUSED IT INTO THINKING IT COULD SINK ITSELF INTO THE PAVEMENT.
OR IT JUST GOT WASHED UP THERE.
EITHER WAY, I FEEL BAD FOR IT.
IT HAS TO WIGGLE ITSELF BACK OFF THE ROAD INTO THE DIRT OR IT'LL GET RUN OVER BY A CAR.
OR MAYBE THE SUN WILL LEACH OUT ITS MOISTURE UNTIL IT DIES.

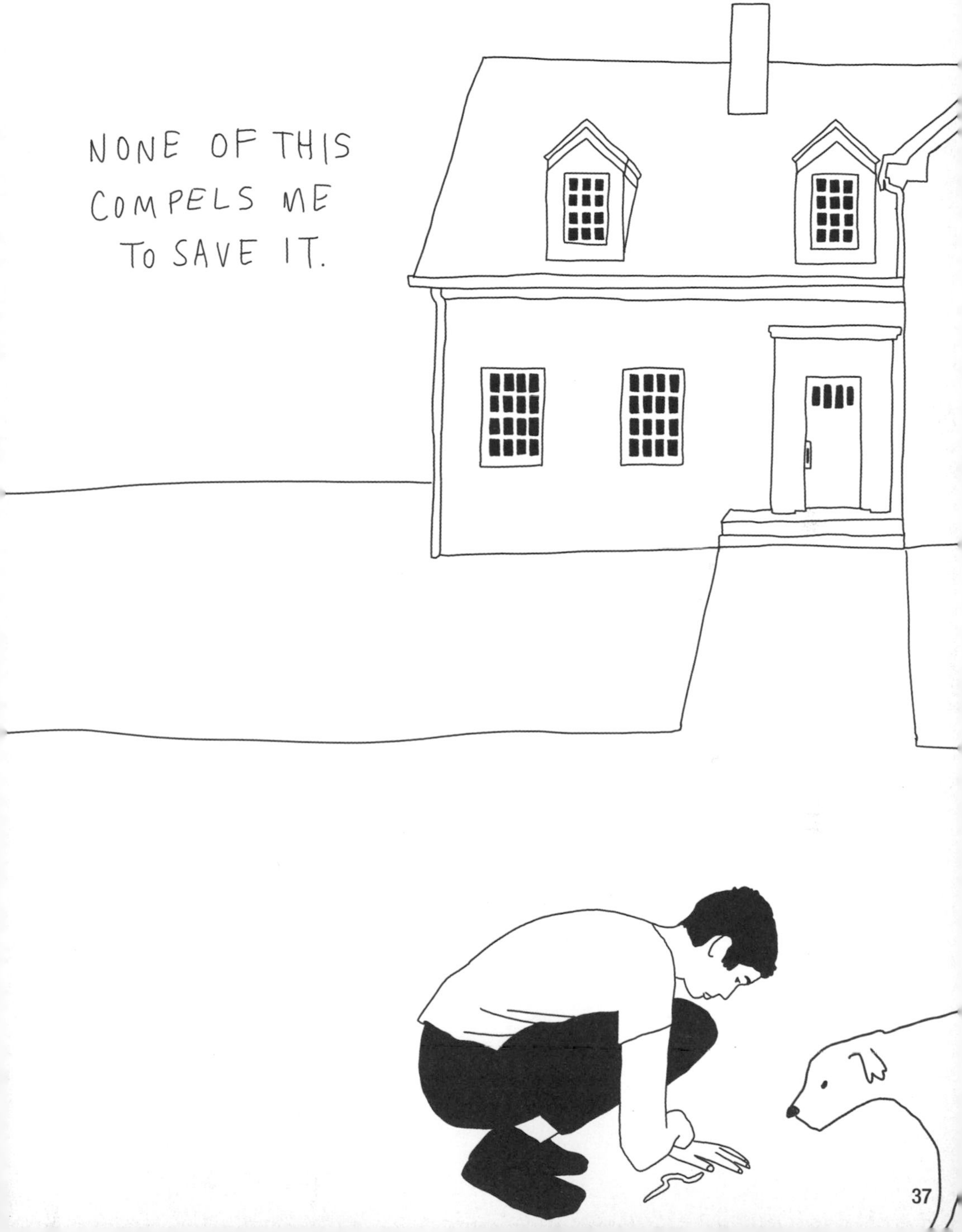
NONE OF THIS COMPELS ME TO SAVE IT.

I WRITE A POEM.

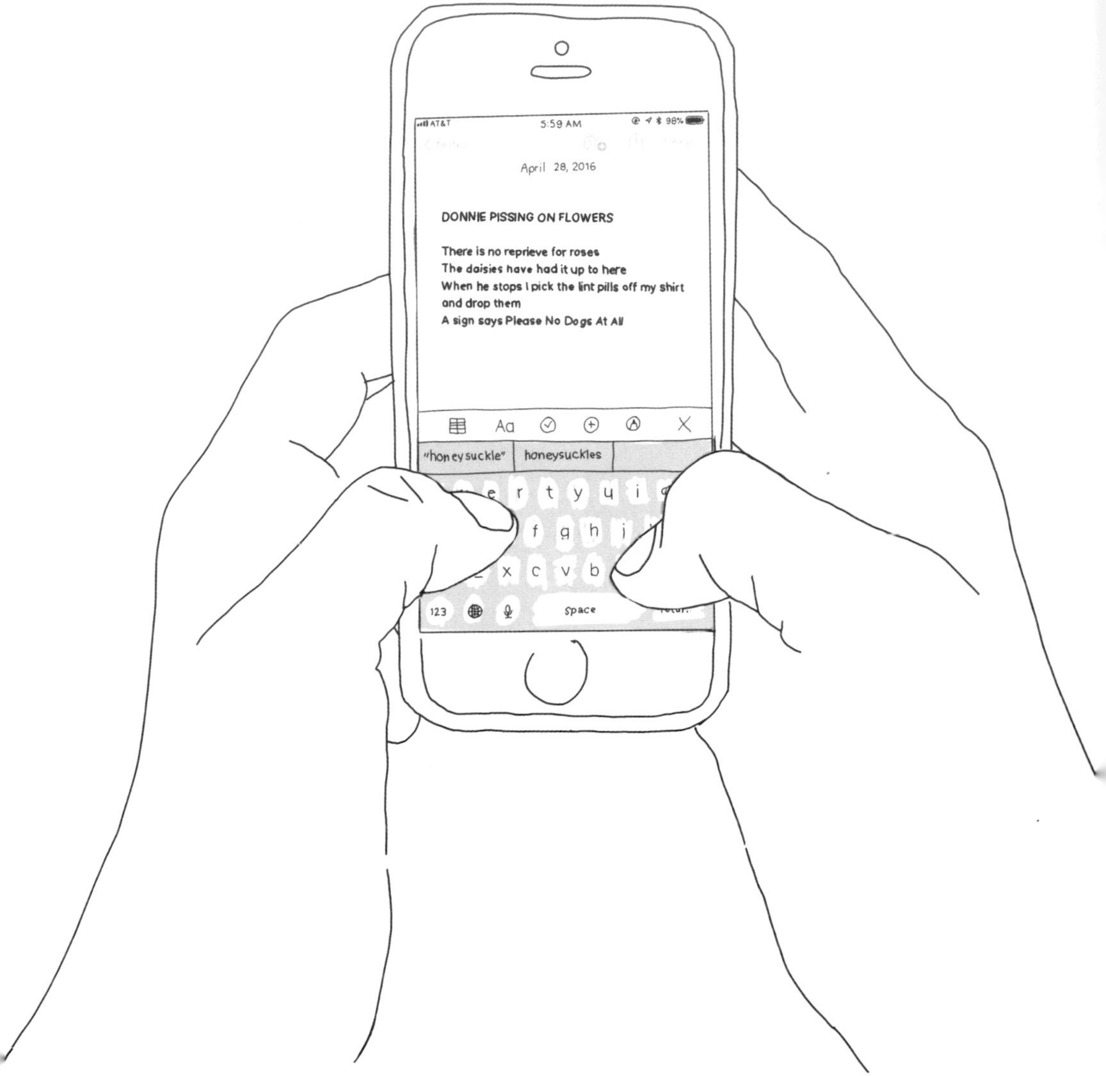
AT&T
5:59 AM
98%
April 28, 2016
DONNIE PISSING ON FLOWERS
There is no reprieve for roses
The daisies have had it up to here
When he stops I pick the lint pills off my shirt and drop them
A sign says Please No Dogs At All
Aa
"honeysuckle"
honeysuckles
123
space

I LEAVE FOR WORK BEFORE MY FAMILY IS AWAKE.

WAIT FOR THE TRAIN

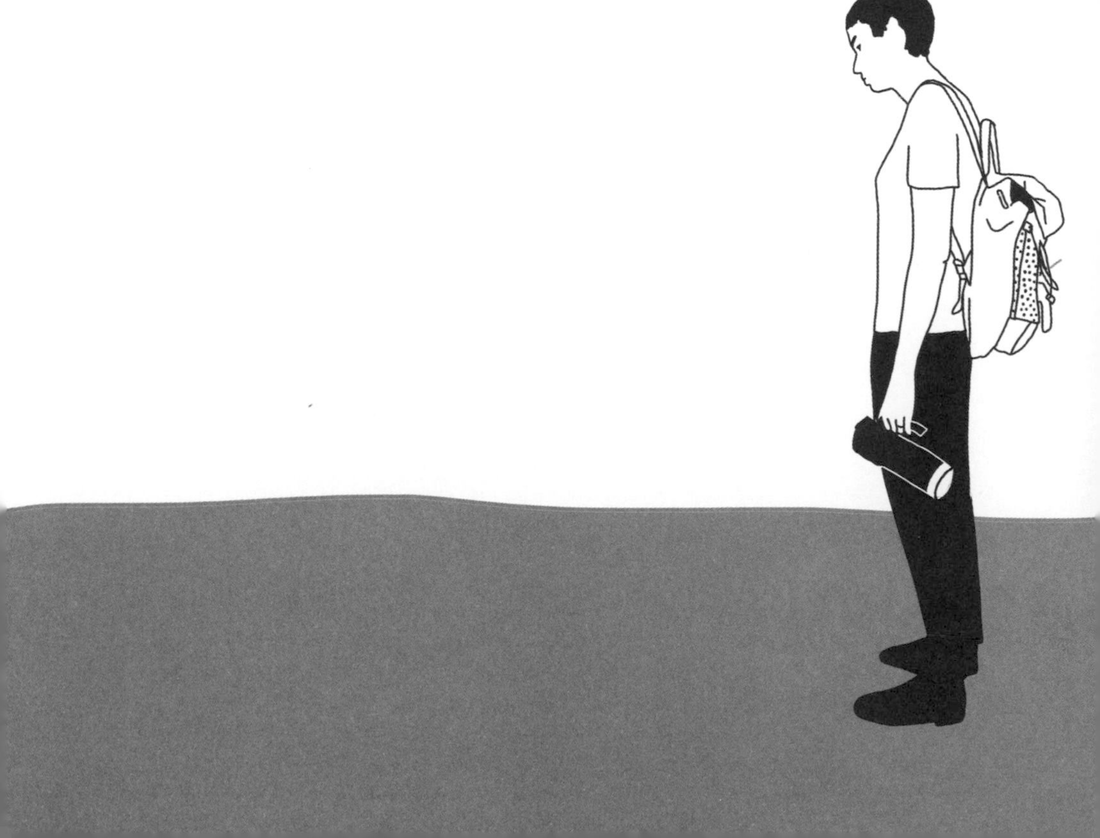

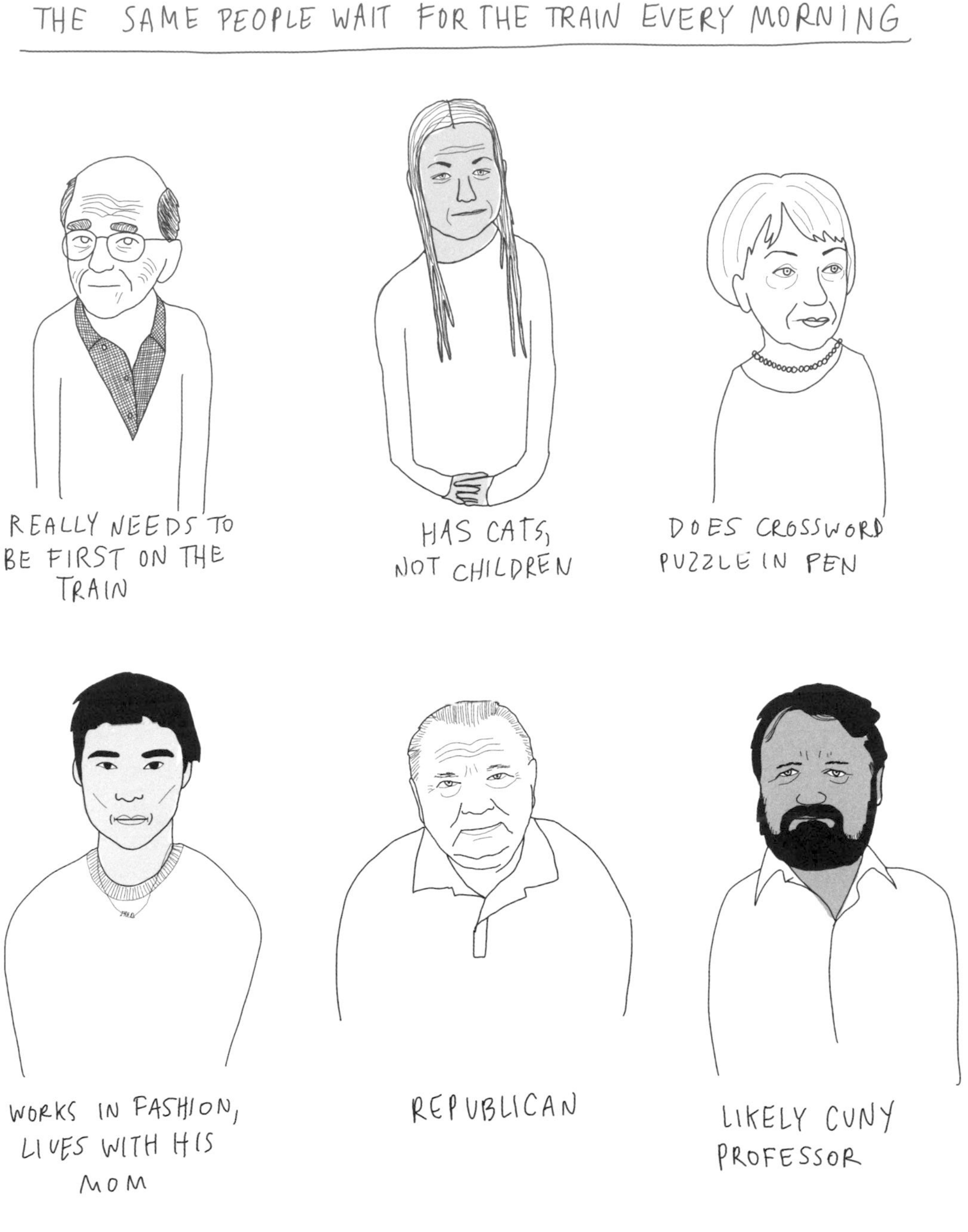
THE SAME PEOPLE WAIT FOR THE TRAIN EVERY MORNING
REALLY NEEDS TO BE FIRST ON THE TRAIN
HAS CATS, NOT CHILDREN
DOES CROSSWORD PUZZLE IN PEN
WORKS IN FASHION, LIVES WITH HIS MOM
REPUBLICAN
LIKELY CUNY PROFESSOR

ONE WOMAN IS FRIENDLY. SHE LIVES IN A CONDO AND WEARS ANORAKS. SHE'S A PERSONAL ASSISTANT TO A GUY WHO OWNS A HEATING AND COOLING BUSINESS. SHE IS MY TRAIN-BEST-FRIEND: NICE TO TALK TO, BUT DOESN'T CONTINUE TALKING ONCE WE GET ON THE TRAIN. MOSTLY WE CHAT ABOUT THE WEATHER AND HOUSING PRICES.

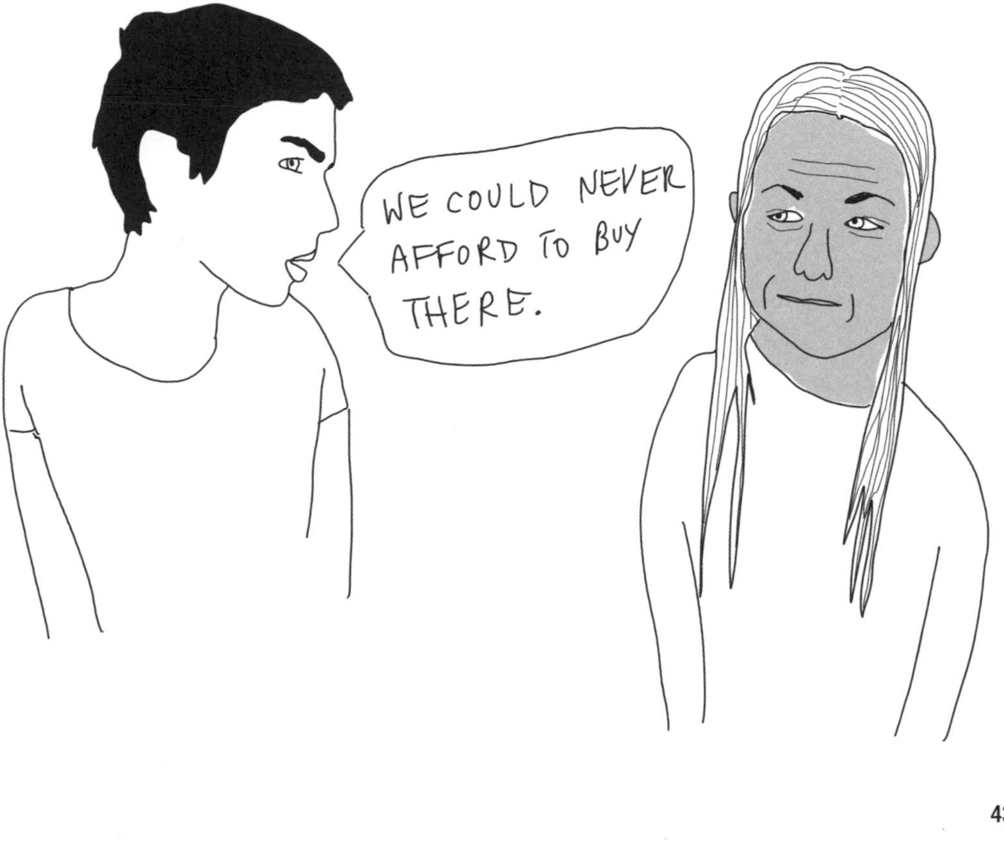
WE COULD NEVER AFFORD TO BUY THERE.

THIS GUY IS A PAIN IN THE ASS. BY THE TIME THE TRAIN GETS TO OUR STOP, THE CARS ARE SO FULL THERE MIGHT ONLY BE ONE WINDOW SEAT LEFT. **THIS GUY HAS TO HAVE IT.** THEN HE PULLS OUT A TERRIBLE NOVEL, SOME MASS-MARKET THRILLER GARBAGE, AND **DOESN'T LOOK OUT THE WINDOW.** IT'S JUST HIM AND JAMES PATTERSON, SOLVING CRIME WITHOUT LOOKING UP.

(ONE THING THAT ALL ALCOHOLICS KNOW IS THAT NO ONE COULD POSSIBLY HAVE BEHAVIORS THAT ARE UNRELATED TO YOU PERSONALLY. HE'S NOT SITTING BY THE WINDOW BECAUSE IT'S NICE, HE IS **TAKING IT AWAY FROM YOU.** THIS IS WHY IT'S CALLED A DISEASE.)

A NEW GUY WALKS UP, SO WE ALL LOOK AT HIM.
HE REMINDS ME OF A GUY I TOOK HOME ONCE AND
MADE OUT WITH IN BED UNTIL MY HAIR MATTED
UP INTO A **RAT'S NEST**. I HAD MY PERIOD SO
WE DION'T HAVE SEX. I THINK HE THOUGHT I WAS
DEMURE. HE WAS SLIGHTLY BALDING AND WORKED
IN MAGAZINES, BOTH OF WHICH I FOUND TO BE
IMPRESSIVE AND GENTLY AUTHORITATIVE. HIS
NAME WAS FRED.

NEW GUY

FRED

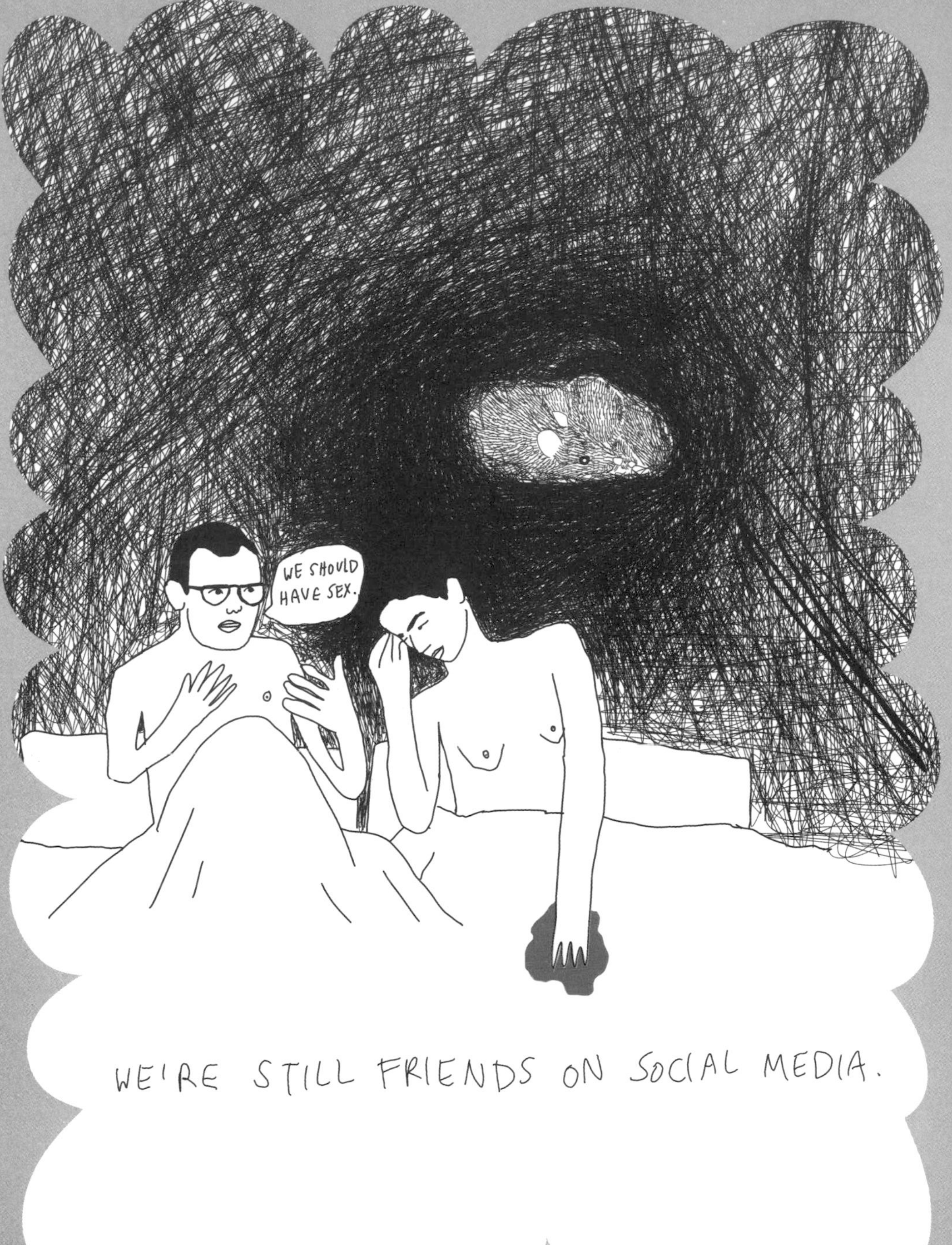
WE SHOULD HAVE SEX.
WE'RE STILL FRIENDS ON SOCIAL MEDIA.

A MAN IN A BLUE SUIT AND SNEAKERS LOOKS AT ME FOUR TIMES WHILE I WAIT FOR THE TRAIN.

(IT'S IMPORTANT THAT I KEEP YOU HERE, ON THIS COMMUTE. I WANT YOU TO UNDERSTAND WHAT IT'S LIKE TO BE CONSTANTLY REMINDED OF WHAT YOU ARE: DESIRABLE + VISIBLE OR UNDESIRABLE + INVISIBLE. WITH THE FIRST COMES A CONSTANT + VAGUE SENSE OF THREAT. WITH THE SECOND COMES LONELINESS. THIS IS WHAT IT MEANS TO BE A

WOMAN IN PUBLIC.)

WAIT A MINUTE. LET'S GO BACK AGAIN.
I WANT TO TALK ABOUT ARTHUR.

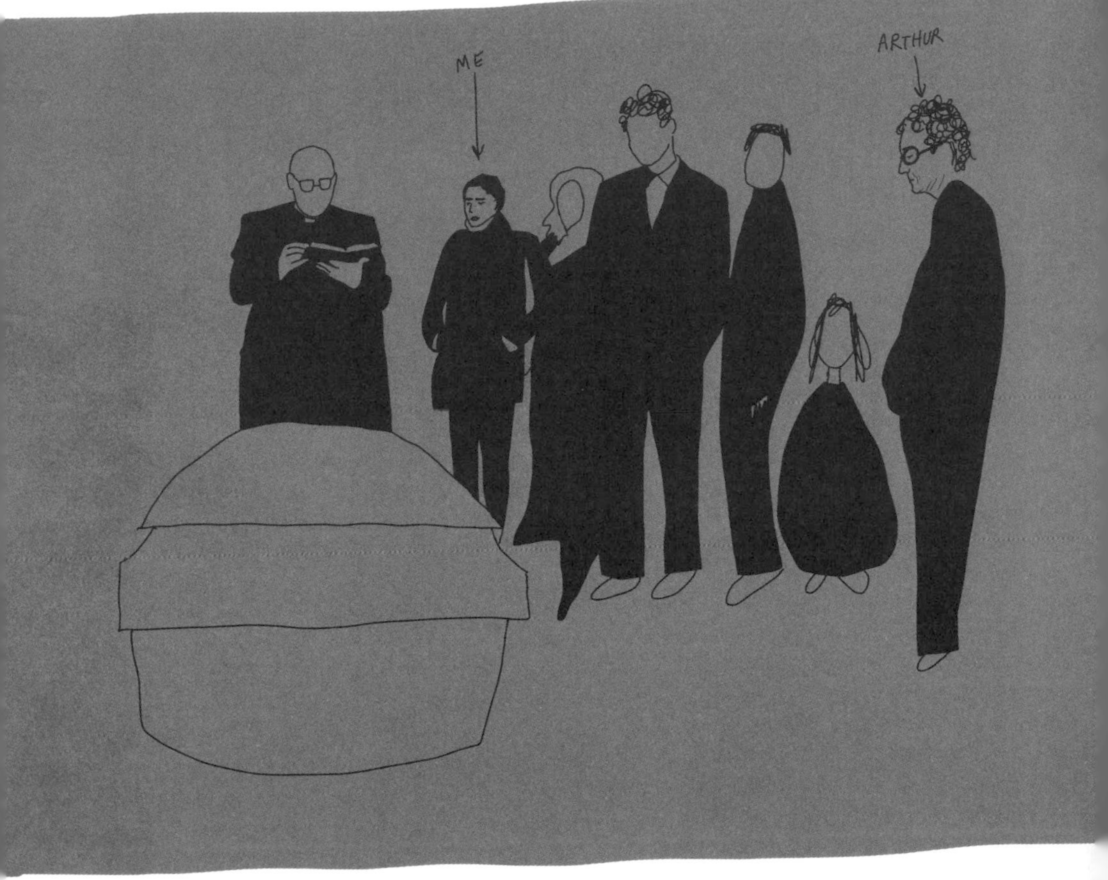

ME
ARTHUR

I MET ARTHUR AT MY GRANDFATHER'S FUNERAL.

MY GRANDFATHER WAS A PROFESSOR. ARTHUR WAS HIS STUDENT IN THE 1970s.

WHEN WE MET, ARTHUR WAS A PROFESSOR AT A COMMUNITY COLLEGE. I WAS A RECENT COLLEGE GRADUATE.

OBVIOUSLY WE HAD A LOT IN COMMON.

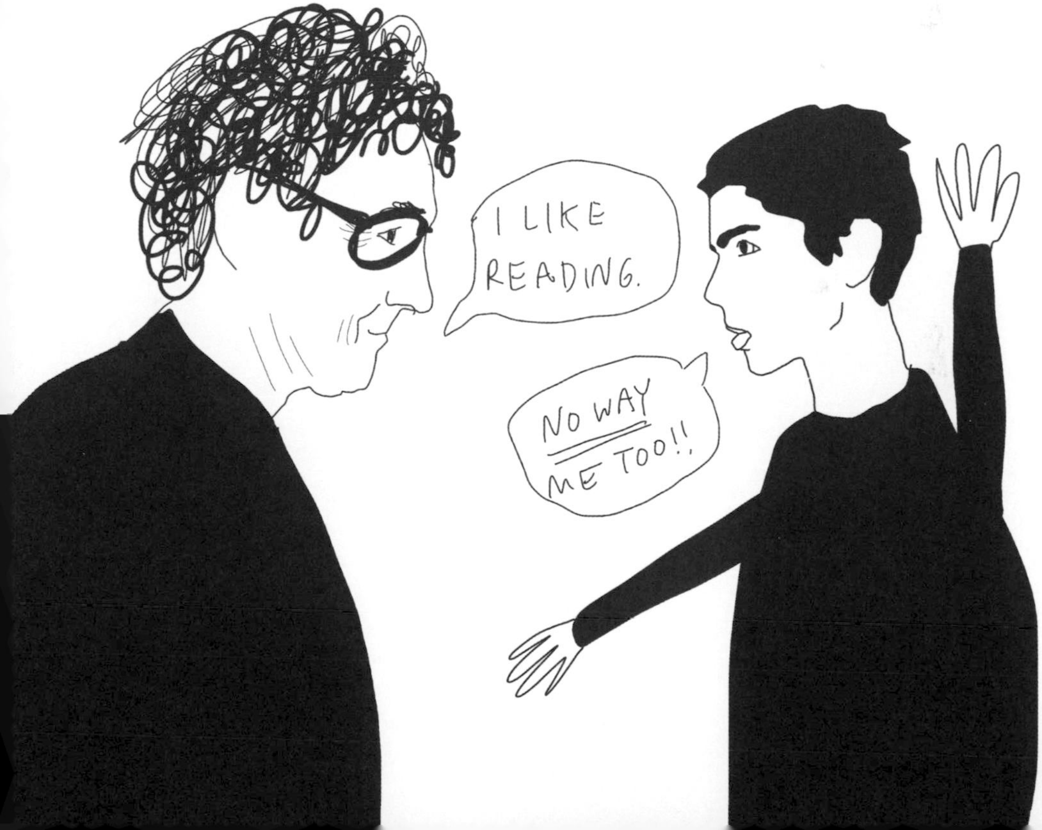
I LIKE READING.
NO WAY ME TOO!!

WE BECAME PEN PALS AND TALKED ON THE
PHONE FOR HOURS.

Dearest Erin,
I was thinking of you in my garden
today as I planted a patch of eggplants.
They love sunlight + water.
Did you ever realize that love
is a weed? Like dandelions,
love persists.   Love,
                          Arthur

DEAR ARTHUR,
    KIERKEGAARD IS _AMAZING!!!!_
I CAN'T BELIEVE I'D
NEVER READ THE FIRST
4 PAGES OF FEAR + TREMB-
LING BEFORE.
COOL ABOUT YOUR GARDEN. IT'S
COLD HERE. I'M GONNA GO
DRINK UNTIL I FORGET WHAT
TEMPERATURE IS.
                LOVE,
                      ERIN

← HE EXCLUSIVELY WROTE
ON OLD LADY CARDS
WITH FLOWERS ON THE
FRONT AND TALKED NON-
STOP ABOUT HIS GARDEN.

I LIVED WITH MY PARENTS AND WROTE ON
LOOSELEAF LEFT OVER FROM HIGH SCHOOL.

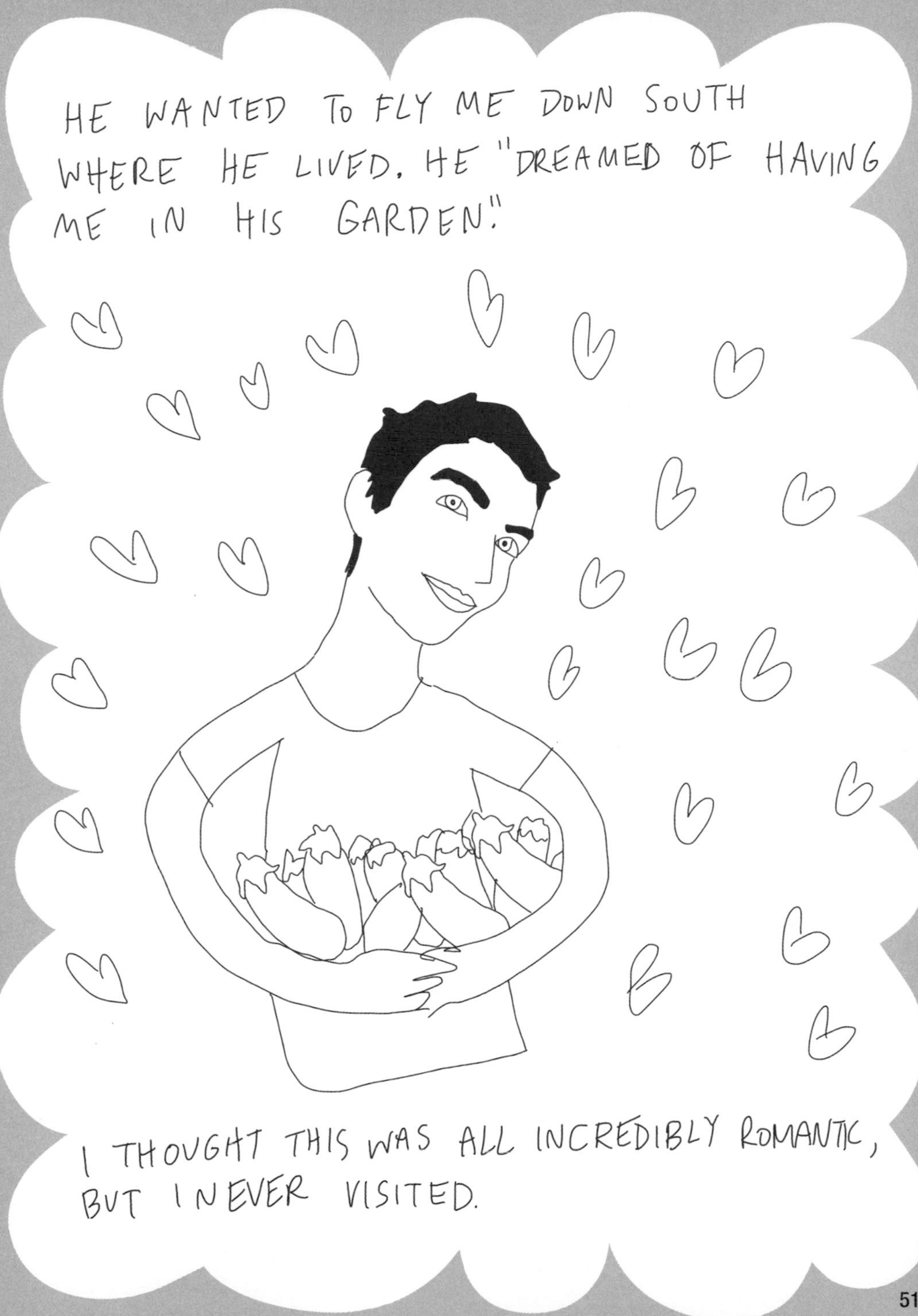
HE WANTED TO FLY ME DOWN SOUTH WHERE HE LIVED. HE "DREAMED OF HAVING ME IN HIS GARDEN."
I THOUGHT THIS WAS ALL INCREDIBLY ROMANTIC, BUT I NEVER VISITED.

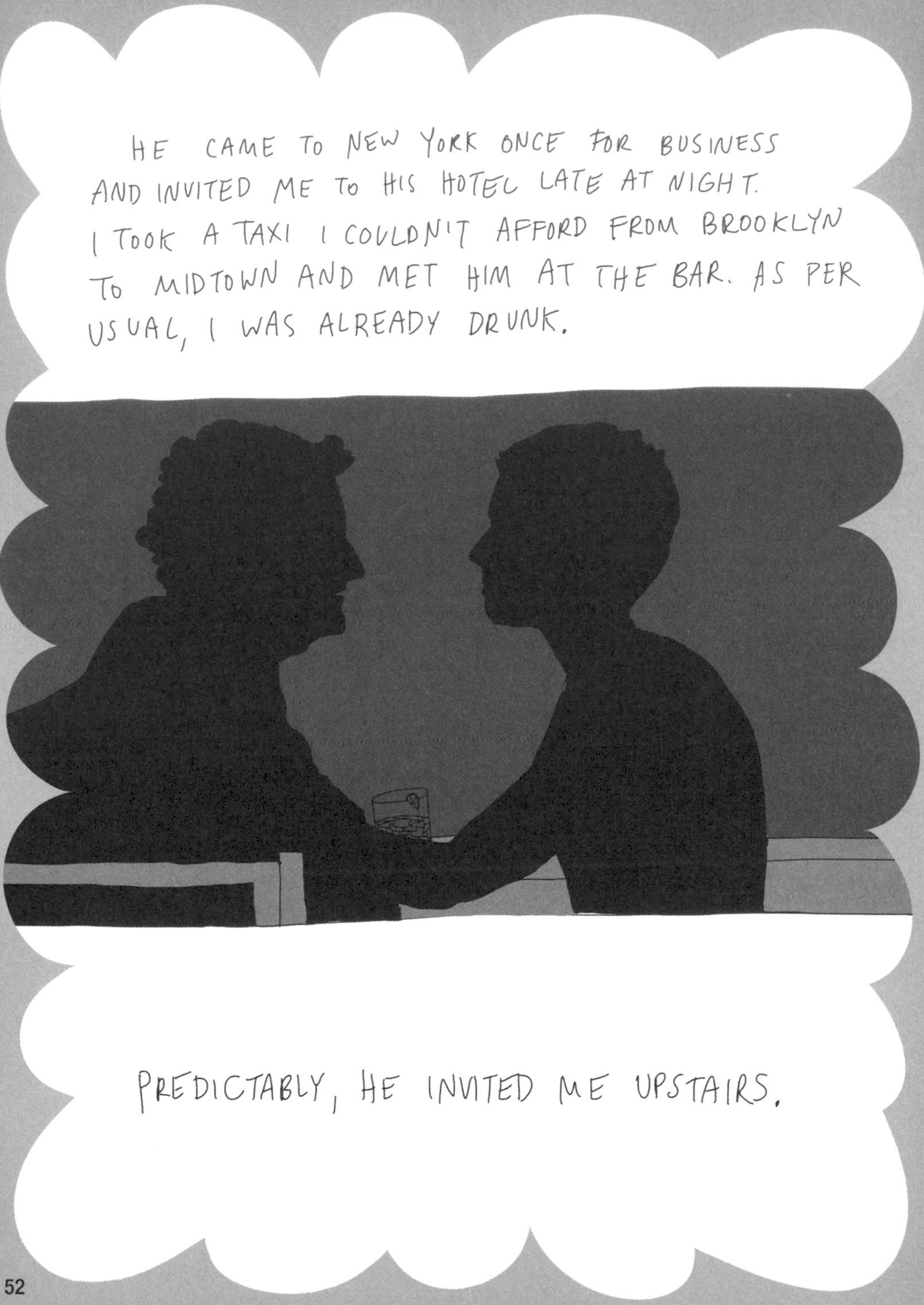
HE CAME TO NEW YORK ONCE FOR BUSINESS AND INVITED ME TO HIS HOTEL LATE AT NIGHT. I TOOK A TAXI I COULDN'T AFFORD FROM BROOKLYN TO MIDTOWN AND MET HIM AT THE BAR. AS PER USUAL, I WAS ALREADY DRUNK.
PREDICTABLY, HE INVITED ME UPSTAIRS.

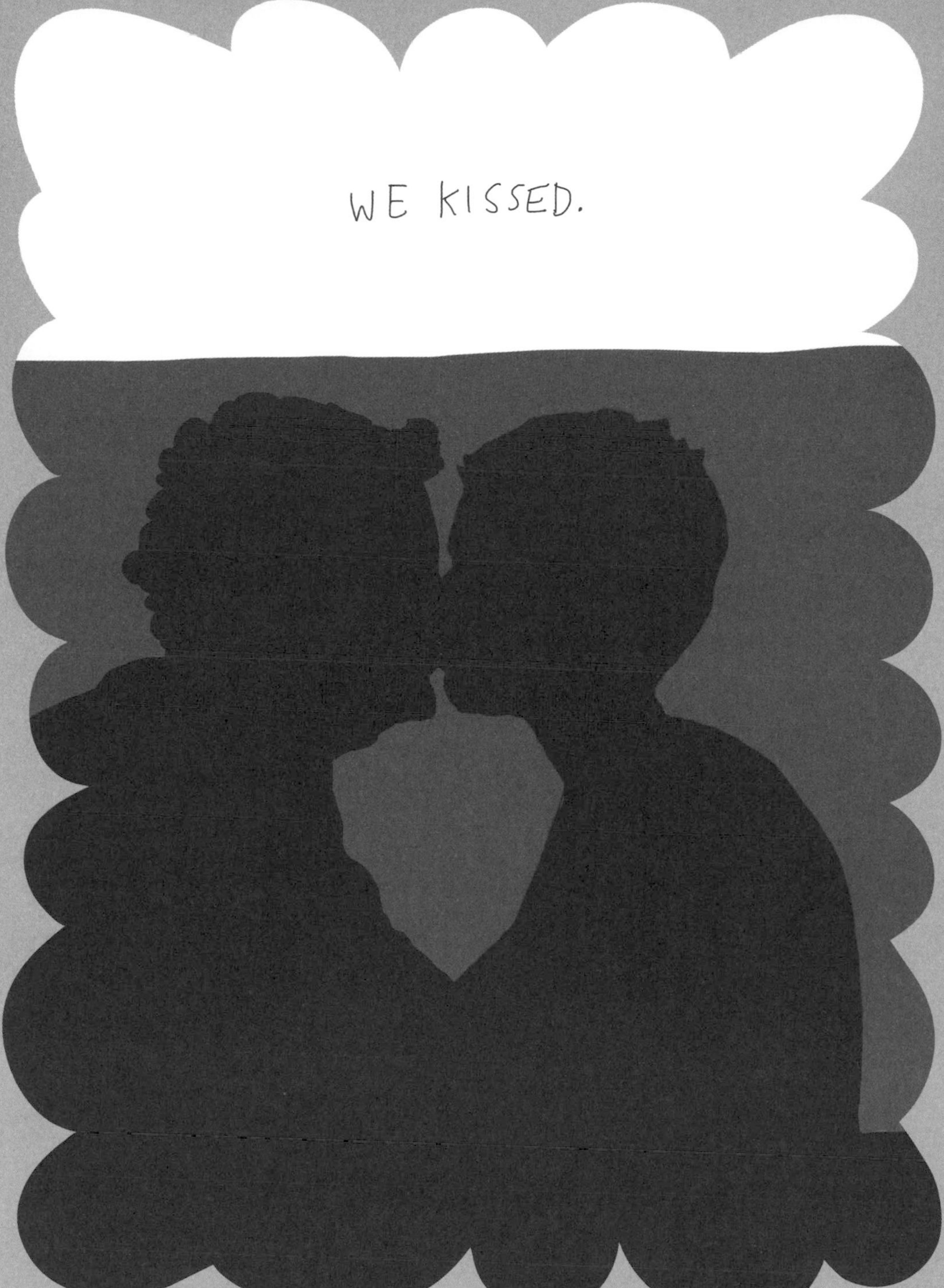
WE KISSED.

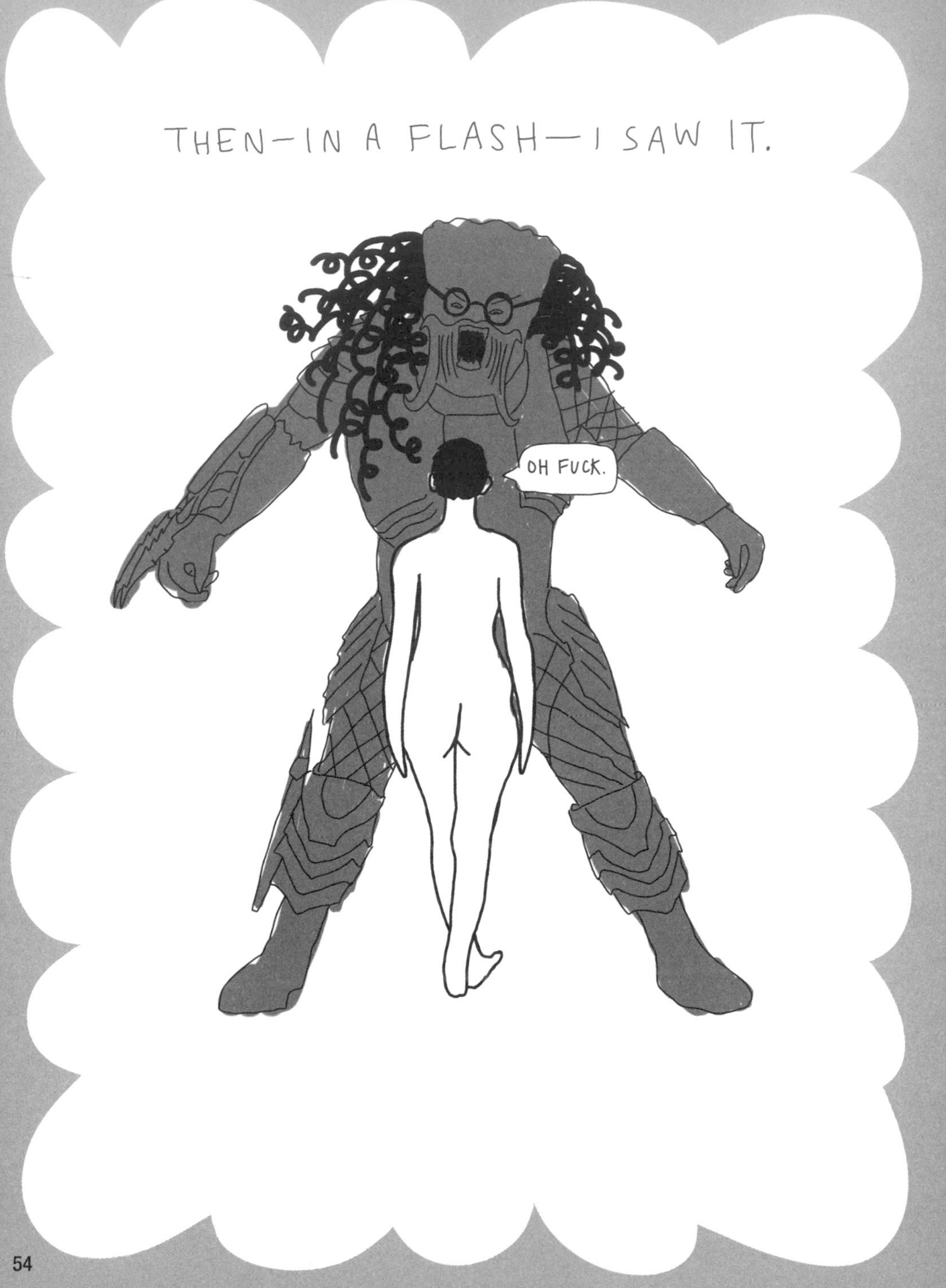
THEN—IN A FLASH—I SAW IT.
OH FUCK.

IN HIM, IN ALL MEN, I TRIED TO DISAPPEAR.
THIS IS DIFFERENT THAN OTHER DISAPPEARING.
IT'S ABOUT WANTING DESPERATELY TO BE
SEEN.

IN THE MOMENT BEFORE HE
CONSUMES ME, I SEE IT. ON HIS FACE
AND IN HOW HUNGRY HE IS.

HE DOESN'T SEE ME AT ALL.

BLINDED BY THE THICK BRUME OF HIS
OWN THUNDEROUS NEED.

HE'S GONNA EAT YOU UP. RAW. SPINDLY
BONES AND JELLY LEGS. WONKY EYE,
PUBIC HAIR, SUNKEN POSTURE.

I COULD NOT DISAPPEAR — TO
DISAPPEAR, YOU HAD TO HAVE BEEN
THERE IN THE FIRST PLACE.

GET THE FUCK OUT OF THERE, GIRL.

(I TOLD MYSELF.)

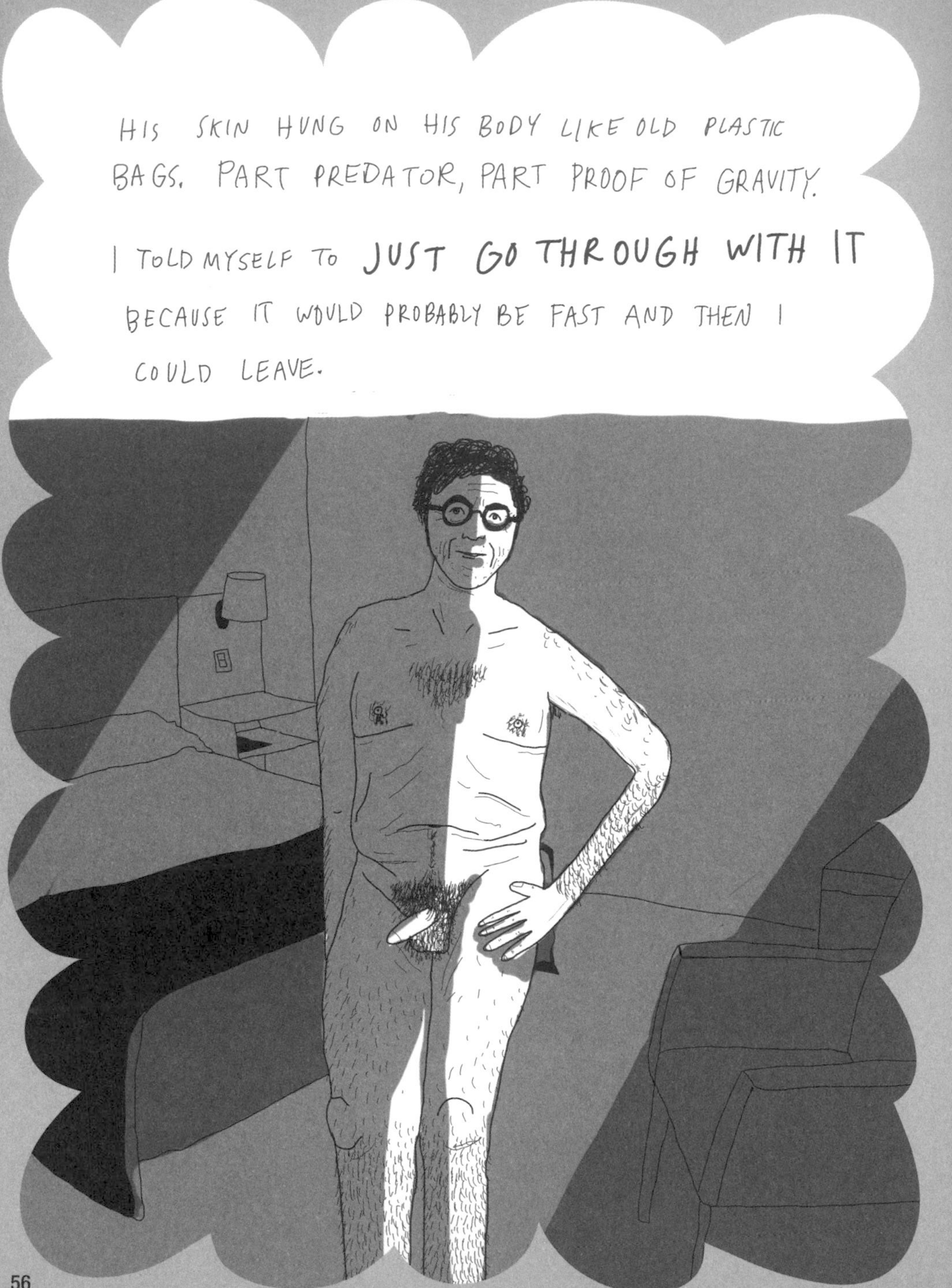
HIS SKIN HUNG ON HIS BODY LIKE OLD PLASTIC BAGS. PART PREDATOR, PART PROOF OF GRAVITY.
I TOLD MYSELF TO JUST GO THROUGH WITH IT BECAUSE IT WOULD PROBABLY BE FAST AND THEN I COULD LEAVE.

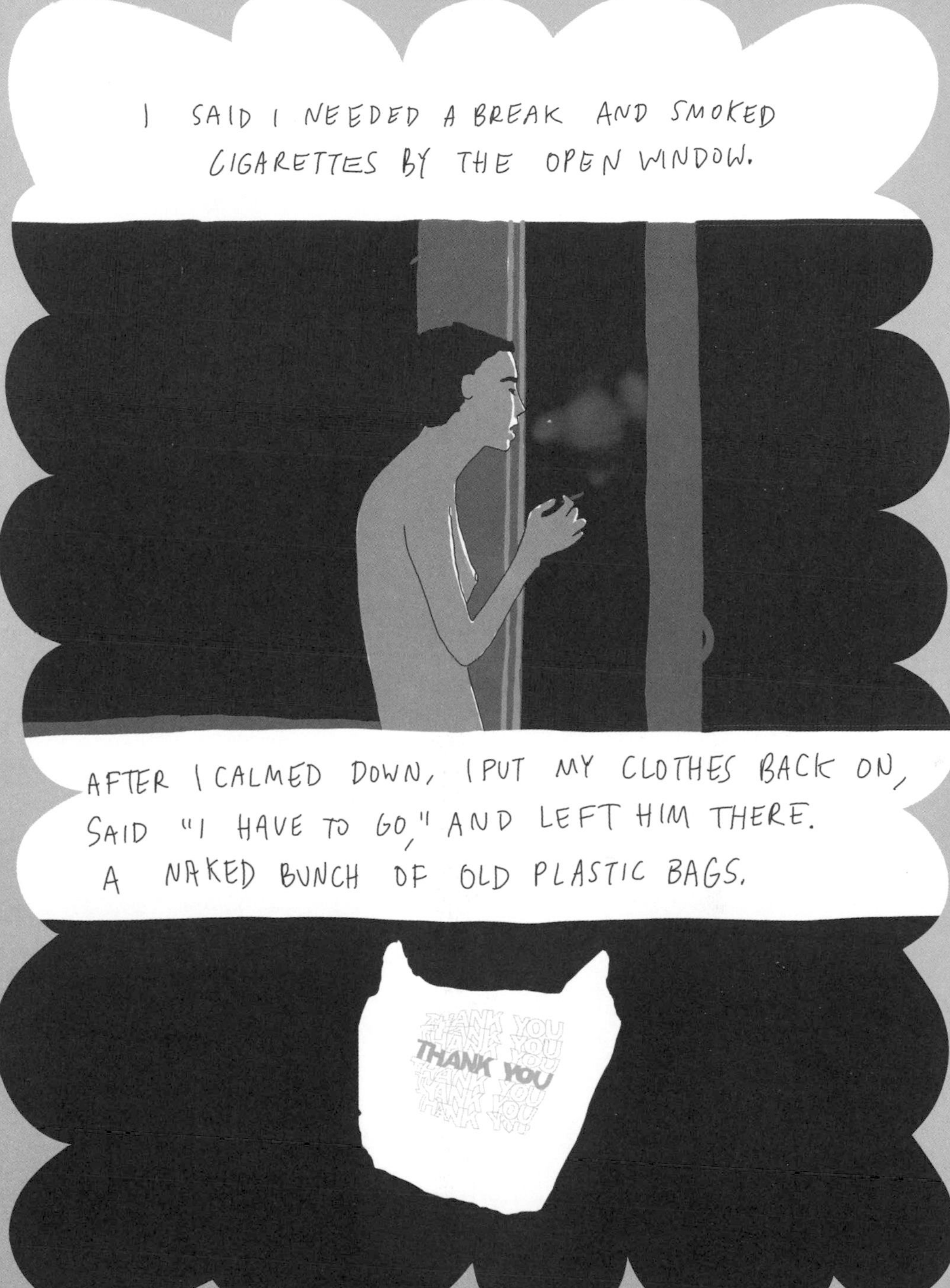
I SAID I NEEDED A BREAK AND SMOKED CIGARETTES BY THE OPEN WINDOW.
AFTER I CALMED DOWN, I PUT MY CLOTHES BACK ON, SAID "I HAVE TO GO," AND LEFT HIM THERE. A NAKED BUNCH OF OLD PLASTIC BAGS.
THANK YOU

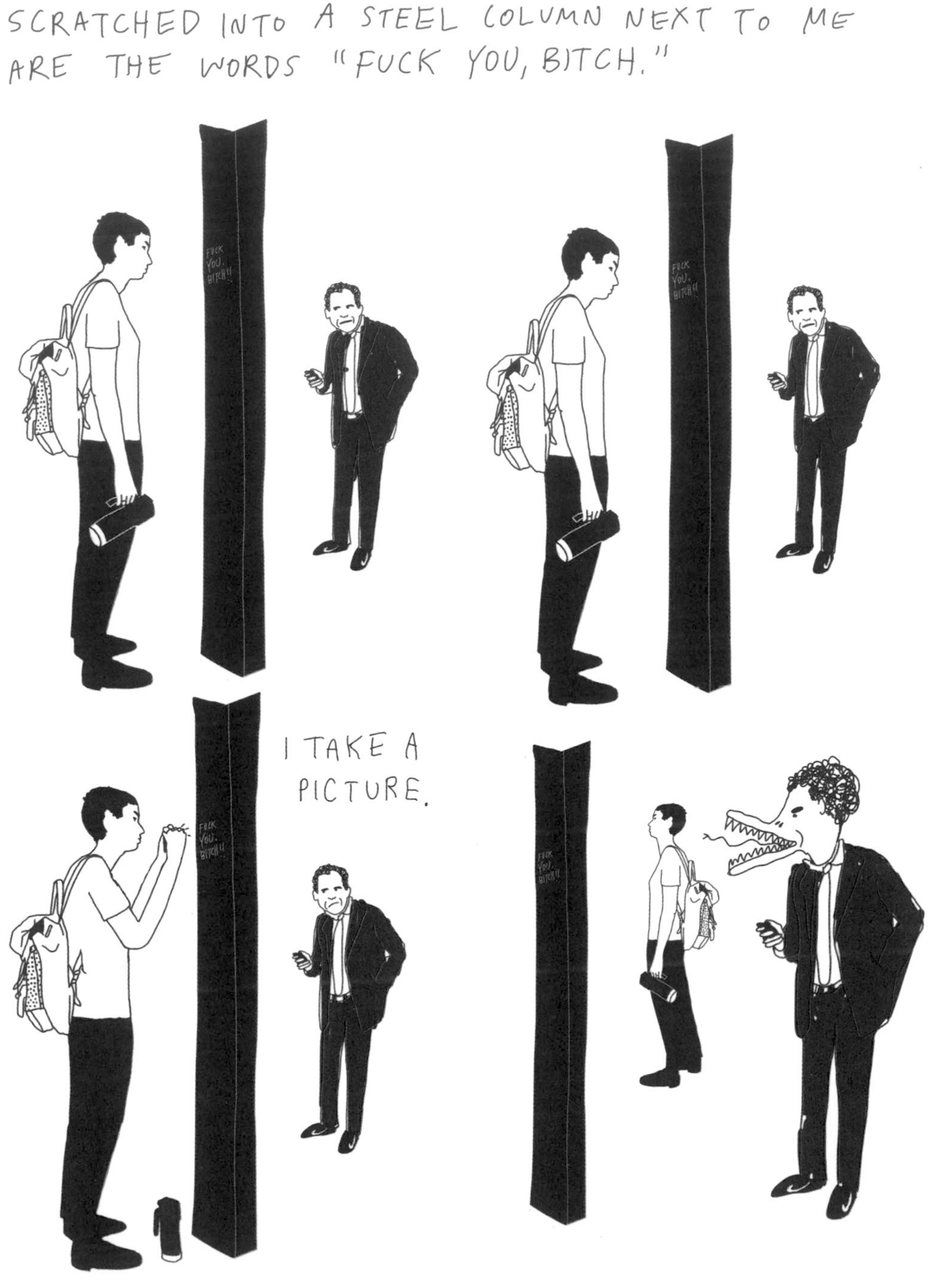
SCRATCHED INTO A STEEL COLUMN NEXT TO ME ARE THE WORDS "FUCK YOU, BITCH."
FUCK YOU, BITCH!!
FUCK YOU, BITCH!!
FUCK YOU, BITCH!!
I TAKE A PICTURE.
FUCK YOU, BITCH!!

RIDE THE TRAIN

I SIT DOWN, AND THE MAN WHO WAS LOOKING AT ME WHILE I WAS JUST STANDING THERE SITS ACROSS FROM ME, ONE ROW DOWN, EVEN THOUGH THERE ARE OTHER SEATS CLOSER TO THE DOOR. AFTER HE SITS, HE LOOKS AT ME AGAIN.

I PRETEND NOT TO NOTICE.

WHEN HE'S NOT LOOKING, I TAKE A PICTURE OF HIS SHOES.

IT'S A SMALL PERSONAL INVASION, NOT ON PAR WITH HIS RELENTLESS STARING, BUT IT'S ALL I HAVE THE COURAGE OR CARE FOR.

I SIT ON THE SAME SEAT ON THE TRAIN EVERY MORNING. ONE STOP AFTER MINE, THE SAME GUY GETS ON. HE PASSES BY THE EMPTY SEATS JUST LIKE MINE WITH THE SAME SEATS OPEN AND FINDS ME AND SITS NEXT TO ME. WE DON'T KNOW EACH OTHER. WE'VE BEEN SITTING TOGETHER SO LONG THAT NOW HE SAYS GOOD MORNING.

HE TAKES HIS iPAD OUT OF HIS BACKPACK, WHICH LOOKS LIKE THIS. ———▶

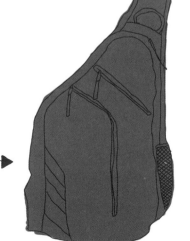

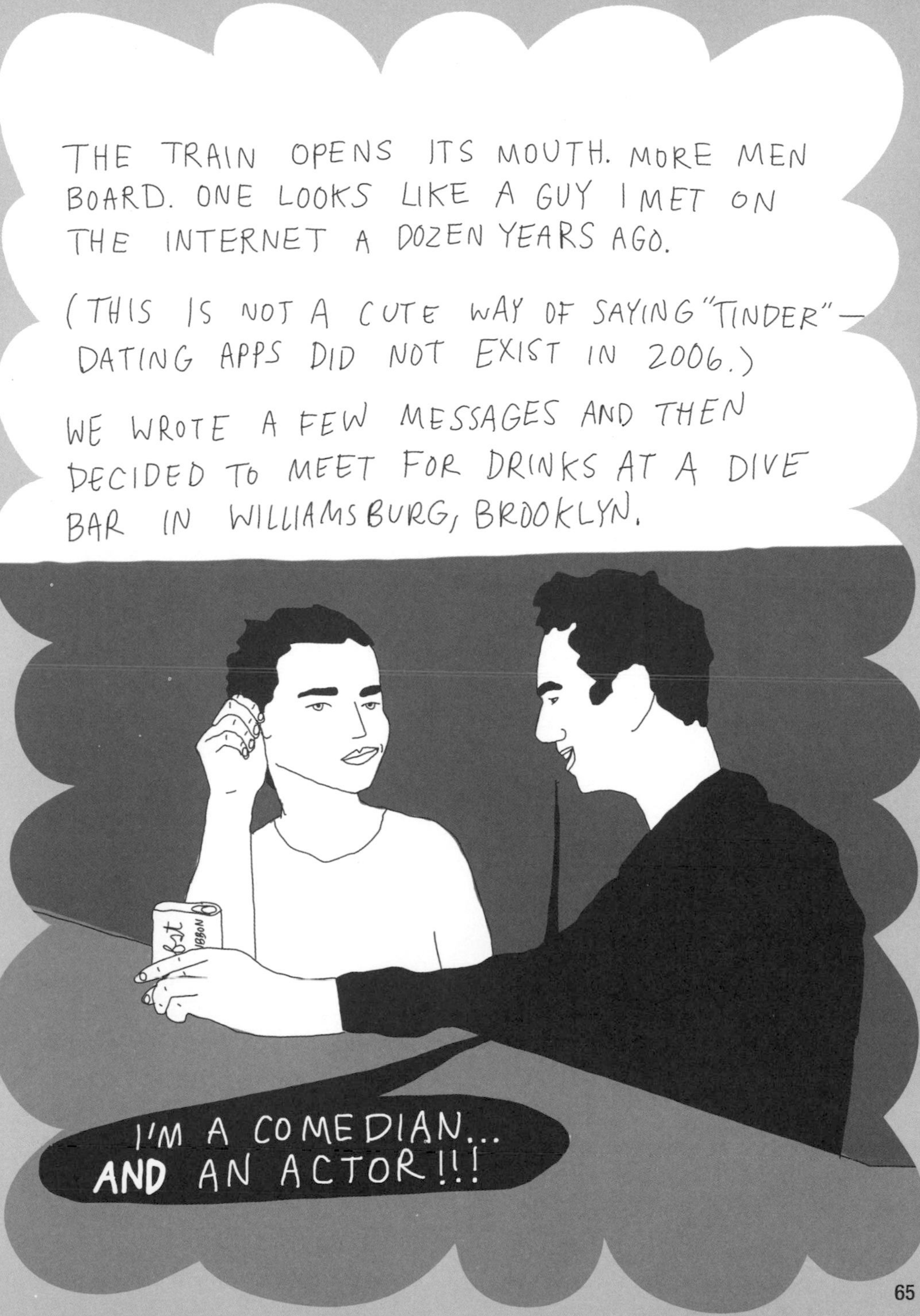
THE TRAIN OPENS ITS MOUTH. MORE MEN BOARD. ONE LOOKS LIKE A GUY I MET ON THE INTERNET A DOZEN YEARS AGO.
(THIS IS NOT A CUTE WAY OF SAYING "TINDER"— DATING APPS DID NOT EXIST IN 2006.)
WE WROTE A FEW MESSAGES AND THEN DECIDED TO MEET FOR DRINKS AT A DIVE BAR IN WILLIAMSBURG, BROOKLYN.
I'M A COMEDIAN... AND AN ACTOR!!!

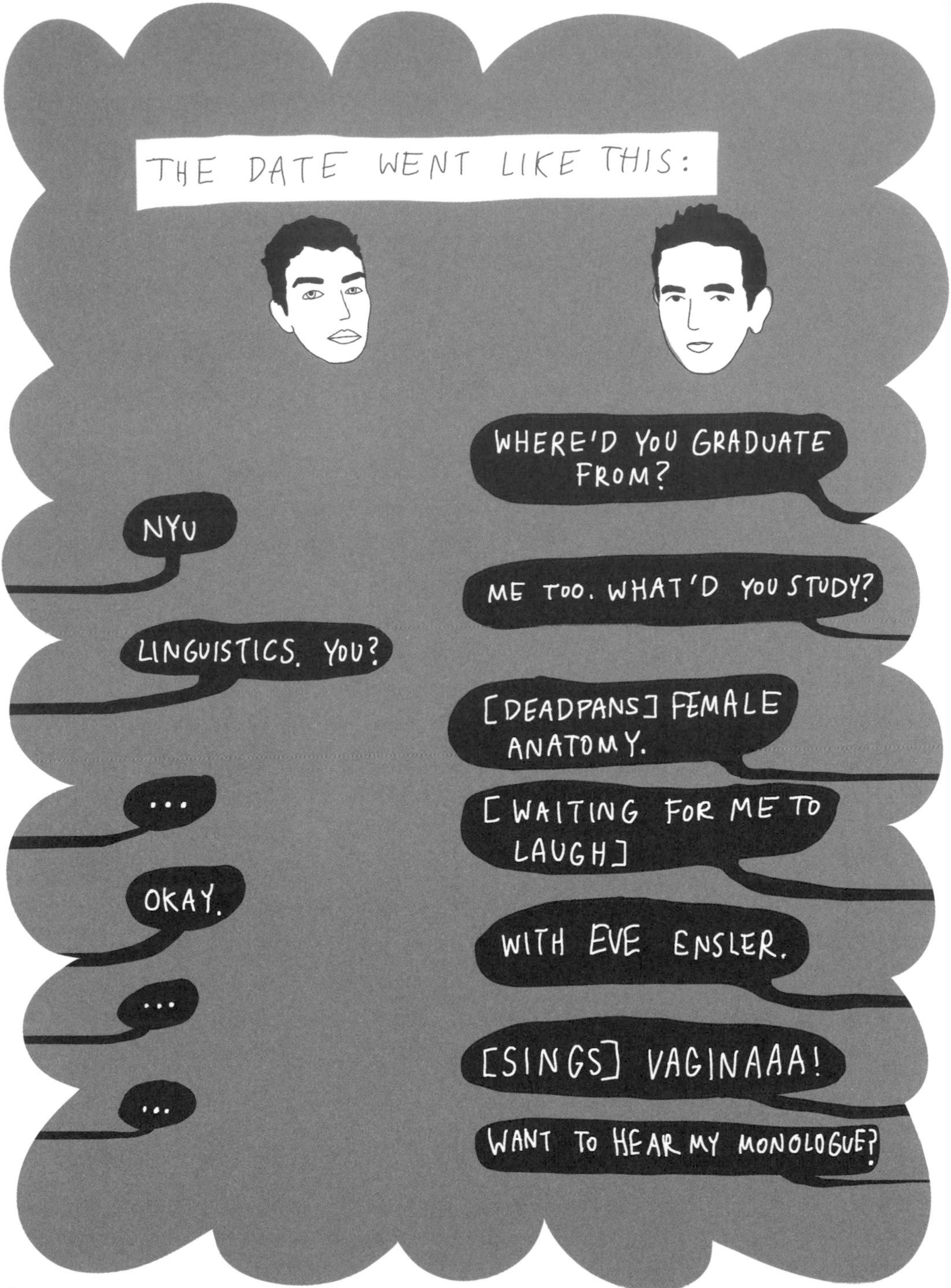
THE DATE WENT LIKE THIS:
WHERE'D YOU GRADUATE FROM?
NYU
ME TOO. WHAT'D YOU STUDY?
LINGUISTICS. YOU?
[DEADPANS] FEMALE ANATOMY.
...
[WAITING FOR ME TO LAUGH]
OKAY.
WITH EVE ENSLER.
...
[SINGS] VAGINAAA!
...
WANT TO HEAR MY MONOLOGUE?

EVERYTHING I SAID CREATED AN
OPPORTUNITY FOR HIM TO PERFORM.
I REALIZED QUICKLY THAT I WAS NOT
ON THIS DATE AS A PARTICIPANT, BUT
AS A WITNESS TO HIS DRAMATIC
PORTRAYAL OF A MAN ON A DATE.

DATE WITH
RYAN

TOMATOMETER ❓

✳ **2%**

Average Rating: .2/10
Reviews Counted: 2
Fresh: 1
Rotten: 1

All Critics | Top Critics

Critics Consensus: *Date with Ryan* chronicles the extremely uncomfortable first date between a grandiose narcissist and a young alcoholic, desperate for male attention.

AUDIENCE SCORE ❓

🗑 **3%**
liked it

Average Rating: 0/5
User Ratings: 6

ADD YOUR RATING

(– NOT INTERESTED) (+ CAN'T LOOK AWAY) ★★★★★

ADD A REVIEW (OPTIONAL)

Post

SO, I DID THE ONLY REASONABLE THING I COULD THINK OF: I GOT DRUNK AND INVITED HIM OVER.
WE MADE OUT...
HICCUP

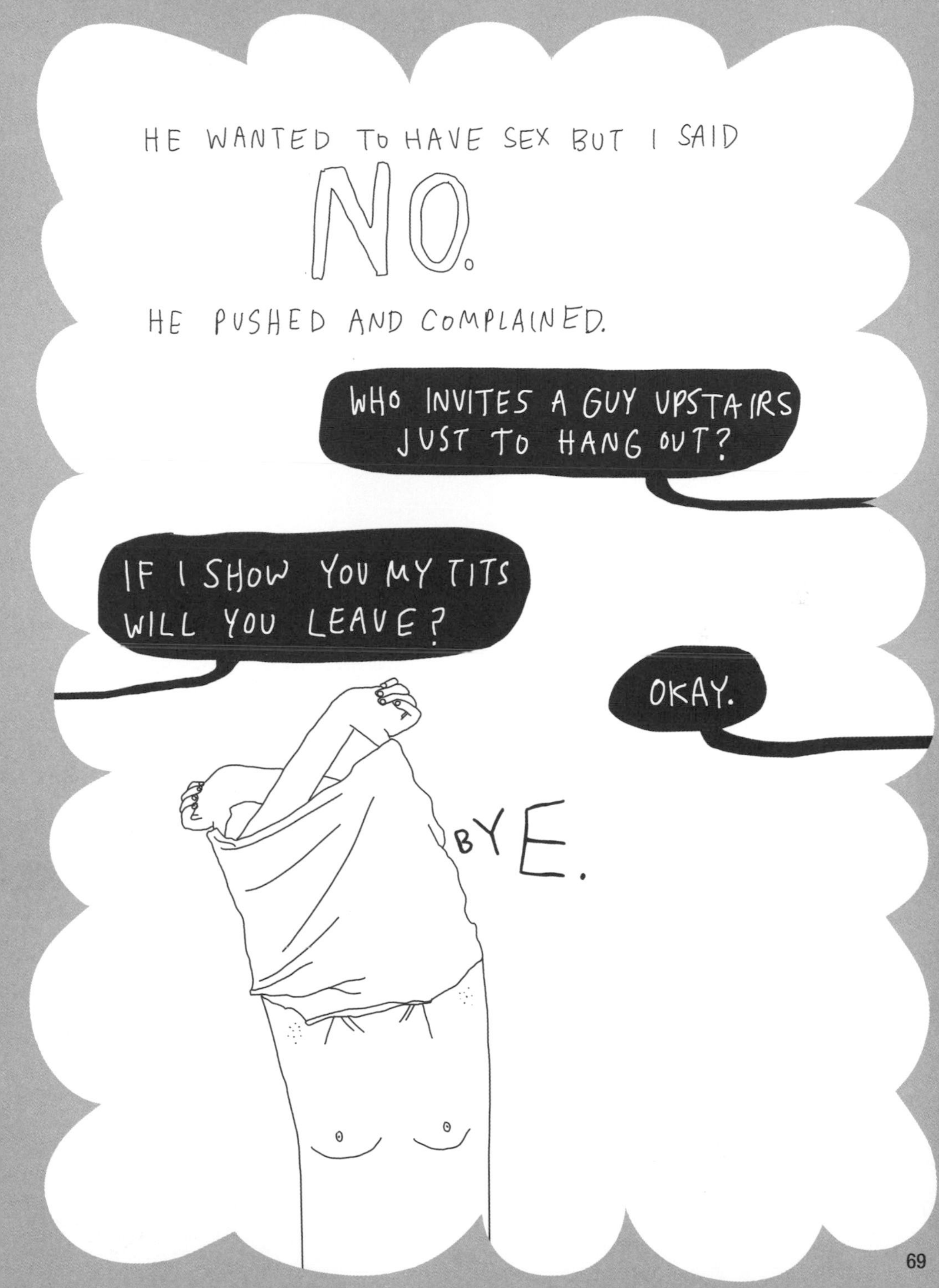
HE WANTED TO HAVE SEX BUT I SAID
NO.
HE PUSHED AND COMPLAINED.
WHO INVITES A GUY UPSTAIRS JUST TO HANG OUT?
IF I SHOW YOU MY TITS WILL YOU LEAVE?
OKAY.
BYE.

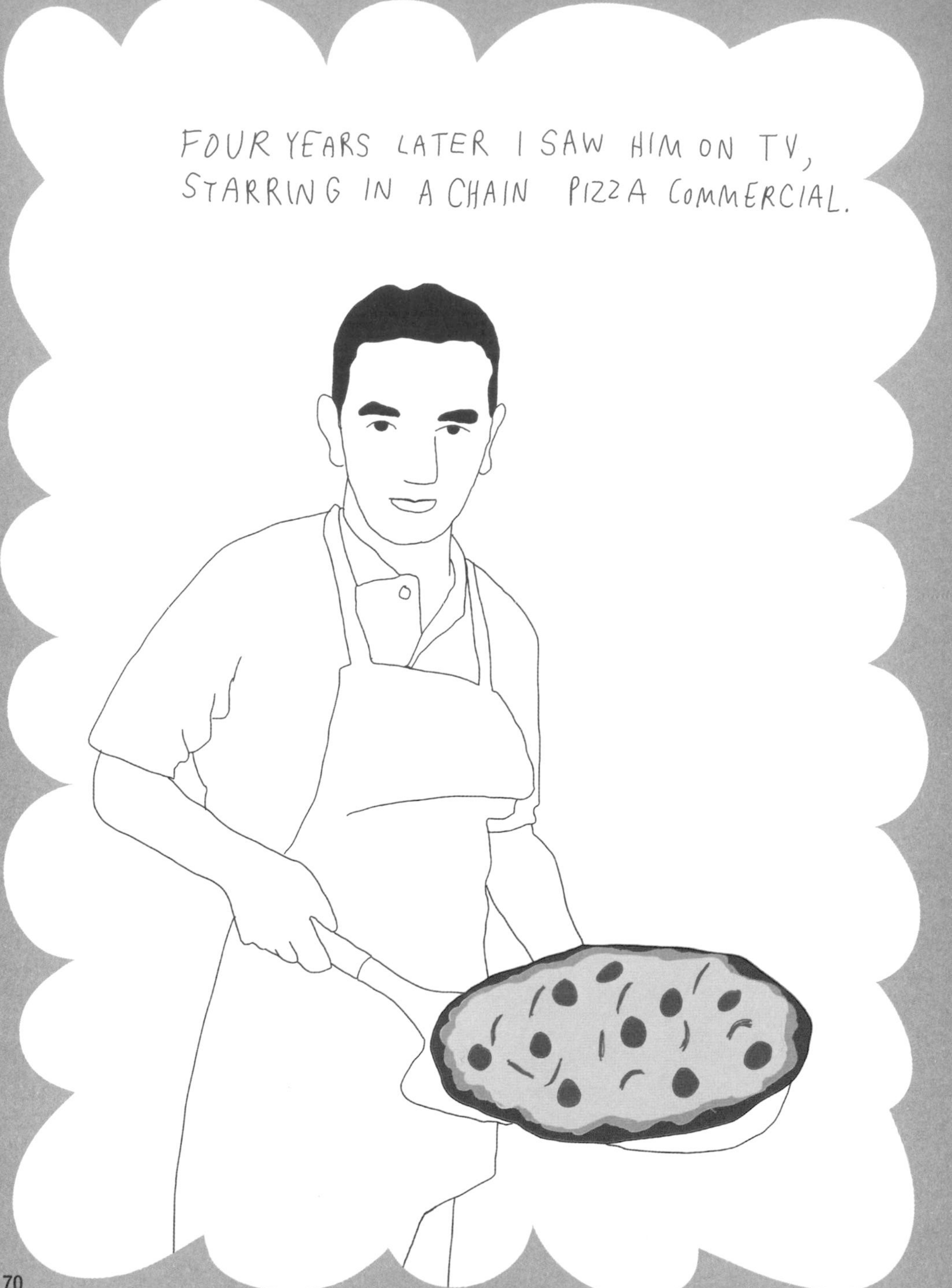
FOUR YEARS LATER I SAW HIM ON TV, STARRING IN A CHAIN PIZZA COMMERCIAL.

ON THE TRAIN (WE ARE BACK ON THE TRAIN) I READ ANY POETRY CAIT TELLS ME TO, EVERYTHING EMILY BOOKS PUBLISHES. I READ BRAVE BOOKS BY BRILLIANT WOMEN. I READ:

I LOVE DICK
Chris Kraus
ERIN BELIEU
SLANT SIX
THE GIFT
BARBARA BROWNING
THE ARGONAUTS
MAGGIE NELSON
CAIT
VALLEYSPEAK
Bad Feminist
Roxane Gay
AFTER CLAUDE
IRIS OWENS
DON'T LET ME BE LONELY
AN AMERICAN LYRIC
CLAUDIA RANKINE
EILEEN
OTTESSA MOSHFEGH

(I DON'T READ BOOKS BY MEN BECAUSE I FEEL SUFFICIENTLY WELL-VERSED IN THE HUMAN MALE EXPERIENCE FROM MY EDUCATION.)

WHEN A PASSAGE IS PARLICULARLY GUTTING, I PUT MY FINGER ON THE LAST WORD TO SAVE MY PLACE AND LOOK UP OUT THE WINDOW TO THINK.

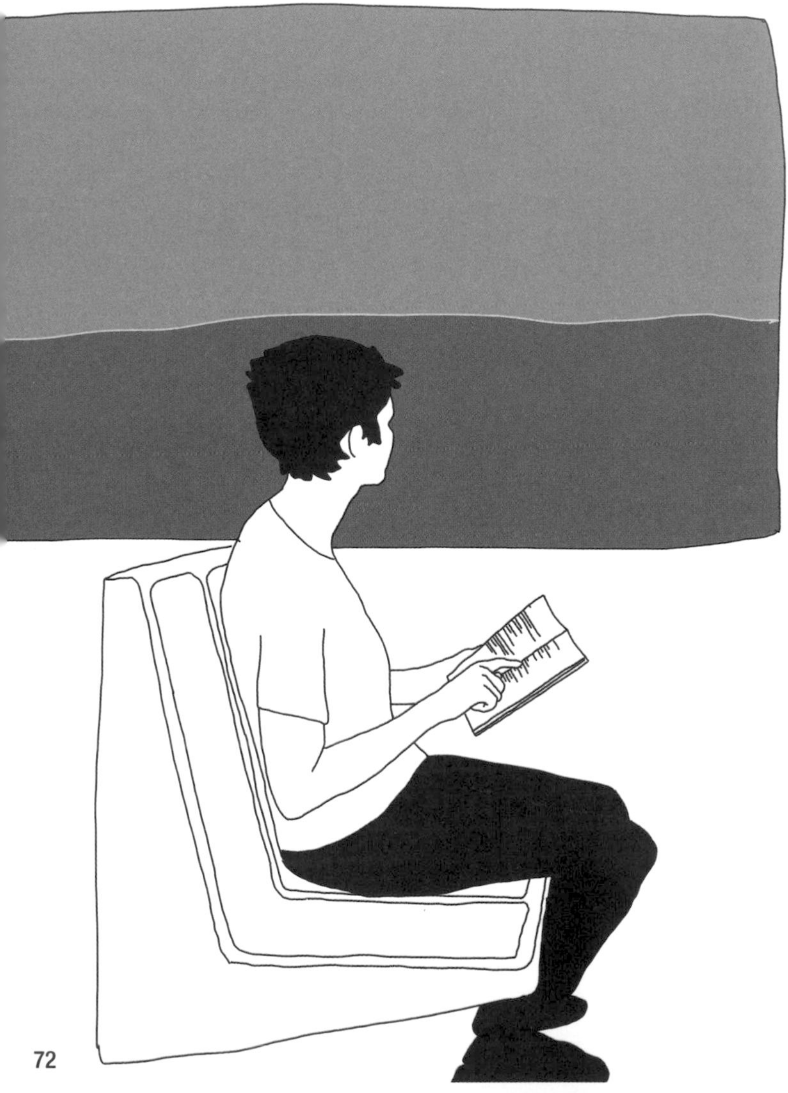

I WATCH THE EXPENSIVE HOUSES AND MANICURED BACKYARDS GLIDE BY WHILE I THINK ABOUT WHAT MAGGIE NELSON SAYS MARY ROACH SAYS ABOUT THE ASTOUNDING NUMBER OF NERVES IN THE HUMAN ASSHOLE. IT'S SO THAT THE ASSHOLE CAN DISTINGUISH BETWEEN SOLID, LIQUID, AND GAS.

KEY
NERVES
BUTT
BUTTHOLE
VAGINA
PEEHOLE
CLIT

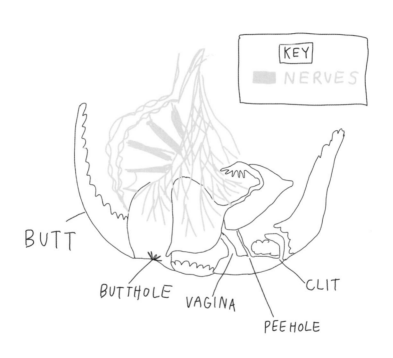

I NEVER APPRECIATED MY ABILITY TO DO THAT BEFORE. BUT IT'S TRUE THAT I CAN DISTINGUISH BETWEEN A SHIT AND A FART WITHOUT THINKING ABOUT IT.

I MAKE INDISCREET MARGINALIA.

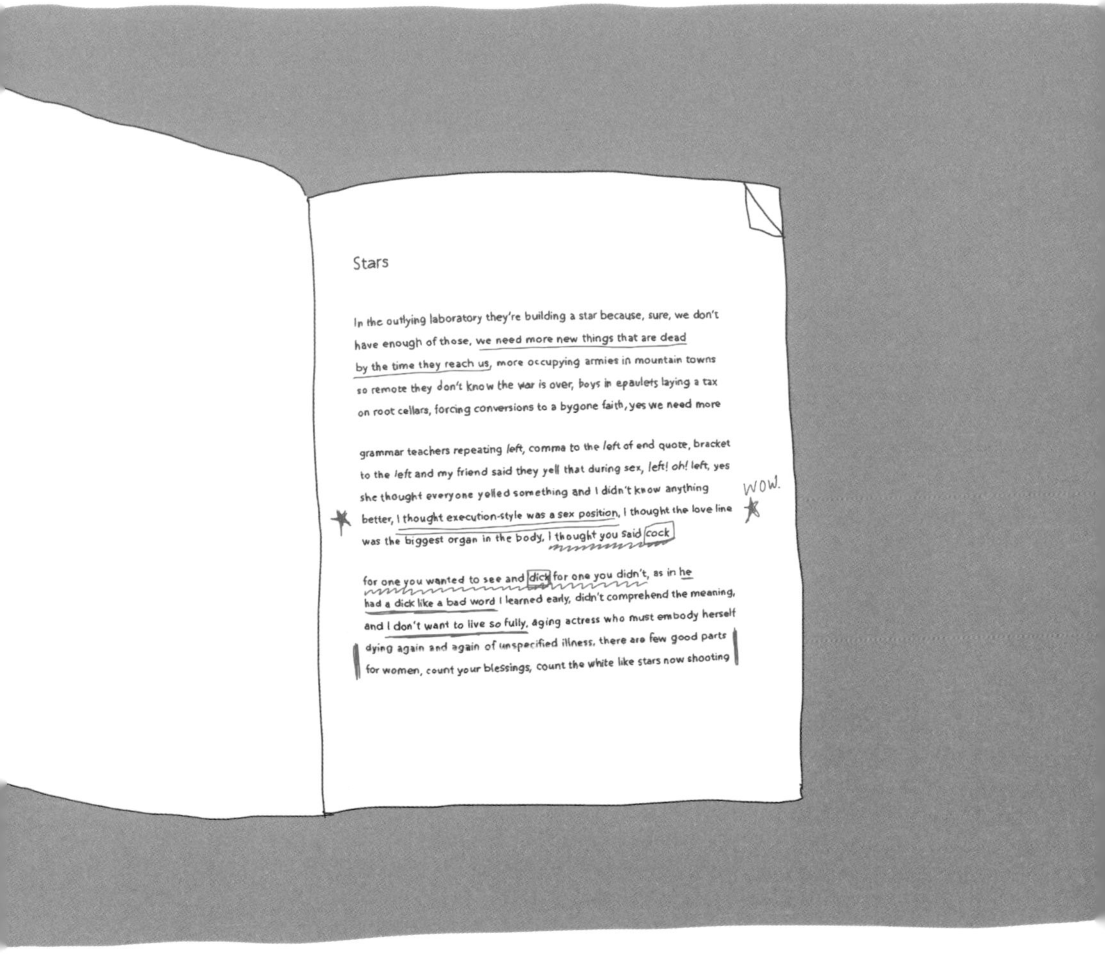
Stars
In the outlying laboratory they're building a star because, sure, we don't
have enough of those, we need more new things that are dead
by the time they reach us, more occupying armies in mountain towns
so remote they don't know the war is over, boys in epaulets laying a tax
on root cellars, forcing conversions to a bygone faith, yes we need more
grammar teachers repeating left, comma to the left of end quote, bracket
to the left and my friend said they yell that during sex, left! oh! left, yes
she thought everyone yelled something and I didn't know anything
better, I thought execution-style was a sex position, I thought the love line
was the biggest organ in the body, I thought you said cock
for one you wanted to see and dick for one you didn't, as in he
had a dick like a bad word I learned early, didn't comprehend the meaning,
and I don't want to live so fully, aging actress who must embody herself
dying again and again of unspecified illness, there are few good parts
for women, count your blessings, count the white like stars now shooting
WOW.

WHEN I FORGET A PEN, I BORROW ONE.

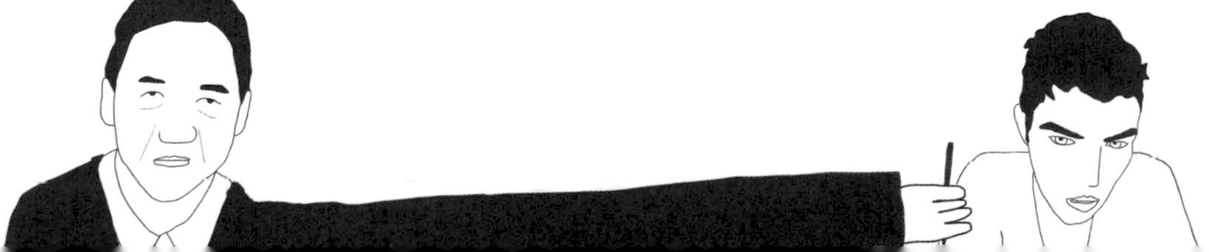

NATALIE SHAPERO SAYS IN A POEM THAT SHE
THOUGHT "EXECUTION-STYLE WAS A SEX POSITION,"
AND I UNDERSTAND THIS COMPLETELY.

THIS WAS
RECONFIRMED BY
CHILDBIRTH WHEN
I WAS SLICED
OPEN ACROSS
THE MIDDLE
IN THE SHAPE
OF A

SMILE

WHILE I WAS
STILL AWAKE.

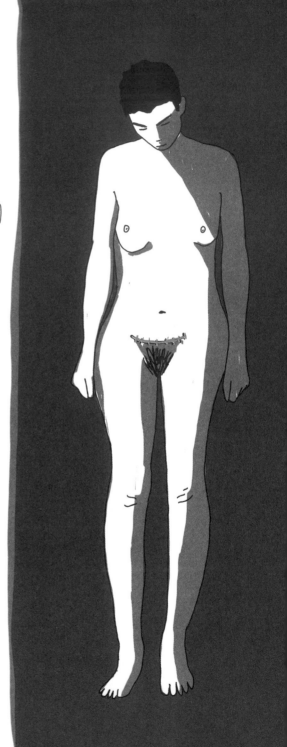

THE BODY REMEMBERS THINGS THAT THE MIND WOULD RATHER FORGET.

I FIGHT ALL DAY FOR CONTROL OF MY BODY, PUBLICLY AND PRIVATELY. FOR HOW I'M ALLOWED TO BE HANDLED AND TOUCHED AND LOOKED AT. FOR WHEN I AM ALLOWED TO SHIT AND WHEN TO HOLD IT. FOR WHEN TO EAT AND HOW AND WHEN TO STOP OR RISK FATNESS AND UNDESIRABILITY.

MY MIND WOULD LIKE TO FORGET WHAT IT FEELS LIKE TO BE TREATED ONLY AS A BODY, AN ASSEMBLY OF HOLES.

BUT THE BODY AND ITS COLONIES EXPLODE WITH NEED.

TO DENY THESE TWO PARTS IS TO DENY YOUR OWN HUMANITY.

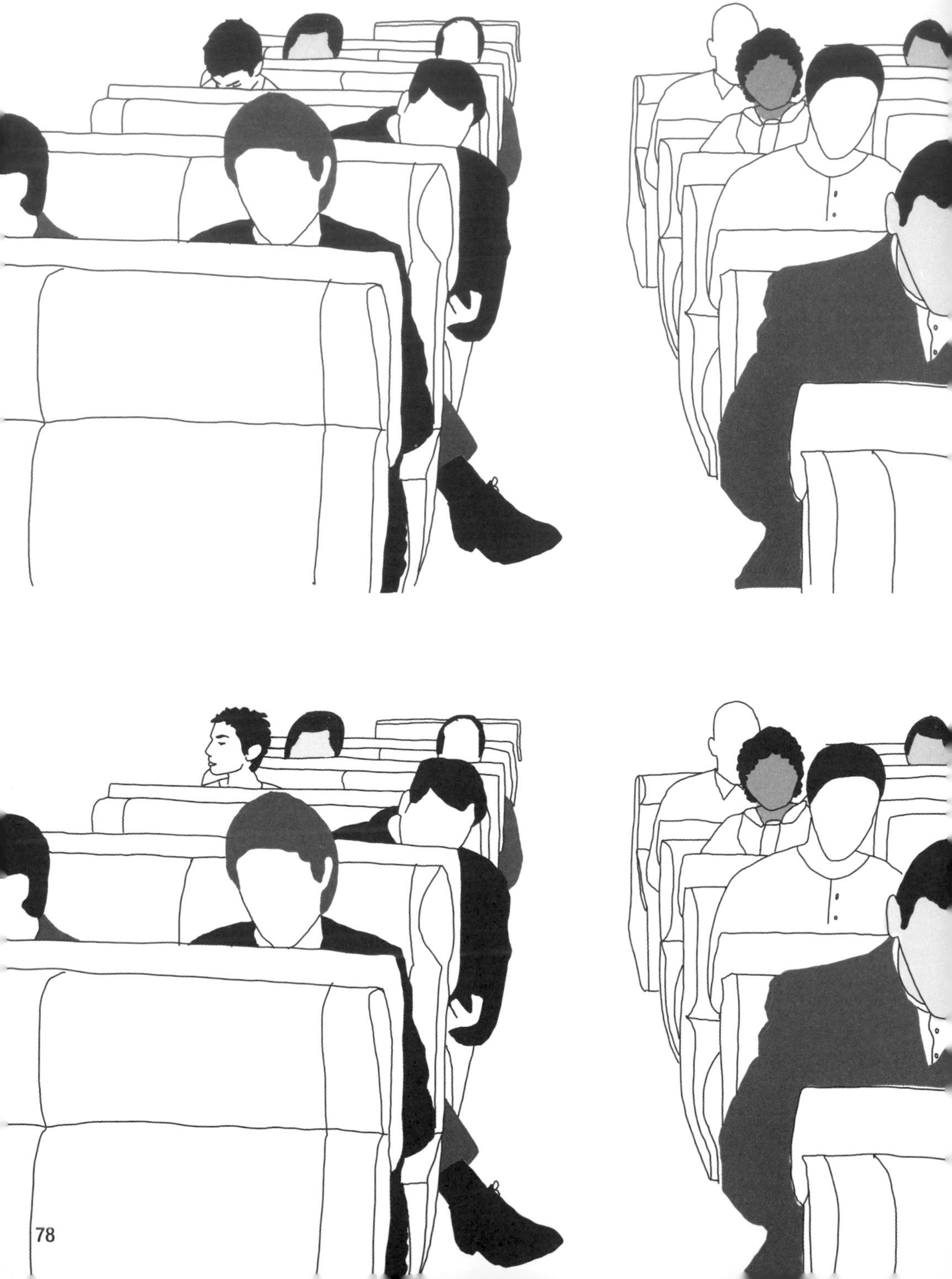

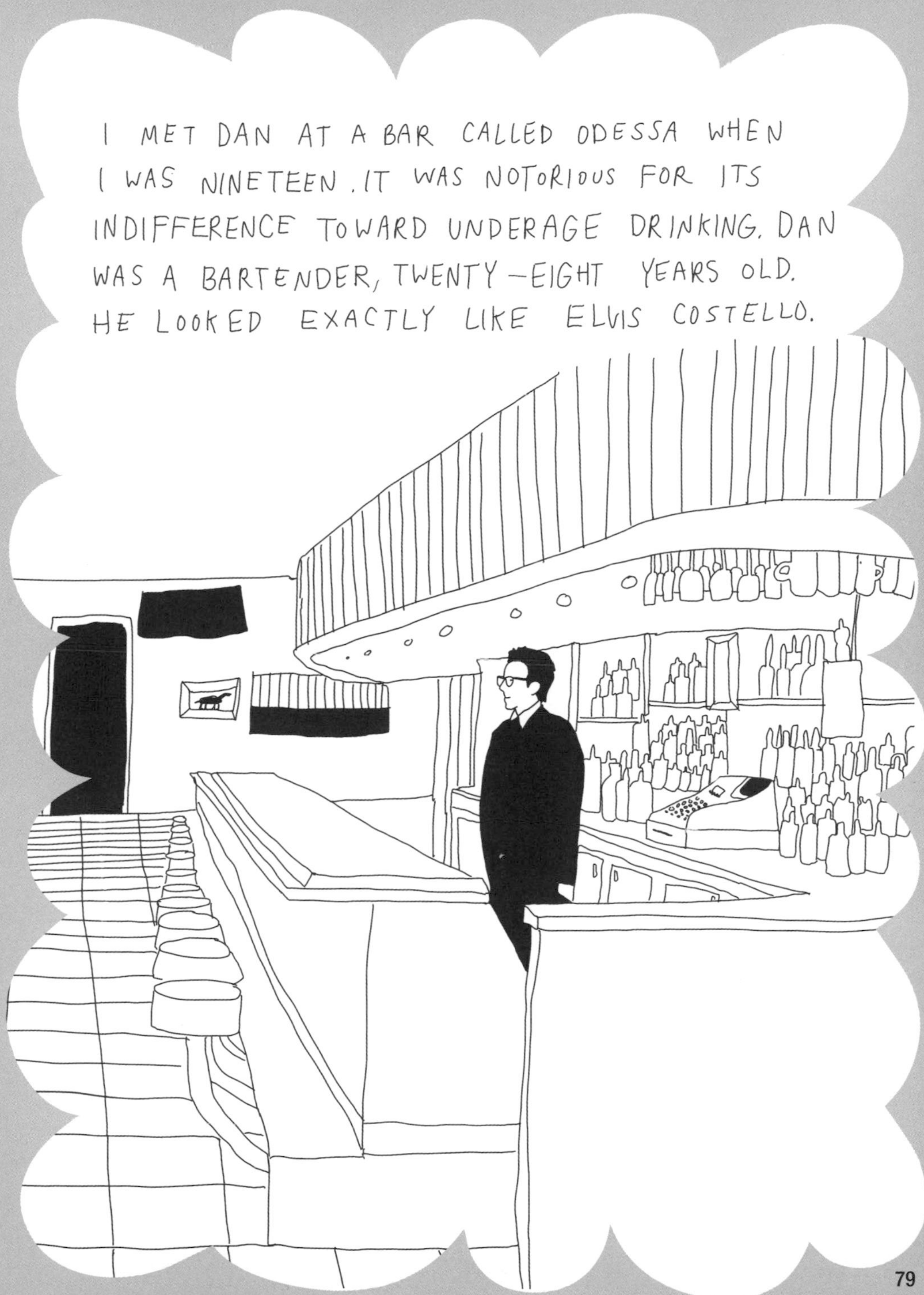
I MET DAN AT A BAR CALLED ODESSA WHEN I WAS NINETEEN. IT WAS NOTORIOUS FOR ITS INDIFFERENCE TOWARD UNDERAGE DRINKING. DAN WAS A BARTENDER, TWENTY-EIGHT YEARS OLD. HE LOOKED EXACTLY LIKE ELVIS COSTELLO.

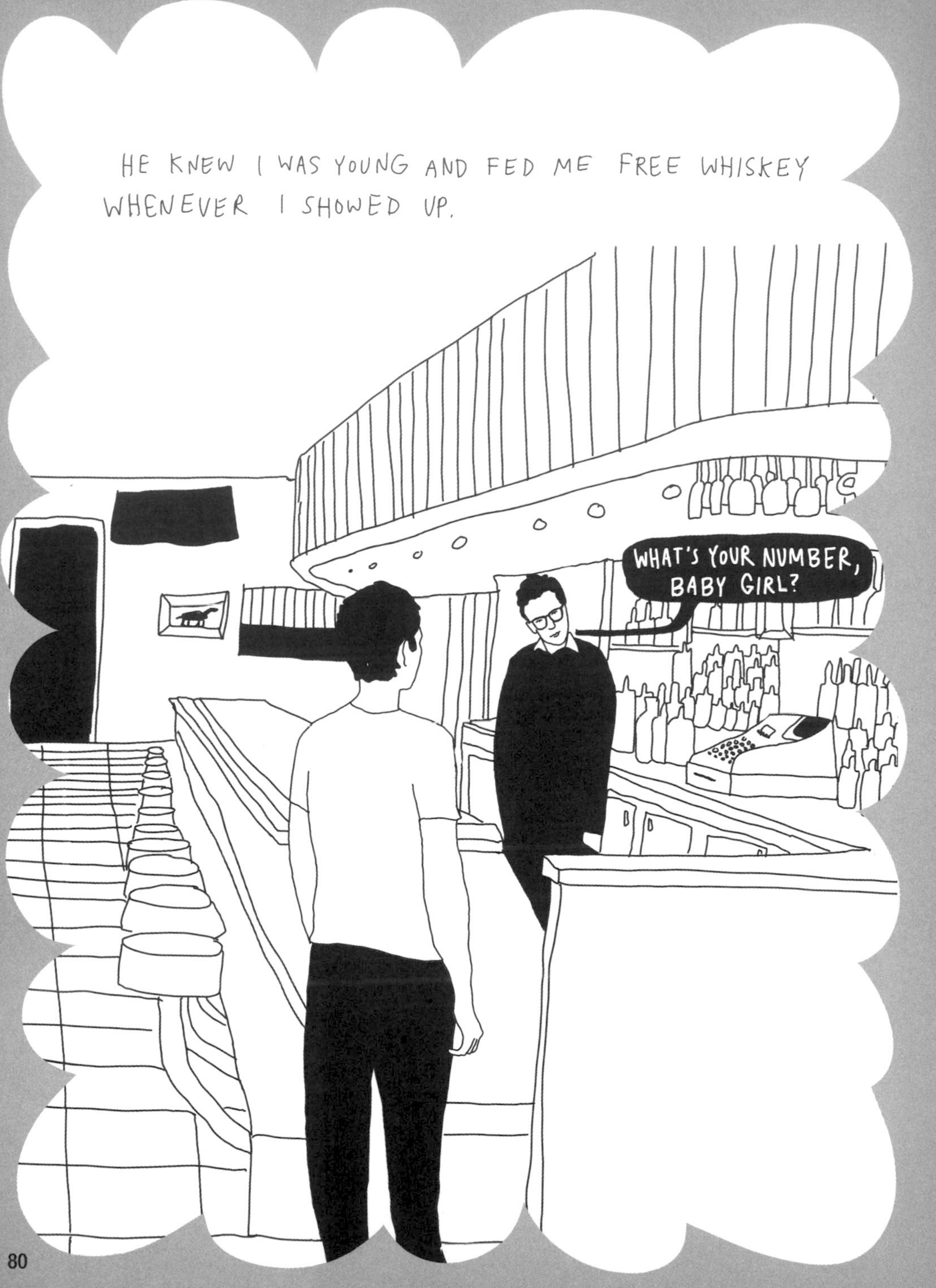
HE KNEW I WAS YOUNG AND FED ME FREE WHISKEY WHENEVER I SHOWED UP.
WHAT'S YOUR NUMBER, BABY GIRL?

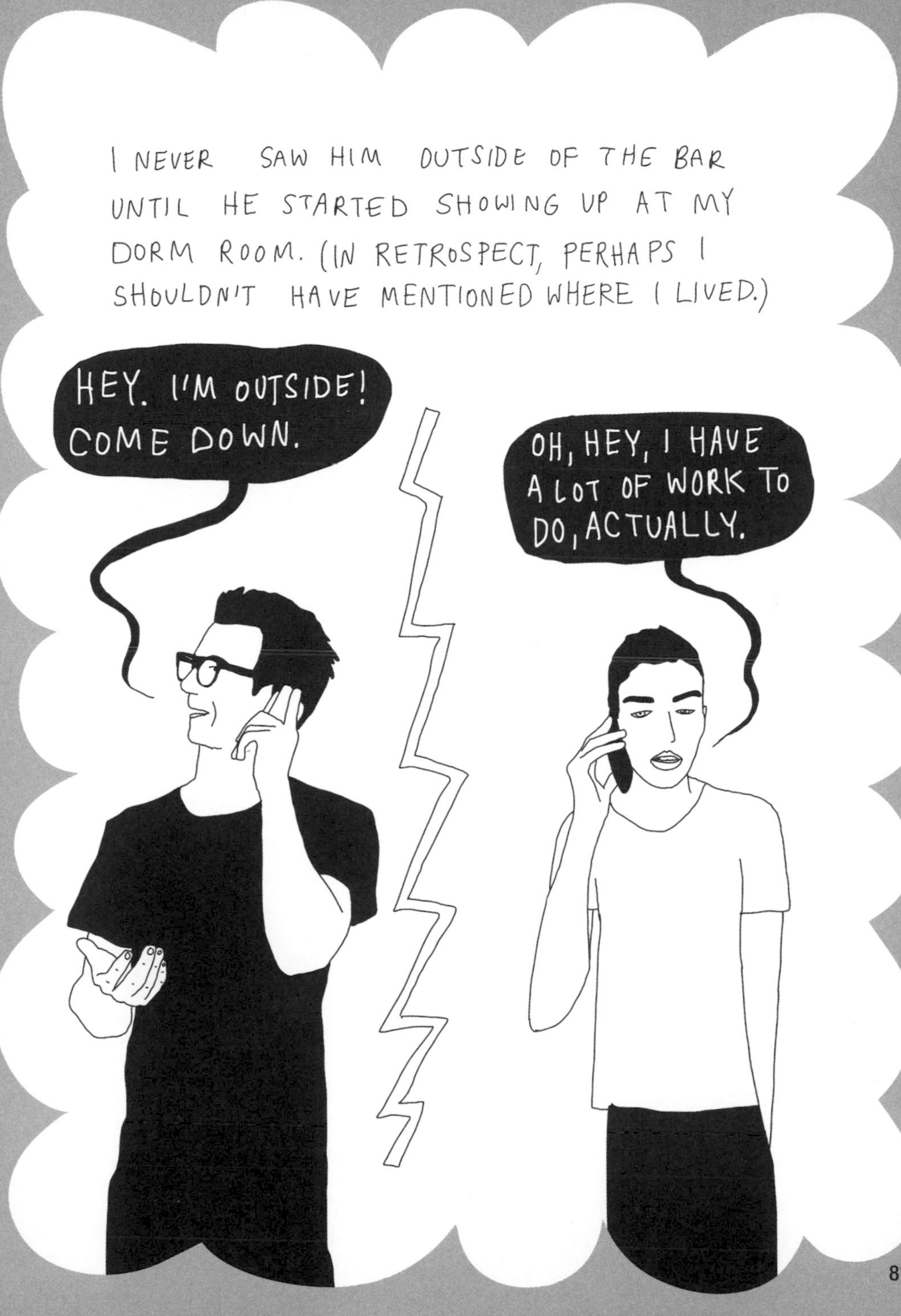
I NEVER SAW HIM OUTSIDE OF THE BAR UNTIL HE STARTED SHOWING UP AT MY DORM ROOM. (IN RETROSPECT, PERHAPS I SHOULDN'T HAVE MENTIONED WHERE I LIVED.)
HEY. I'M OUTSIDE! COME DOWN.
OH, HEY, I HAVE A LOT OF WORK TO DO, ACTUALLY.

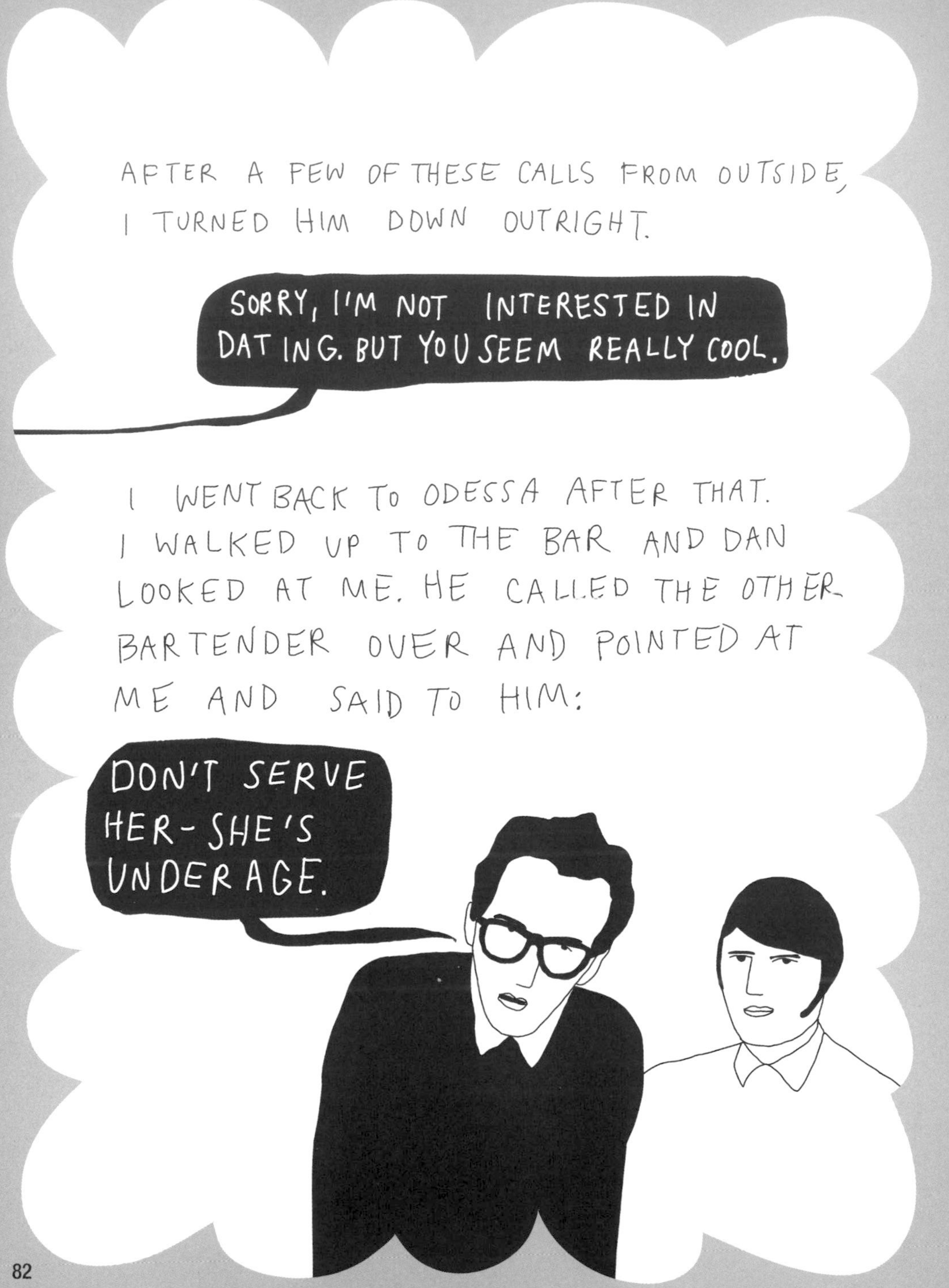
AFTER A FEW OF THESE CALLS FROM OUTSIDE, I TURNED HIM DOWN OUTRIGHT.
SORRY, I'M NOT INTERESTED IN DATING. BUT YOU SEEM REALLY COOL.
I WENT BACK TO ODESSA AFTER THAT. I WALKED UP TO THE BAR AND DAN LOOKED AT ME. HE CALLED THE OTHER BARTENDER OVER AND POINTED AT ME AND SAID TO HIM:
DON'T SERVE HER-SHE'S UNDERAGE.

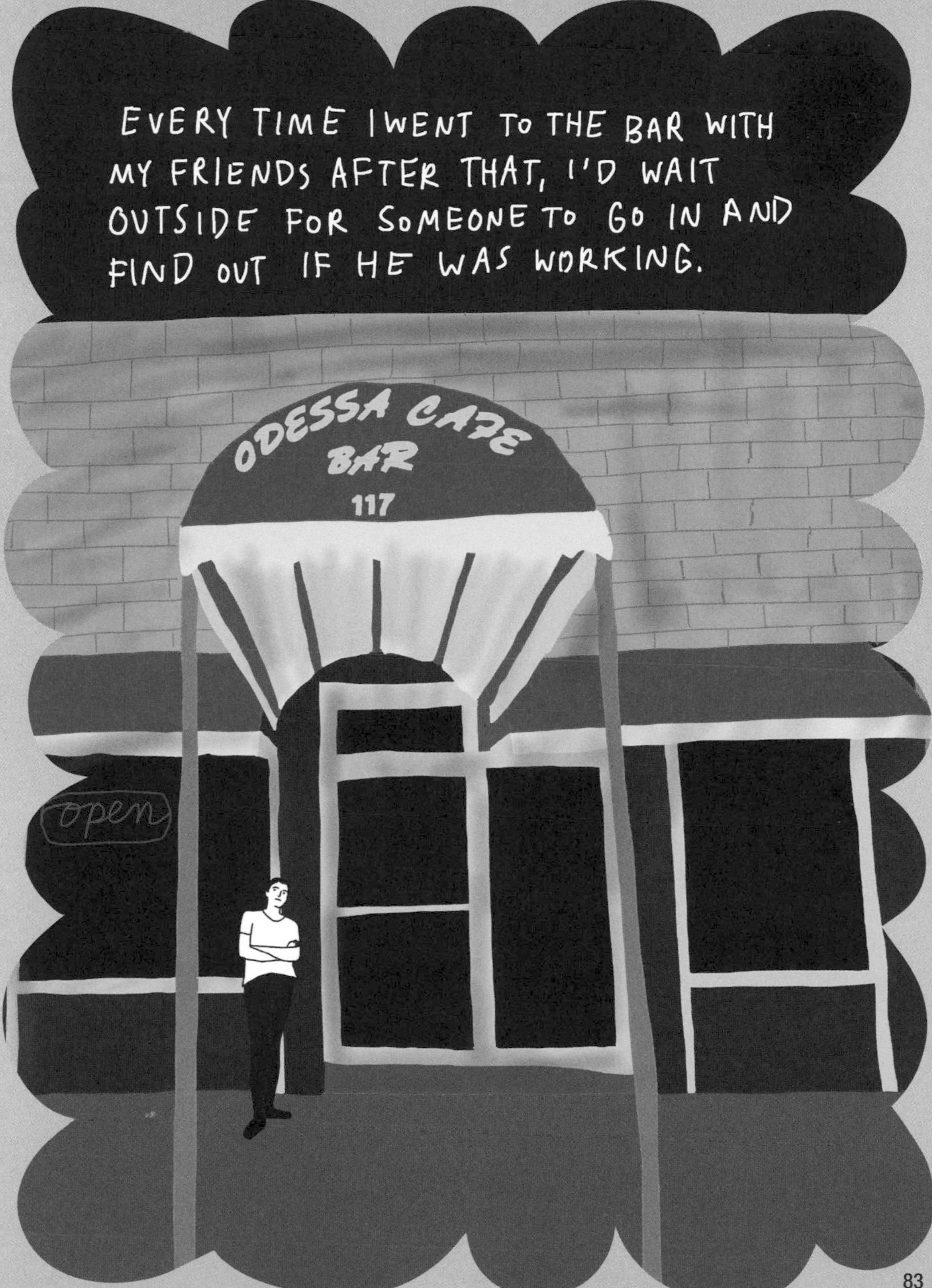
EVERY TIME I WENT TO THE BAR WITH MY FRIENDS AFTER THAT, I'D WAIT OUTSIDE FOR SOMEONE TO GO IN AND FIND OUT IF HE WAS WORKING.
ODESSA CAFE
BAR
117
open

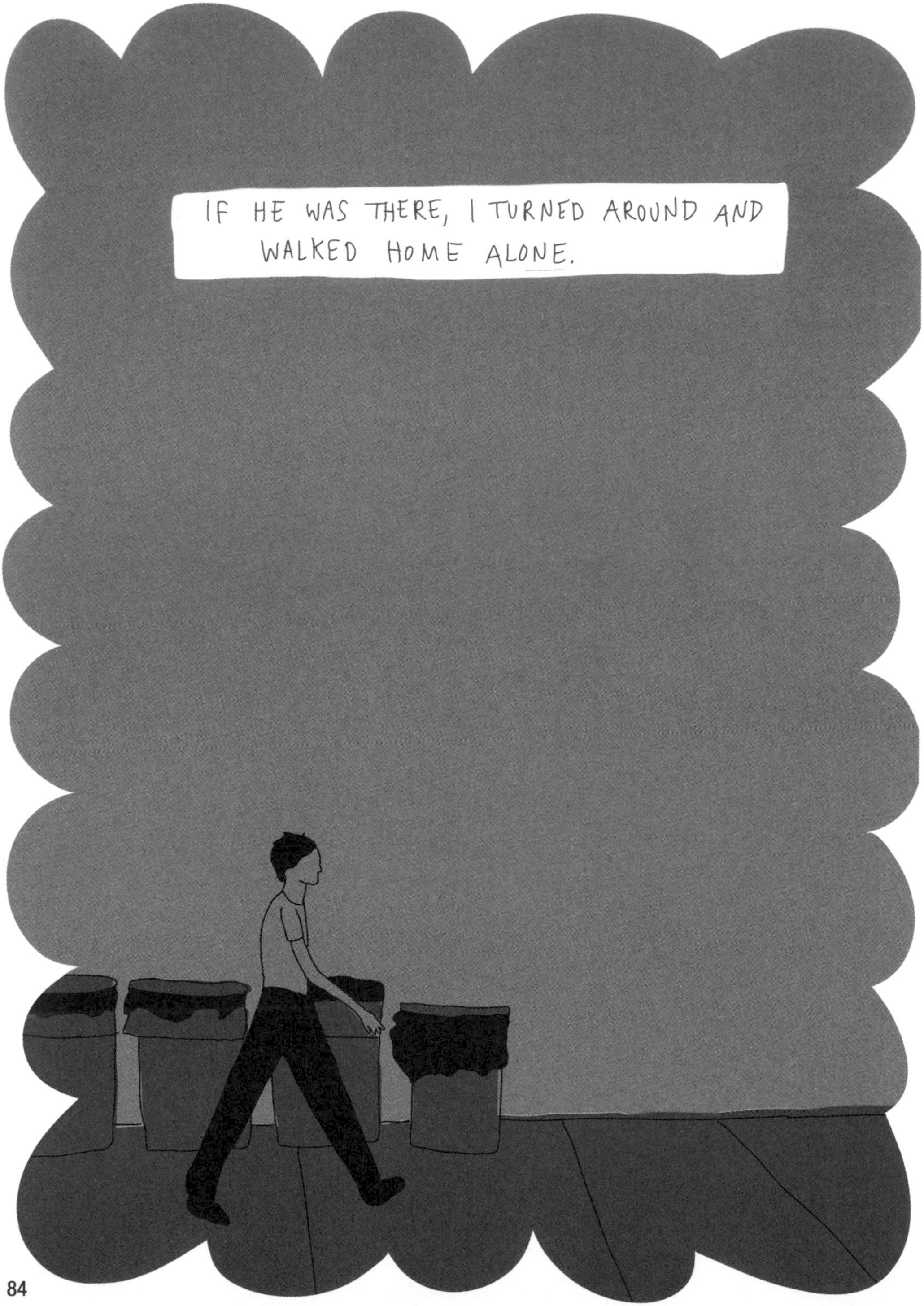
IF HE WAS THERE, I TURNED AROUND AND WALKED HOME ALONE.

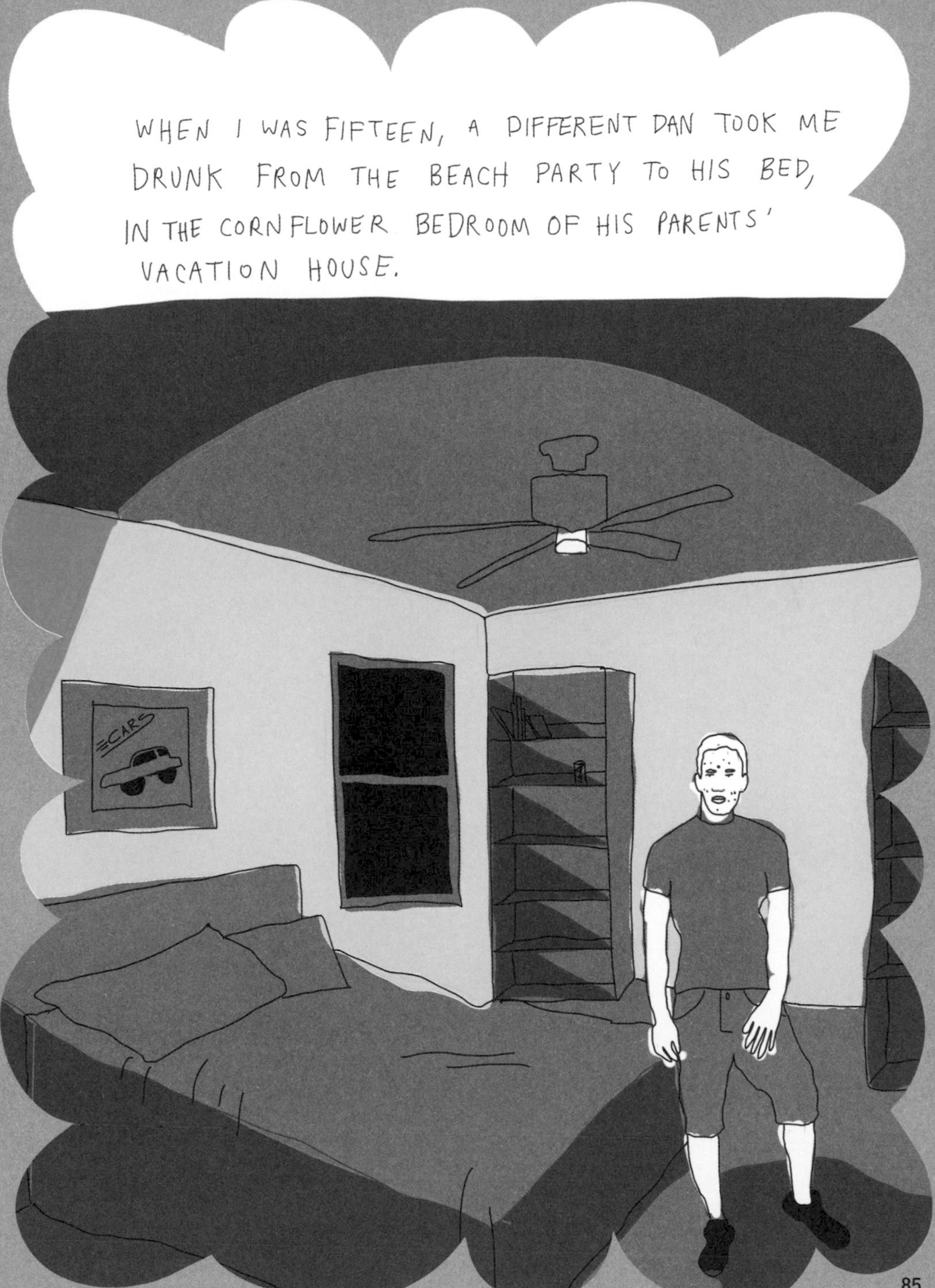
WHEN I WAS FIFTEEN, A DIFFERENT DAN TOOK ME DRUNK FROM THE BEACH PARTY TO HIS BED, IN THE CORNFLOWER BEDROOM OF HIS PARENTS' VACATION HOUSE.
CARS

WE KISSED, CLIMBED INTO HIS BED, AND THERE IT WAS...

THE FIRST
DICK
I EVER SAW

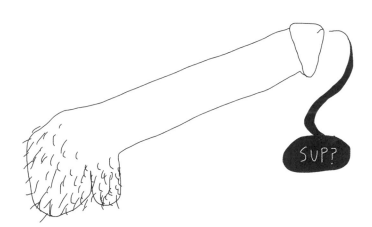

SUP?

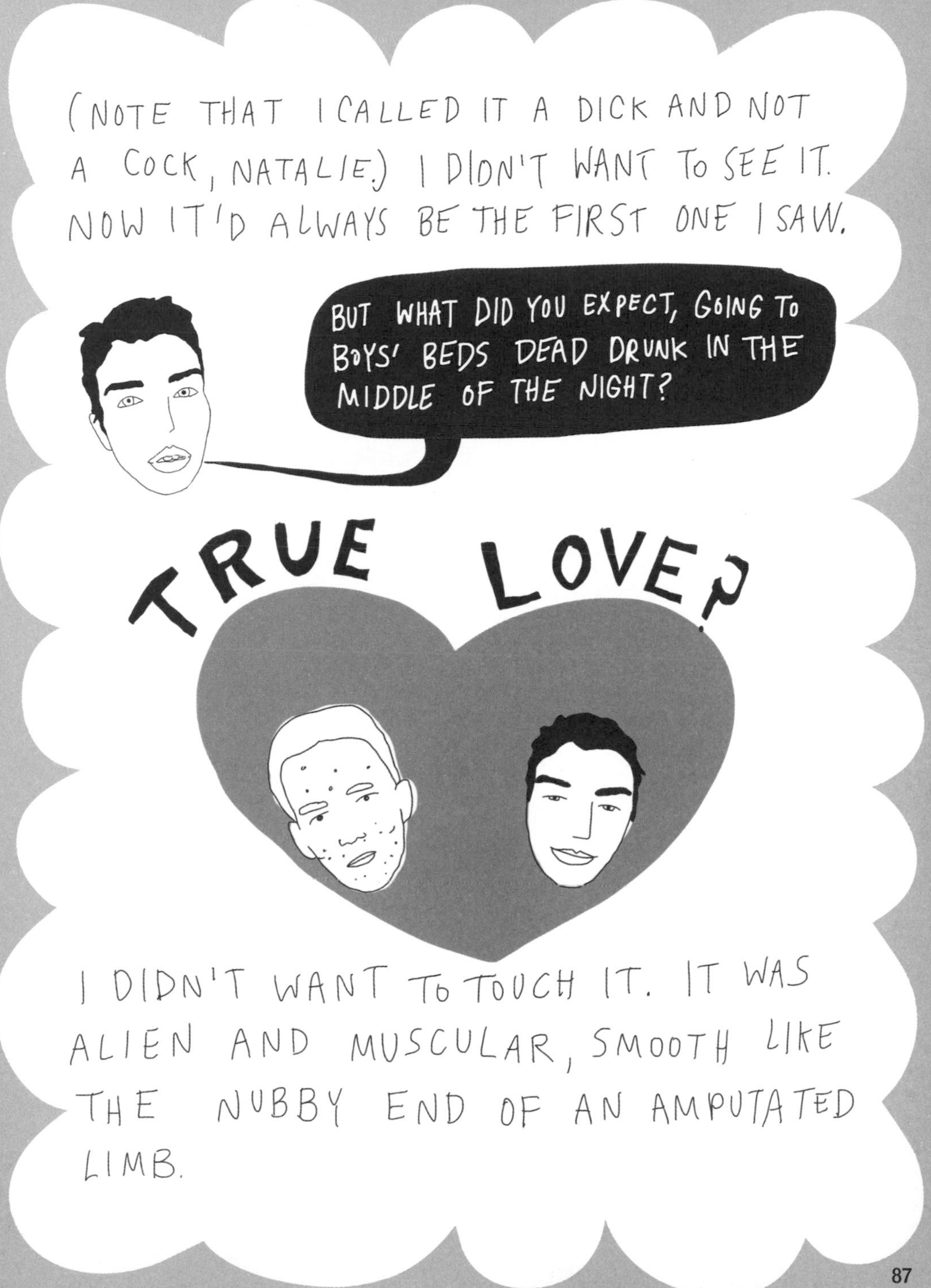
(NOTE THAT I CALLED IT A DICK AND NOT A COCK, NATALIE.) I DIDN'T WANT TO SEE IT. NOW IT'D ALWAYS BE THE FIRST ONE I SAW.
BUT WHAT DID YOU EXPECT, GOING TO BOYS' BEDS DEAD DRUNK IN THE MIDDLE OF THE NIGHT?
TRUE LOVE?
I DIDN'T WANT TO TOUCH IT. IT WAS ALIEN AND MUSCULAR, SMOOTH LIKE THE NUBBY END OF AN AMPUTATED LIMB.

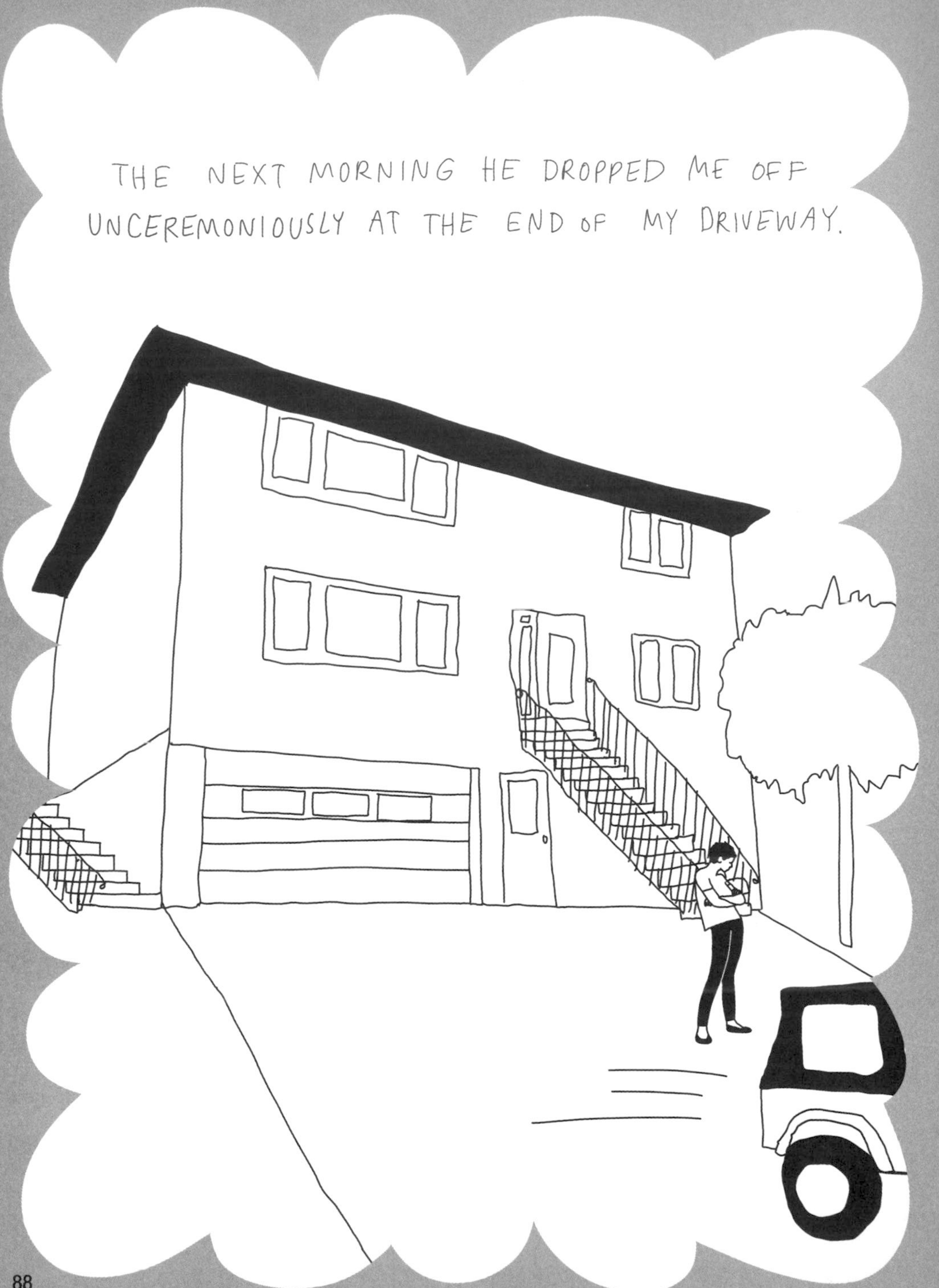
THE NEXT MORNING HE DROPPED ME OFF UNCEREMONIOUSLY AT THE END OF MY DRIVEWAY.

THE TRAIN ROLLS PAST THE TREES AND BRICK-AND-BROWN APARTMENT COMPLEXES. SOMEWHERE AROUND YONKERS, IT CHANGES...

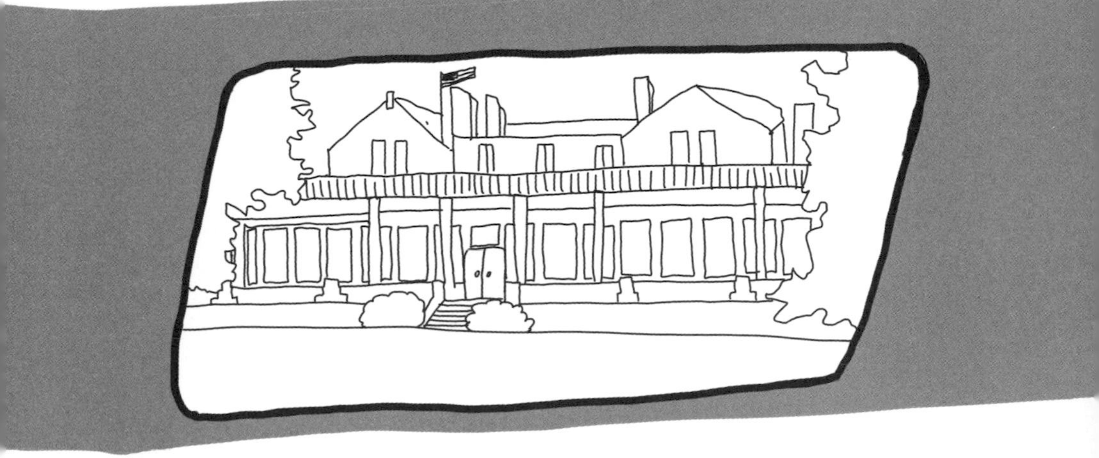

FROM MILLION-DOLLAR HOMES...

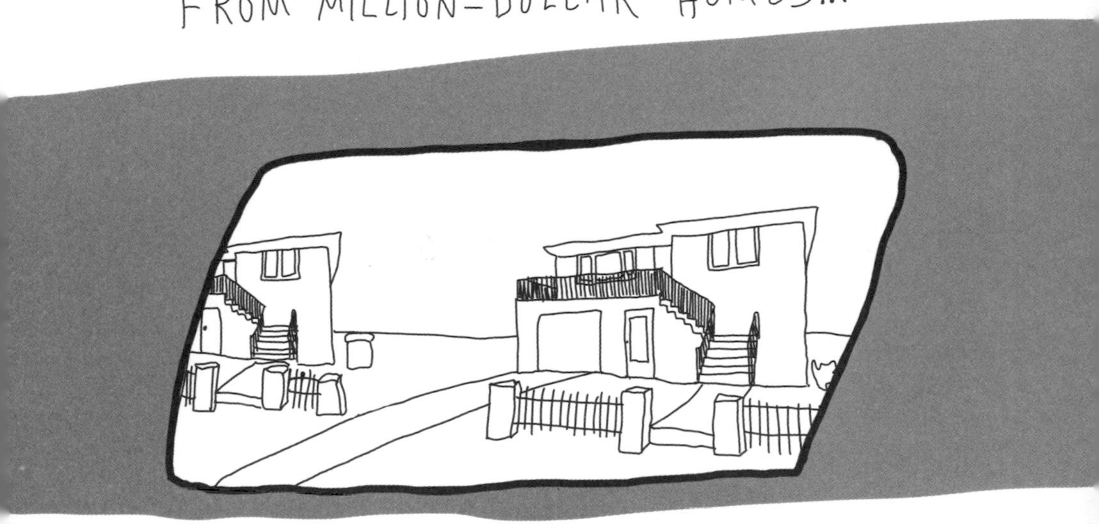

TO RENTABLE MULTIFAMILY UNITS.

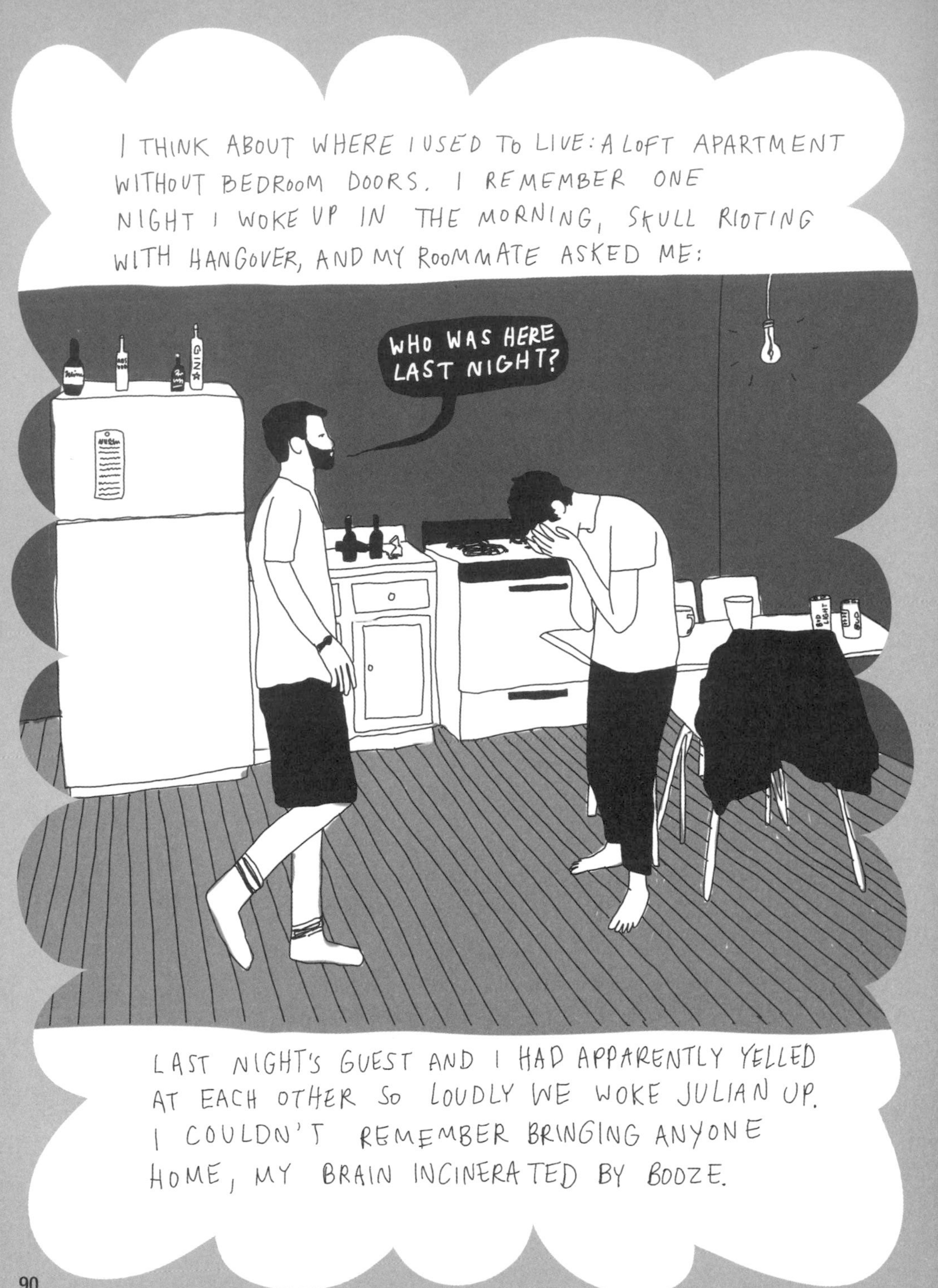
I THINK ABOUT WHERE I USED TO LIVE: A LOFT APARTMENT WITHOUT BEDROOM DOORS. I REMEMBER ONE NIGHT I WOKE UP IN THE MORNING, SKULL RIOTING WITH HANGOVER, AND MY ROOMMATE ASKED ME:
WHO WAS HERE LAST NIGHT?
LAST NIGHT'S GUEST AND I HAD APPARENTLY YELLED AT EACH OTHER SO LOUDLY WE WOKE JULIAN UP. I COULDN'T REMEMBER BRINGING ANYONE HOME, MY BRAIN INCINERATED BY BOOZE.

I WONDER WHO HE WAS AND WHY I BROUGHT HIM HOME AND WHAT HE WAS SO ANGRY ABOUT.

ALL THE MORNINGS I WOKE UP AND COULDN'T REMEMBER WHETHER I'D HAD SEX THE NIGHT BEFORE, I'D FINGER MYSELF TO SEE IF I WAS SORE.

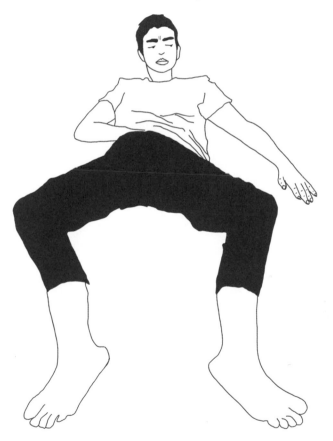

ON THAT MORNING, I WAS SURE I HADN'T HAD SEX.

THIS ALL MIGHT SOUND WEIRD TO YOU IF YOU'RE UNFAMILIAR WITH ALCOHOLISM.

ALCOHOLICS, LIKE OTHER ADDICTS, ARE OBLIVION JUNKIES. IT'S A KIND OF PEACE-SEEKING THROUGH ABSOLUTE PHYSICAL, EMOTIONAL, AND SPIRITUAL OBLITERATION.

FUCKING IS LIKE THAT TOO — AT ITS CLIMAX, A LOSS OF SELF.

TO SURROUND MYSELF WITH MEN WHO THOUGHT LITTLE OF MY VALUE FELT NATURAL, SINCE MUCH OF MY RECREATIONAL HOURS WERE SPENT IN OR ATTEMPTING A BLACKOUT.

BLACKOUTS ARE EUPHORIC, QUIET, TWILIGHT BIRTH. EXISTENCE WITHOUT TIME OR PRESENCE OR PHYSICALITY OR CONSEQUENCE.

YOU DON'T FEAR DEATH.

(OR MEN OR RAPE OR STRANGERS AT ALL).

IMAGINE MOVING THROUGH THE WORLD WITHOUT FEAR OR ANXIETY.

IT'S ABSOLUTE, PERFECT FREEDOM.

SO YOU BRING STRANGERS HOME, BECAUSE IN THIS SACRED DARKNESS, INTIMACY IS NOT A THREAT, IT'S A COMPULSION.

THE DARK HAS YOU COVERED.

A BUSINESSMAN AND WOMAN ARE SITTING ACROSS FROM ME ON THE TRAIN, ARGUING.

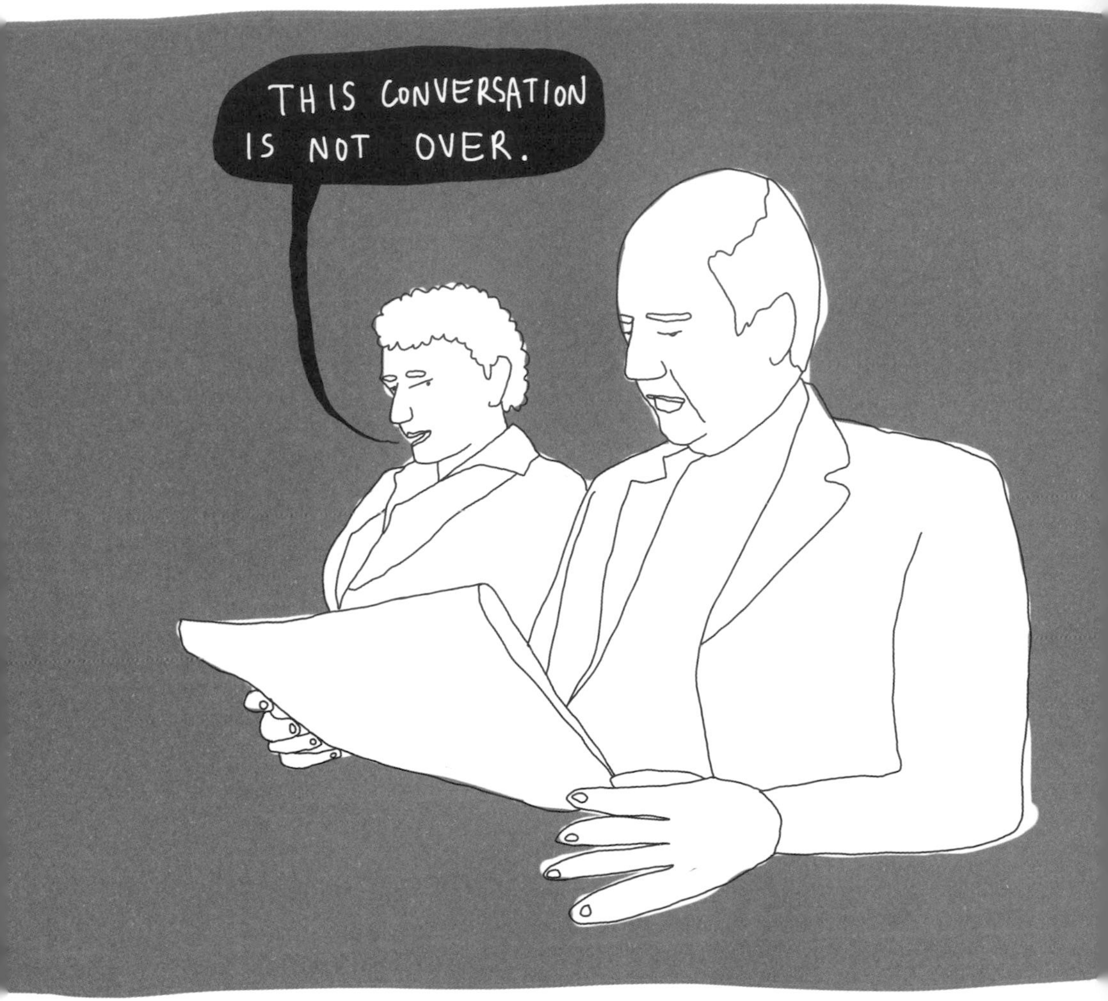
THIS CONVERSATION IS NOT OVER.

THEY GET UP. EVERYONE GETS UP. WE ALL WALK OFF THE TRAIN.

IT'S A SLOW MERGE UP A LONG, THIN INTESTINE TOWARDS THE TORSO OF GRAND CENTRAL. UP THE GUT INSTEAD OF DOWN.

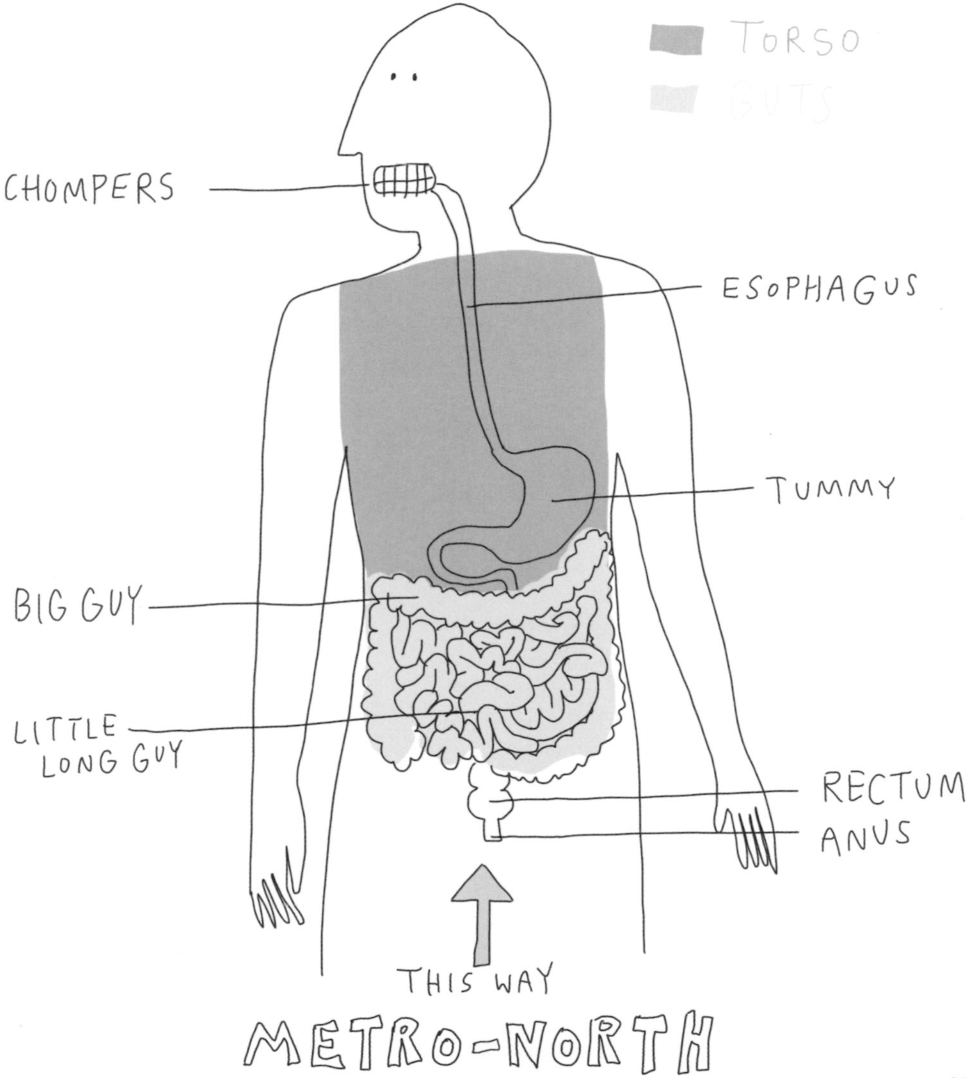
TORSO
GUTS
CHOMPERS
ESOPHAGUS
TUMMY
BIG GUY
LITTLE LONG GUY
RECTUM
ANUS
THIS WAY
METRO-NORTH

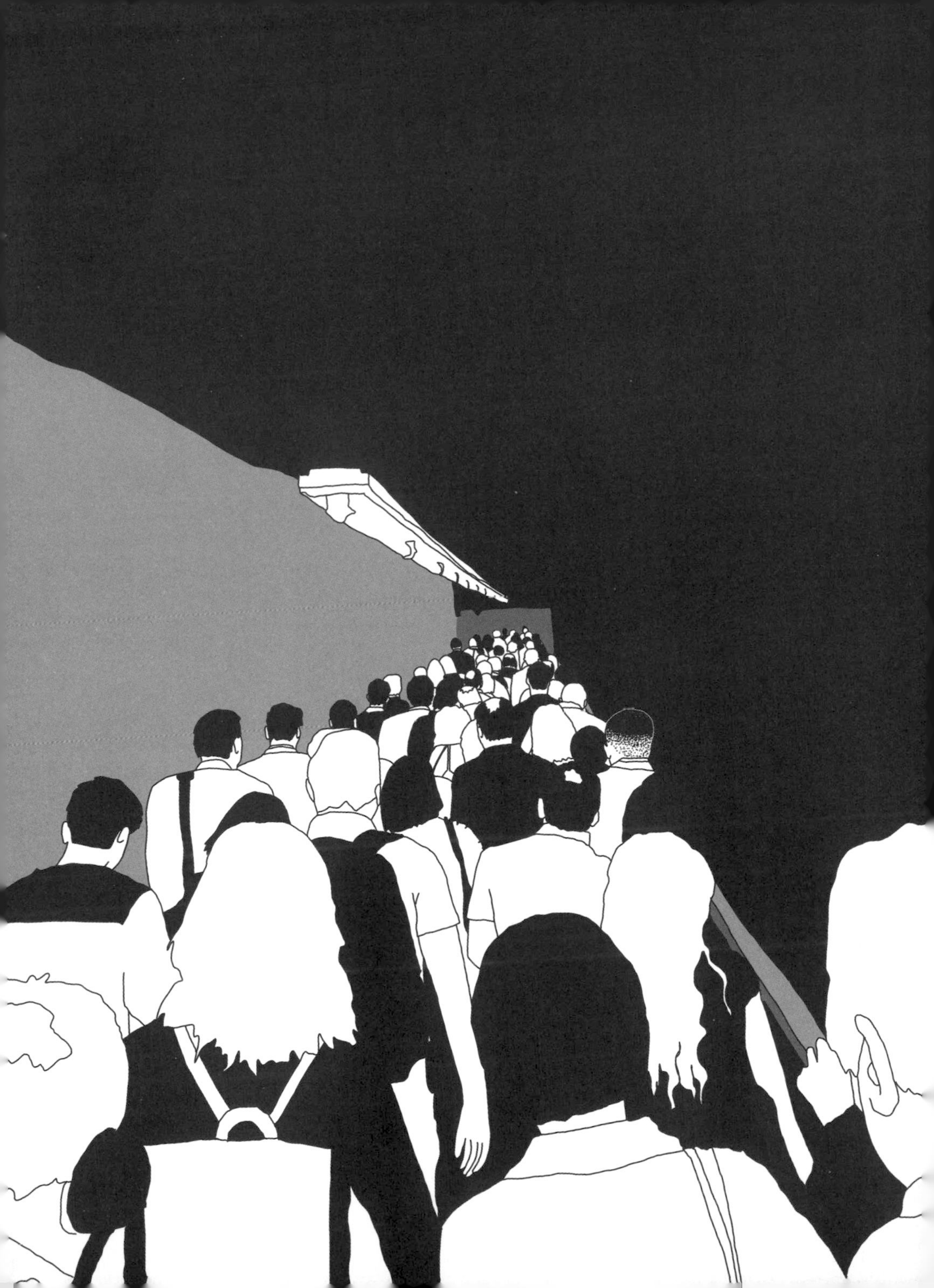

WALK TO WORK

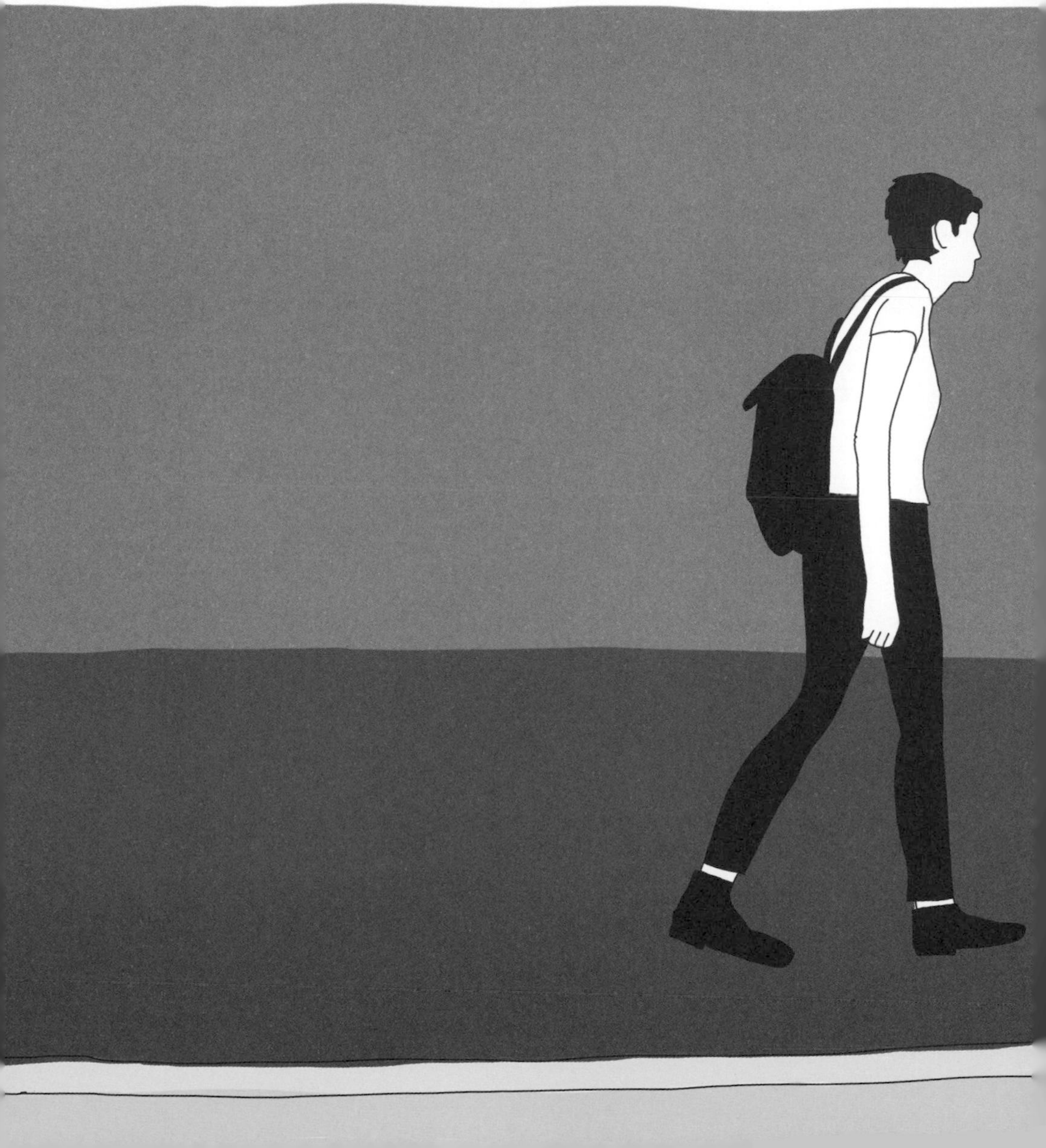

A MAN AND I BUMP INTO EACH OTHER ON THE STREET.

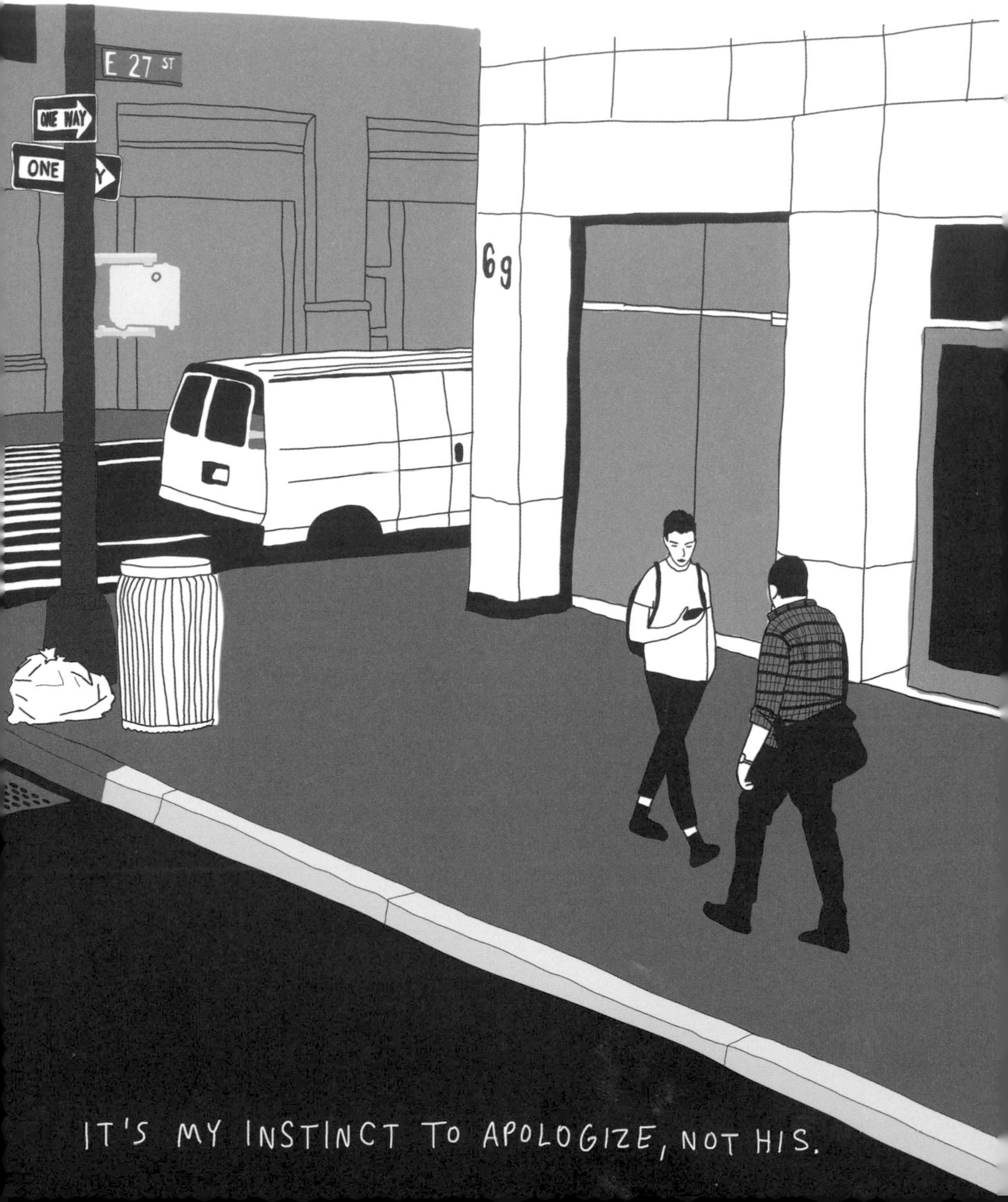
E 27 ST
ONE WAY
ONE
69
IT'S MY INSTINCT TO APOLOGIZE, NOT HIS.

I TELL MYSELF FOR THE FIRST OF TEN TIMES THAT DAY TO STOP SAYING I'M SORRY.

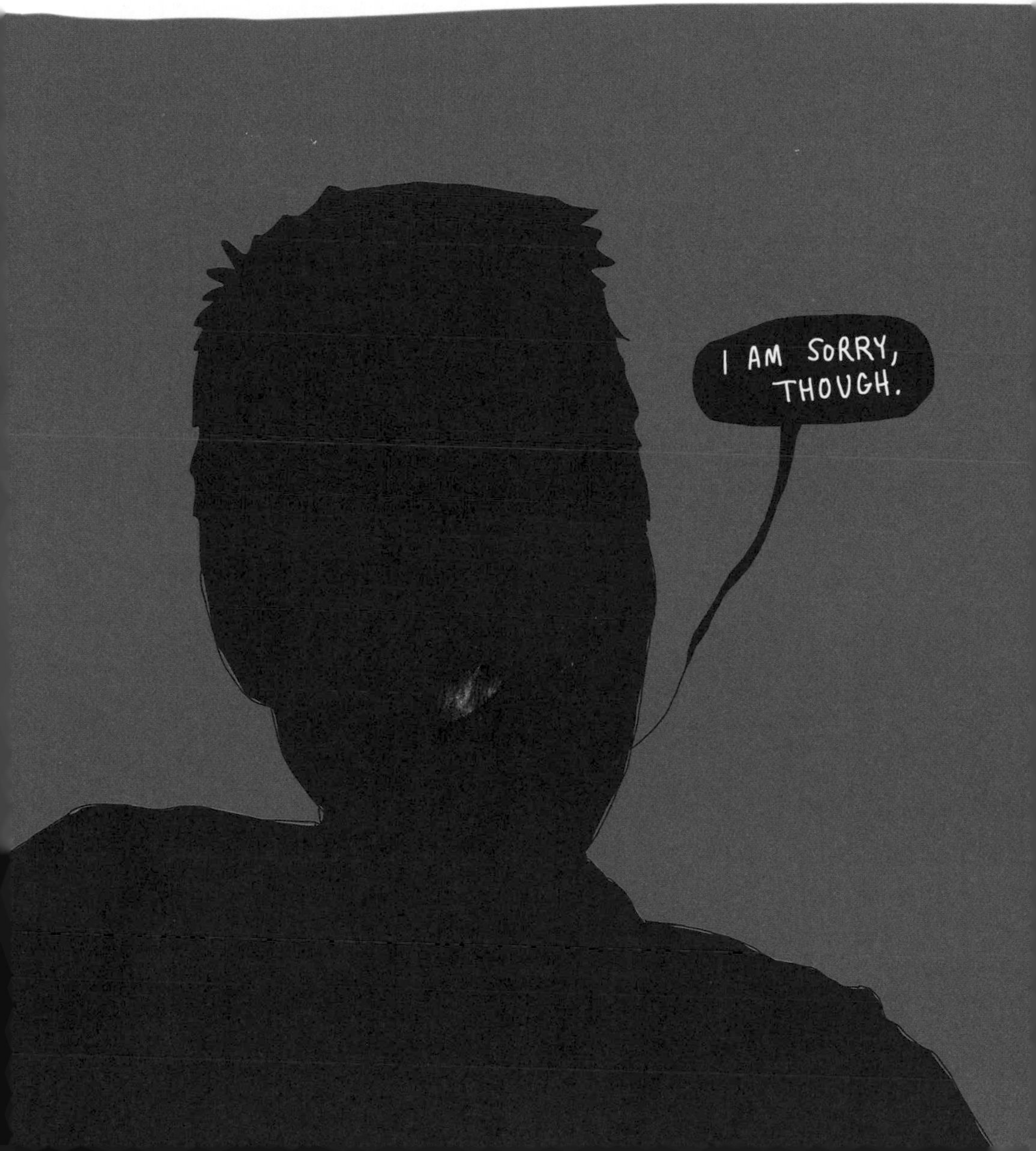
I AM SORRY, THOUGH.

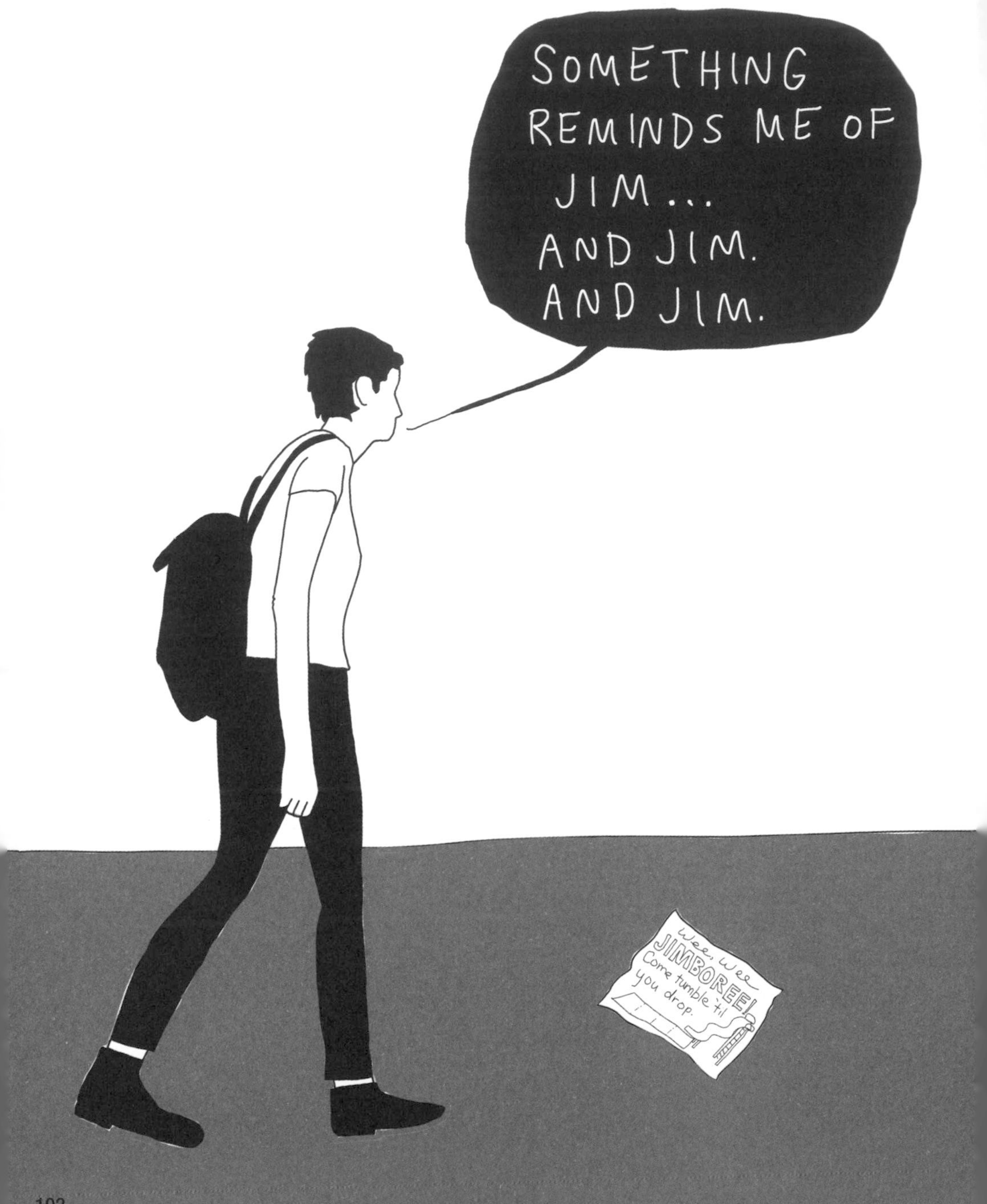
SOMETHING REMINDS ME OF JIM... AND JIM. AND JIM.
Wee, Wee JIMBOREE! Come tumble 'til you drop.

I WALK PAST A GYM.

3 JIMS

I'M AN ARTIST SO I'LL LOOK THIS WAY.

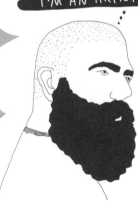

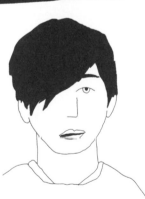

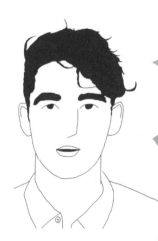

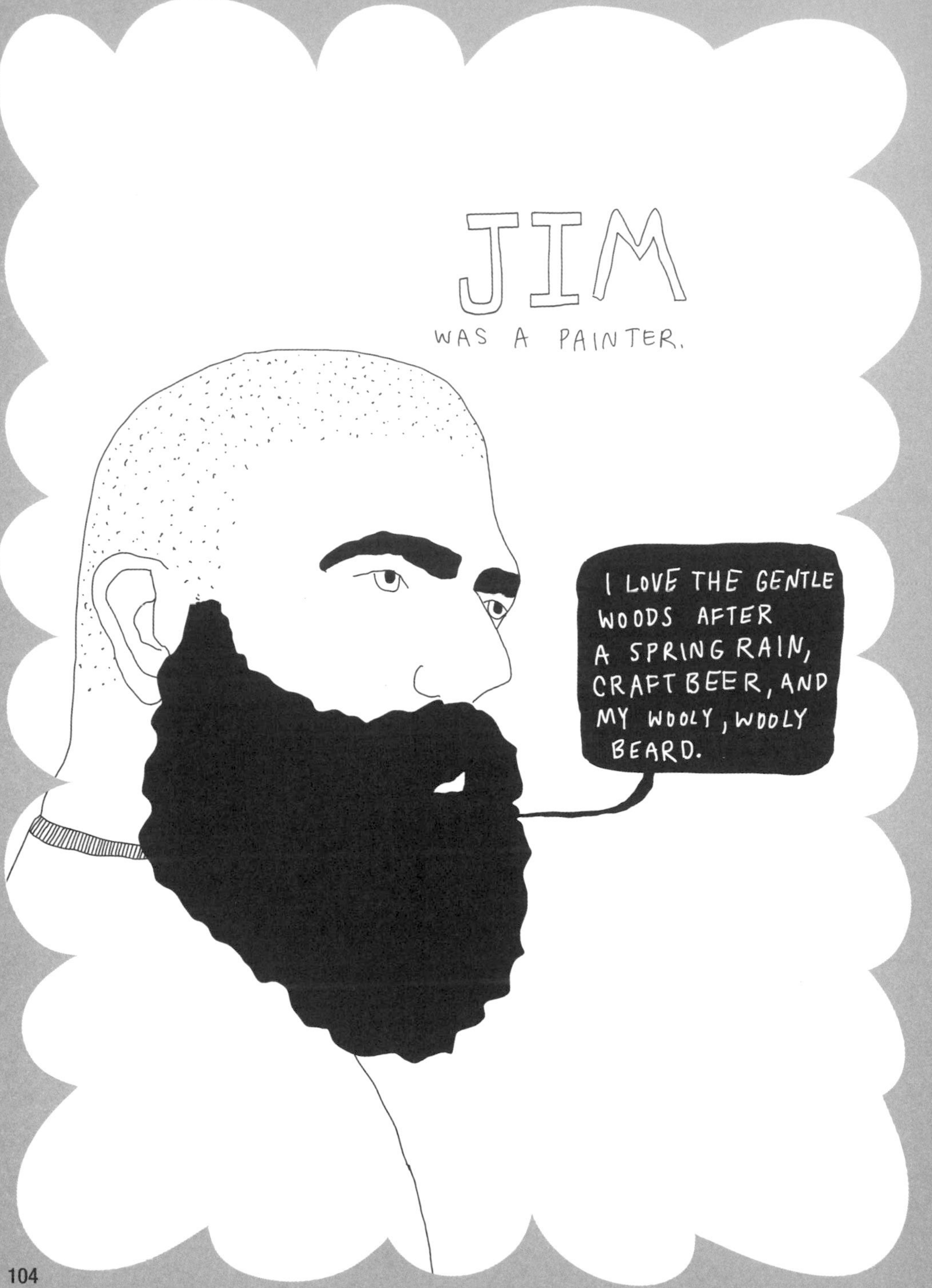
JIM
WAS A PAINTER.
I LOVE THE GENTLE WOODS AFTER A SPRING RAIN, CRAFT BEER, AND MY WOOLY, WOOLY BEARD.

I TOLD MY FRIEND KATE WHO WAS GOING THROUGH A DIVORCE (WITH A MONSTER) THAT SHE WOULD LIKE HIM. I INVITED THEM OVER. WHEN WE ALL GOT DRUNK I FLIRTED WITH HIM HARD UNTIL KATE GAVE UP AND LEFT.

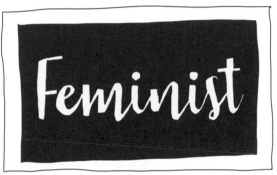

ONCE HE WAS ON TOP, INSIDE, I WANTED IT TO STOP. I WAITED FIVE MINUTES. I DIDN'T KNOW HOW TO ESCAPE THIS THING I'D WANTED, WHICH I'D ONLY WANTED BECAUSE KATE HAD WANTED IT. (NO HONOR AMONG DRUNKS.) (KATE'S NOT A DRUNK, SO IT WAS JUST ME WITHOUT HONOR.)

STOP STOP STOP STOP STOP STOP ..

I SAID IN MY MIND.

KATE WAS DIVORCING AN EMOTIONAL TERRORIST, A MAN WHO PREFERRED MUCH YOUNGER WOMEN. I SAID TO HER... YOU SHOULD MEET THIS MUSICIAN. OK. SHE SAID.

I HADN'T BLACKED OUT. WHEN I REALIZED I COULD STILL FEEL, IT WAS ONLY TERROR. STOP. I WANT YOU TO STOP.

HE KEPT SLAMMING INTO ME. BUT I'M SO CLOSE HE SAID.

KATE WAS MY BEST FRIEND.

STOP. I WANT YOU TO STOP.

SHE MOVED ONTO MY COUCH THE MORNING HER HUSBAND'S NINETEEN-YEAR-OLD MISTRESS SHOWED UP AT HER DOOR.

BUT I'M SO CLOSE.

STAY AS LONG AS YOU WANT, I SAID, THROUGH THE CLOTTED GAUZE OF ANOTHER HANGOVER. I LOVE YOU. STAY. STAY.

STOP. I WANT YOU TO STOP.

KATE LEFT THAT NIGHT WITHOUT PROTEST.

BUT I'M SO CLOSE.

AFTER HE LEFT I FELT ASHAMED AND DISGUSTING. I BROKE THE MIX CD HE'D LEFT FOR ME AND THREW IT IN THE GARBAGE.

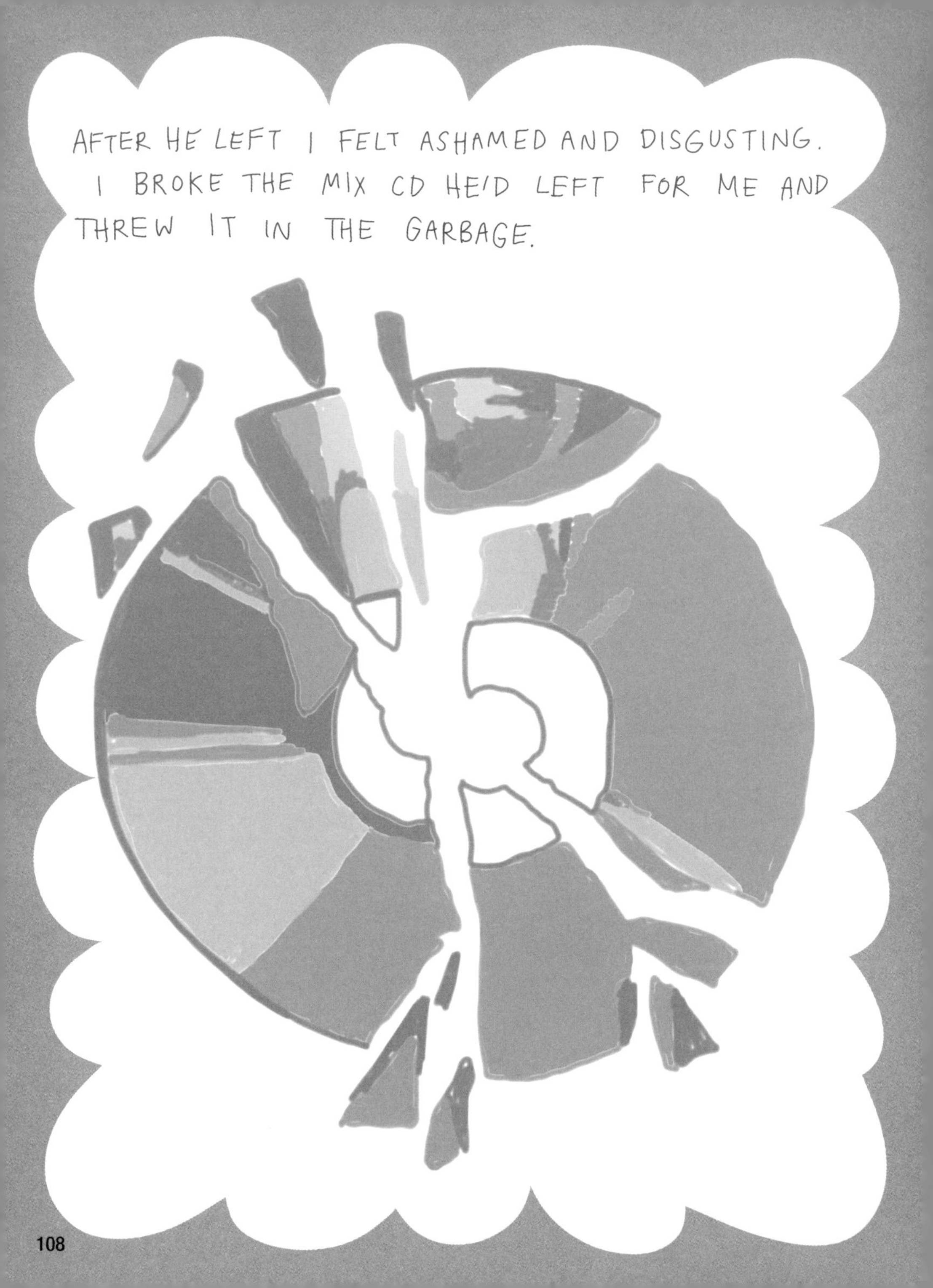

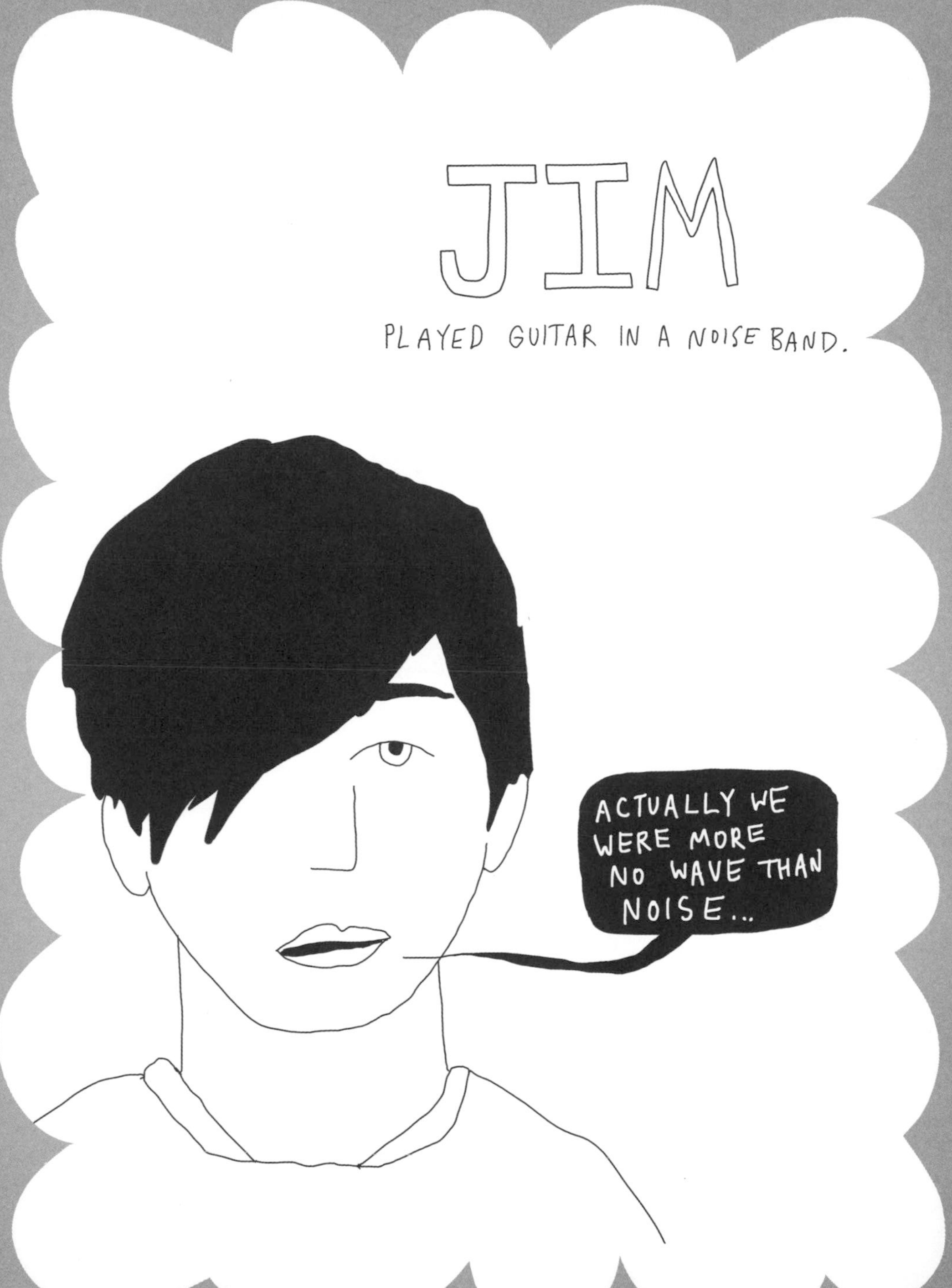
JIM
PLAYED GUITAR IN A NOISE BAND.
ACTUALLY WE WERE MORE NO WAVE THAN NOISE...

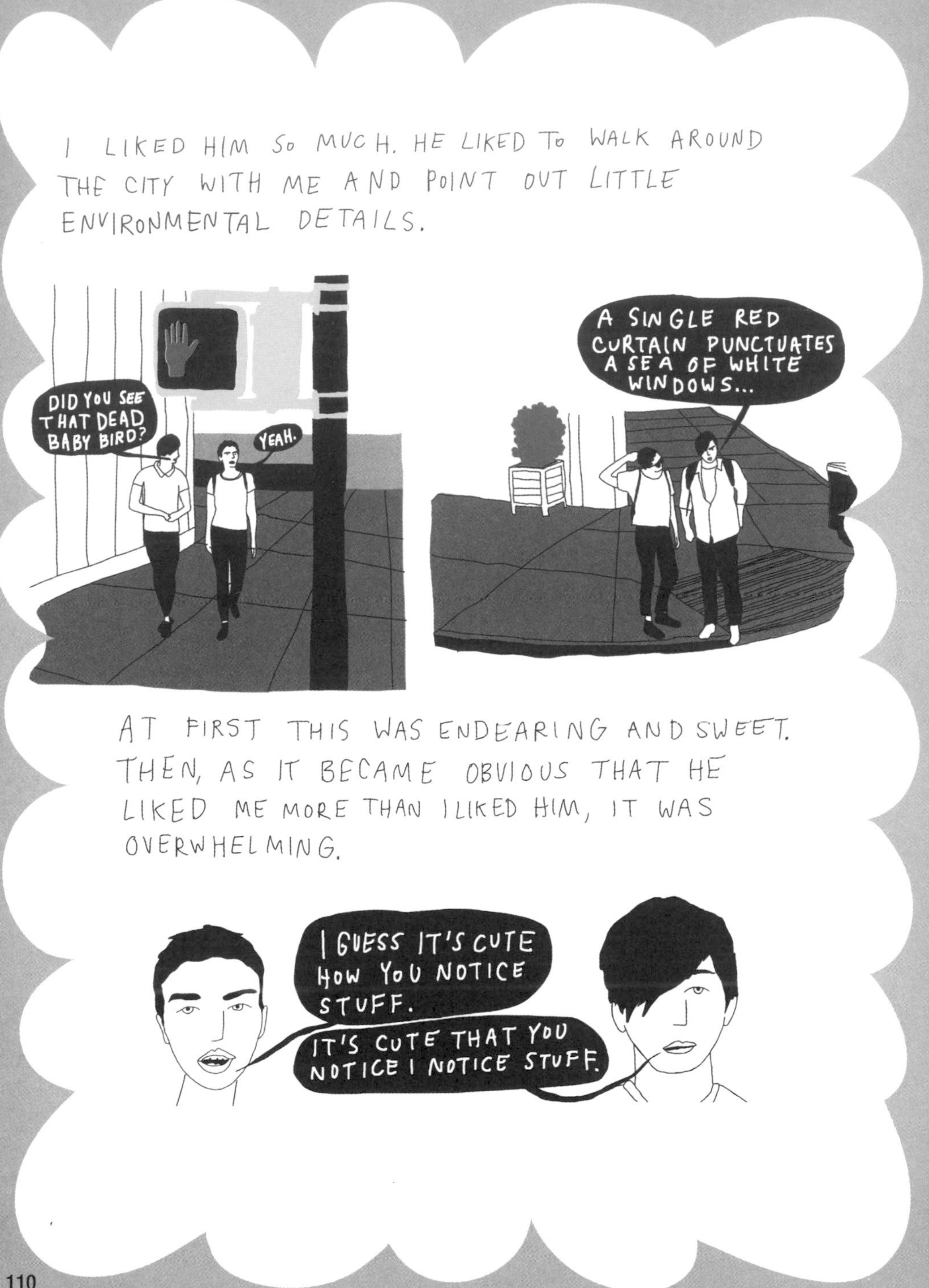
I LIKED HIM SO MUCH. HE LIKED TO WALK AROUND THE CITY WITH ME AND POINT OUT LITTLE ENVIRONMENTAL DETAILS.
DID YOU SEE THAT DEAD BABY BIRD?
YEAH.
A SINGLE RED CURTAIN PUNCTUATES A SEA OF WHITE WINDOWS...
AT FIRST THIS WAS ENDEARING AND SWEET. THEN, AS IT BECAME OBVIOUS THAT HE LIKED ME MORE THAN I LIKED HIM, IT WAS OVERWHELMING.
I GUESS IT'S CUTE HOW YOU NOTICE STUFF.
IT'S CUTE THAT YOU NOTICE I NOTICE STUFF.

SO I TOLD ALL MY FRIENDS HE WAS HOPPY IN BED, LIKE A BUNNY. THEY MADE FUN OF HIM BEHIND HIS BACK. I FELT SO BAD ABOUT IT I DUMPED HIM.

I WOULD HAVE DONE ANYTHING TO RID MYSELF OF THIS RARE THREAT OF INTIMACY. (THERE WAS NO GREATER VIOLENCE THAN AFFECTION.)

JIM
WAS MY EX'S FRIEND.
ERIN THINKS I MIGHT'VE WORKED IN CONSTRUCTION BUT CAN'T REMEMBER.

I THREW A PARTY AND SEDUCED HIM. I SAY "SEDUCED," BUT IT WAS ONE OF THOSE THINGS WHERE TWO PEOPLE KNOW EACH OTHER FOR A WHILE AND DON'T HAVE SEX AND THEN ONE DAY JUST TRY IT OUT. ALSO, I WAS DRUNK.

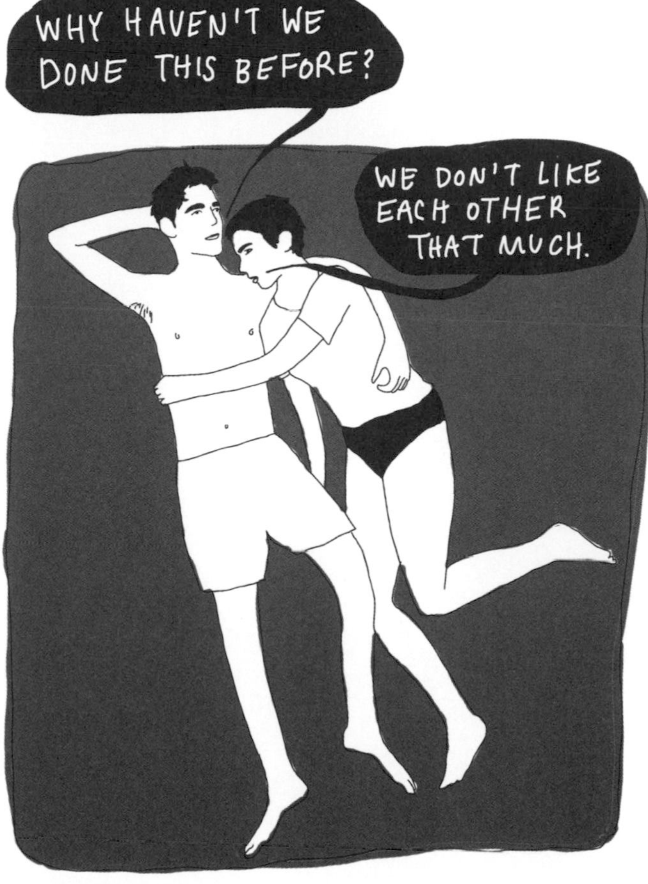
WHY HAVEN'T WE DONE THIS BEFORE?
WE DON'T LIKE EACH OTHER THAT MUCH.

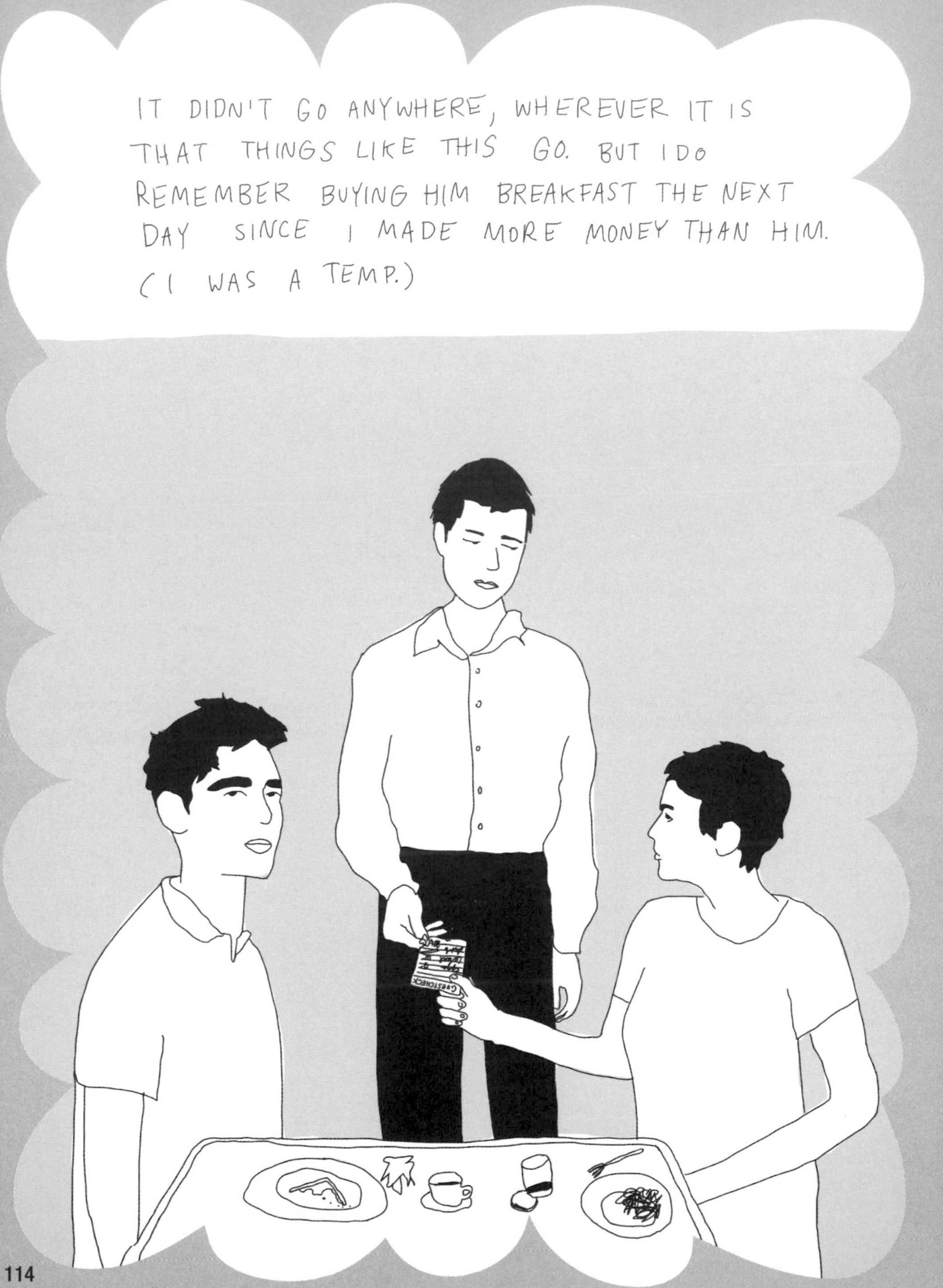
IT DIDN'T GO ANYWHERE, WHEREVER IT IS THAT THINGS LIKE THIS GO. BUT I DO REMEMBER BUYING HIM BREAKFAST THE NEXT DAY SINCE I MADE MORE MONEY THAN HIM. (I WAS A TEMP.)

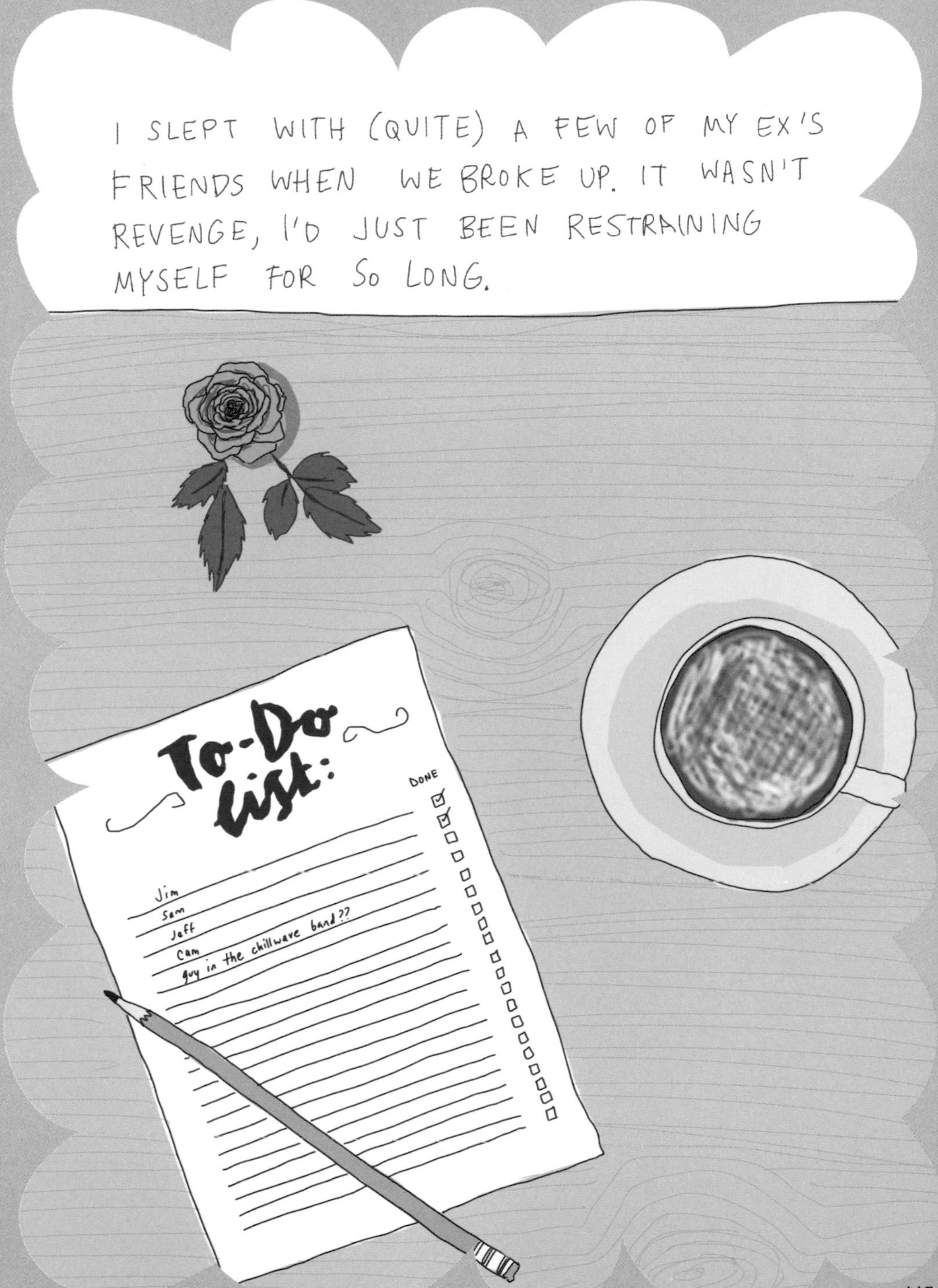
I SLEPT WITH (QUITE) A FEW OF MY EX'S FRIENDS WHEN WE BROKE UP. IT WASN'T REVENGE, I'D JUST BEEN RESTRAINING MYSELF FOR SO LONG.
To-Do List:
DONE
Jim
Sam
Jeff
Cam
guy in the chillwave band??

SPEAKING OF, MY EX JASON USED TO WORK AT A BOOKSTORE AND HAD THIS REGULAR CUSTOMER, A WOMAN WHO ONLY ORDERED BOOKS ON THE PHONE AND HAD THEM SHIPPED TO HER HOUSE. (THIS WAS BEFORE AMAZON.)

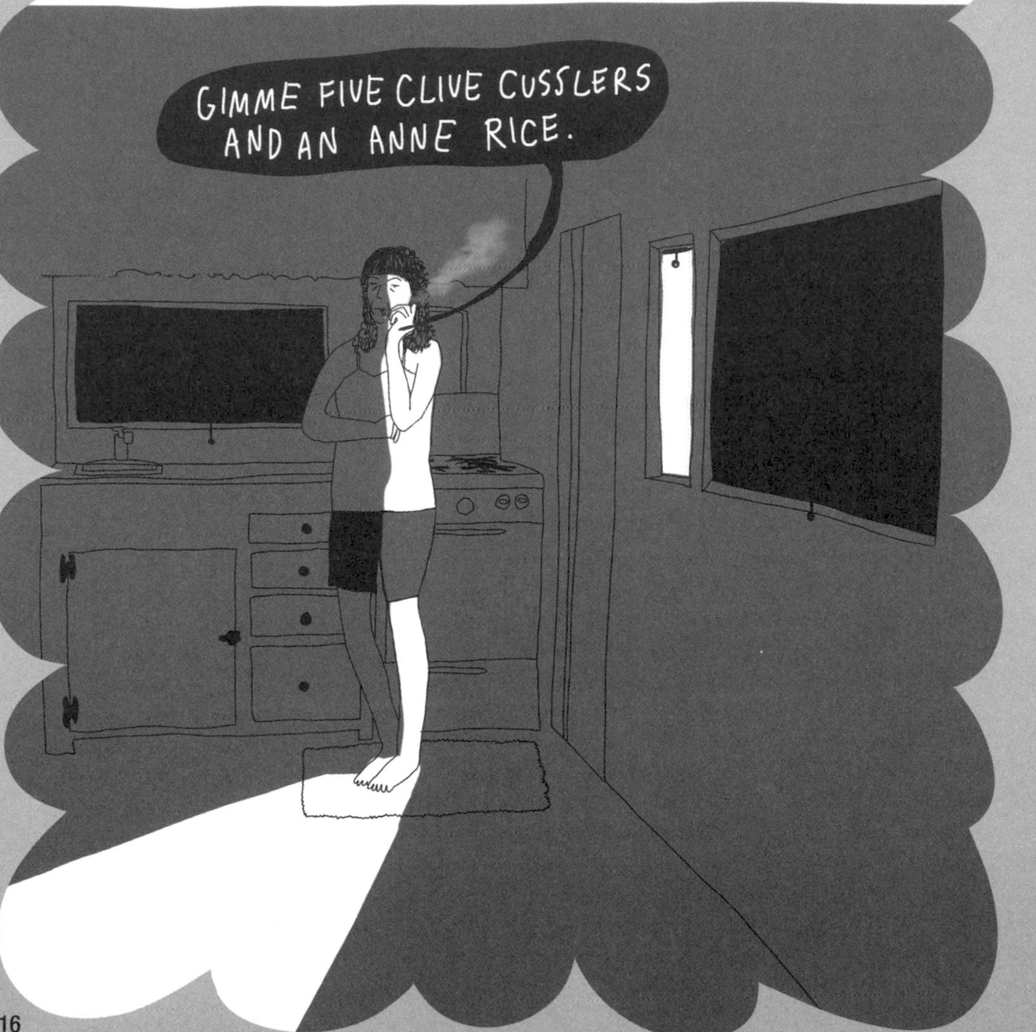
GIMME FIVE CLIVE CUSSLERS AND AN ANNE RICE.

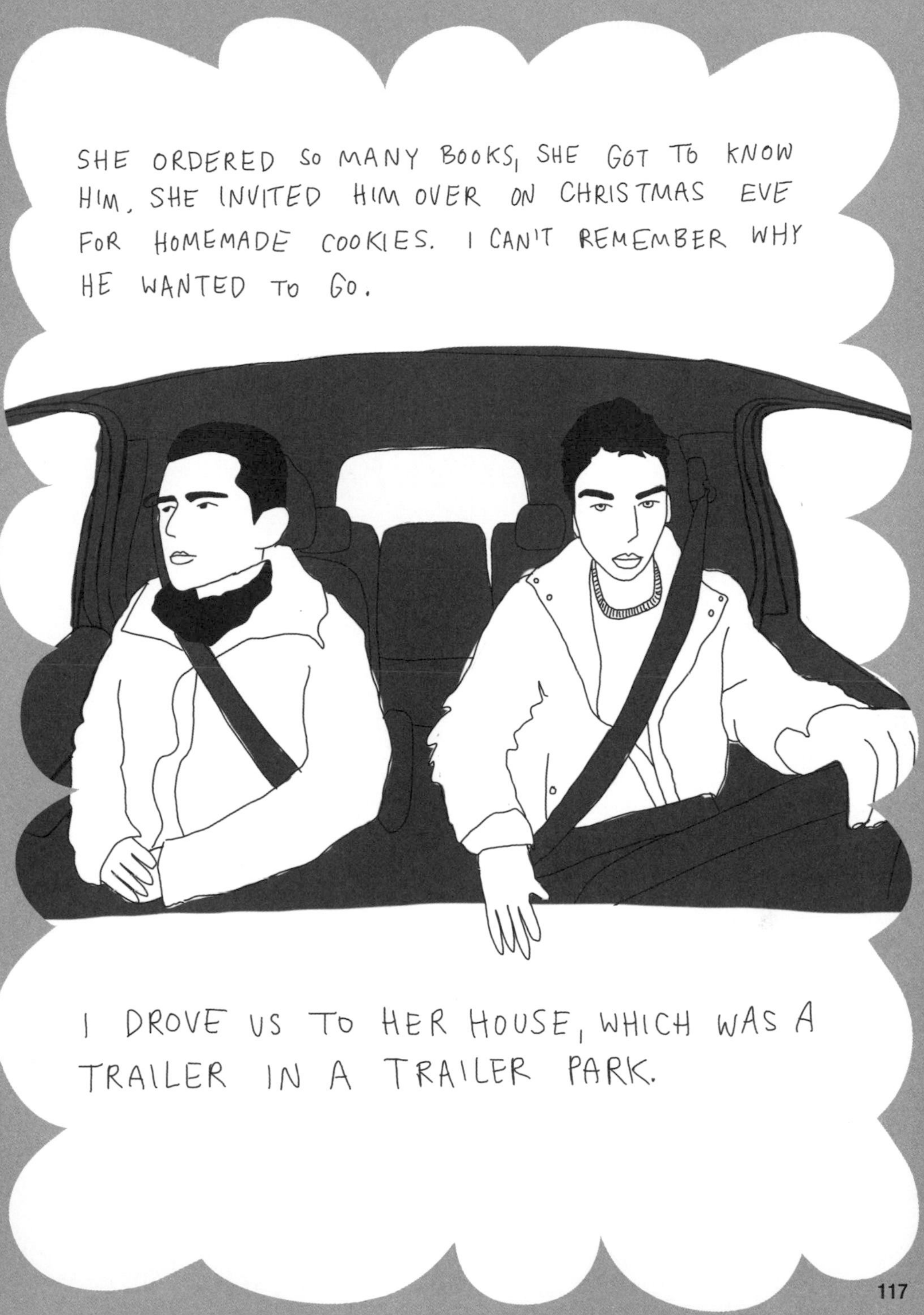
SHE ORDERED SO MANY BOOKS, SHE GOT TO KNOW HIM, SHE INVITED HIM OVER ON CHRISTMAS EVE FOR HOMEMADE COOKIES. I CAN'T REMEMBER WHY HE WANTED TO GO.
I DROVE US TO HER HOUSE, WHICH WAS A TRAILER IN A TRAILER PARK.

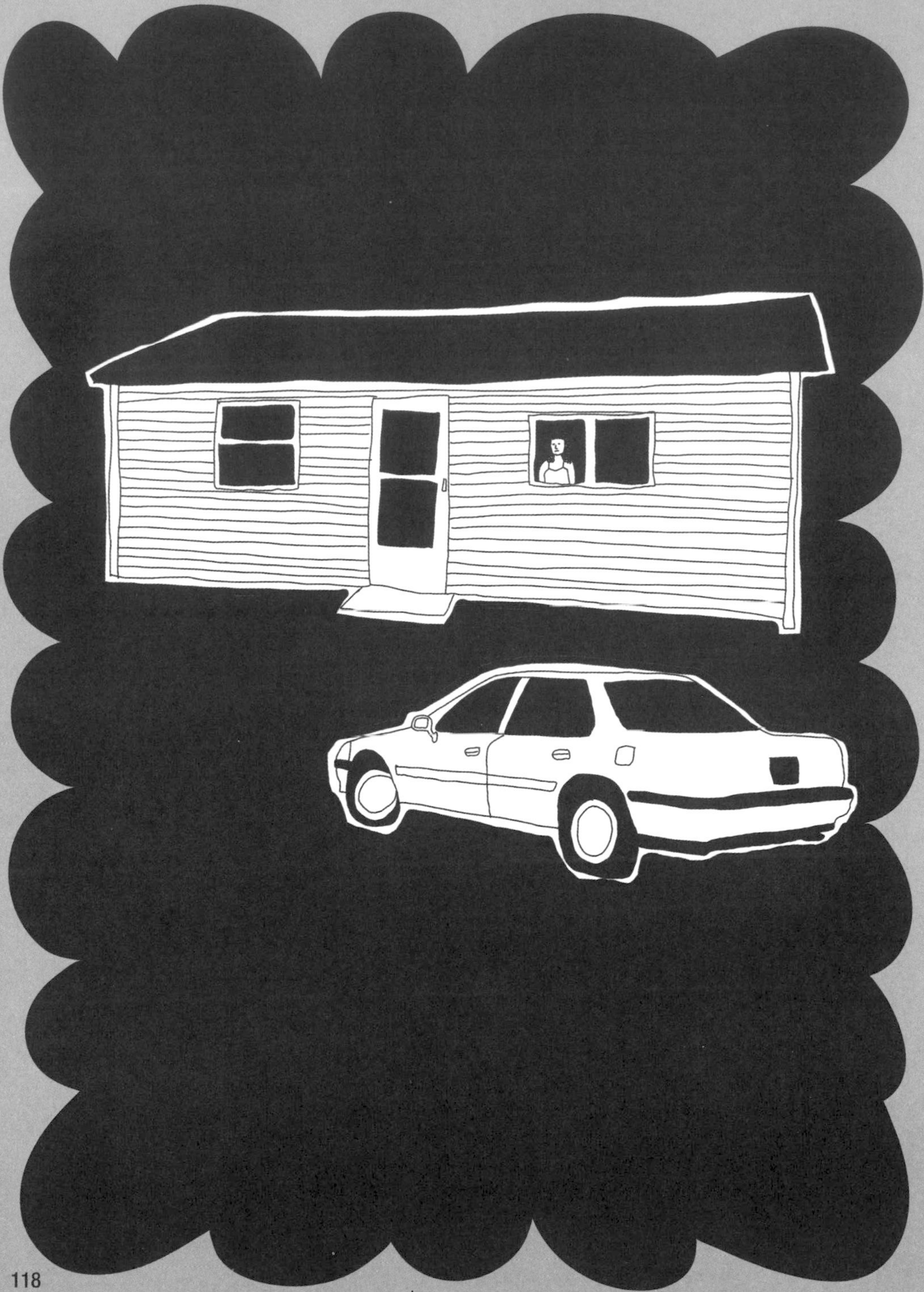

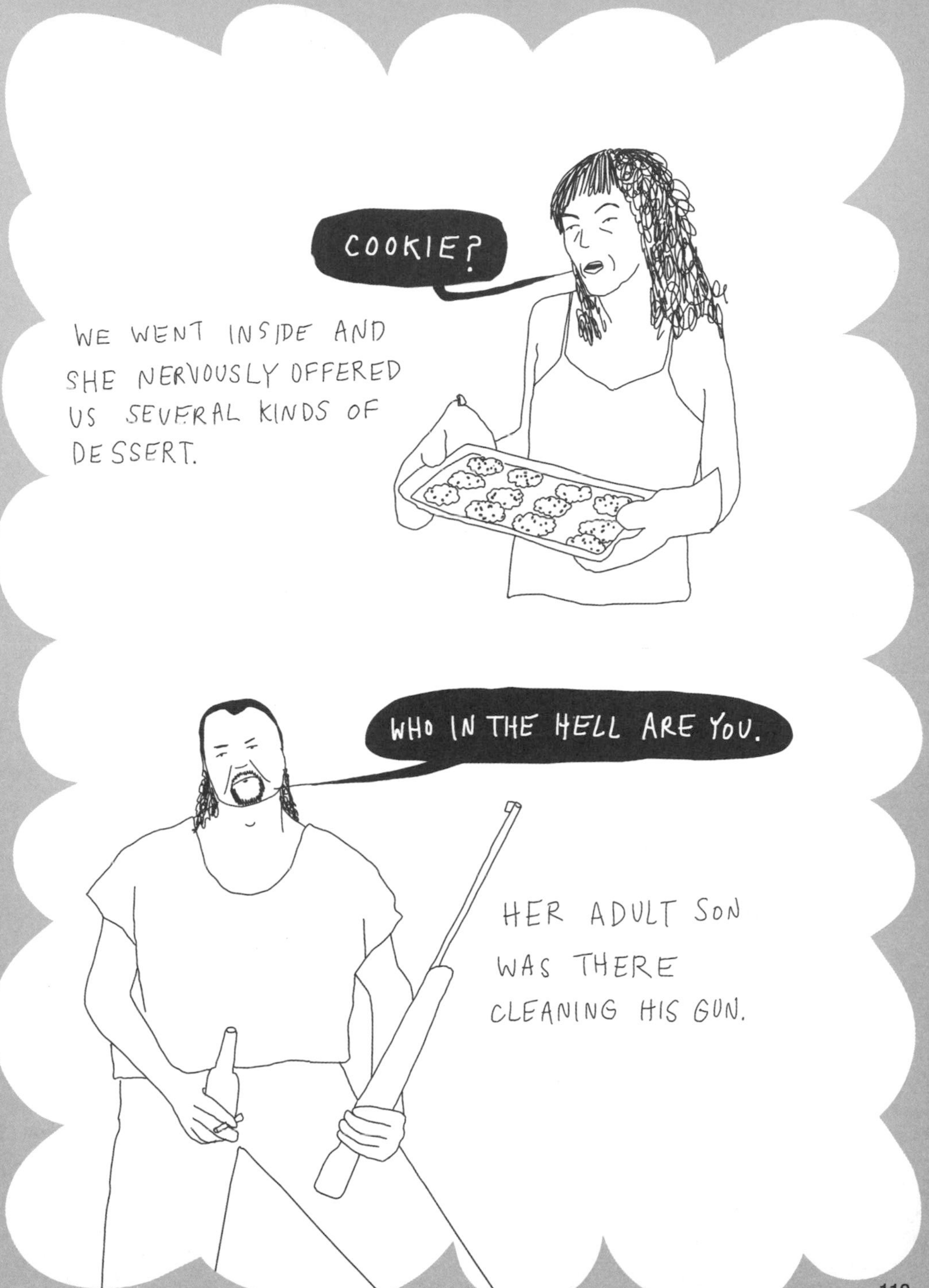
COOKIE?
WE WENT INSIDE AND SHE NERVOUSLY OFFERED US SEVERAL KINDS OF DESSERT.
WHO IN THE HELL ARE YOU.
HER ADULT SON WAS THERE CLEANING HIS GUN.

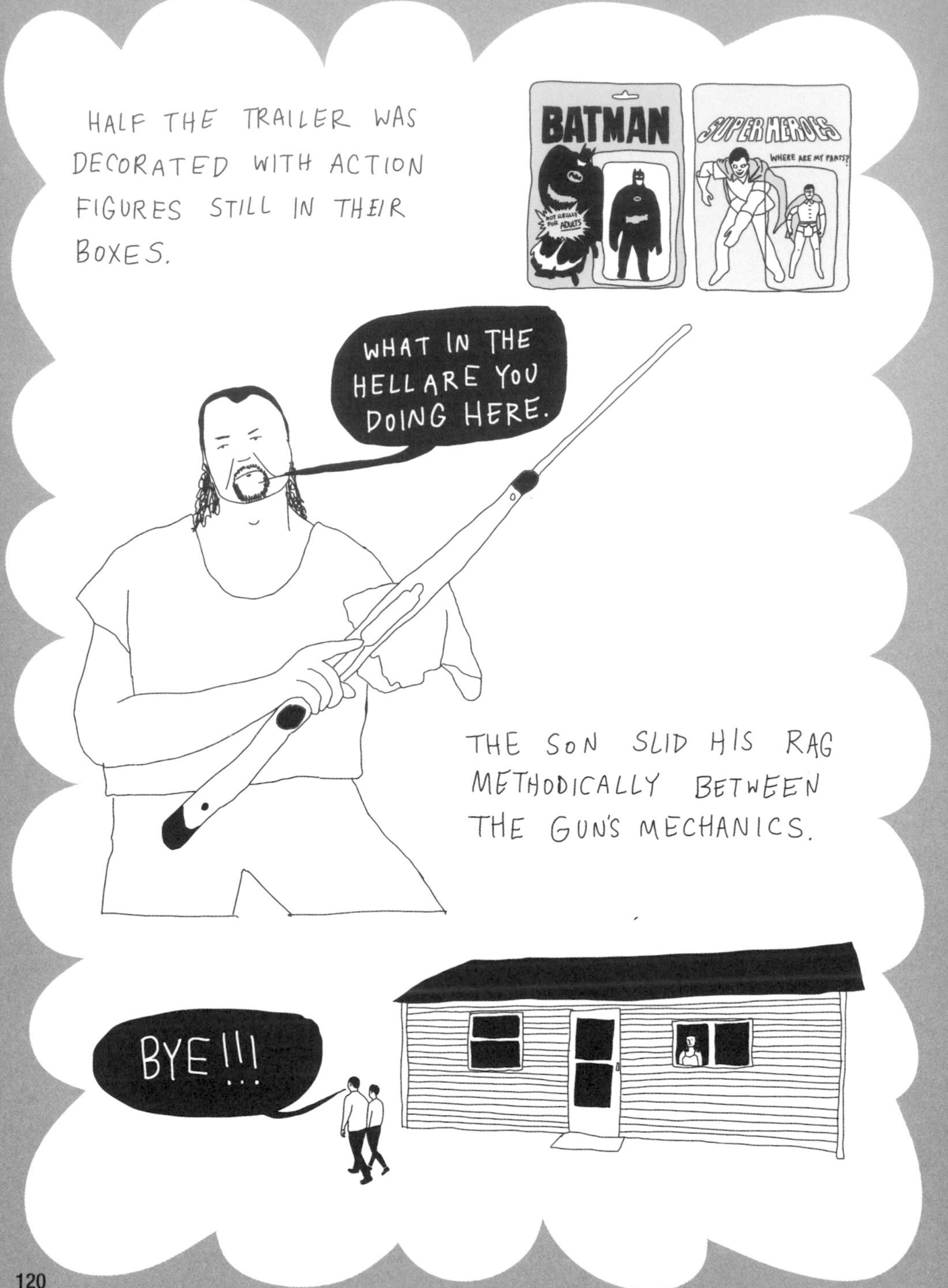
HALF THE TRAILER WAS DECORATED WITH ACTION FIGURES STILL IN THEIR BOXES.
BATMAN
NOT REALLY FOR ADULTS
SUPER HEROES
WHERE ARE MY PANTS?
WHAT IN THE HELL ARE YOU DOING HERE.
THE SON SLID HIS RAG METHODICALLY BETWEEN THE GUN'S MECHANICS.
BYE!!!
...

WE WENT BACK TO MY PARENTS' HOUSE, GOT DRUNK, AND LAUGHED ABOUT HOW HE COULD'VE KILLED US.

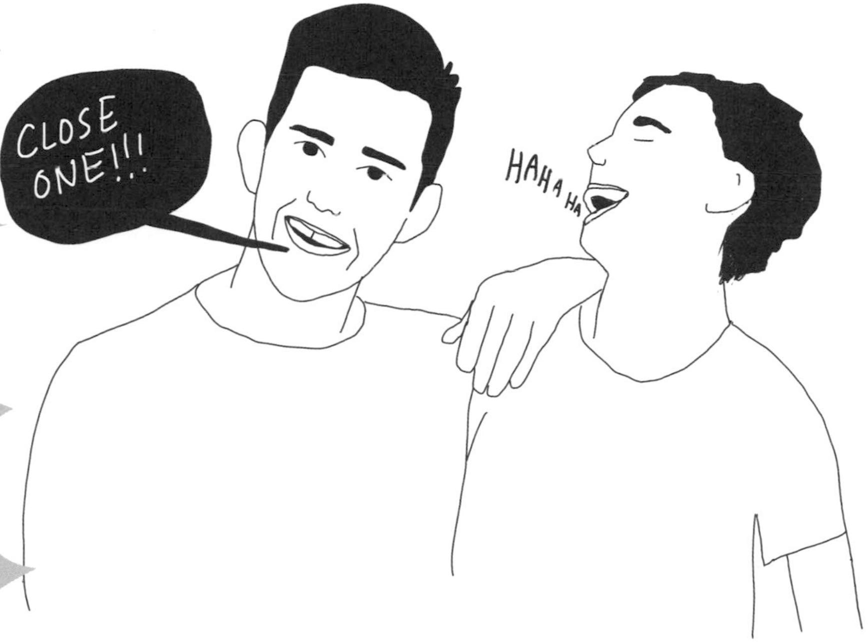
CLOSE ONE!!!
HAHAHA

IT WAS THE FIRST TIME.

WE HAD ANAL SEX. NOT BECAUSE IT WAS PLEASURABLE FOR ME, BUT BECAUSE IT FELT APPROPRIATELY VIOLENT AND VIOLATING. (IT WAS MY IDEA; HE MERELY COMPLIED.)

THINKING ABOUT JASON REMINDS ME OF MY OTHER EX, JEFF. JEFF GAVE ME A HEAVY WHITE BOX ON VALENTINE'S DAY. I TOOK OFF THE PAPER AND RIBBON, REMOVED THE TOP, AND UNFOLDED THE LIPS OF TISSUE PAPER.

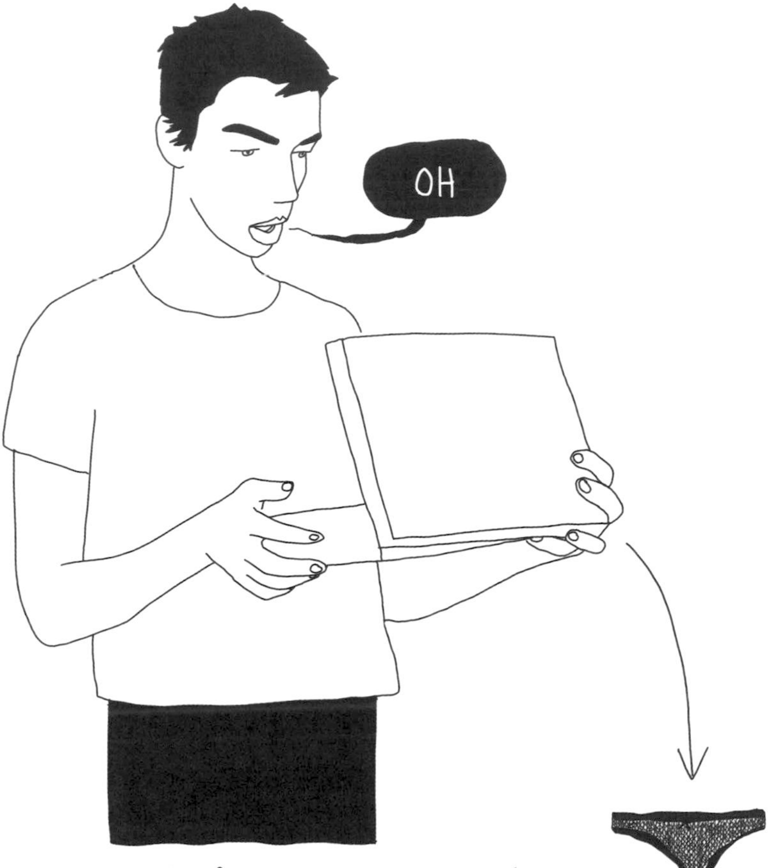
OH

A PAIR OF BLACK UNDERWEAR.

LOOK UNDERNEATH.

I TOOK THE TISSUE PAPER OUT OF THE BOX.

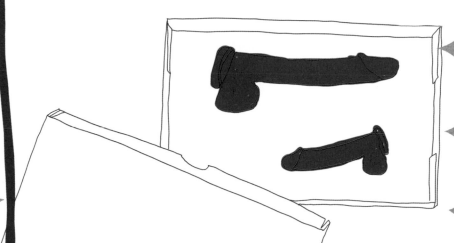

THE BIG ONE'S FOR YOU AND THE LITTLE ONE'S FOR ME.

WHEN I LATER BROKE UP WITH HIM (UNRELATED* TO THE VALENTINE'S GIFT), HE CALLED ME AND HUNG UP SO INCESSANTLY THAT I HAD TO THREATEN HIM WITH A RESTRAINING ORDER TO MAKE IT STOP.

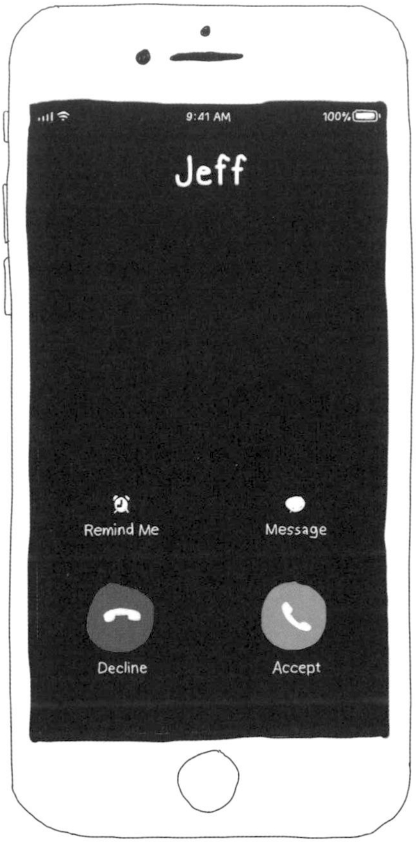
9:41 AM
100%
Jeff
Remind Me
Message
Decline
Accept

* YOU KNOW, UNRELATED BUT... RELATED.

ONE OF THE THINGS I'M MOST STRUCK BY WHEN I THINK ABOUT THAT RELATIONSHIP NOW IS:

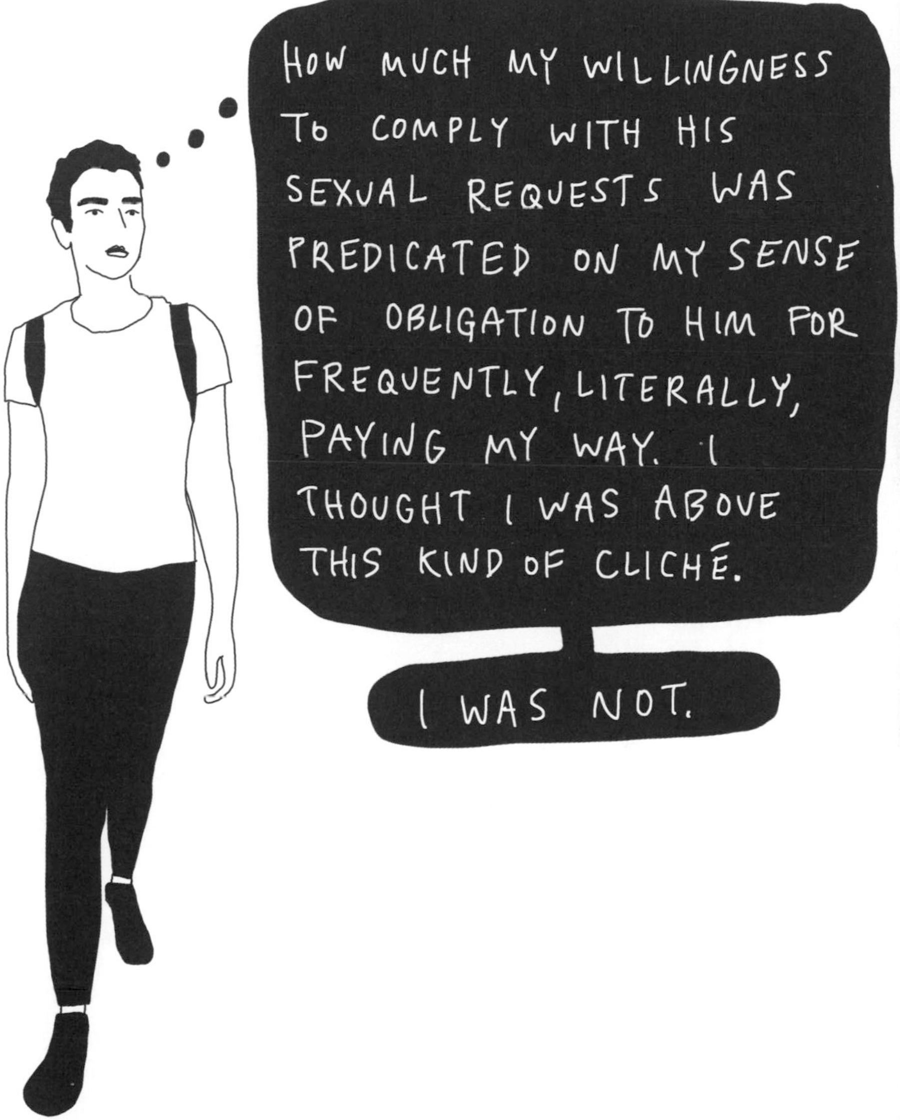
HOW MUCH MY WILLINGNESS TO COMPLY WITH HIS SEXUAL REQUESTS WAS PREDICATED ON MY SENSE OF OBLIGATION TO HIM FOR FREQUENTLY, LITERALLY, PAYING MY WAY. I THOUGHT I WAS ABOVE THIS KIND OF CLICHÉ.
I WAS NOT.

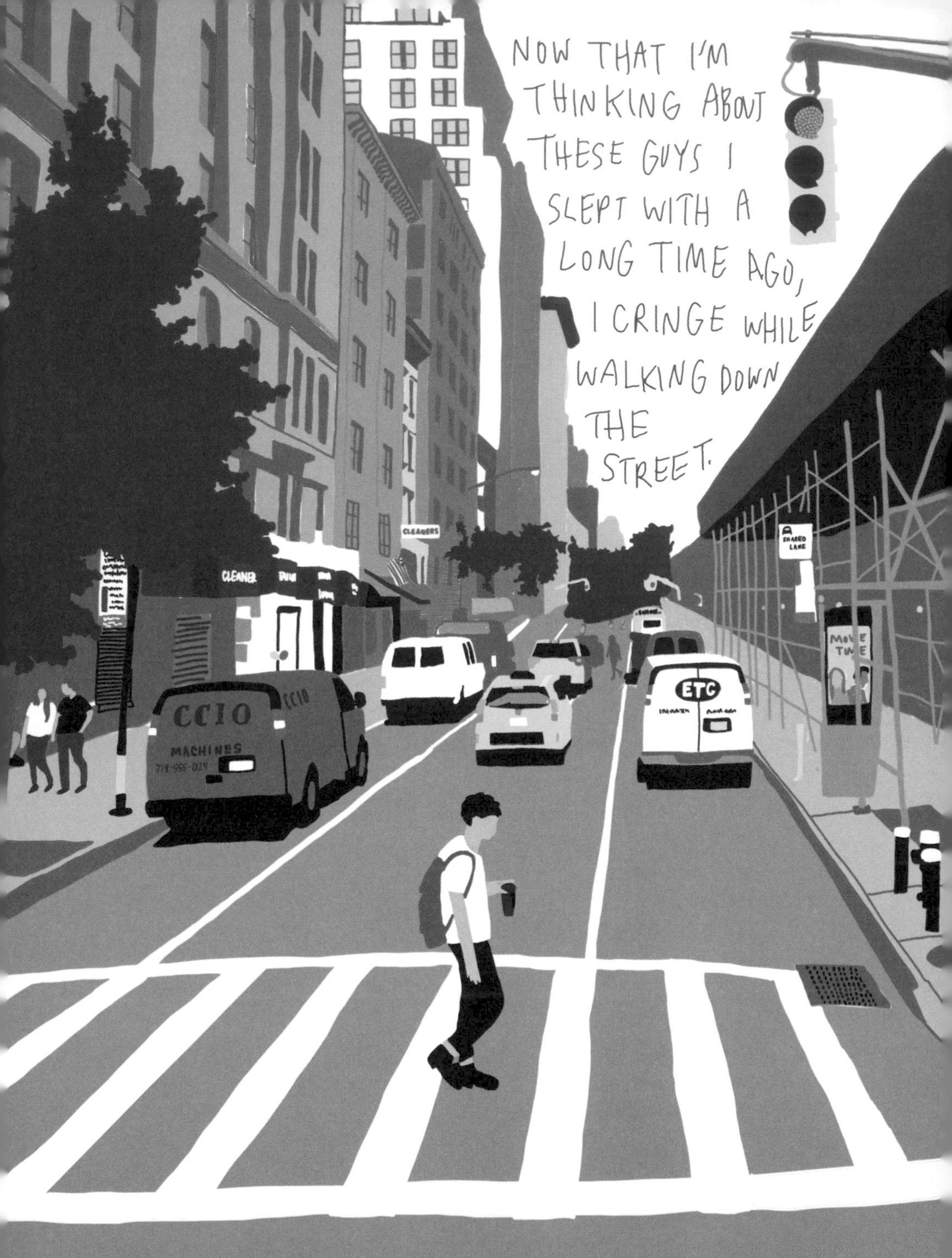
NOW THAT I'M THINKING ABOUT THESE GUYS I SLEPT WITH A LONG TIME AGO, I CRINGE WHILE WALKING DOWN THE STREET.
CLEANER
CLEANERS
CCIO
MACHINES
ETC
SHARED LANE

I MET KARL ON A DATING WEBSITE. HE WAS SOME KIND OF PRETENTIOUS GRADUATE STUDENT. RUSSIAN LITERATURE, I THINK.

Karl, 28
Brooklyn, New York

About

Dostoevsky is my homeboy. I love cleverness, pickled foods, whiskey, inner turmoil, and short walks off a long bridge. You should be a reader, visionary, expert at crosswords, and sex goddess. Let me feed you eggs while sharing my PlayStation.

Detailed Info

Ethnicity	White / Caucasian
Height	5'10"
Politics	Other
Has Kids	None

iMac

HE GAVE ME A BAD, FEAR-FOR-YOUR-LIFE TYPE OF FEELING.

ONE NIGHT I WAS LONELY AND WE GCHATTED.
HE WAS THE ONLY PERSON I KNEW ONLINE.

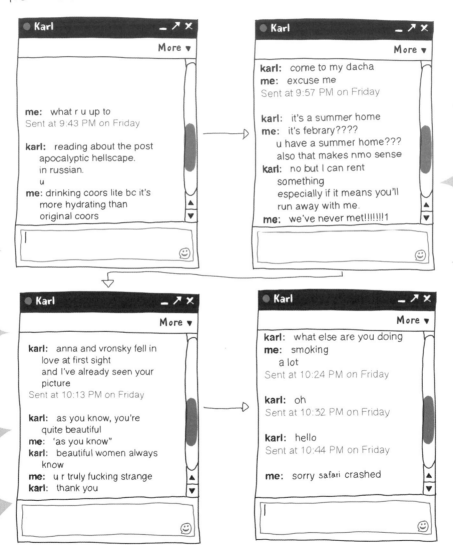

Karl — ⤢ ✕

More ▾

me: what r u up to
Sent at 9:43 PM on Friday

karl: reading about the post
apocalyptic hellscape.
in russian.
u
me: drinking coors lite bc it's
more hydrating than
original coors

☺

Karl — ⤢ ✕

More ▾

karl: come to my dacha
me: excuse me
Sent at 9:57 PM on Friday

karl: it's a summer home
me: it's febrary????
u have a summer home???
also that makes nmo sense
karl: no but I can rent
something
especially if it means you'll
run away with me.
me: we've never met!!!!!!1

☺

Karl — ⤢ ✕

More ▾

karl: anna and vronsky fell in
love at first sight
and I've already seen your
picture
Sent at 10:13 PM on Friday

karl: as you know, you're
quite beautiful
me: 'as you know'
karl: beautiful women always
know
me: u r truly fucking strange
karl: thank you

☺

Karl — ⤢ ✕

More ▾

karl: what else are you doing
me: smoking
a lot
Sent at 10:24 PM on Friday

karl: oh
Sent at 10:32 PM on Friday

karl: hello
Sent at 10:44 PM on Friday

me: sorry safari crashed

☺

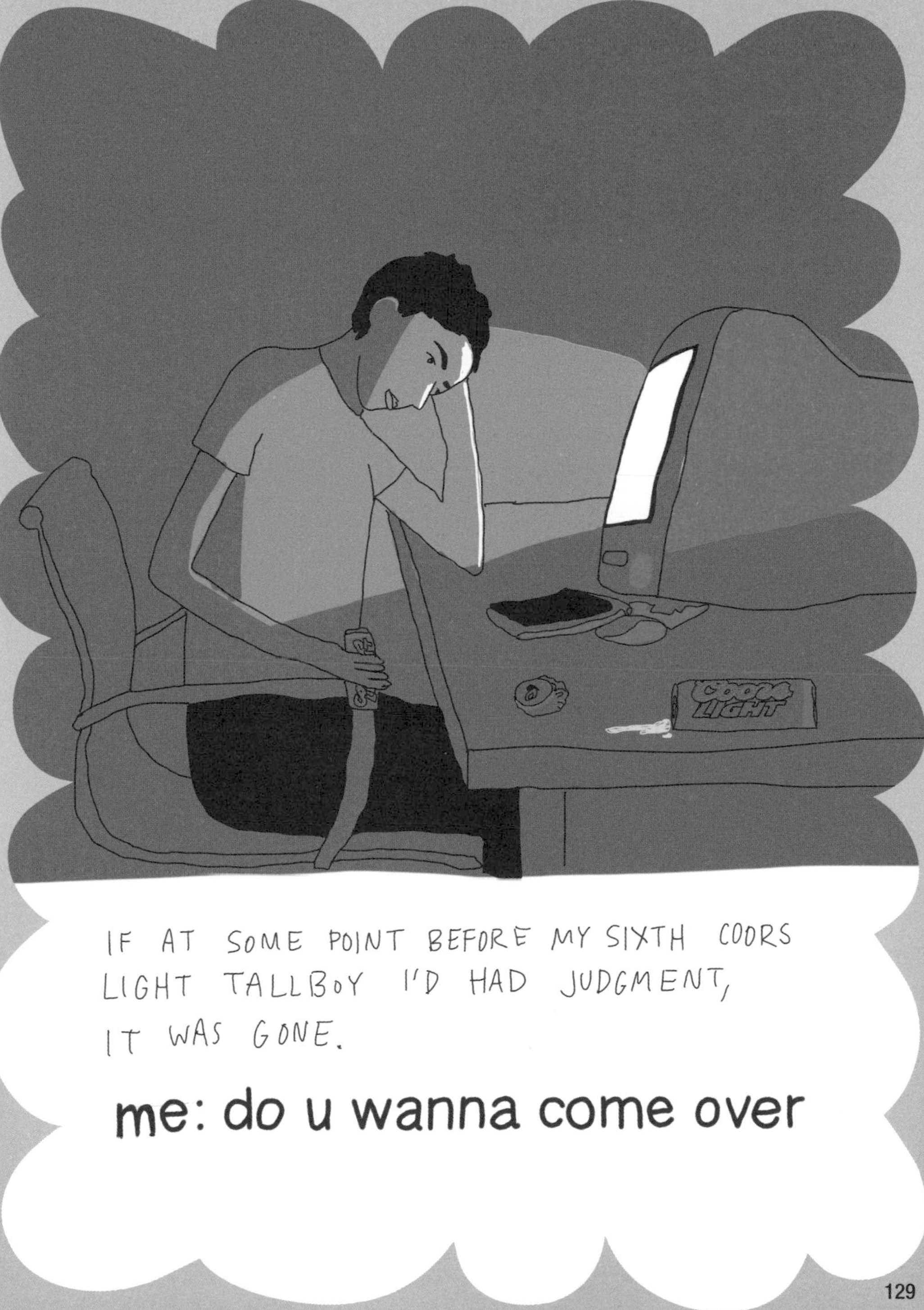
LIGHT
IF AT SOME POINT BEFORE MY SIXTH COORS LIGHT TALLBOY I'D HAD JUDGMENT, IT WAS GONE.
me: do u wanna come over

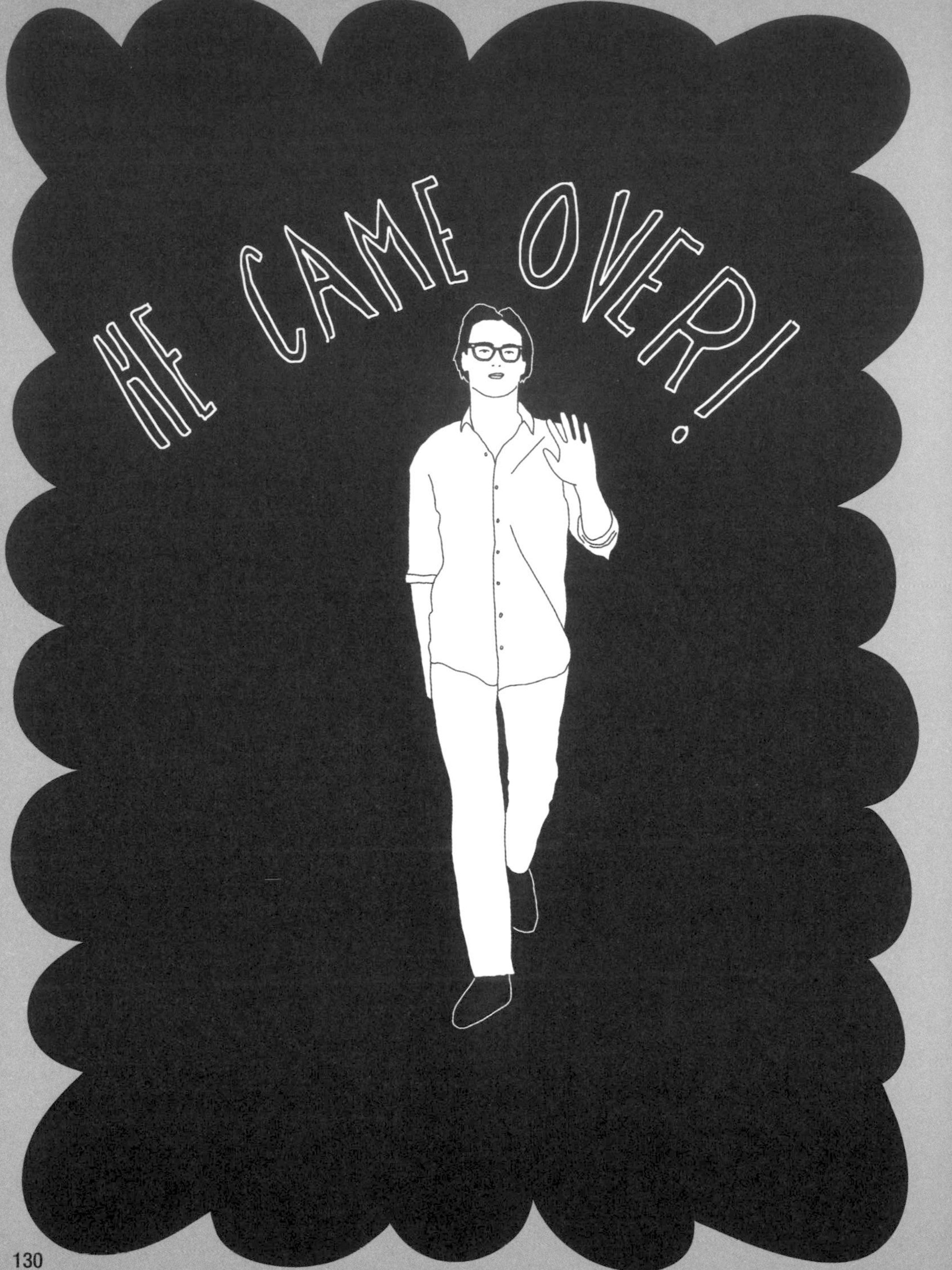
HE CAME OVER!

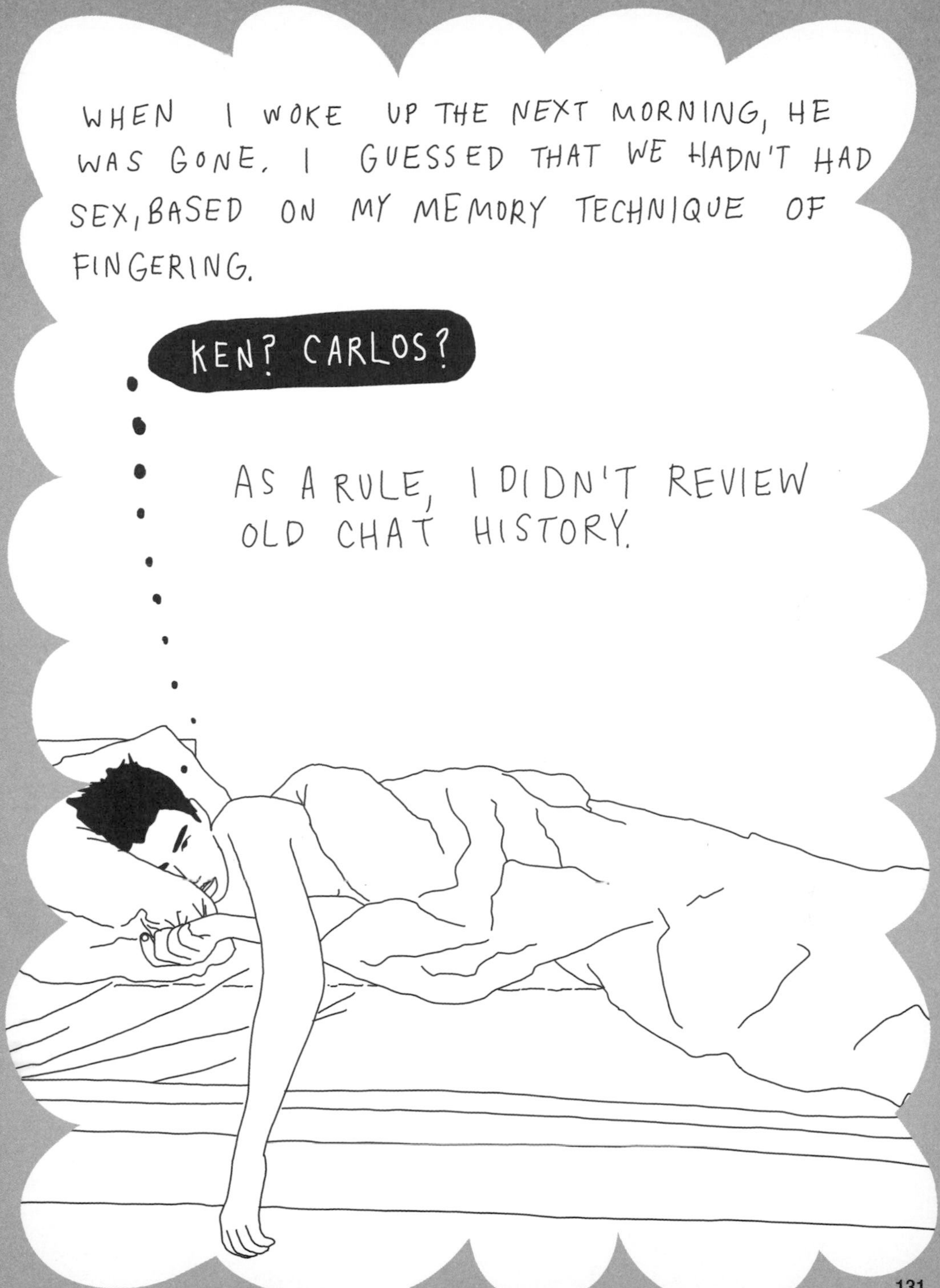
WHEN I WOKE UP THE NEXT MORNING, HE WAS GONE. I GUESSED THAT WE HADN'T HAD SEX, BASED ON MY MEMORY TECHNIQUE OF FINGERING.
KEN? CARLOS?
AS A RULE, I DIDN'T REVIEW OLD CHAT HISTORY.

I FOUND A NOTE FROM HIM ON
MY BED.

little enigma—

with love one can live even without happiness

— fyodor dostoevsky

it was a pleasure to watch you sleep.

karl

I NEVER SAW HIM AGAIN.

10 THE NUMBER OF MEN WHO LOOK ME IN THE EYE WHILE I WALK TO WORK.

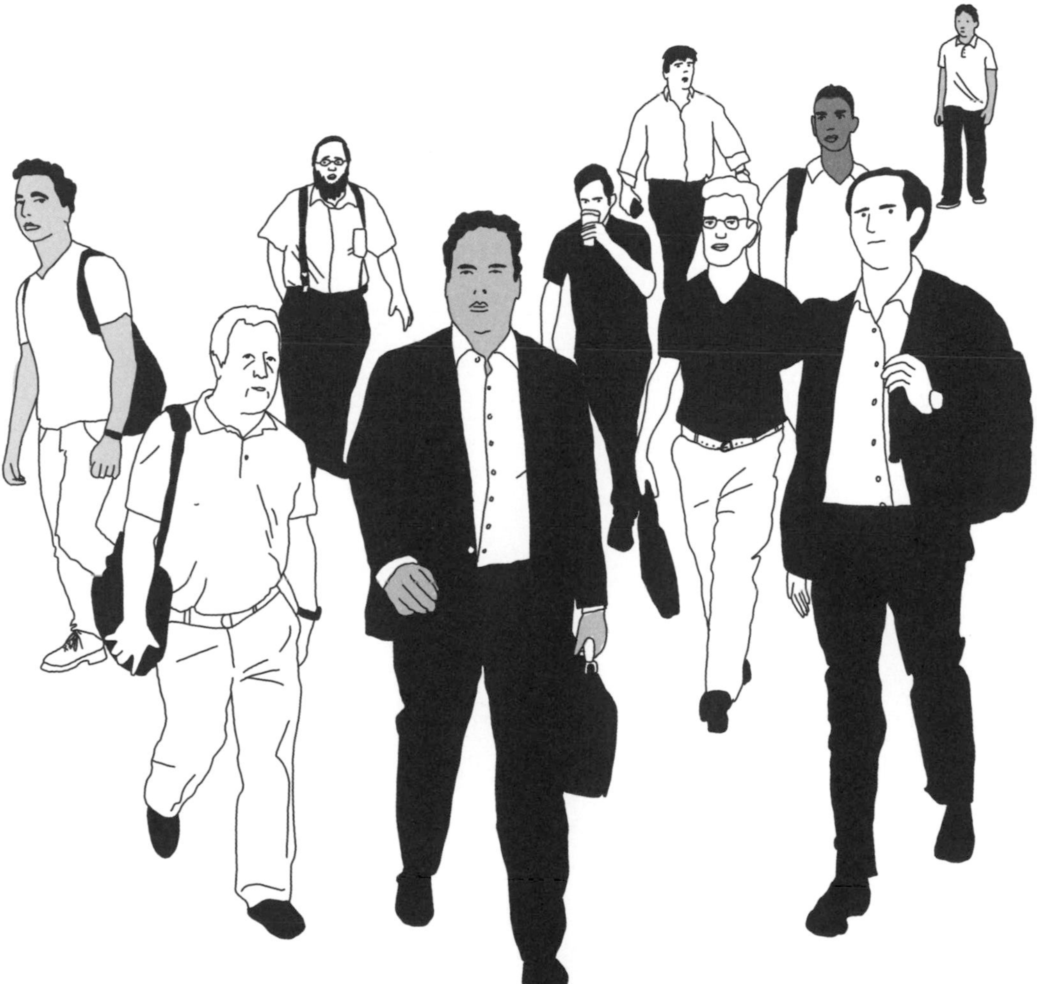

OTHER THINGS I SEE:

VACANCY

A HOTEL RECOMMENDS
STAYING THE NIGHT

A WOMAN
VACUUMS A
STORE
BEFORE IT
OPENS

"THESE ARE VERY
SPECIAL TREES".
PLEASE CURB YOUR DOG
THANK YOU

TREE URGENCY IN
A PLANTER WITH
NO TREES

A NOTICE THAT
LINDSAY LOHAN
WENT TO A BAR
IN 2006

A PHOTOREALISTIC
STEAK

A MANNEQUIN
IN LINGERIE

A PREGNANT WOMAN

A SHEEP DOG WITH
A HIGH PONYTAIL

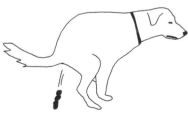

A DOG POOPING
(NO PONYTAIL)

I STOP FOR BREAKFAST.

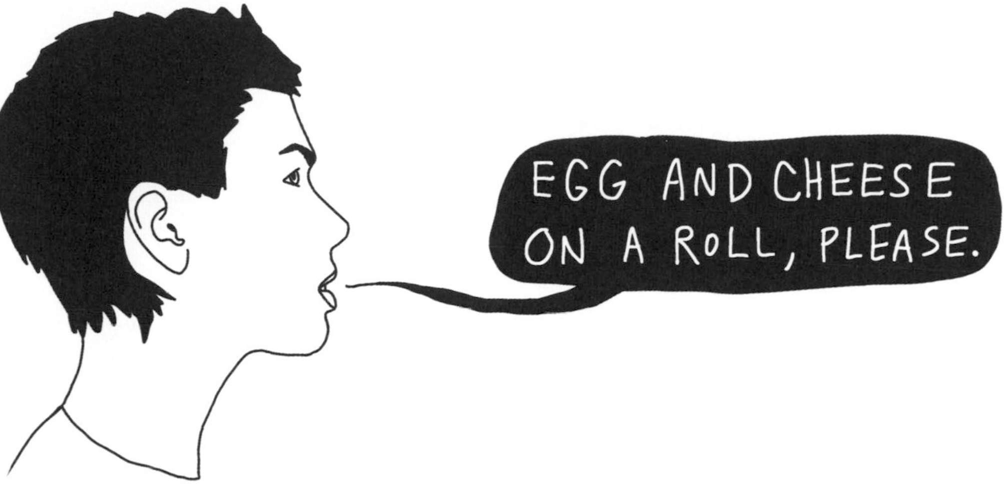
EGG AND CHEESE ON A ROLL, PLEASE.

I PAY FOR IT.

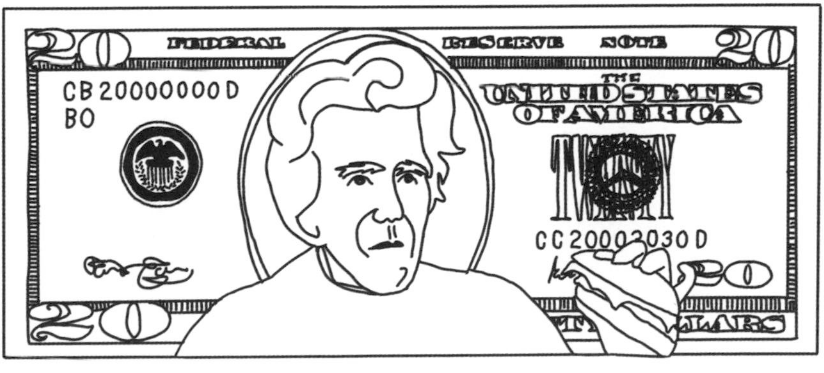
CB 20000000 D
BO

I WAIT AT THE COUNTER WHILE A WOMAN MAKES IT.

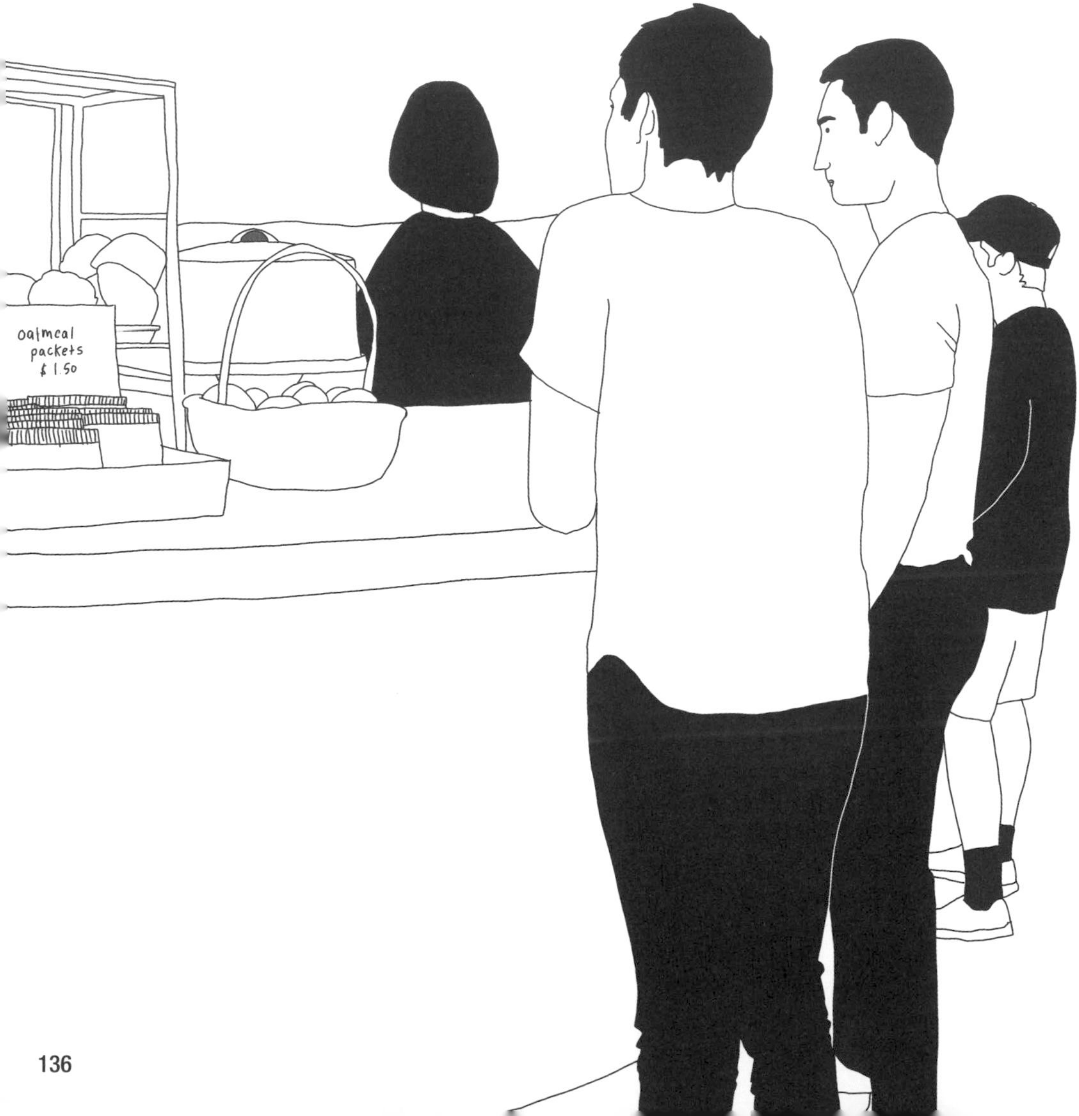
oatmeal
packets
$ 1.50

A MAN OGLES A WOMAN WALKING BY, BREASTS BOUNCING IN A TIGHT TOP.

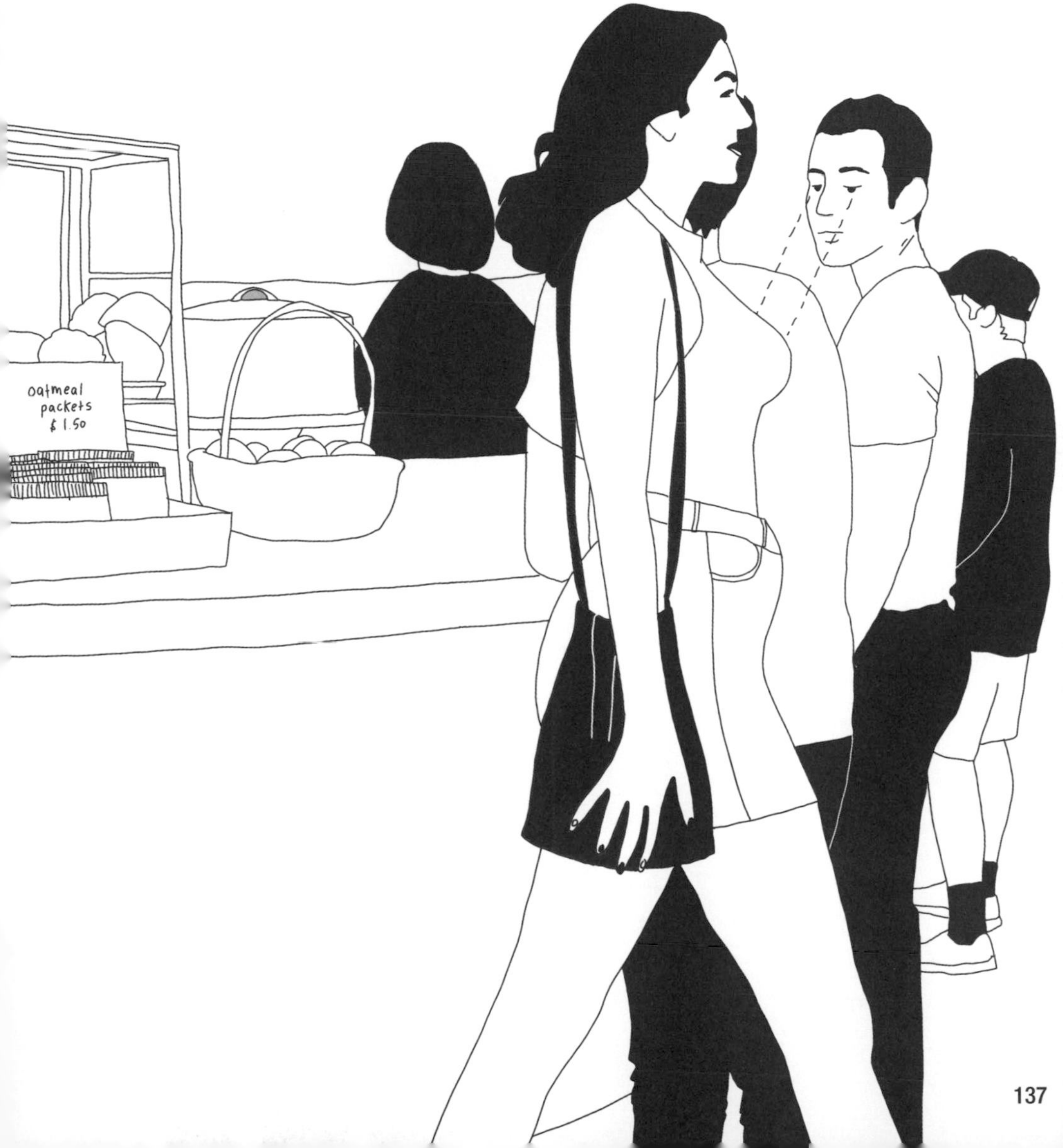
oatmeal
packets
$1.50

MY SANDWICH IS READY. I TAKE IT AND LEAVE.

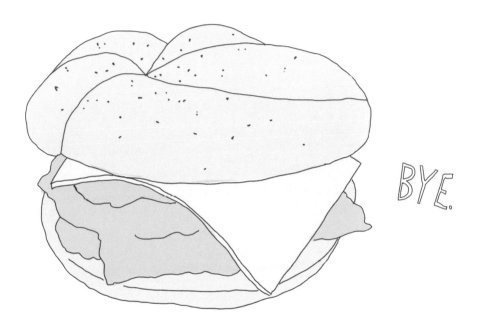

BYE.

I GET TO WORK, OPEN THE FOIL, AND WORRY SOMEONE WILL SMELL THE HOT FOOD AND THINK I'M GROSS.

I WORK FOR A WHILE.

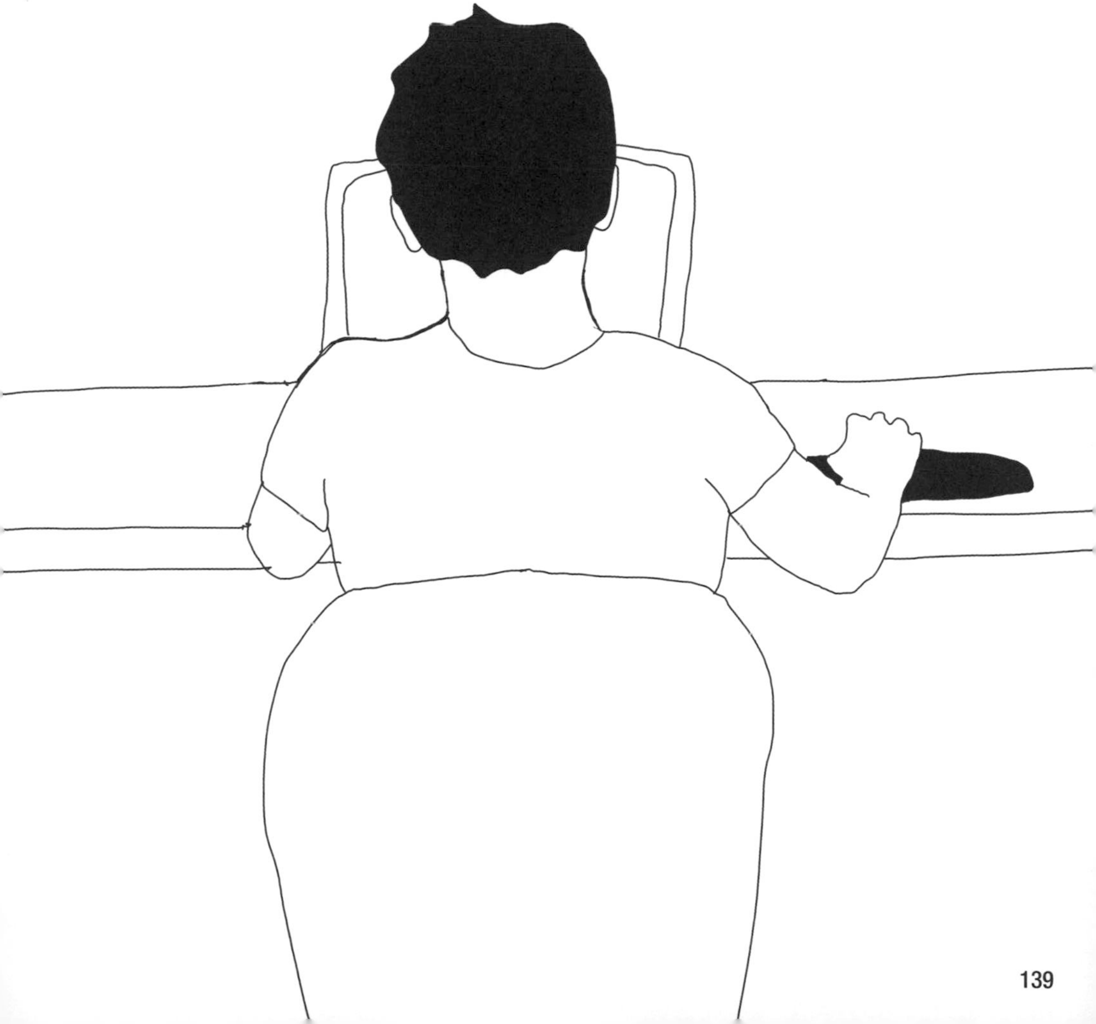

TAKE A BREAK

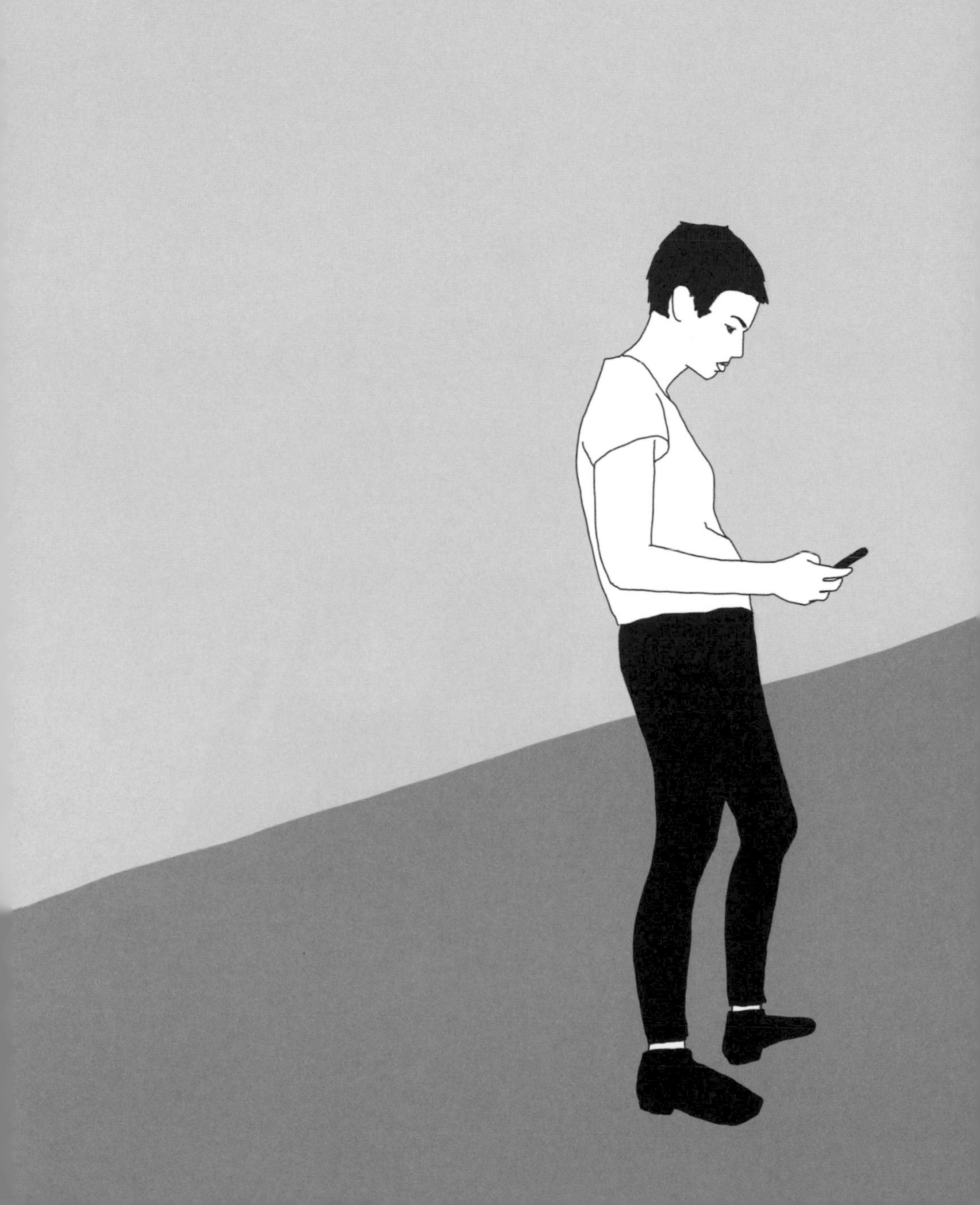

MY COWORKER ANDREW INVITES ME OUT FOR A COFFEE. WE WALK IN THE PARK. HE TELLS ME I SHOULD BE MORE FORGIVING OF PSYCHOANALYSIS AS A CONCEPT.

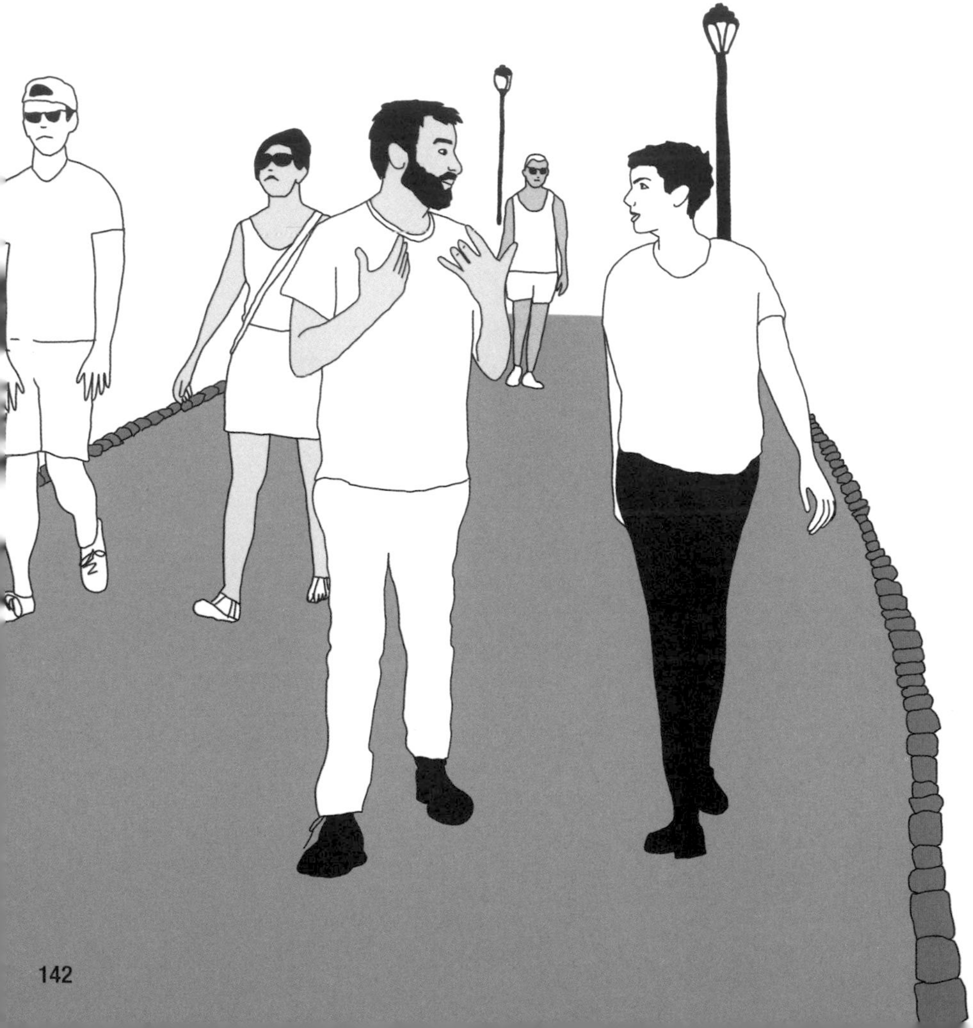

HE HAS A PhD AND YEARS OF PSYCHOANALYSIS UNDER HIS BELT* AND WHETHER FREUD IS GOOD OR BAD IS NOT AN ACCEPTABLE TOPIC OF DISCUSSION.

HE WAS A GENIUS.

* NOTE THAT WE DO NOT WORK IN ANY FIELD RELATED TO PSYCHOLOGY; WE ARE CANCER RESEARCHERS.

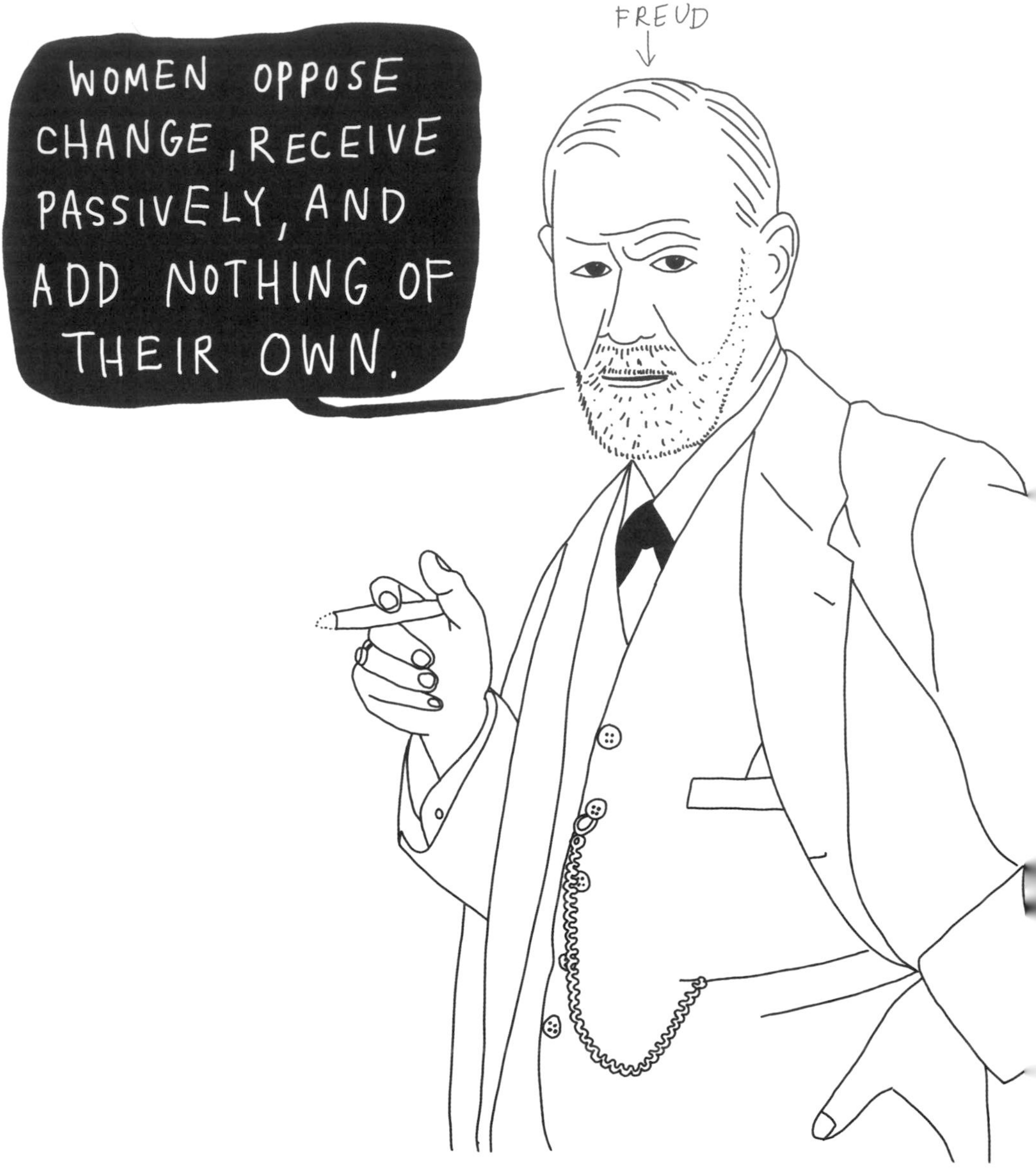
WOMEN OPPOSE CHANGE, RECEIVE PASSIVELY, AND ADD NOTHING OF THEIR OWN.
FREUD

I DON'T LIKE FREUD.

MEN ARE ABLE TO DISMISS THE DEFICIENCIES OF OTHER SCHOLARLY MEN AS PRODUCTS OF THEIR TIME RATHER THAN RECOGNIZING THEM AS BIGOTS WHO HELPED TO PERPETUATE CENTURIES OF OPPRESSION.

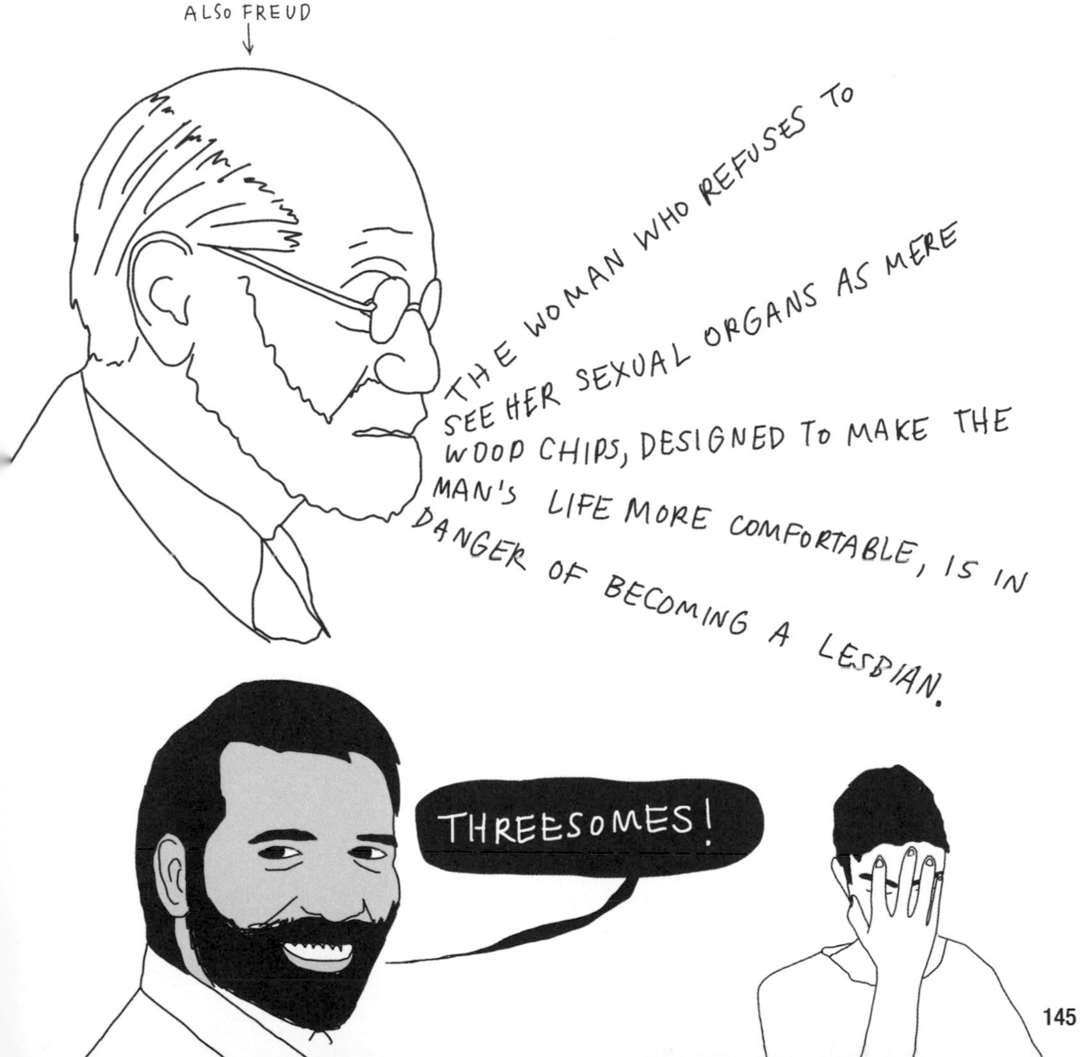
ALSO FREUD
THE WOMAN WHO REFUSES TO SEE HER SEXUAL ORGANS AS MERE WOOD CHIPS, DESIGNED TO MAKE THE MAN'S LIFE MORE COMFORTABLE, IS IN DANGER OF BECOMING A LESBIAN.
THREESOMES!

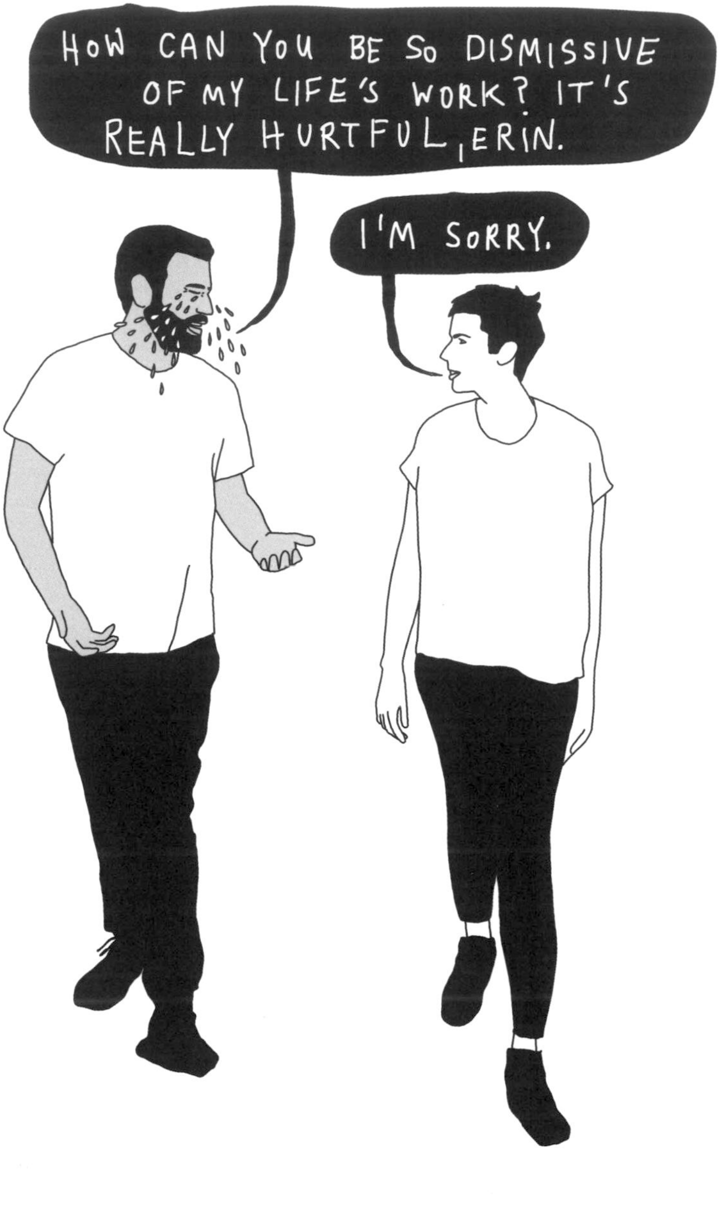
HOW CAN YOU BE SO DISMISSIVE OF MY LIFE'S WORK? IT'S REALLY HURTFUL, ERIN.
I'M SORRY.

LONG
GREEN
STICK
STALKS
NEATLY
EXPLODE
WITH
PURPLE
FLOWERS
ALONG
THE
PATH.

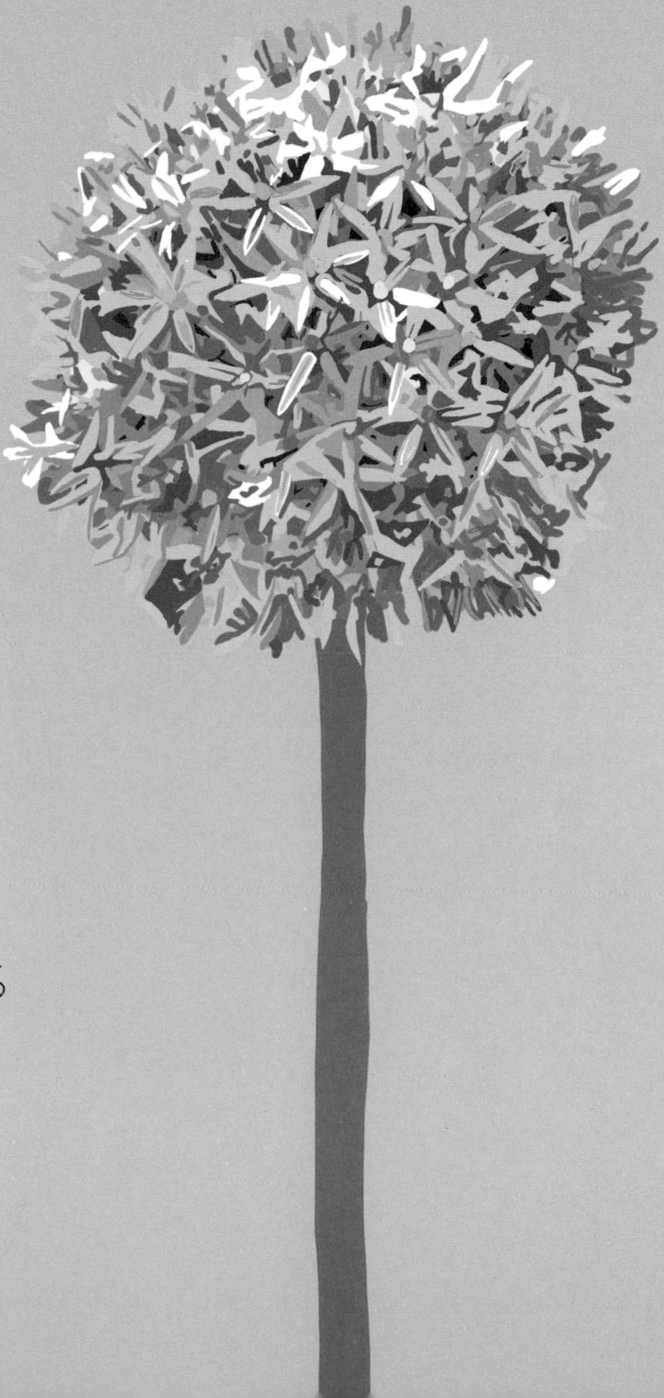

HE TELLS ME A FACT ABOUT SEX.

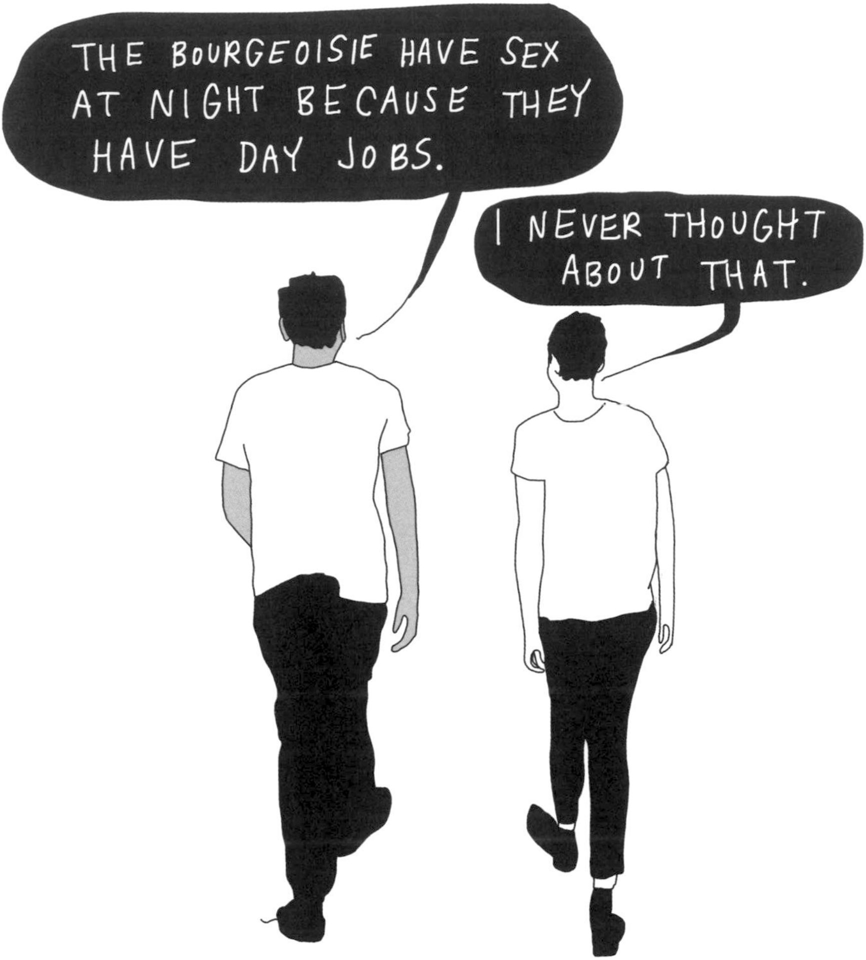
THE BOURGEOISIE HAVE SEX AT NIGHT BECAUSE THEY HAVE DAY JOBS.
I NEVER THOUGHT ABOUT THAT.

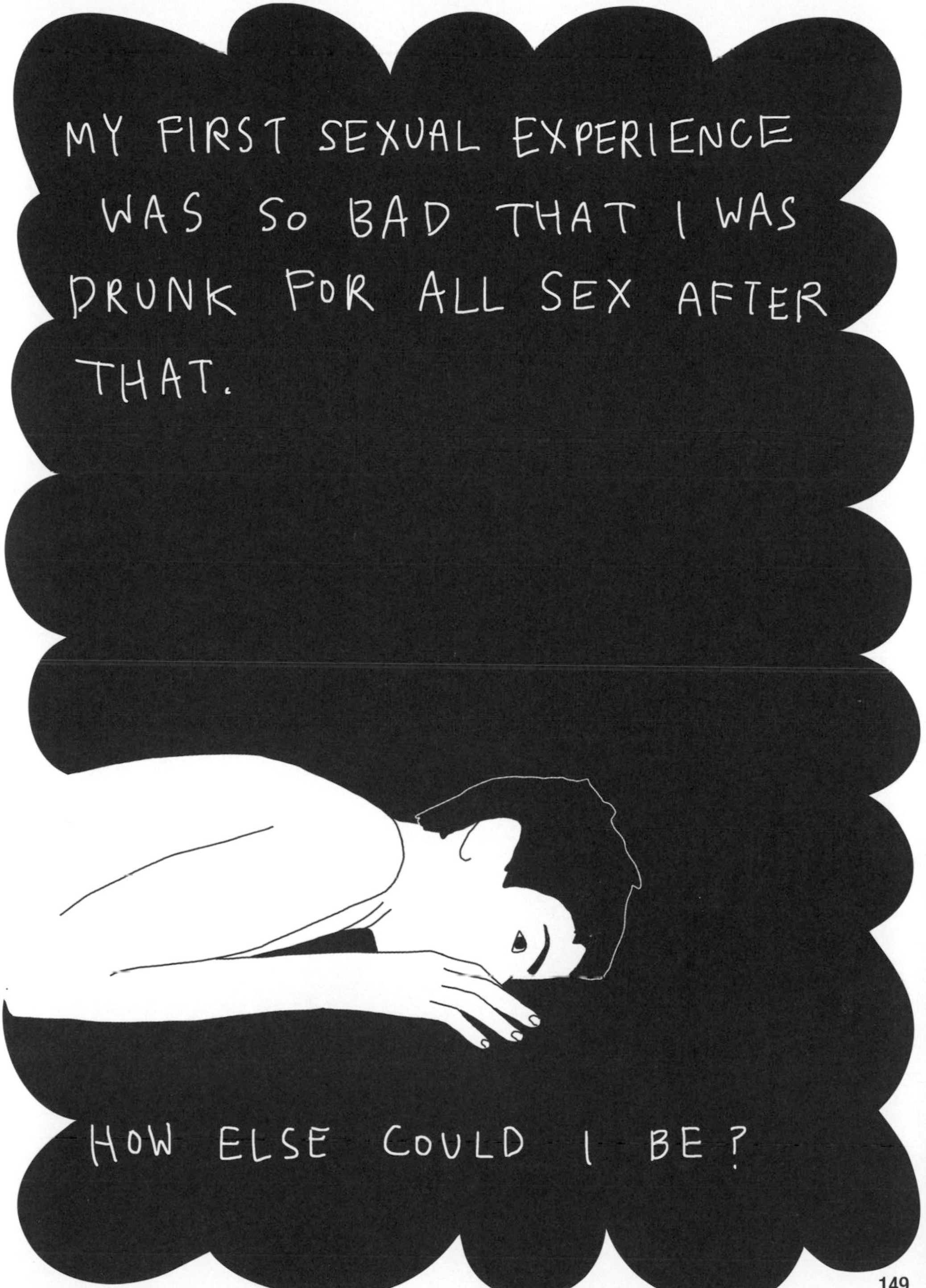
MY FIRST SEXUAL EXPERIENCE WAS SO BAD THAT I WAS DRUNK FOR ALL SEX AFTER THAT.
HOW ELSE COULD I BE?

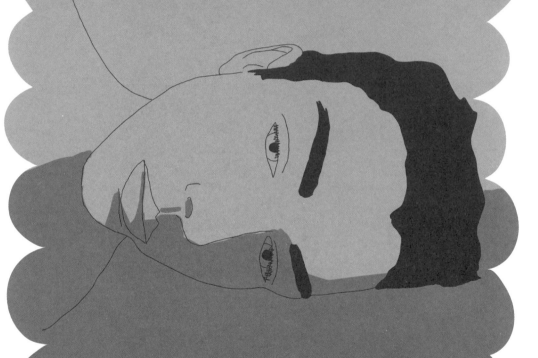

NIGHT ALWAYS WORKED BEST FOR ME
BECAUSE OF THE DARKNESS AND THE DRINKING.

BUT IT IS ALSO TRUE THAT I MOSTLY WORKED
DURING THE DAY.

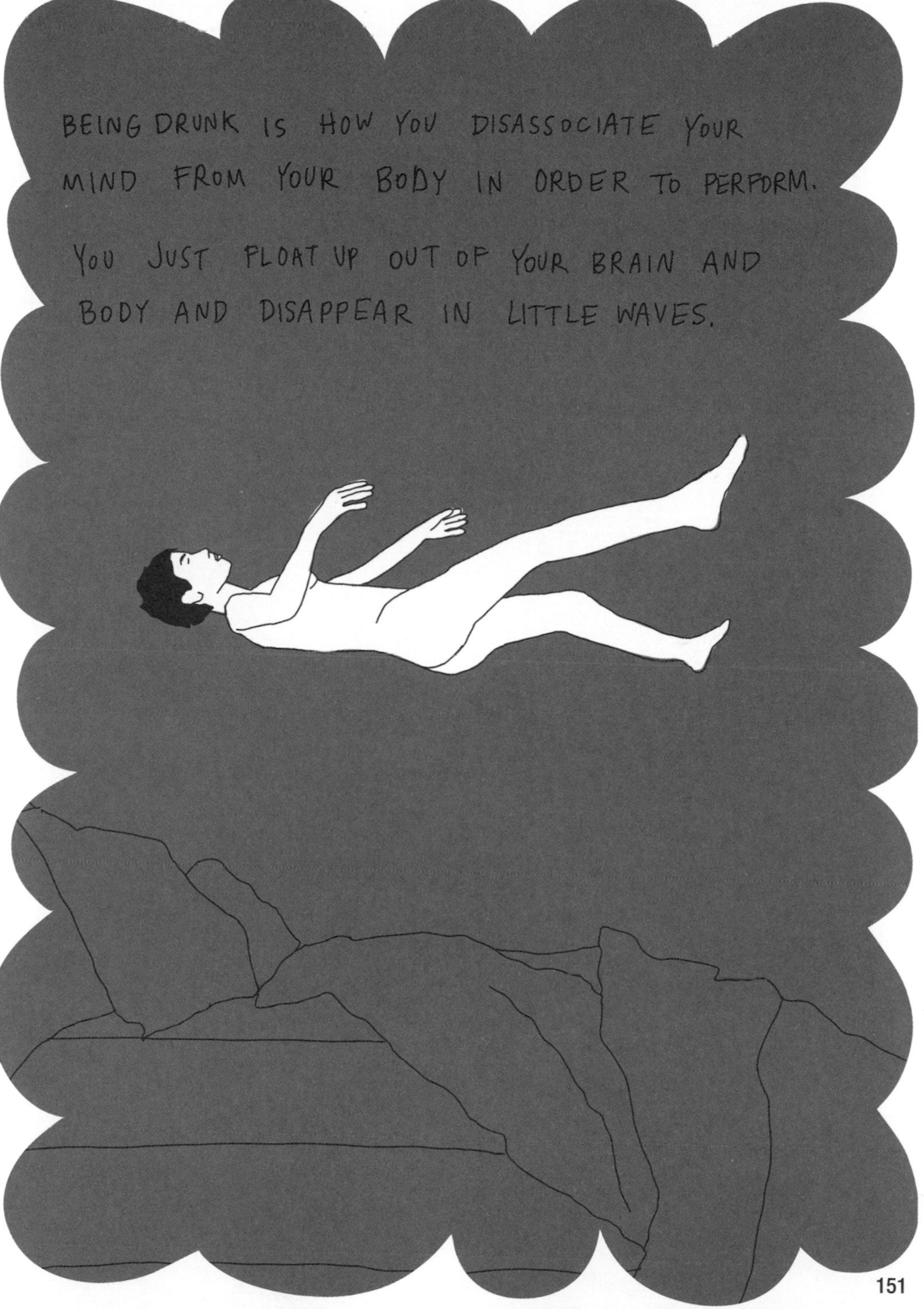
BEING DRUNK IS HOW YOU DISASSOCIATE YOUR MIND FROM YOUR BODY IN ORDER TO PERFORM.
YOU JUST FLOAT UP OUT OF YOUR BRAIN AND BODY AND DISAPPEAR IN LITTLE WAVES.

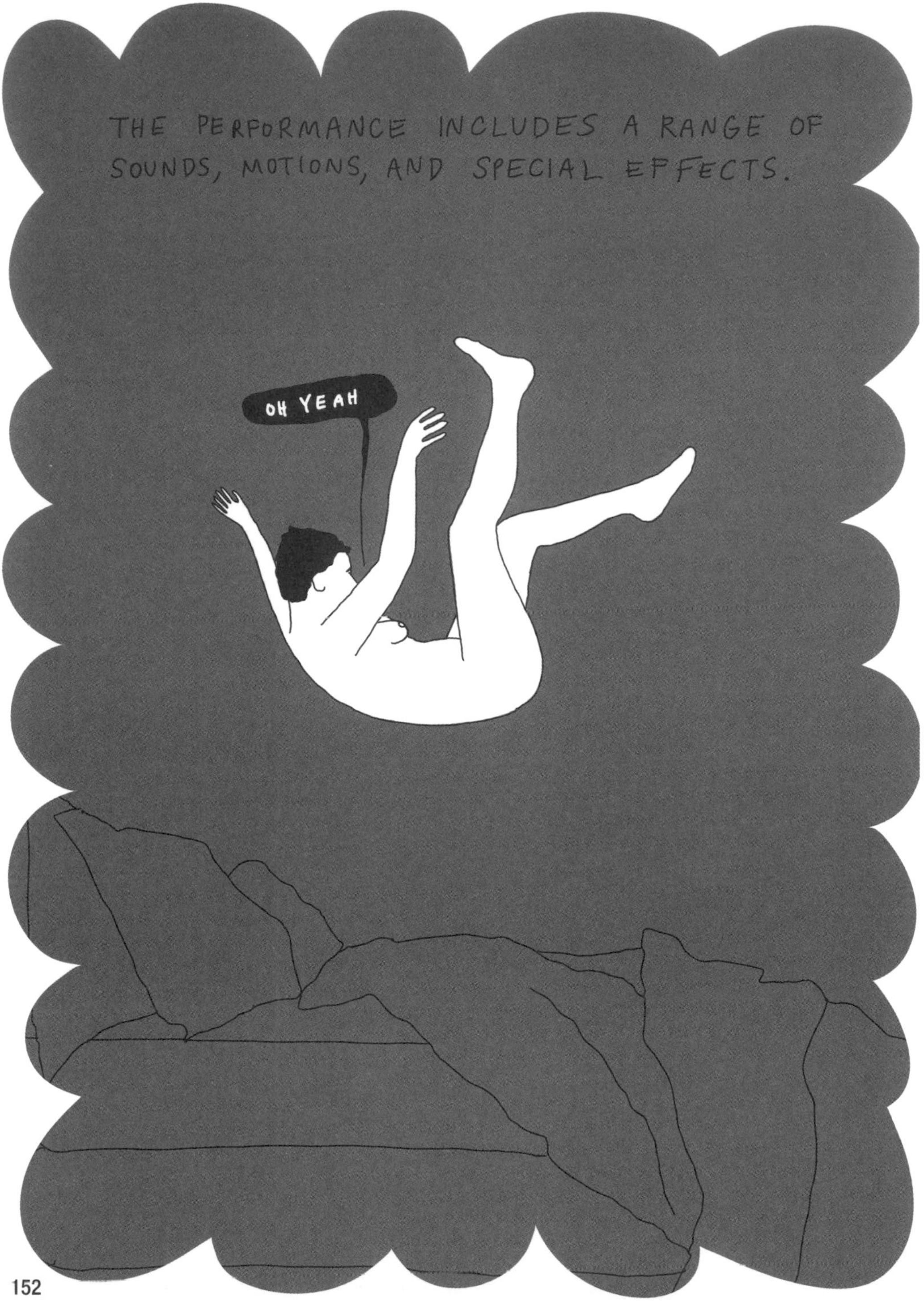
THE PERFORMANCE INCLUDES A RANGE OF SOUNDS, MOTIONS, AND SPECIAL EFFECTS.
OH YEAH

LIKE IF YOU LIE ON YOUR BACK, YOUR BELLY FALLS
CONCAVE UNDER A PILE OF RIBS.
YOU LOOK SKINNY.
IT'S EASIER FOR THEM TO PICK THE MEAT
OFF THE BONE.

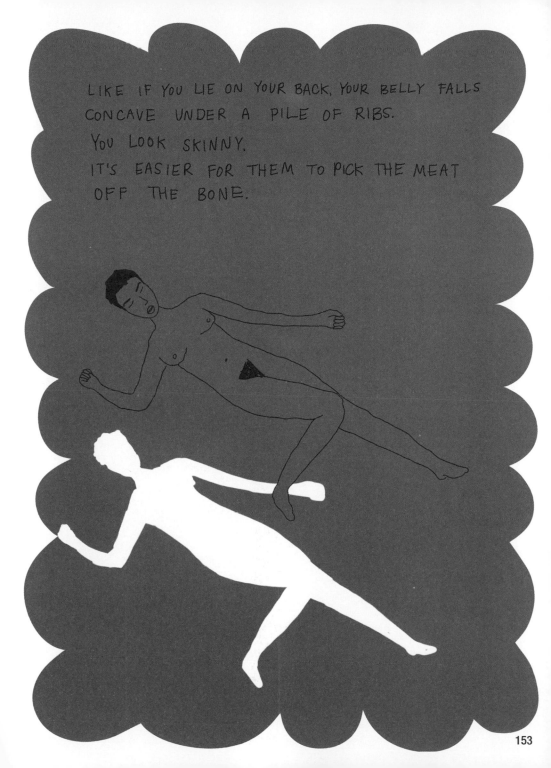

WE GET OUR COFFEES AND WALK BACK TO THE OFFICE.

I SIT AT MY DESK POKING A KEYBOARD FOR THREE MORE HOURS.

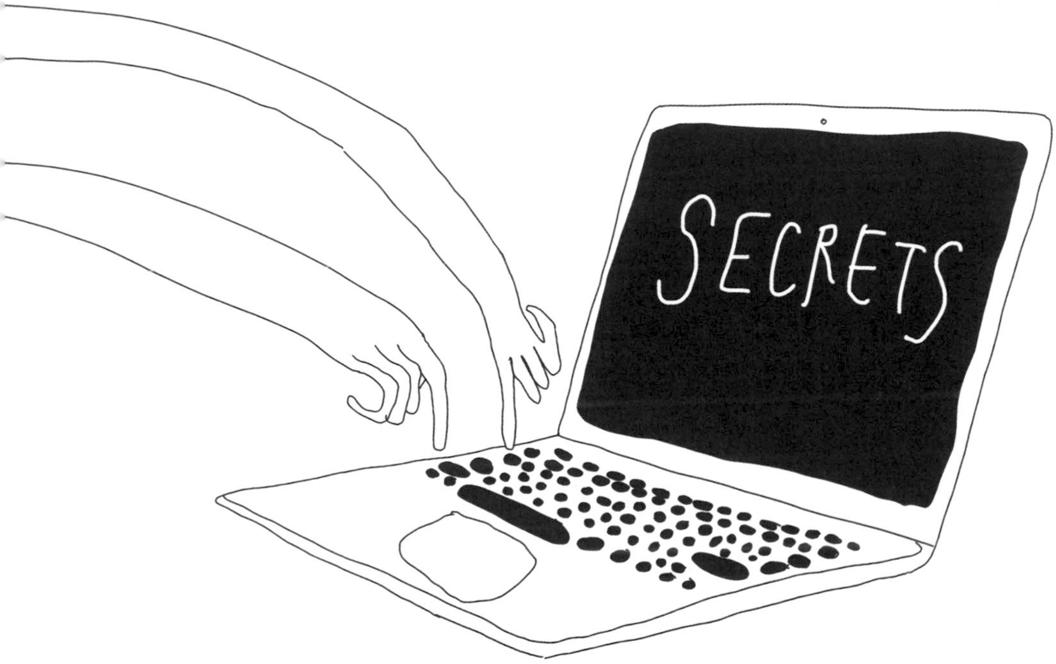
SECRETS

WALK BACK TO THE STATION

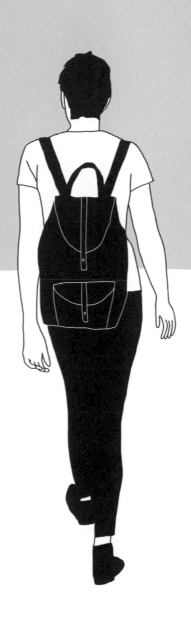

I LEAVE THE OFFICE TO WALK BACK TO THE TRAIN.

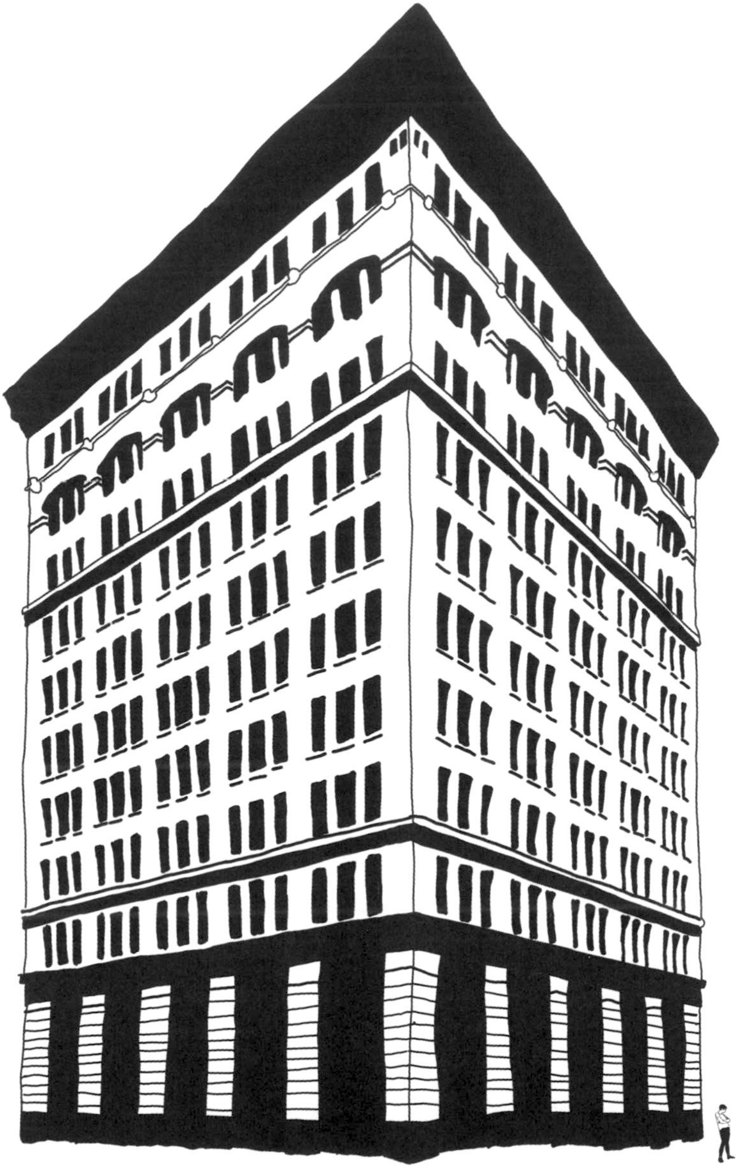

THERE IS A (PRESUMABLY) VERY EXPENSIVE
SPECIALTY COUCH STORE ON MADISON
AVENUE.

flowers or something???

display for 3 books

I SAY "VERY EXPENSIVE" BECAUSE THERE
ARE ONLY EVER TWO COUCHES ON
DISPLAY, AND THE RENT IS PROBABLY
$10,000 A MONTH.

IF I OWNED A COUCH LIKE THAT, I IMAGINE STAINS FROM OTHER PARTS OF THE HOUSE WOULD MAGICALLY MIGRATE TO IT.

peanut butter
period blood
milk (gross)
blueberries

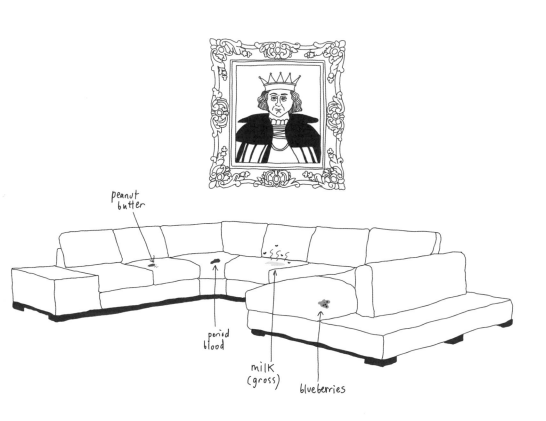

THERE ARE HALF-NAKED WOMEN EVERYWHERE ON THE STREET. THIS IS HOW WE'VE DECIDED ITEMS SHOULD BE SOLD.

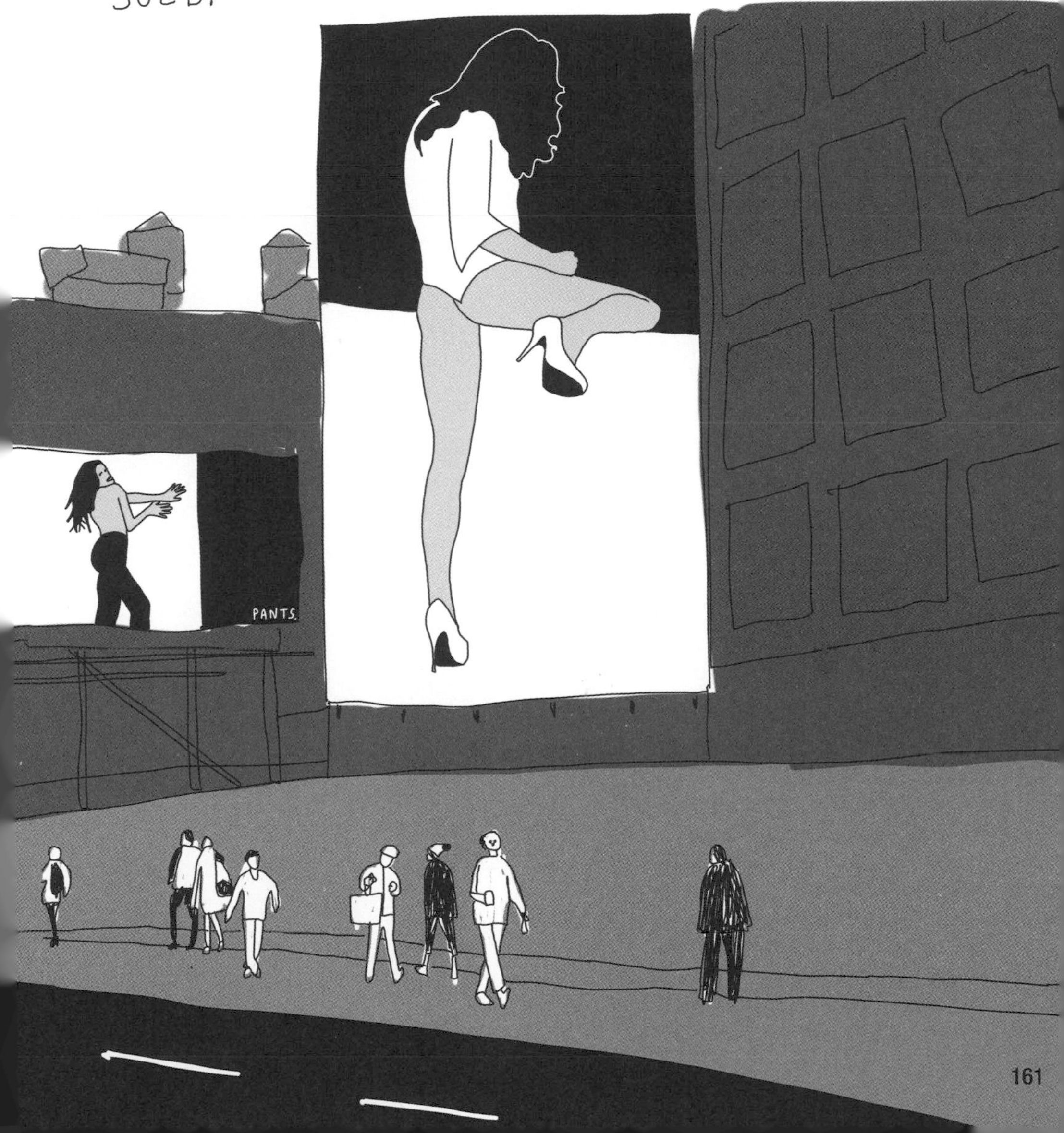
PANTS.

THE VODKA TRUCK HAS A HUGE SANDY ASS ON THE BACK OF IT.

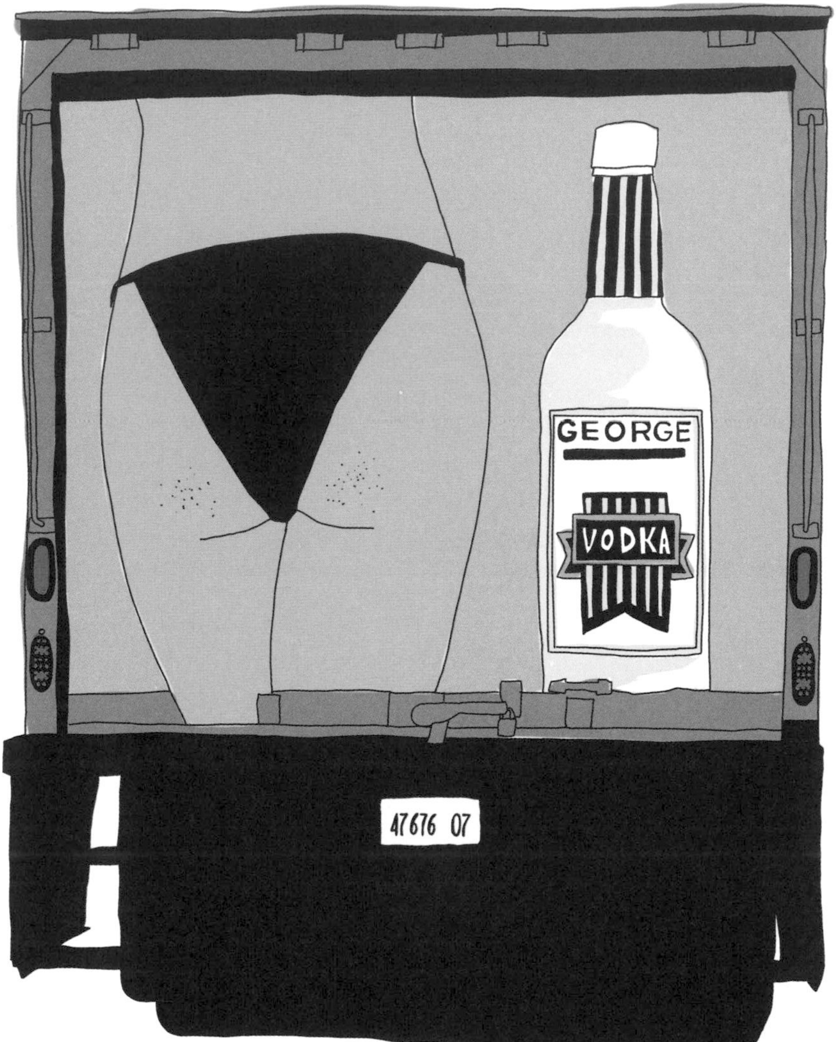
GEORGE
VODKA
47676 07

AN IN-STORE TV DISPLAY PLAYS VIDEO OF A WOMAN MOVING FURNITURE IN A BATHING SUIT.

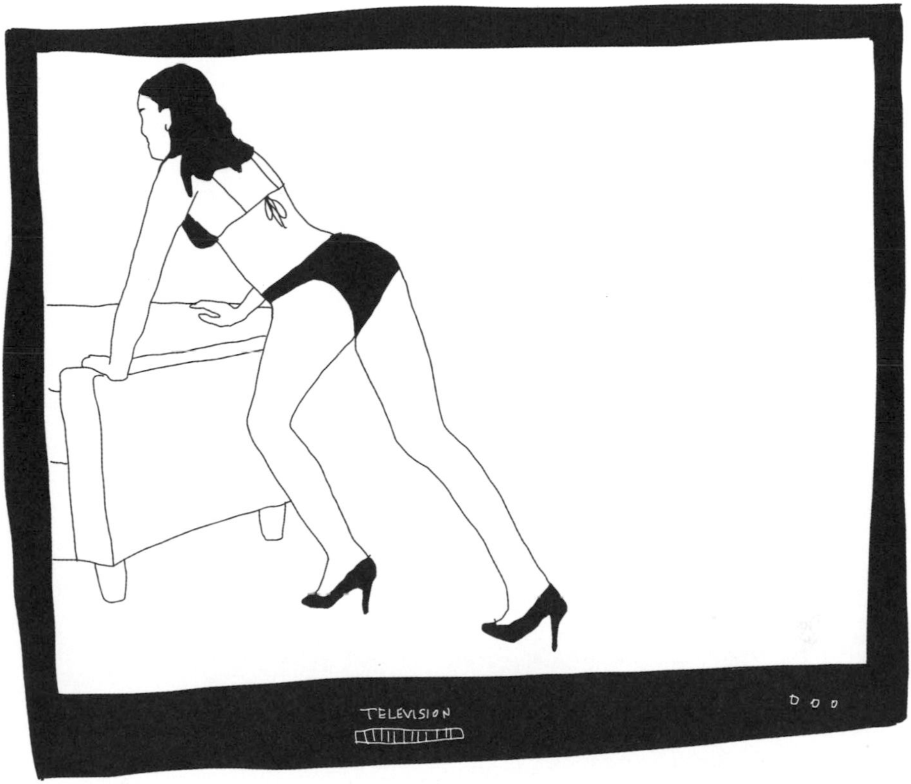
TELEVISION

WHO DOES ANYTHING IN A BATHING SUIT BESIDES REGRET PREVIOUS FOOD AND EXERCISE DECISIONS?

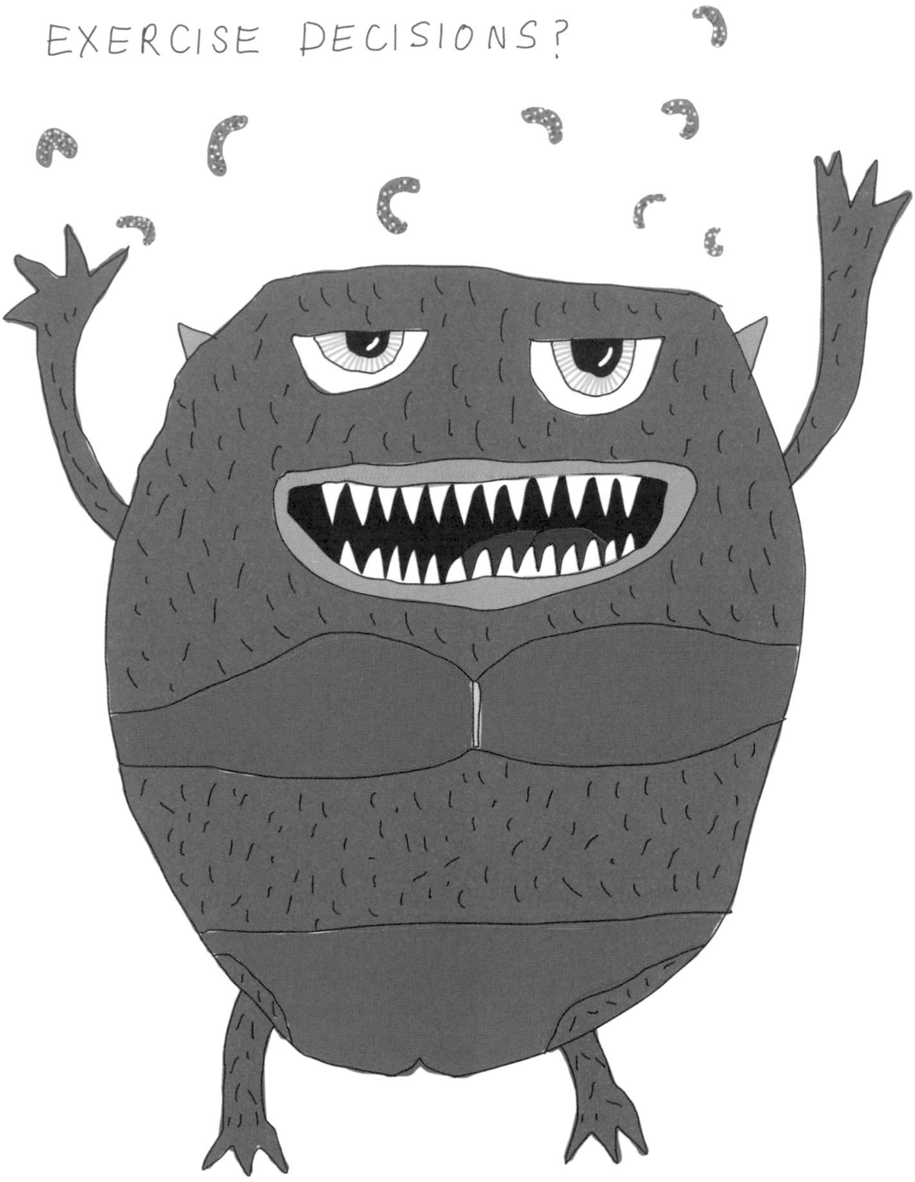

I WAS NEVER SKINNY ENOUGH.

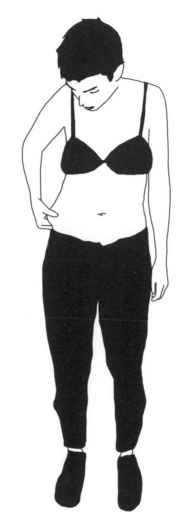

(LADIES—THIS IS A TRAP. THERE WILL
ALWAYS BE TOO MUCH OF YOU—FAT, NOISE,
AGE — EVERY WAY YOU TAKE UP SPACE IS
UNDESIRABLE.)

I WAS A MODEL FIVE OR SIX TIMES
AND WAS TOLD EACH OF THOSE TIMES
THAT AT 5'11" AND 125 POUNDS, I
WAS TOO FAT.

THE SAMPLE SIZE WON'T FIT THIS ONE.

I WOULD HAVE FELT TOO FAT ANYWAY, EVEN WITHOUT THE PERSONAL FEEDBACK.

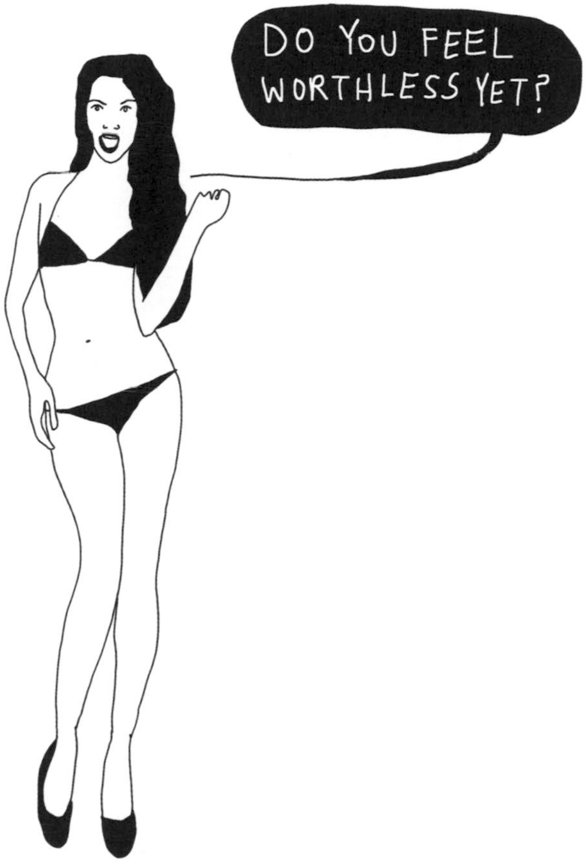
DO YOU FEEL WORTHLESS YET?

I WAS NEVER SKINNY ENOUGH FOR BEN. FOR A WEEK I REALLY LOVED HIM. HE WAS JEWISH AND HAD A CAR, BOTH OF WHICH I FOUND TO BE DESIRABLE ATTRIBUTES.

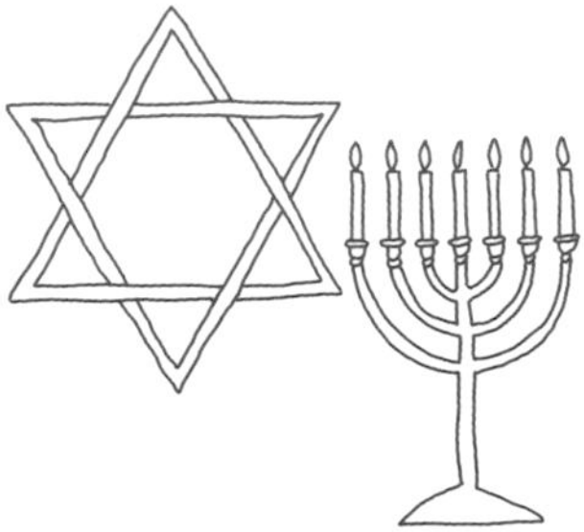

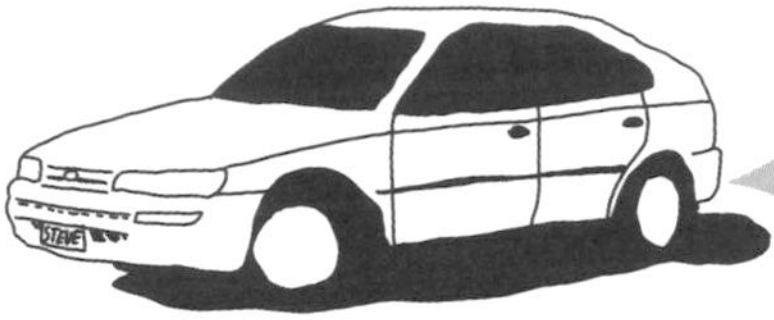

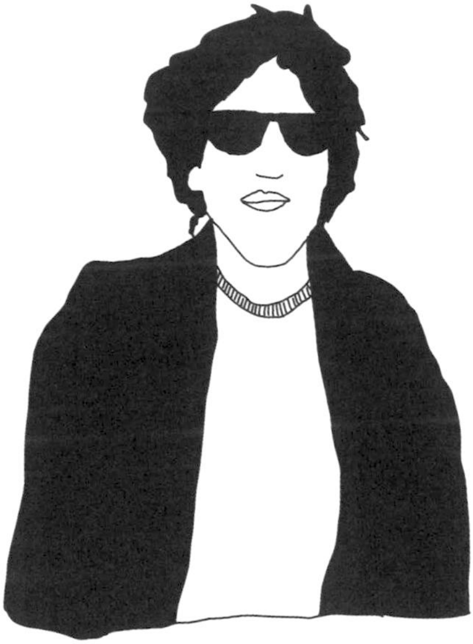

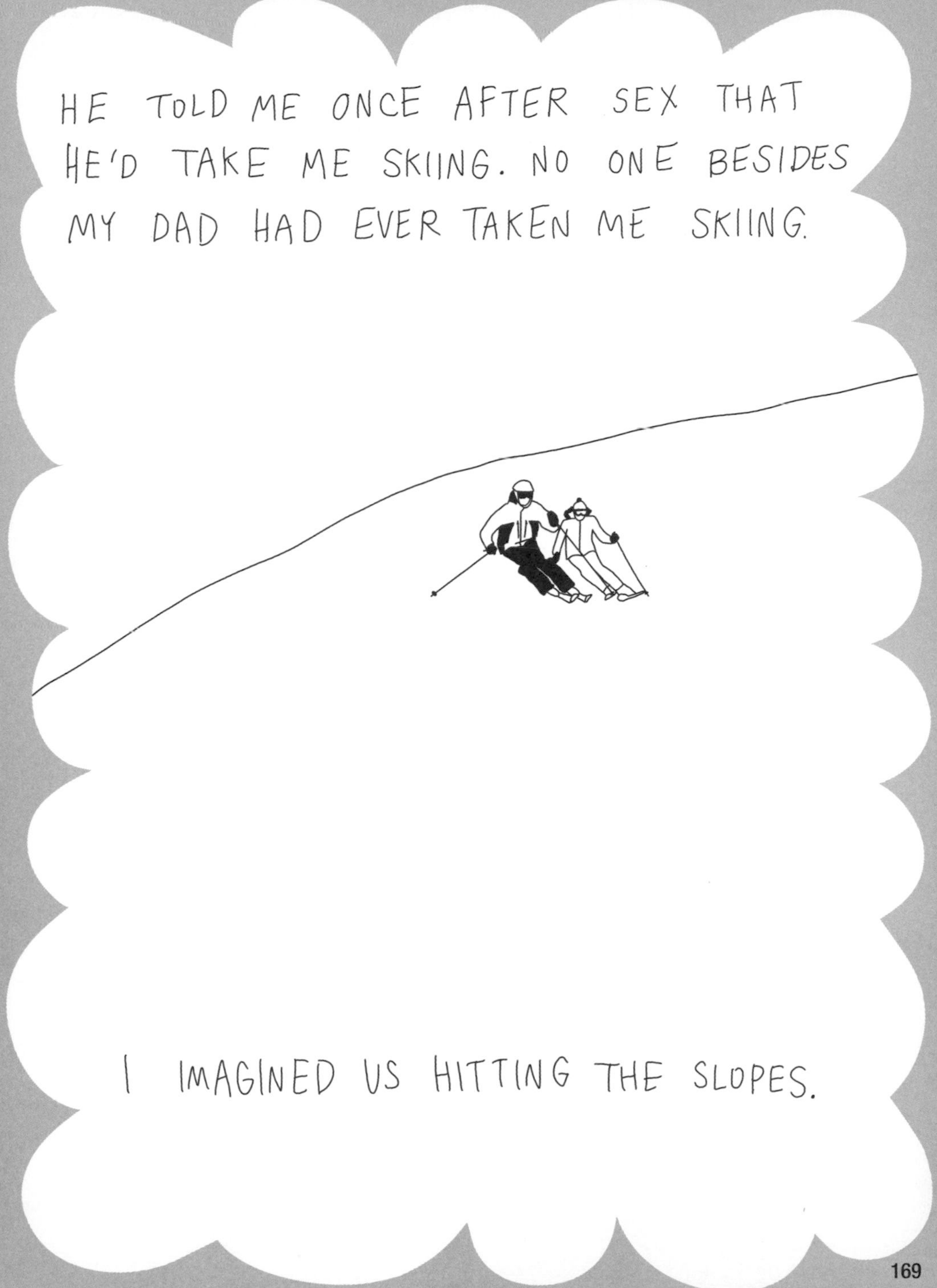
HE TOLD ME ONCE AFTER SEX THAT HE'D TAKE ME SKIING. NO ONE BESIDES MY DAD HAD EVER TAKEN ME SKIING.
I IMAGINED US HITTING THE SLOPES.

HE TALKED A LOT ABOUT HIS EX-GIRLFRIEND, CHLOÉ, WHO WAS PERFECT. I NEVER MET HER BUT THOUGHT A LOT ABOUT WHAT SHE MUST'VE BEEN LIKE.

ASSUMPTIONS ABOUT CHLOÉ:

- THIN
- SMART
- SHORT
- EASYGOING
- NONCOMMITTAL
- LISTENED TO COOL 70S MUSIC
- HAD EXPENSIVE, MINIMALIST OUTFITS
- DIDN'T GET DRUNK
- SMOKED WEED (NO CALORIES)
- ENJOYED GIVING HEAD
- WORE HORIZONTAL STRIPES
- "FORGOT TO EAT BREAKFAST"
- HAD A SAVINGS ACCOUNT

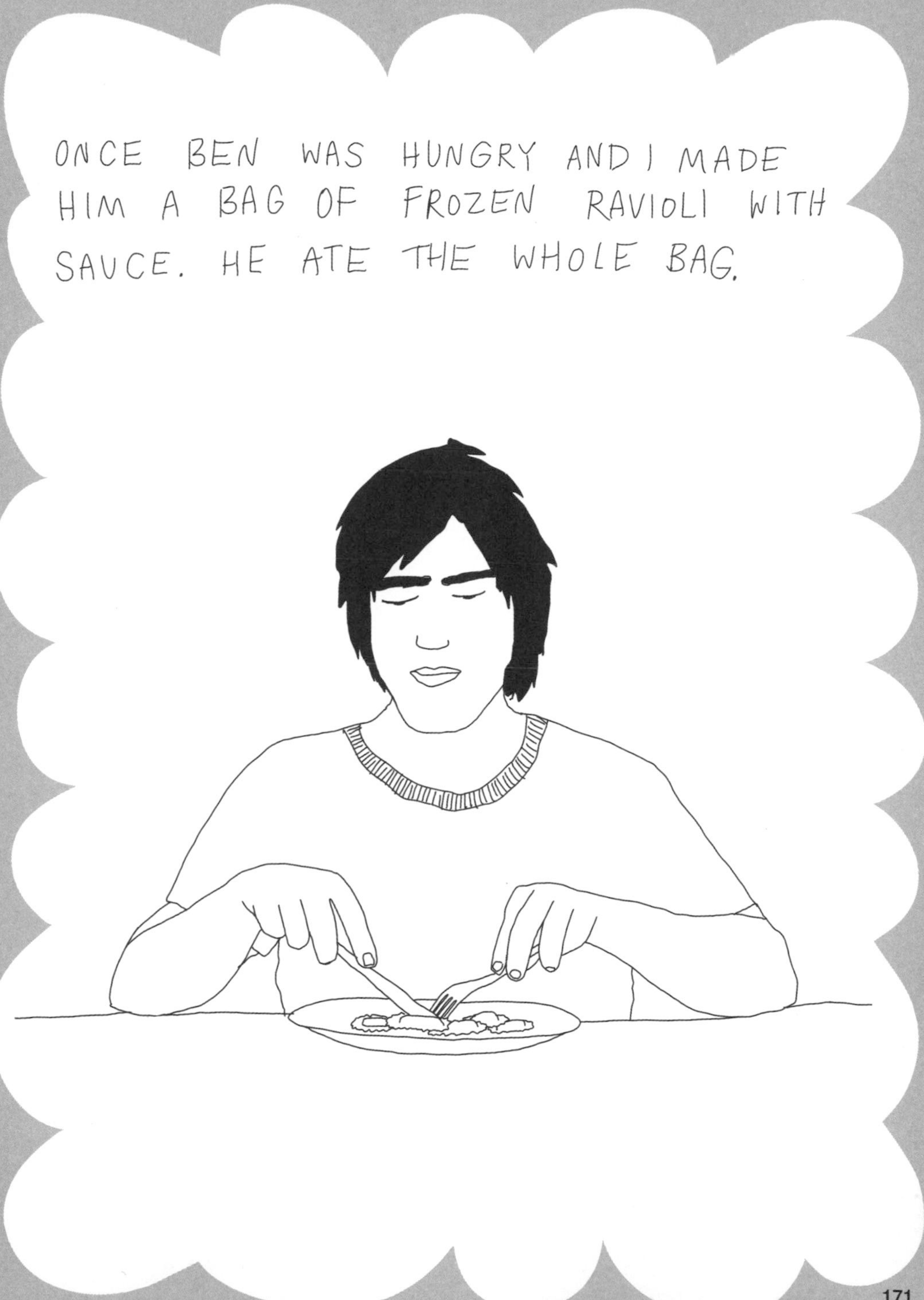
ONCE BEN WAS HUNGRY AND I MADE HIM A BAG OF FROZEN RAVIOLI WITH SAUCE. HE ATE THE WHOLE BAG.

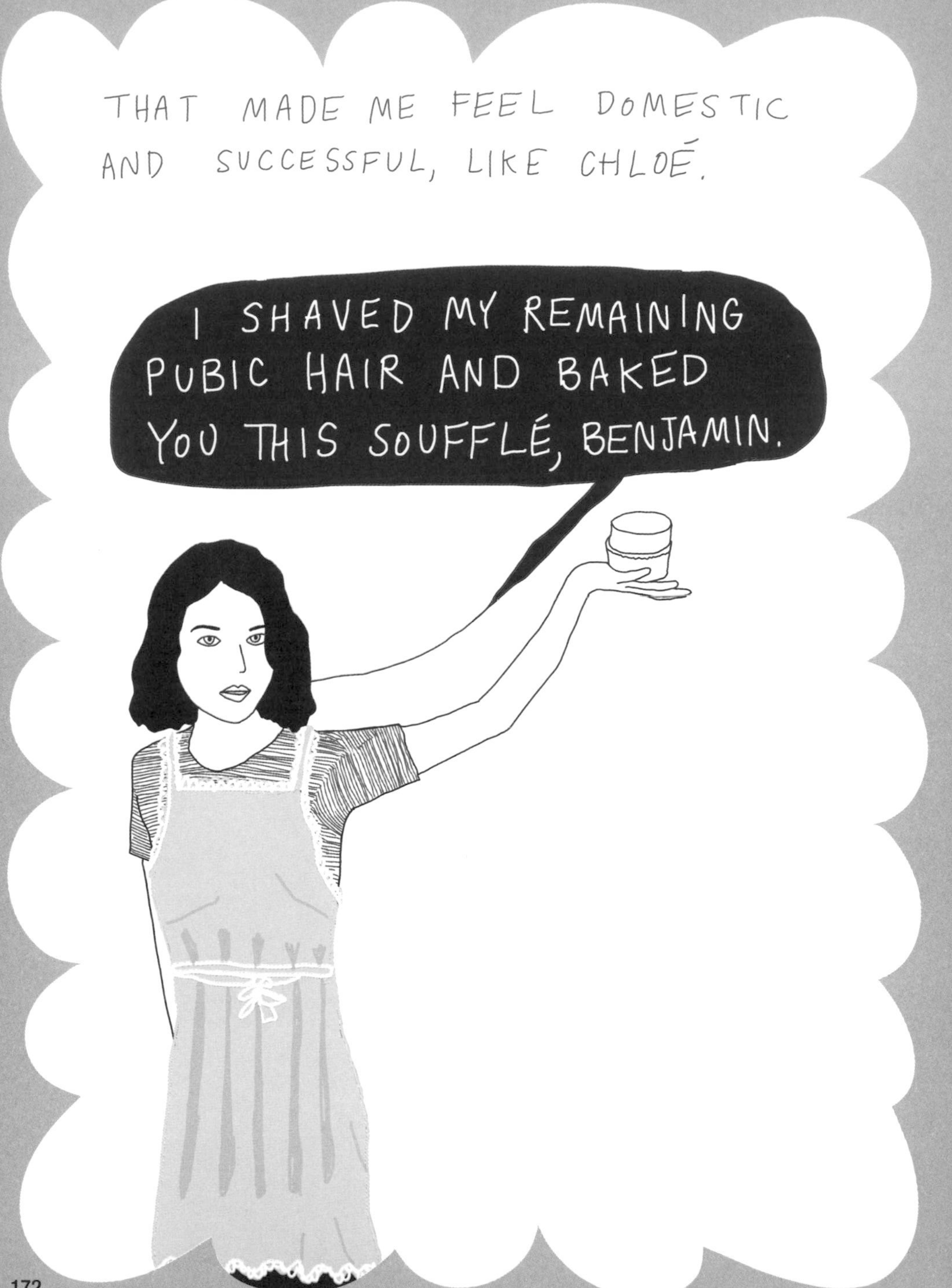
THAT MADE ME FEEL DOMESTIC AND SUCCESSFUL, LIKE CHLOÉ.
I SHAVED MY REMAINING PUBIC HAIR AND BAKED YOU THIS SOUFFLÉ, BENJAMIN.

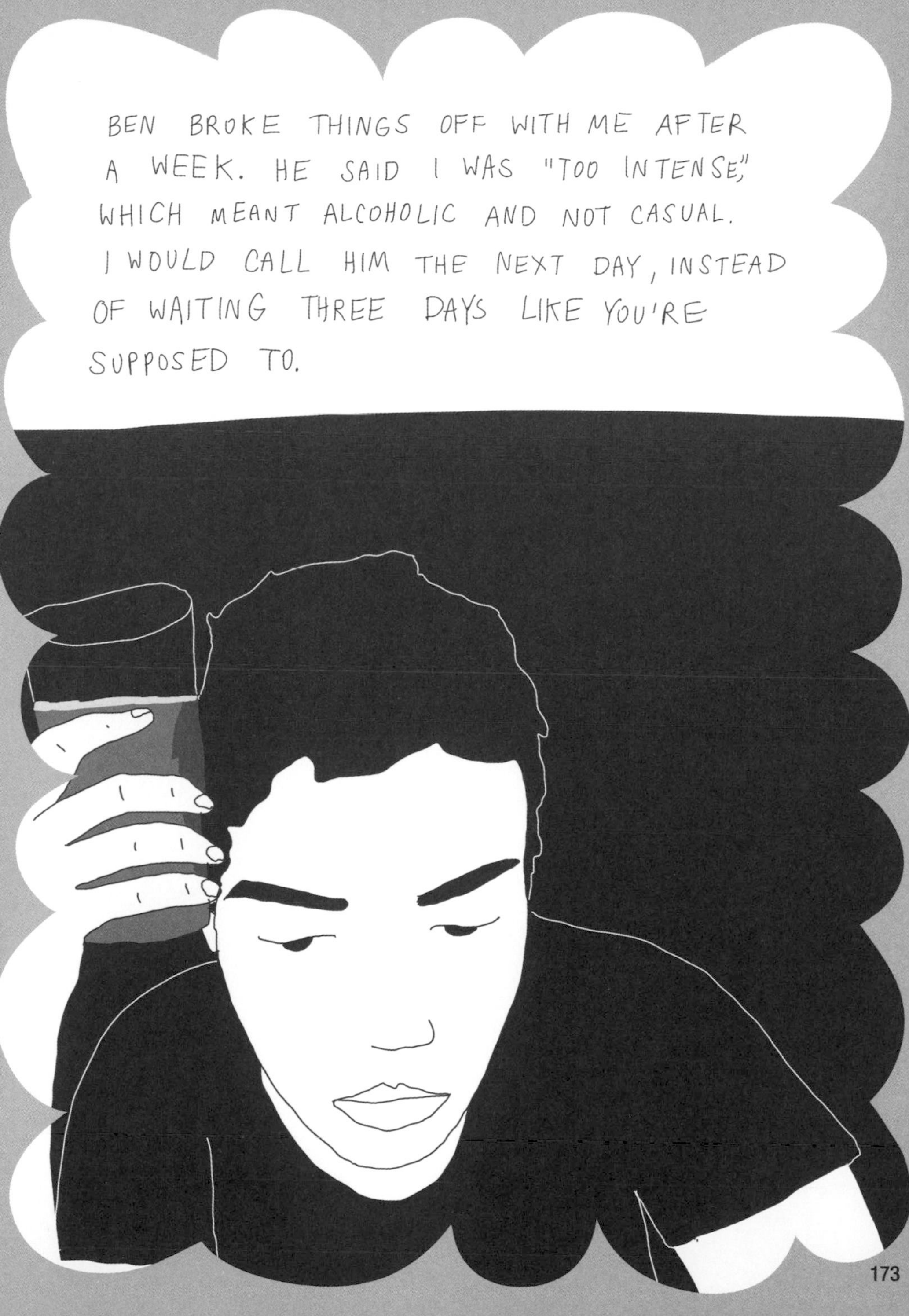
BEN BROKE THINGS OFF WITH ME AFTER A WEEK. HE SAID I WAS "TOO INTENSE," WHICH MEANT ALCOHOLIC AND NOT CASUAL. I WOULD CALL HIM THE NEXT DAY, INSTEAD OF WAITING THREE DAYS LIKE YOU'RE SUPPOSED TO.

I WALK BY...

3

CHICKEN

RESTAURANTS

FUCK YOU

1. A MAN RUBS THE BACK OF A WOMAN'S NECK WHILE SHE EATS A BOWL OF CHICKEN IN A RESTAURANT SPECIALIZING IN CHICKEN. IT LOOKS MORE LIKE A THREAT TO CHOKE THAN A GESTURE OF AFFECTION. SHE LOOKS BORED.

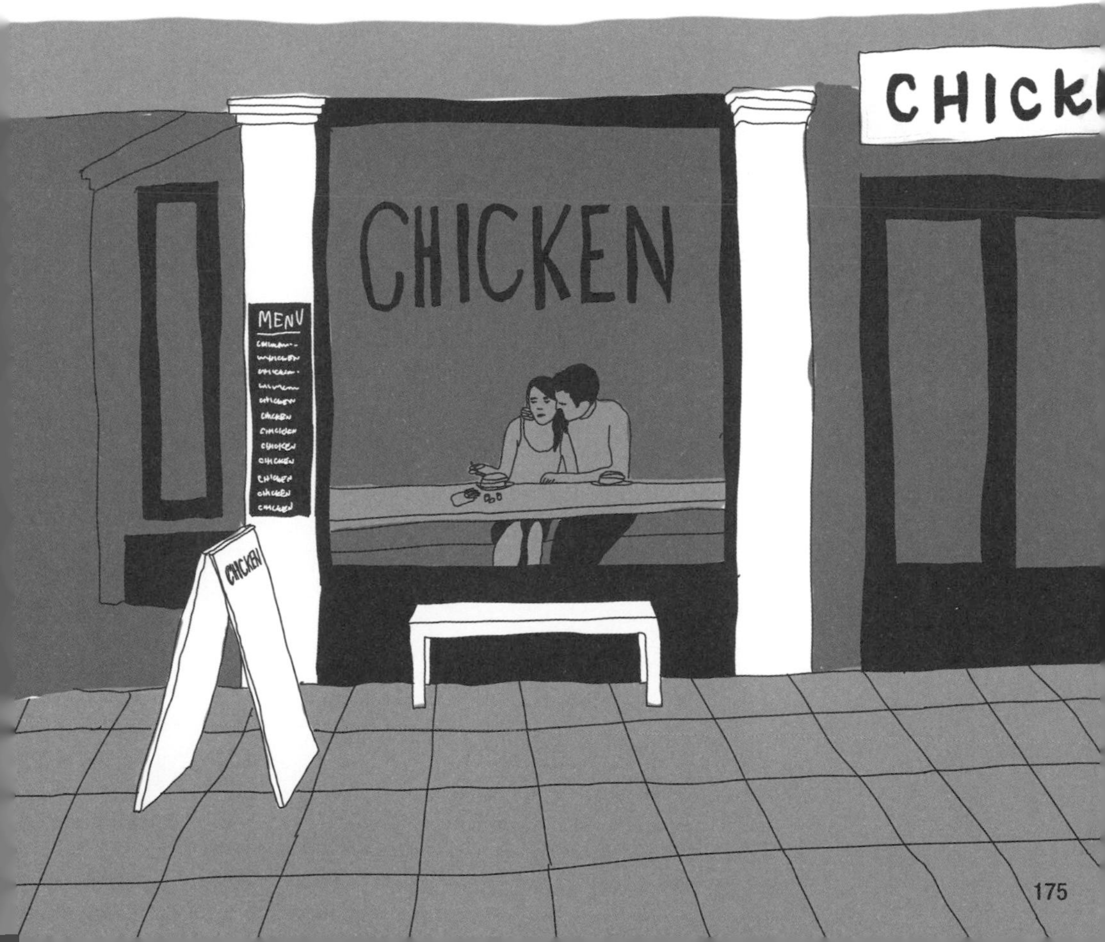
CHICK
CHICKEN
MENU
CHICKEN

2.

LIGHTS FLASH ACROSS THE TOP OF
A HALAL CART, SPELLING WORDS.

YOU ARE THIRSTY, I LIKE IT HERE,
WE HAVE CHICKEN OVER RICE.

3. THE KOREAN CHICKEN RESTAURANT HAD A DJ BOOTH AND A BIG RED SPIRAL STAIRCASE. THEY SHUT IT DOWN AND LEFT A NOTE IN THE WINDOW.

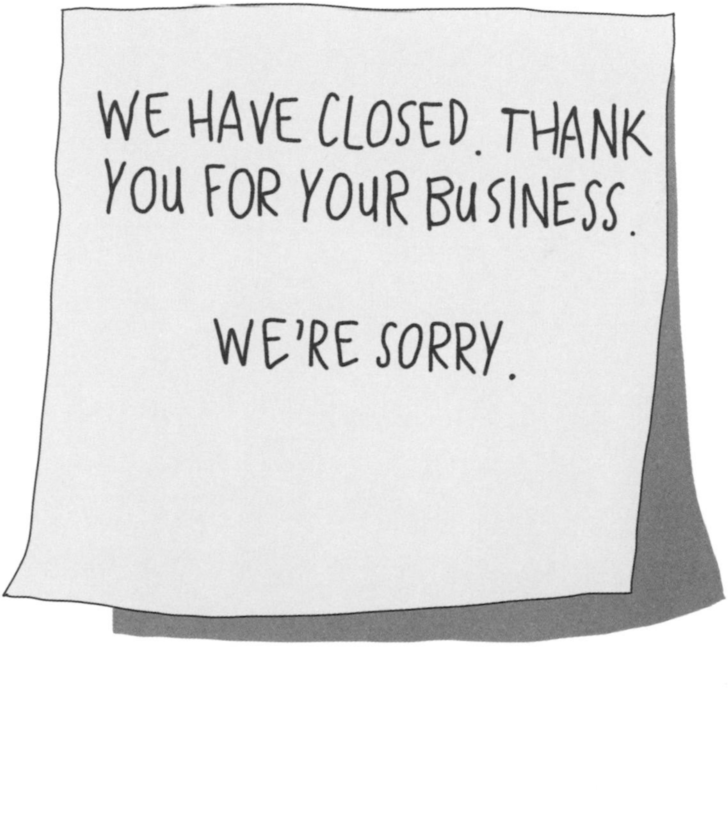
WE HAVE CLOSED. THANK YOU FOR YOUR BUSINESS.
WE'RE SORRY.

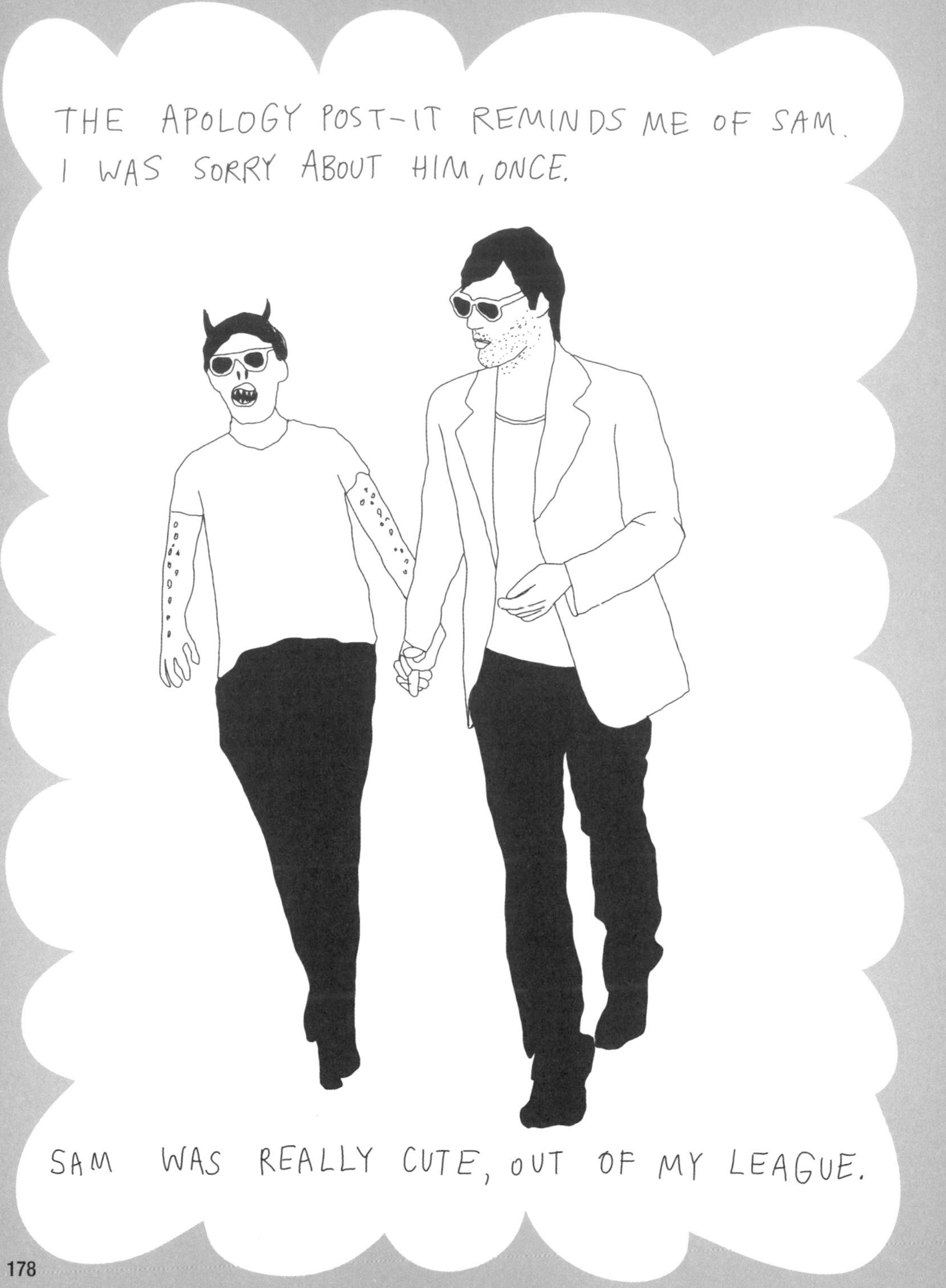
THE APOLOGY POST-IT REMINDS ME OF SAM.
I WAS SORRY ABOUT HIM, ONCE.
SAM WAS REALLY CUTE, OUT OF MY LEAGUE.

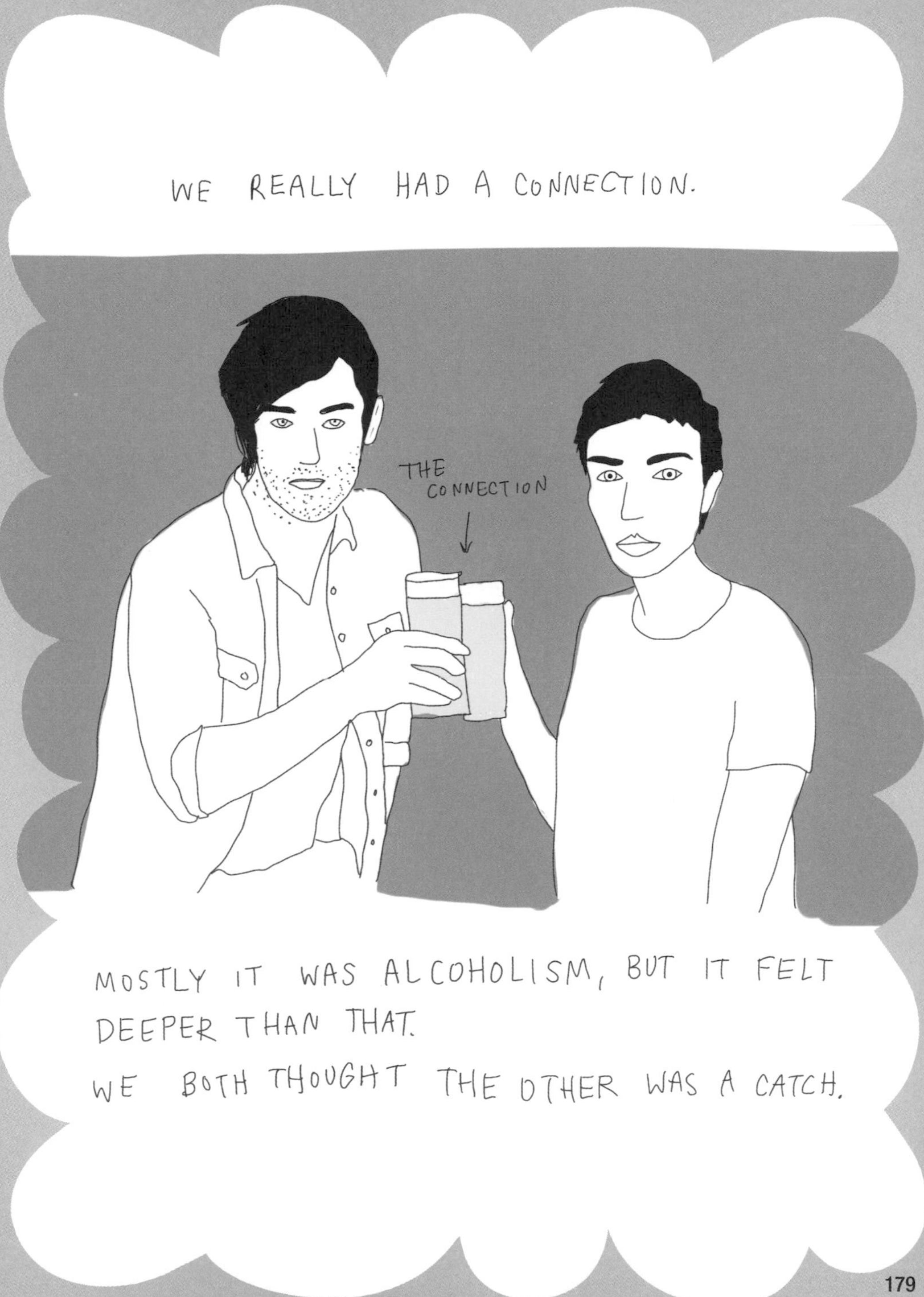
WE REALLY HAD A CONNECTION.
THE CONNECTION
MOSTLY IT WAS ALCOHOLISM, BUT IT FELT DEEPER THAN THAT.
WE BOTH THOUGHT THE OTHER WAS A CATCH.

THE FIRST TIME WE HAD SEX, HE GOT
SWEATY AND SHOOK VIGOROUSLY LIKE HE
WAS DYING ON TOP OF ME.

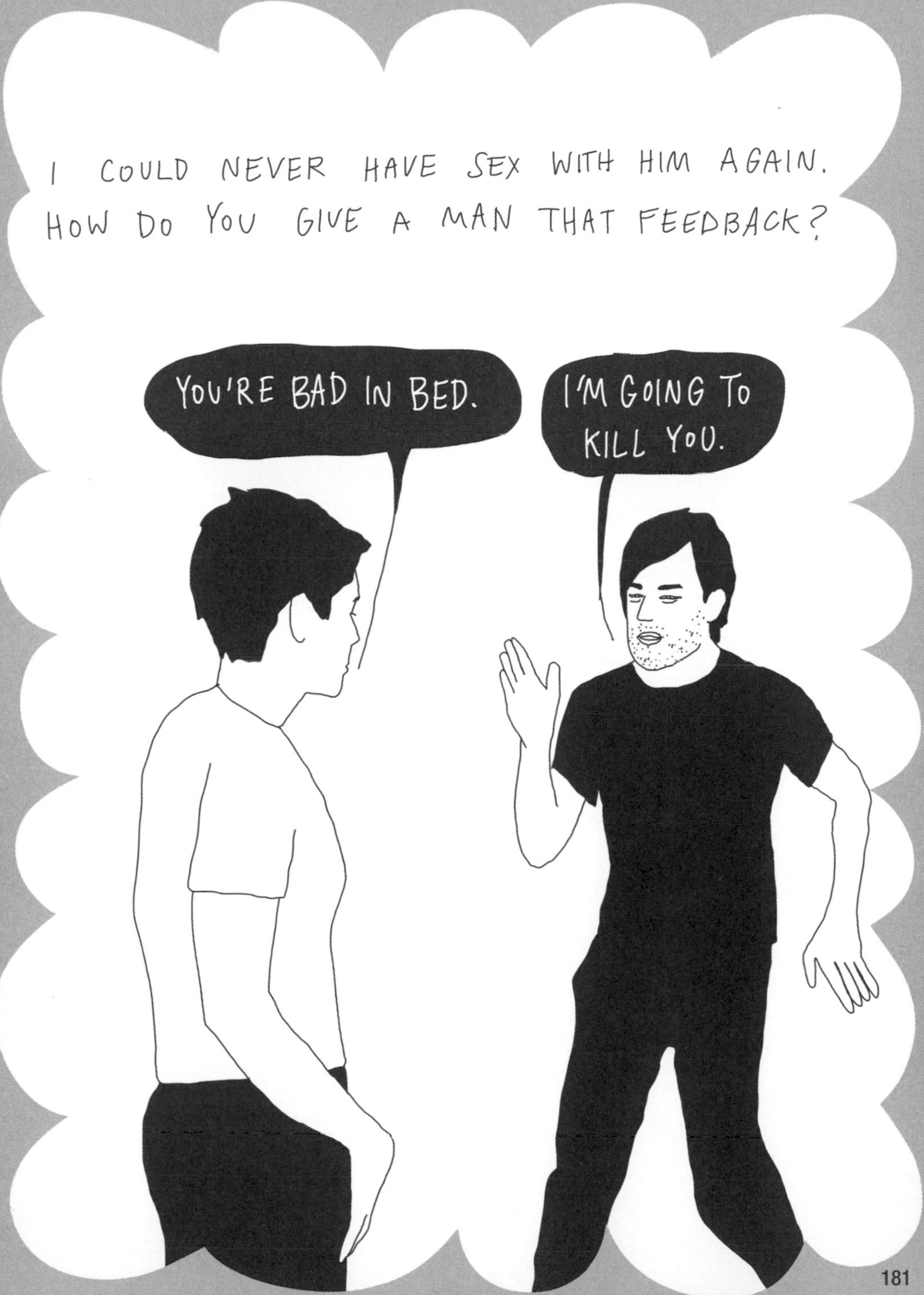
I COULD NEVER HAVE SEX WITH HIM AGAIN.
HOW DO YOU GIVE A MAN THAT FEEDBACK?
YOU'RE BAD IN BED.
I'M GOING TO KILL YOU.

I TOLD HIM I WAS SORRY BUT I WAS MOLESTED BY A FRIEND WHEN I WAS FIVE AND HAD TO DEAL WITH MY ISSUES, IN ORDER TO BREAK IT OFF.

IT'S TRUE THAT I WAS, BUT THAT WASN'T THE REASON I COULDN'T FUCK HIM AGAIN. I JUST COULDN'T FACE IT.

I MOURNED THE LOSS OF MY POTENTIAL
LOVE. HE WORE WHITE POINTY BOOTS AND
WAS A GREAT DANCER. HE DRANK AS MUCH
AS I DID, THOUGH HE METABOLIZED IT BETTER.
WE'D KEEP UP WITH EACH OTHER DRINK FOR
DRINK BUT I'D LOSE MY ABILITY TO WALK
FIRST.

AFTER I DUMPED HIM, HE WROTE ME A LONG LETTER AND PUT FIVE DOLLARS IN THE ENVELOPE FOR A LITERARY MAGAZINE I LAUNCHED ONE ISSUE OF.

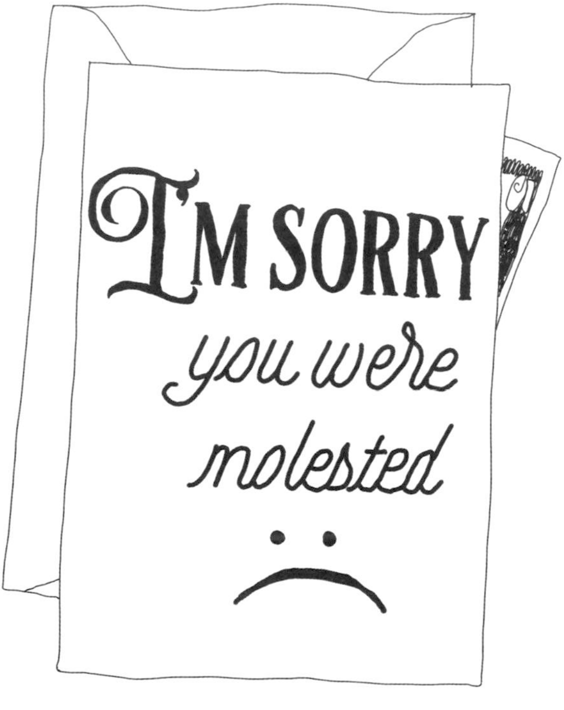
I'M SORRY
you were
molested

I WAS REALLY BLOWN AWAY BY THIS KINDNESS AND REGRETTED MY DISMISSAL OF HIM.

I SAW HIM FIVE YEARS AFTER THAT WHEN
HE WAS IN TOWN FOR WORK.

HE CAME OVER AND SMOKED CIGARETTES IN
MY APARTMENT AND TOLD ME HIS DAD DIED
FROM LUNG CANCER.

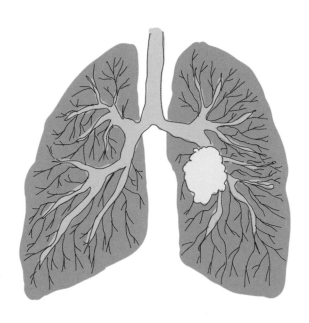

HE TOLD ME I'D GOTTEN FAT.

CLOSER TO THE TRAIN STATION, THE
LANDSCAPE CHANGES FROM
ASPIRATIONAL FURNITURE TO FACTORY
KHAKIS.

ANN TAYLOR

I WONDER ABOUT MY SIZE.

A MAN IN A WHEELCHAIR HOLDS THE DOORS OF GRAND CENTRAL STATION OPEN WITH BOTH ARMS.

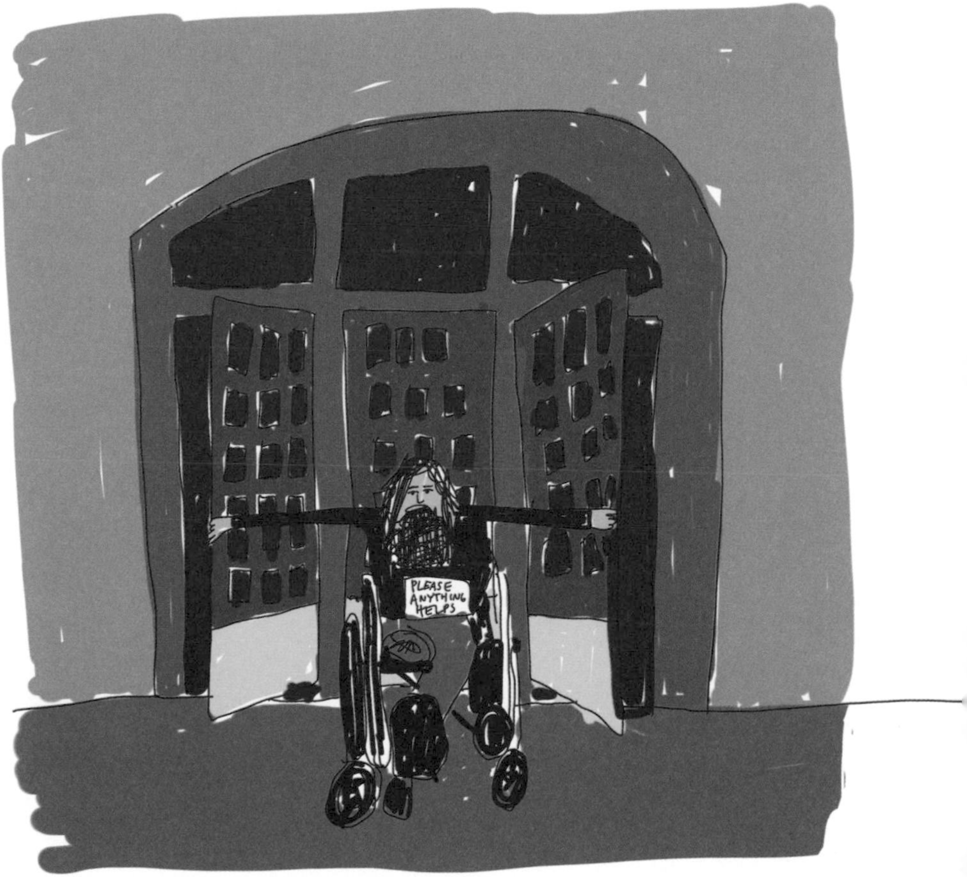
PLEASE ANYTHING HELPS

RIDE THE TRAIN

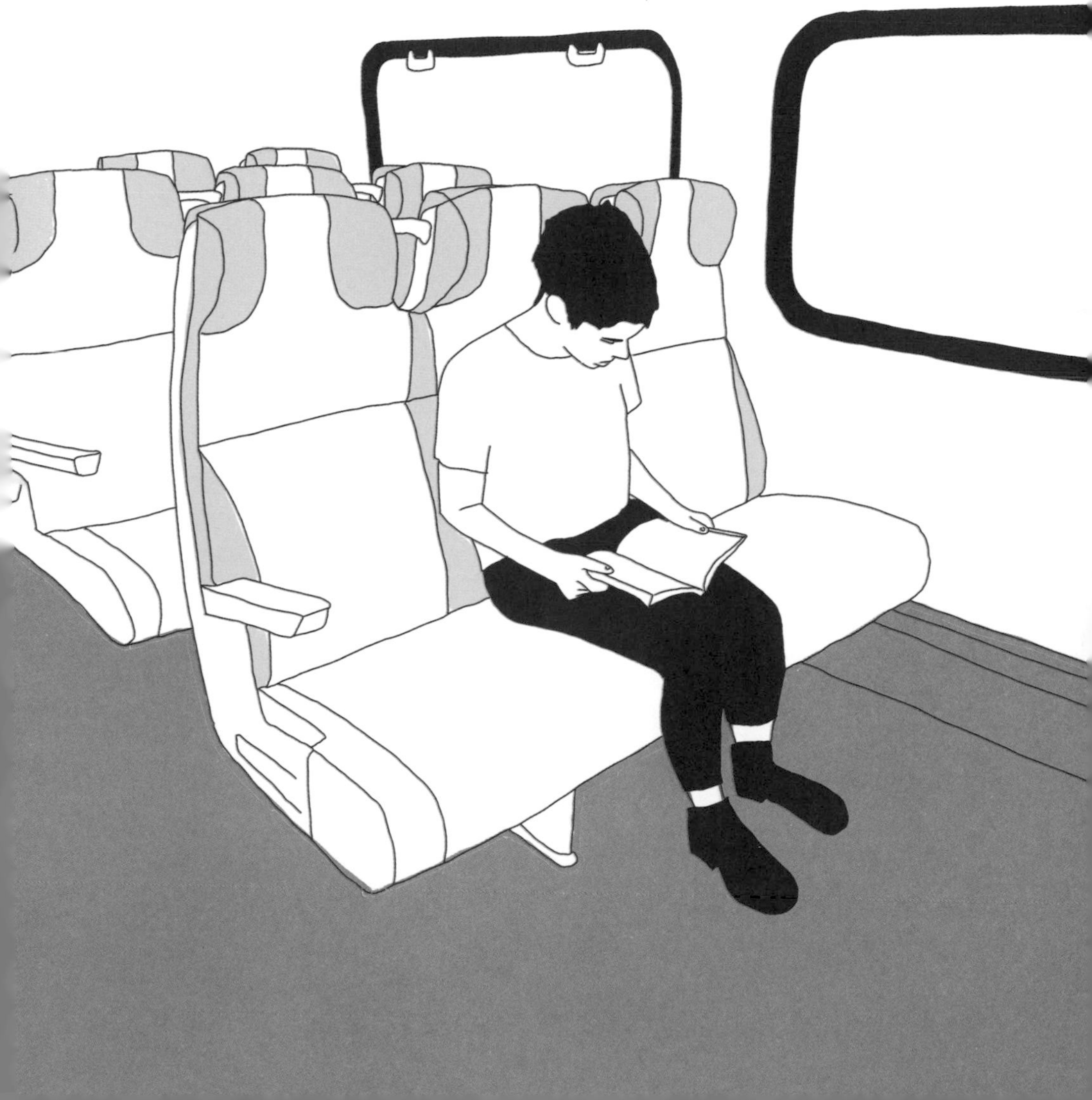

AN OLDER MAN SITS NEXT TO ME. HE LOOKS AT ME FOR A LONG TIME AS HE SITS DOWN. HE HAS A TIE CLIP.

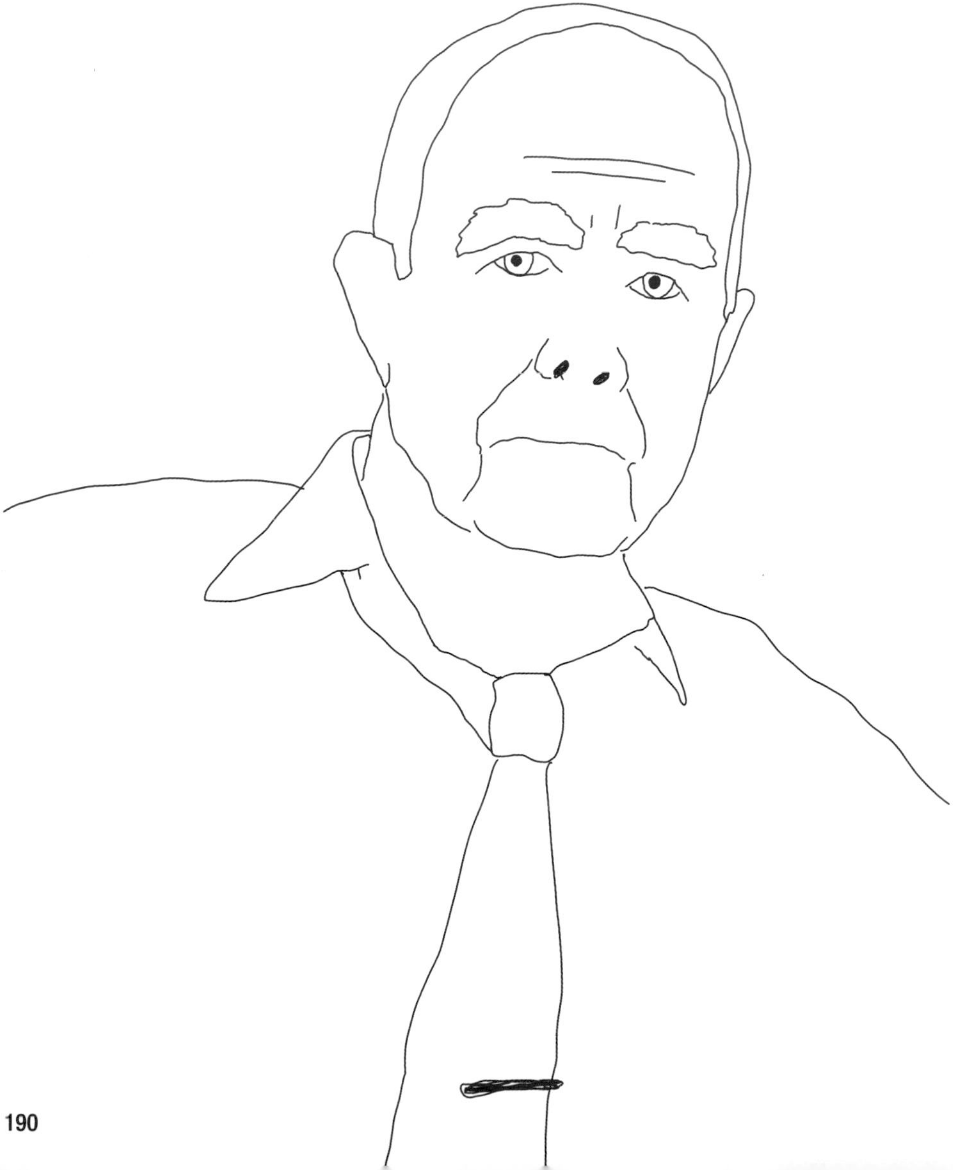

HE READS A 500 PAGE BOOK ABOUT THE MILITARY.

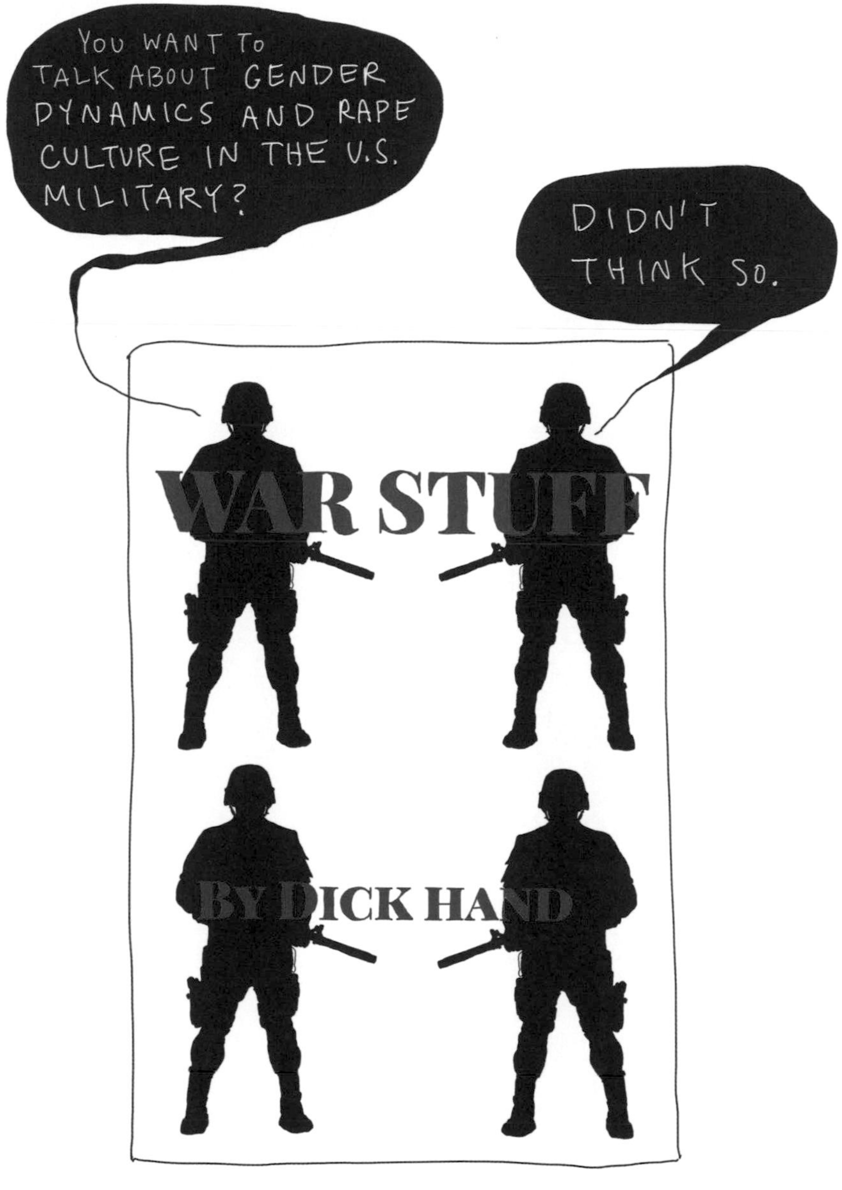
YOU WANT TO TALK ABOUT GENDER DYNAMICS AND RAPE CULTURE IN THE U.S. MILITARY?
DIDN'T THINK SO.
WAR STUFF
BY DICK HAND

HE SIGHS PUNISHINGLY WHEN I AUDIBLY GULP MY WATER. I FEEL LIKE IT'S UPSETTING HIM.

SNIFFLE
GULP
BURP
GLURF
TOOT

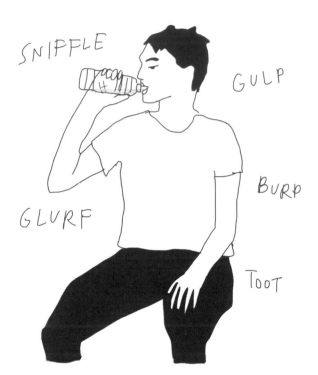

IT IS A FACT THAT WOMEN HAVE BODIES AND TAKE UP SPACE, EVEN WHEN IT IS UNDESIRABLE.

SOUNDS! SMELLS!

I COULD JUST BE TAKING IT PERSONALLY AND IT'S NOT. THE LABORED BREATHING COULD ALSO BE BECAUSE HE'S READ SOME PARTICULARLY GRIM DETAIL OF WAR THAT IS COINCIDENTALLY TIMED TO MY SIPS.

SOME THINGS ARE NOT ABOUT YOU PERSONALLY, I HEAR.

HE COULD ALSO HAVE A MEDICAL
CONDITION THAT I'M NOT AWARE OF.

CHRONIC OBSTRUCTIVE
PULMONARY DISEASE

-LUNG DISEASES
MAKE IT HARD
TO BREATHE.

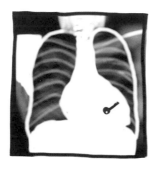

SWALLOWED THE
CAR KEYS

- WHOOPS!

DIPHTHERIA

-A GROSS INFECTION.
VACCINATE !!

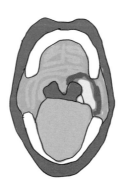

I READ *I LOVE DICK* AND THINK ABOUT A RELATIONSHIP I HAD WITH A MAN IN HIS FORTIES WHEN I WAS TWENTY-THREE.

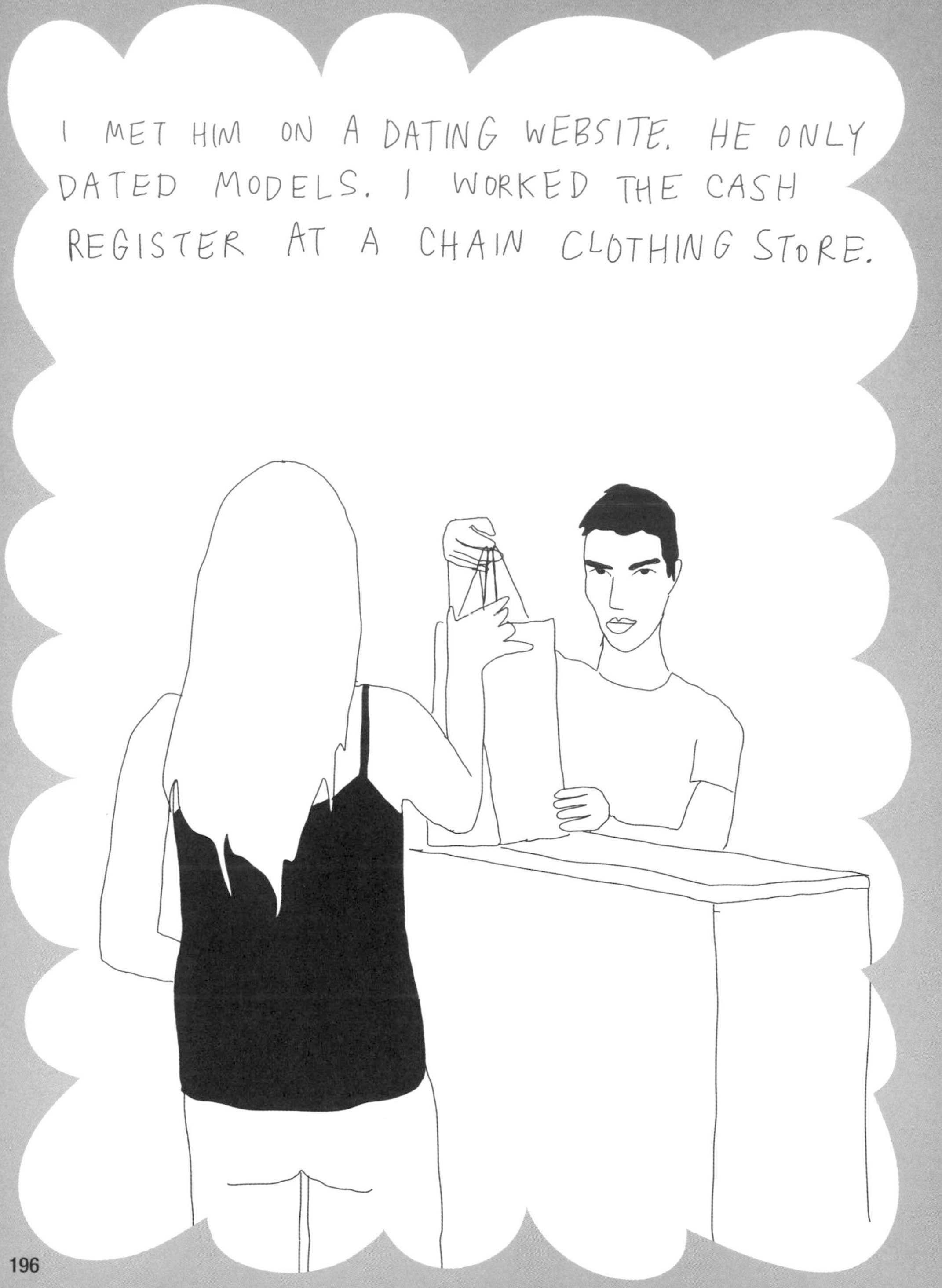
I MET HIM ON A DATING WEBSITE. HE ONLY DATED MODELS. I WORKED THE CASH REGISTER AT A CHAIN CLOTHING STORE.

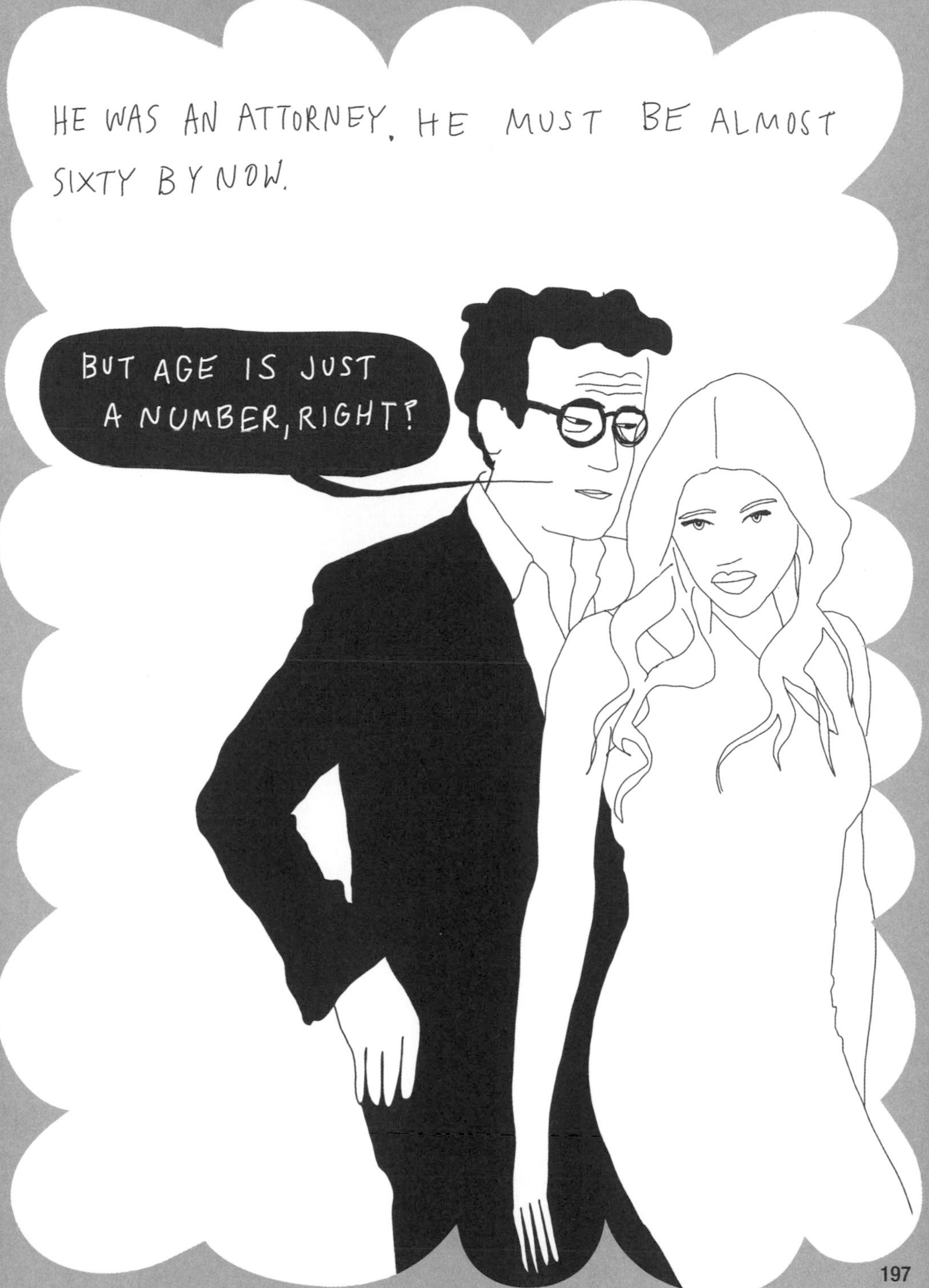
HE WAS AN ATTORNEY. HE MUST BE ALMOST SIXTY BY NOW.
BUT AGE IS JUST A NUMBER, RIGHT?

I DECIDE, ON THE TRAIN, TO WRITE HIM AN EMAIL. I HADN'T SPOKEN TO HIM IN MANY YEARS.

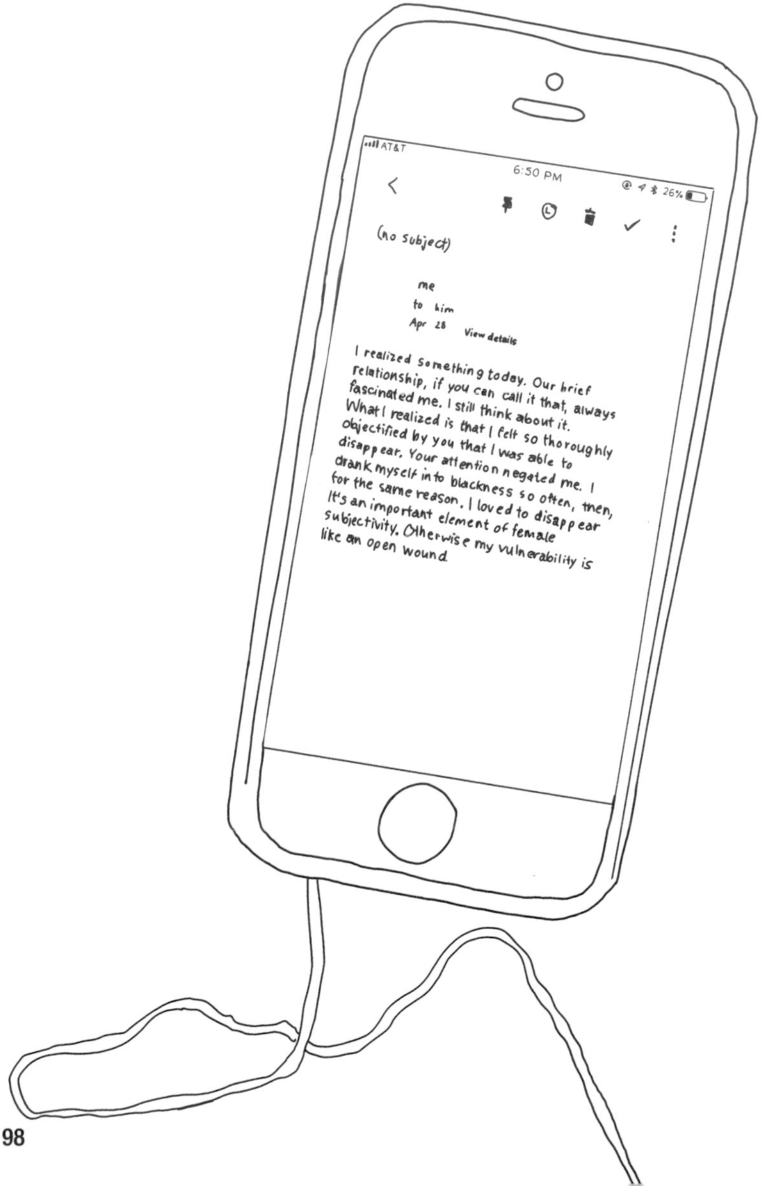
AT&T
6:50 PM
26%
(no subject)
me
to him
Apr 28
View details
I realized something today. Our brief relationship, if you can call it that, always fascinated me. I still think about it. What I realized is that I felt so thoroughly objectified by you that I was able to disappear. Your attention negated me. I drank myself into blackness so often, then, for the same reason. I loved to disappear. It's an important element of female subjectivity. Otherwise my vulnerability is like an open wound.

HE EMAILS ME BACK QUICKLY THREE TIMES:

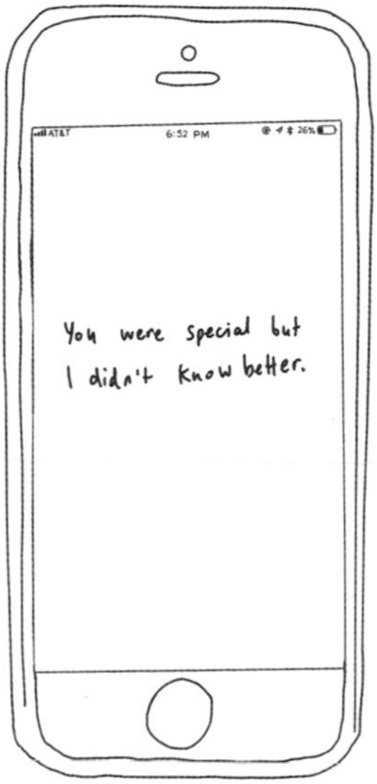
AT&T
6:52 PM
26%
You were special but I didn't know better.

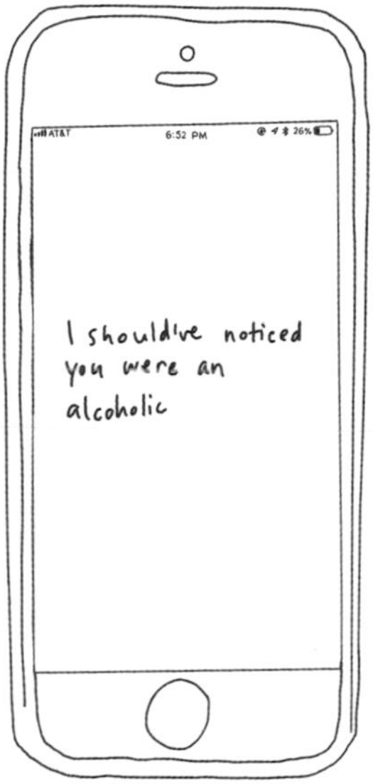
AT&T
6:52 PM
26%
I should've noticed you were an alcoholic

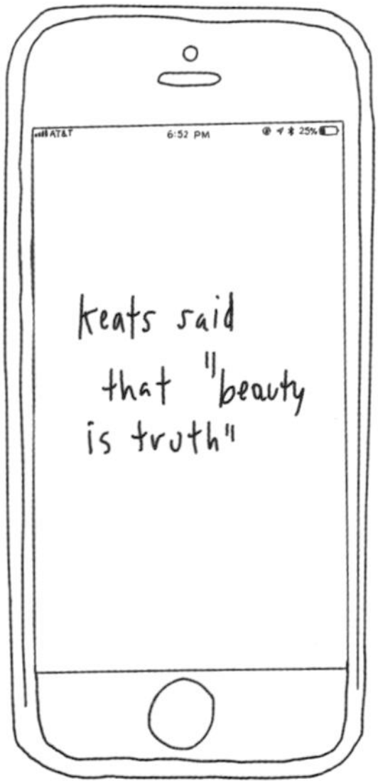
AT&T
6:52 PM
25%
keats said that "beauty is truth"

HOW MANY MEN HAVE USED KEATS TO RATIONALIZE THEIR DESIRE FOR MUCH YOUNGER WOMEN?

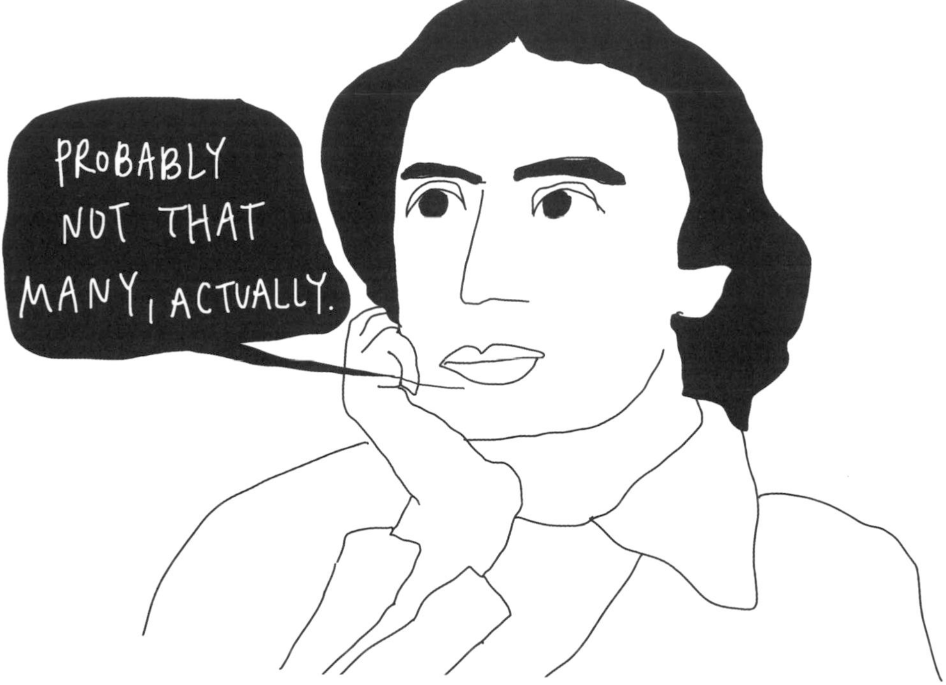
PROBABLY NOT THAT MANY, ACTUALLY.

WHO EVEN READS YOU, KEATS.

IT'S ALREADY DARK OUTSIDE. YOU CAN
SEE THE MOON REFLECT ON THE
WATER. LIGHTS ARE ON IN BUILDINGS
ON THE OTHER SIDE OF THE HUDSON,

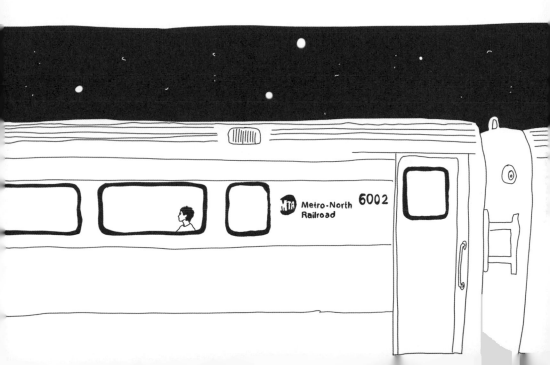

WHEN I'M ABOUT TO GET OFF THE TRAIN AT NIGHT I TAKE INVENTORY OF THE TRAIN CAR. OFTEN I'M THE ONLY WOMAN.

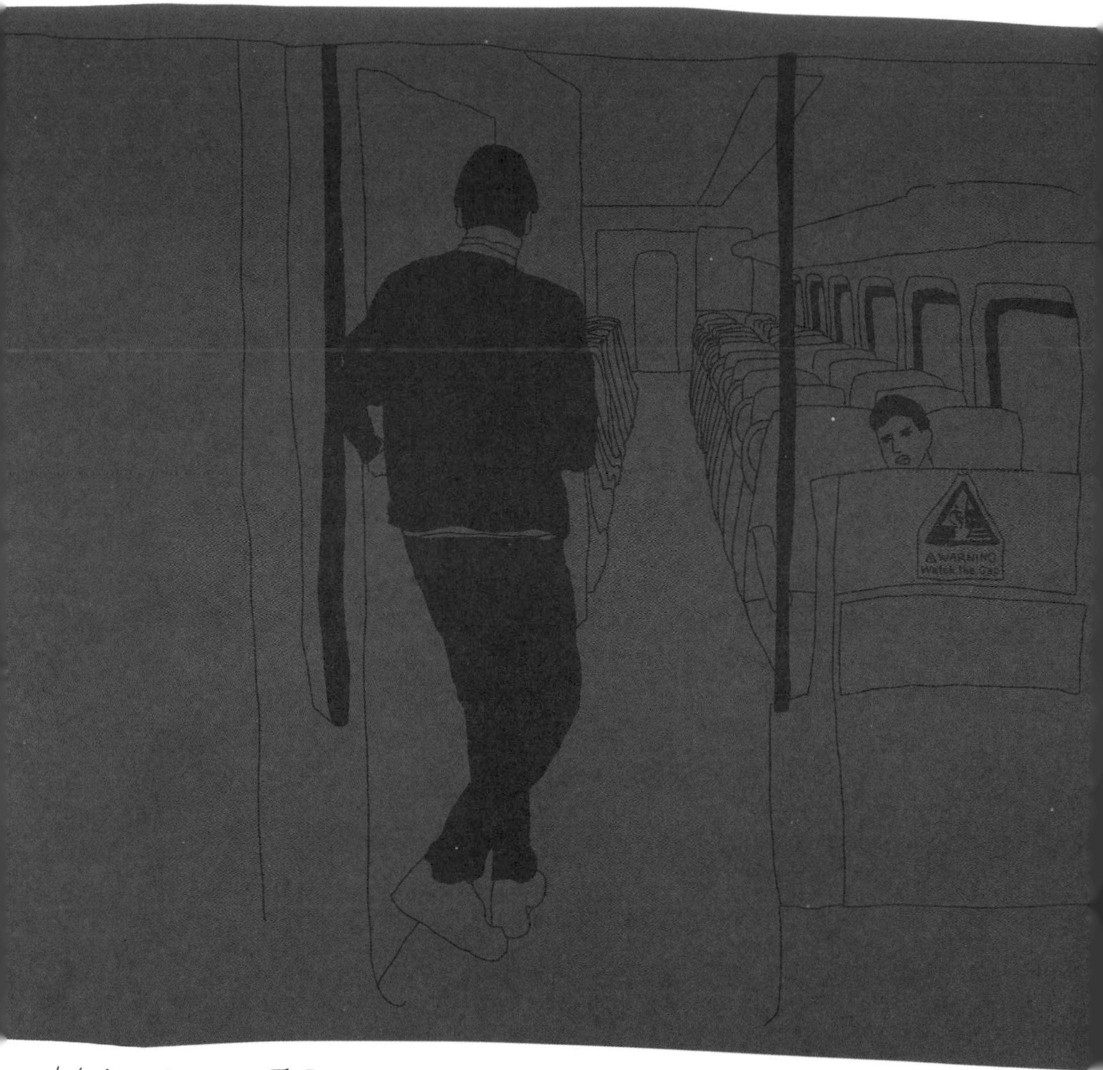
WARNING
Watch the Gap

I'M SCARED.

IT'S ME AND TWO MEN. I DECIDE WHICH ONE OF THEM IS MORE LIKELY TO RAPE ME AND WHICH IS MORE LIKELY TO INTERVENE DURING THE RAPE TO SAVE ME.

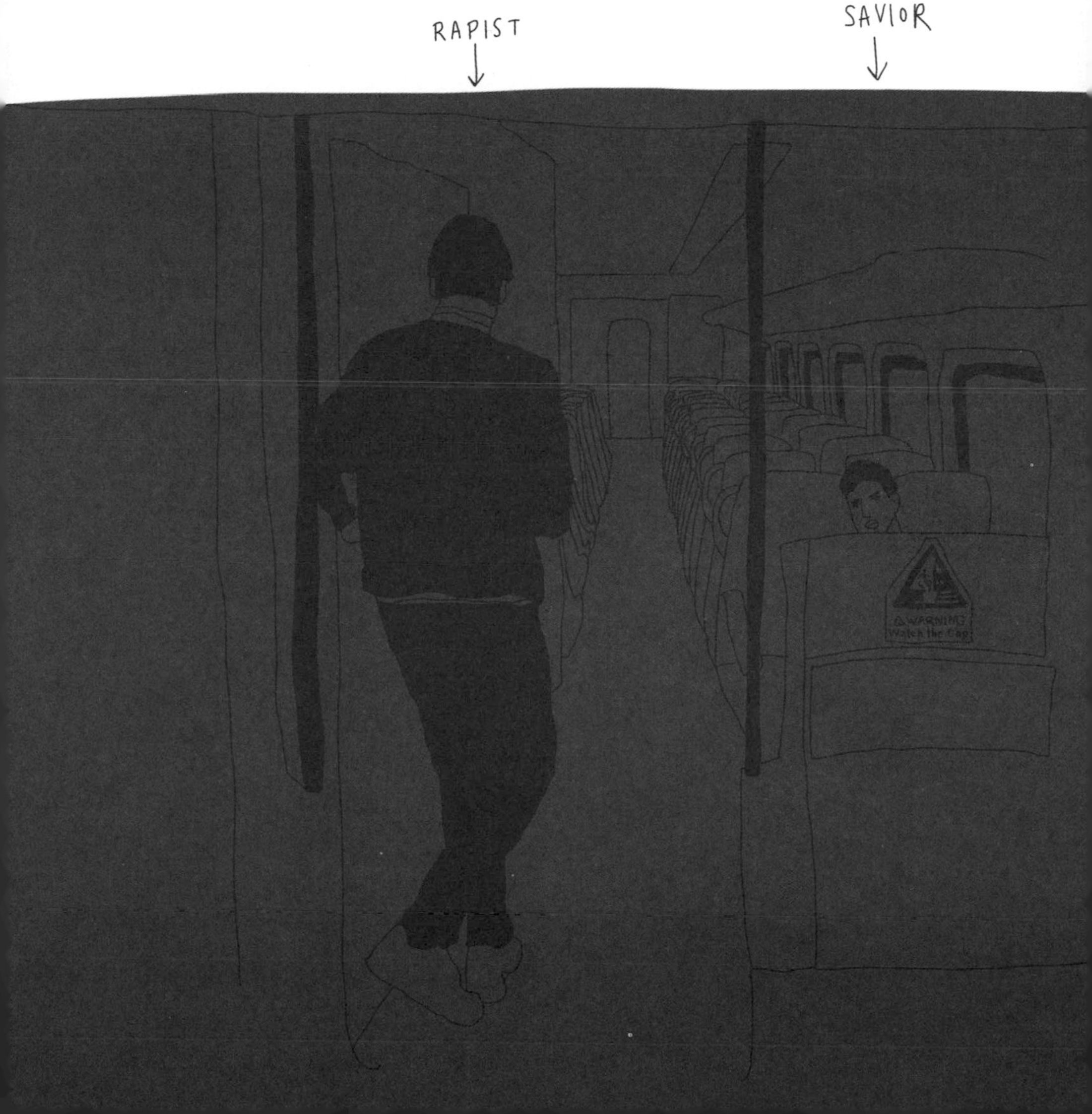
RAPIST
SAVIOR
WARNING
Watch the Gap

RAPING OR SAVING. RAPING OR SAVING. RAPING OR SAVING.

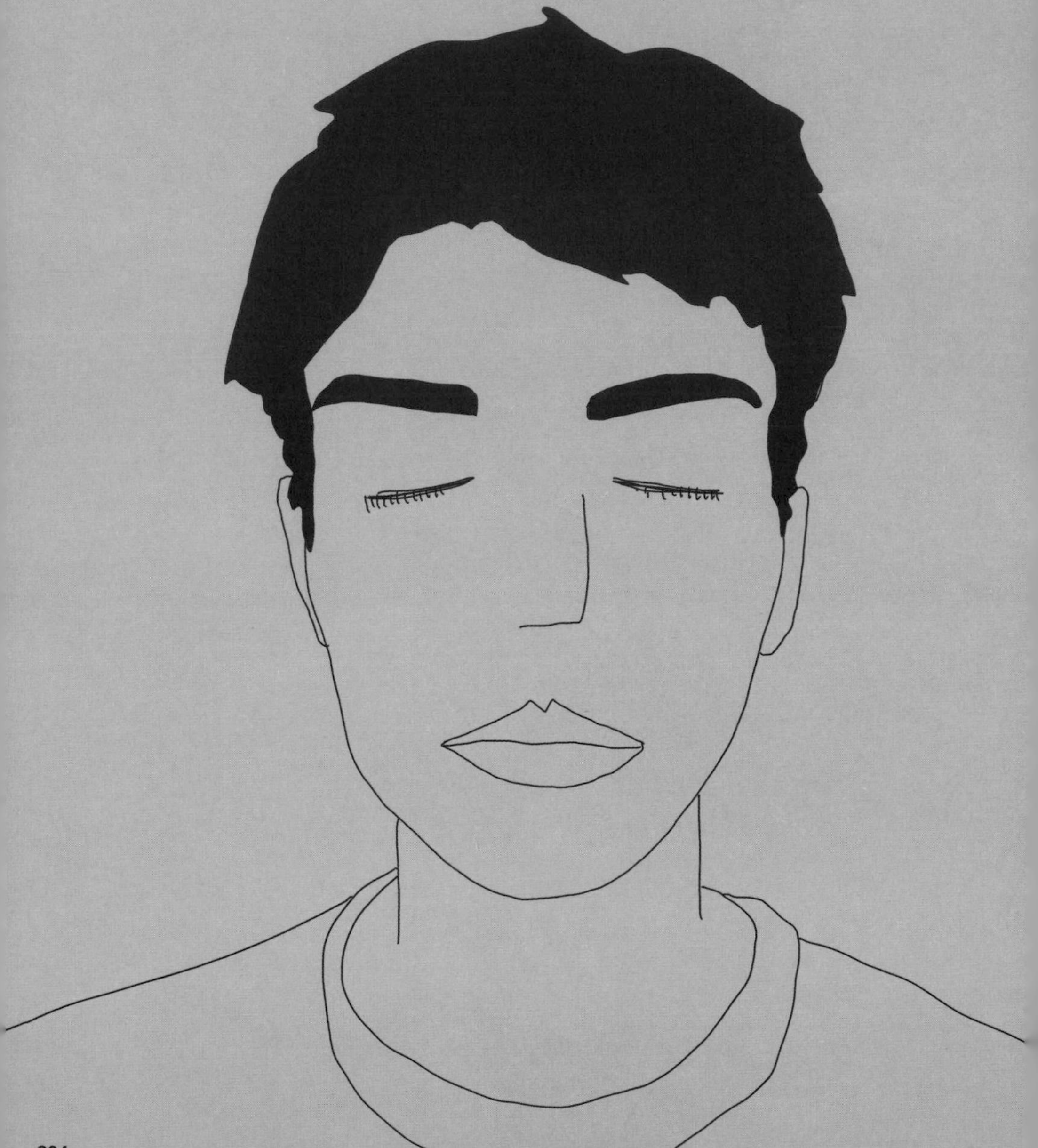

THE ONE WHO IS STARING AT ME IS MORE
LIKELY TO BE THE RAPIST, AND THE INTENSITY
OF THE FEAR IS RELATED TO THE INTENSITY
OF THE STARE AND HIS POSTURE AND A
FEW OTHER VARIABLES.

A MAN WITH HIS HOOD UP IS VERY WORRISOME. IF THERE'S ANOTHER GUY WHO LOOKS LIKE HE'S ON HIS WAY HOME FROM WORK, I COUNT ON HIM TO NOTICE THE RAPING AND CALL THE COPS.

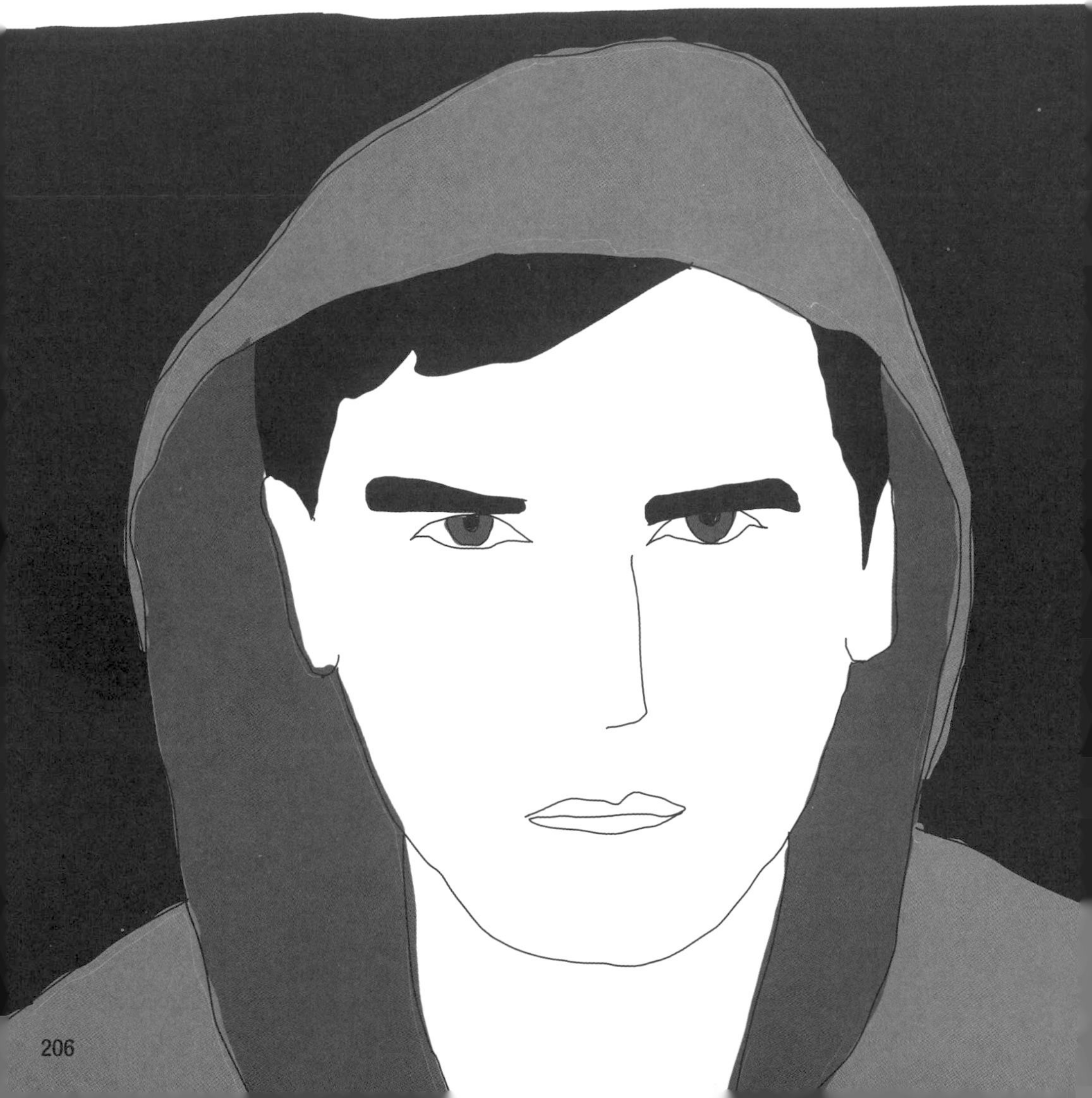

BUT WHAT THE FUCK DO THE COPS DO TO RAPE VICTIMS?

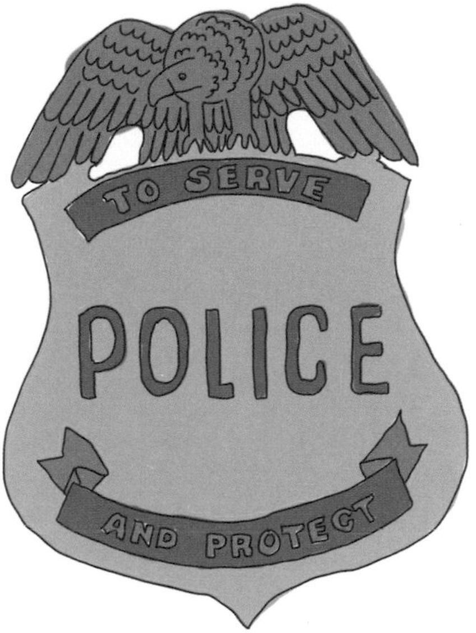
TO SERVE
POLICE
AND PROTECT

DOUBT THEM.

IGNORE THEM.

BURY THEM.

SISTERS, IS THE SYSTEM NOT RIGGED?

THE FIRST DICK I SAW WAS DAN #2'S.

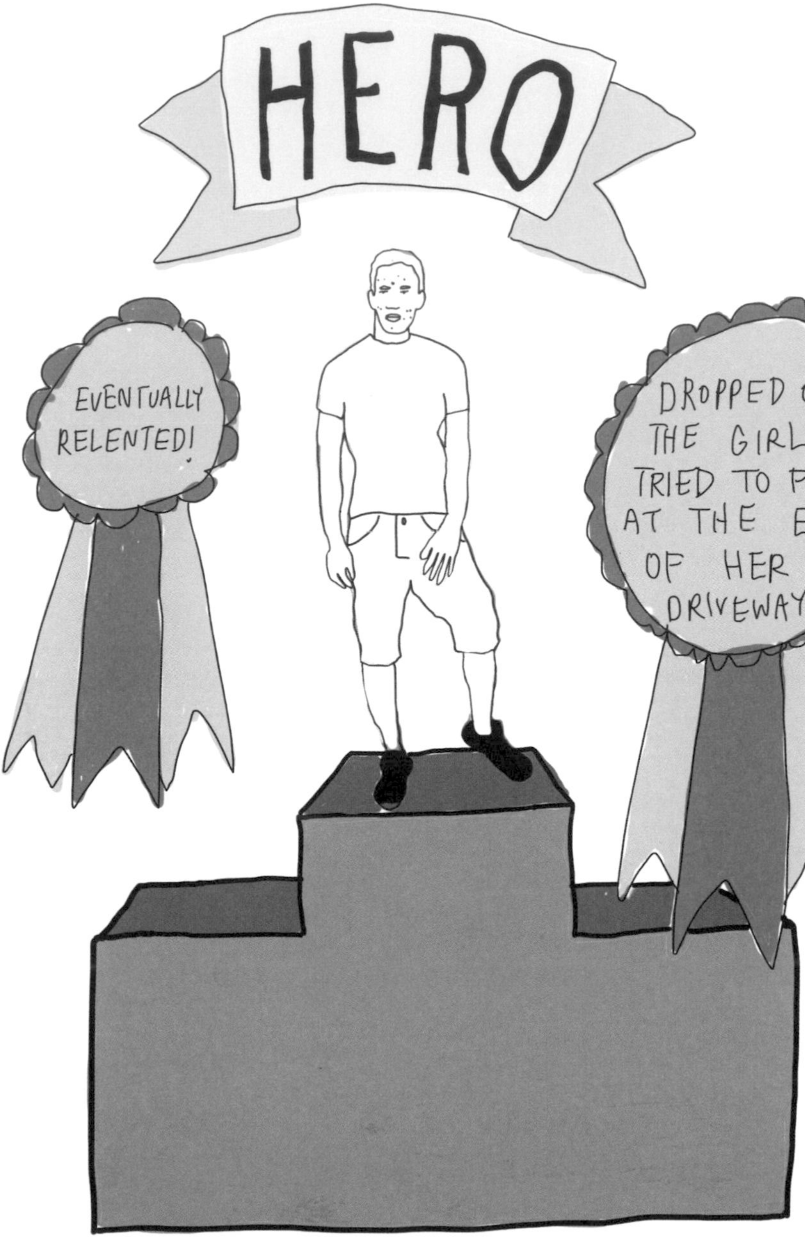
HERO
EVENTUALLY RELENTED!
DROPPED OFF THE GIRL HE TRIED TO FUCK AT THE END OF HER DRIVEWAY!

THE SECOND WAS THAT SAME SUMMER,
A FEW WEEKS LATER.

THE OLDER COUSIN OF A GUY I LIKED
DRAGGED ME DRUNK AWAY FROM A BEACH
PARTY TO A NEIGHBOR'S YARD...

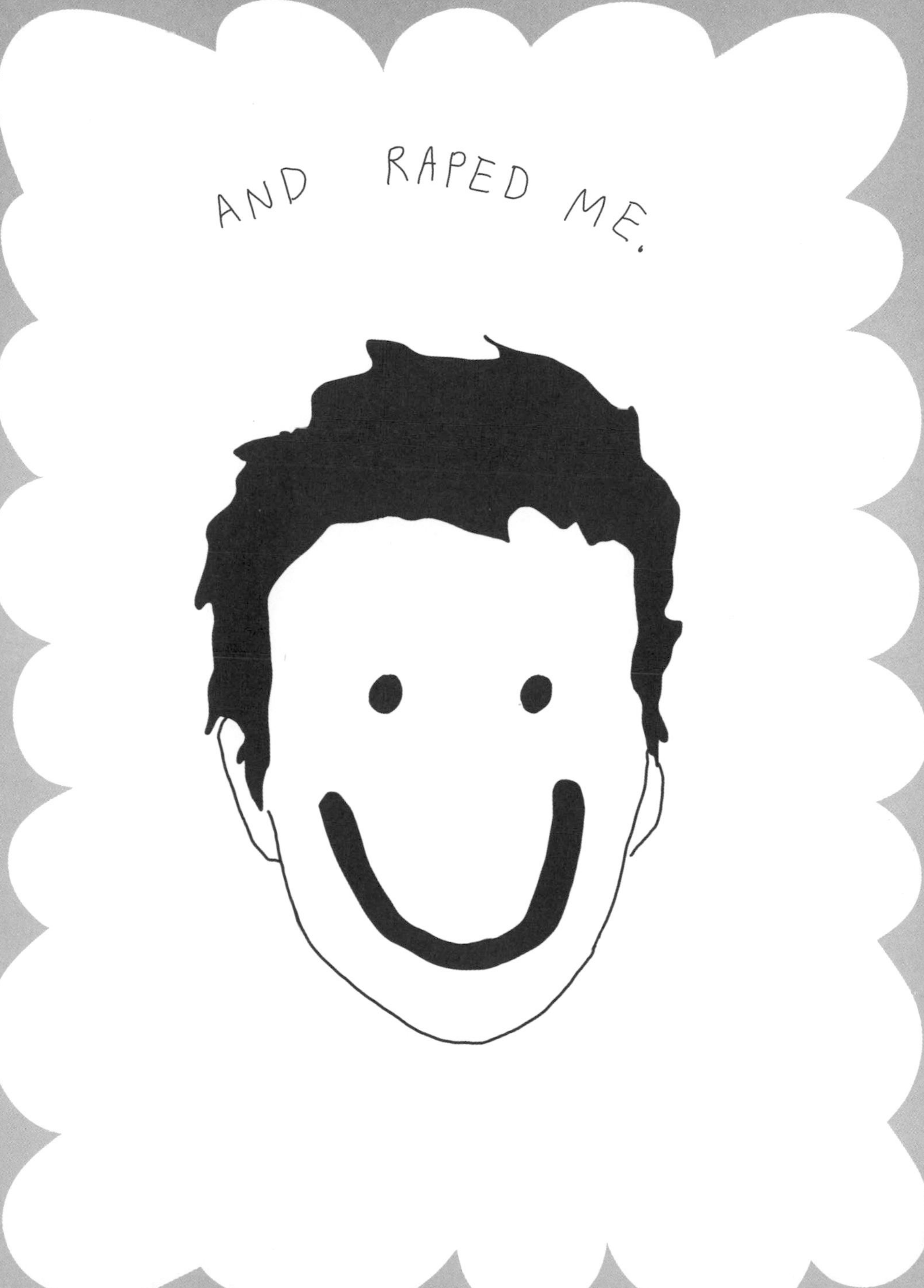
AND RAPED ME.

IT TOOK ME A WHILE TO FIGURE IT OUT.
I THOUGHT IT WAS A HOOKUP.
I THOUGHT IT WAS MY FAULT FOR
BEING DRUNK.

IT WAS MANY YEARS LATER THAT
I WAS GIVEN THE TOOLS TO
UNDERSTAND THAT I

* COULDN'T BREATHE
* WAS PINNED DOWN
* HAD NOT SPOKEN A WORD TO HIM

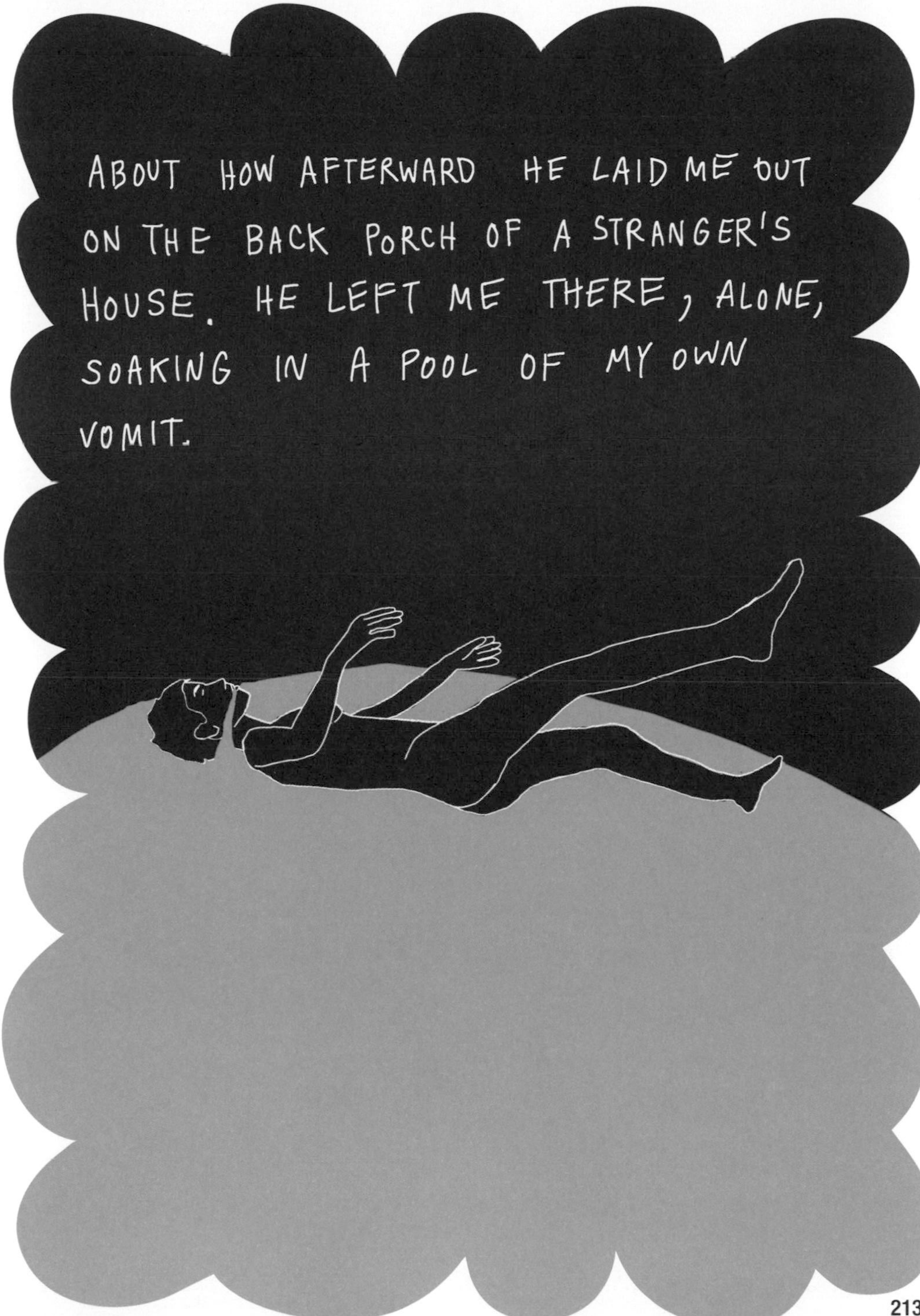
ABOUT HOW AFTERWARD HE LAID ME OUT ON THE BACK PORCH OF A STRANGER'S HOUSE. HE LEFT ME THERE, ALONE, SOAKING IN A POOL OF MY OWN VOMIT.

I THINK ABOUT IT EVERY DAY.

Dear John,
Remember me? Erin. Brown hair?
I'm on a train thinking about you. It's been twenty years.

You taught me so much the night you raped me. Do you consider it a hookup?
Here's what I learned:

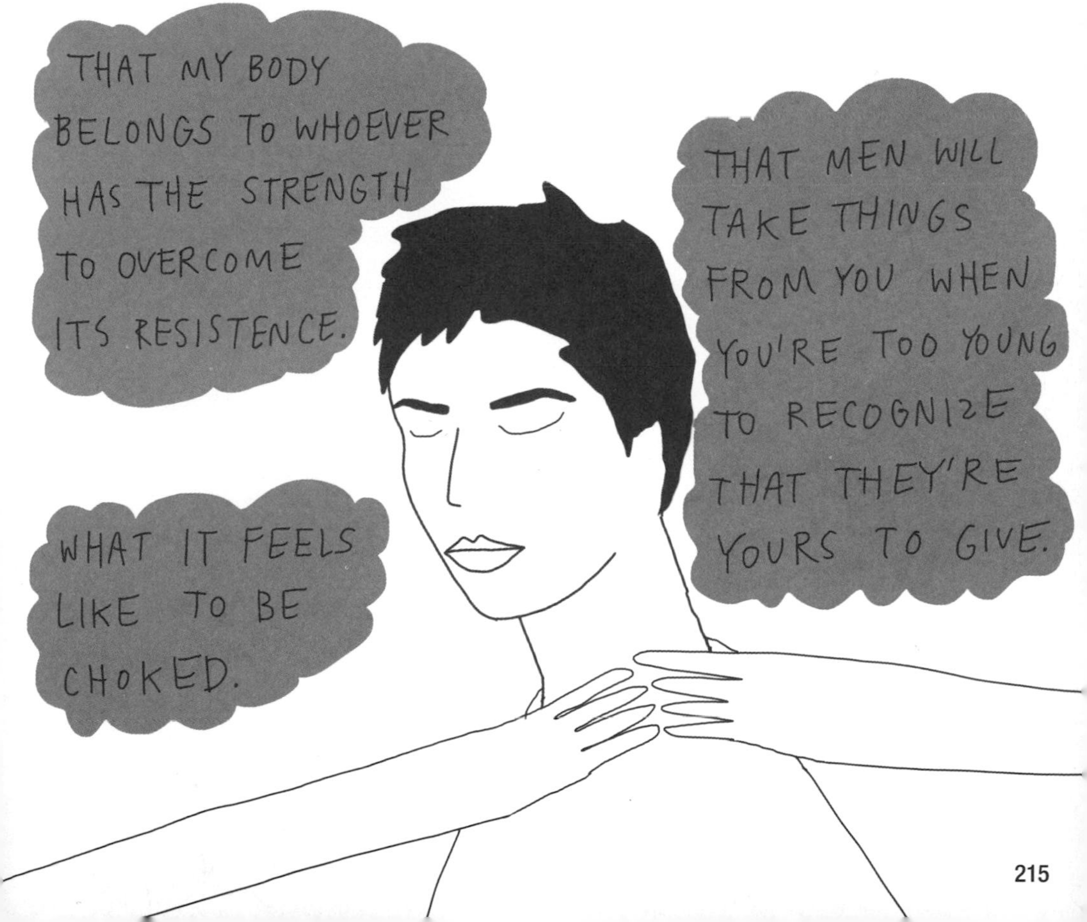
THAT MY BODY BELONGS TO WHOEVER HAS THE STRENGTH TO OVERCOME ITS RESISTENCE.
THAT MEN WILL TAKE THINGS FROM YOU WHEN YOU'RE TOO YOUNG TO RECOGNIZE THAT THEY'RE YOURS TO GIVE.
WHAT IT FEELS LIKE TO BE CHOKED.

THIS IS HOW I LEARNED THAT YOU
CAN DISSOCIATE

IN ORDER

TO SURVIVE

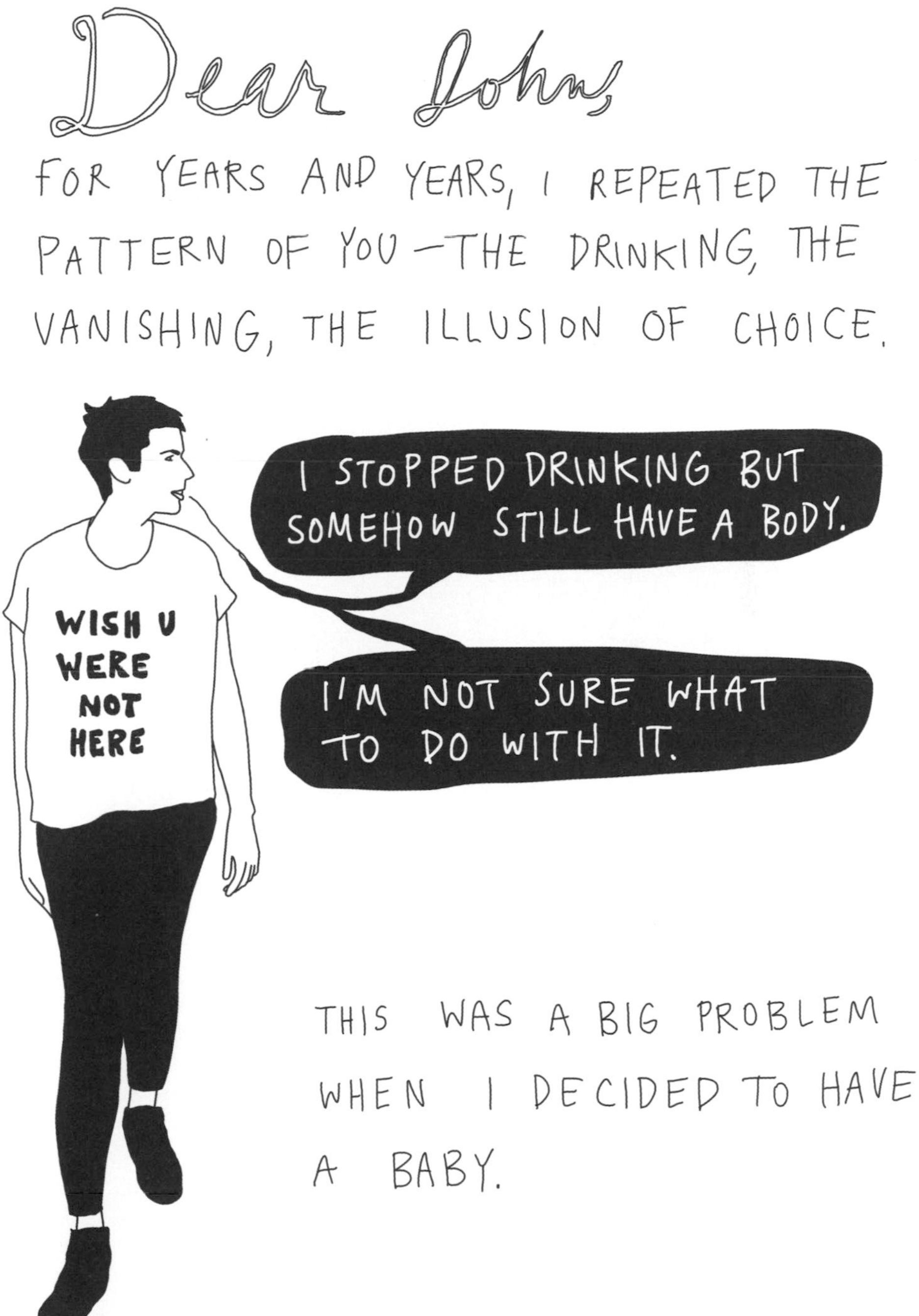
Dear John,
FOR YEARS AND YEARS, I REPEATED THE PATTERN OF YOU—THE DRINKING, THE VANISHING, THE ILLUSION OF CHOICE.
WISH U WERE NOT HERE
I STOPPED DRINKING BUT SOMEHOW STILL HAVE A BODY.
I'M NOT SURE WHAT TO DO WITH IT.
THIS WAS A BIG PROBLEM WHEN I DECIDED TO HAVE A BABY.

I RECOGNIZED THE TERROR OF CHILDBIRTH.
IT WAS MY BODY TRANSACTING AGAINST
MY WILL, A FEELING WITH WHICH YOU
MADE ME INTIMATE, ALL THOSE YEARS AGO.

AFTER FIFTY HOURS OF LABOR, IT
TOOK TWENTY MINUTES TO CUT ME
OPEN AND STITCH ME BACK UP.

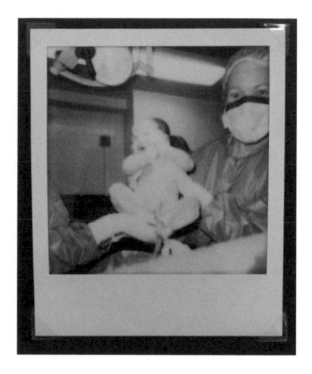

THEY PRESSED HER GUNKY CHEEK
ONTO MINE AND I SOBBED AND SOBBED
AND WAITED FOR MY INSIDES TO GO
BACK INSIDE.

Dear John,

FOR HOURS A DAY, I COMMUTE.

IT'S ME, AND THEM, AND YOU, AND OUR SECRET
TITS, ASSHOLES, AND ERECTIONS IN SENSIBLE
SHOES AND DRY-CLEAN-ONLY SLACKS
PERFORMING BODILY AUTONOMY AND
READING QUIETLY ABOUT THE NEXT WORLD WAR.

WE SIT ON THE TRAIN AND REMEMBER THE BROWN BAG LUNCH WE LEFT ON THE COUNTER, THE REPORT THAT WAS DUE YESTERDAY, THE PERMISSION SLIP THAT NEVER GOT SIGNED.

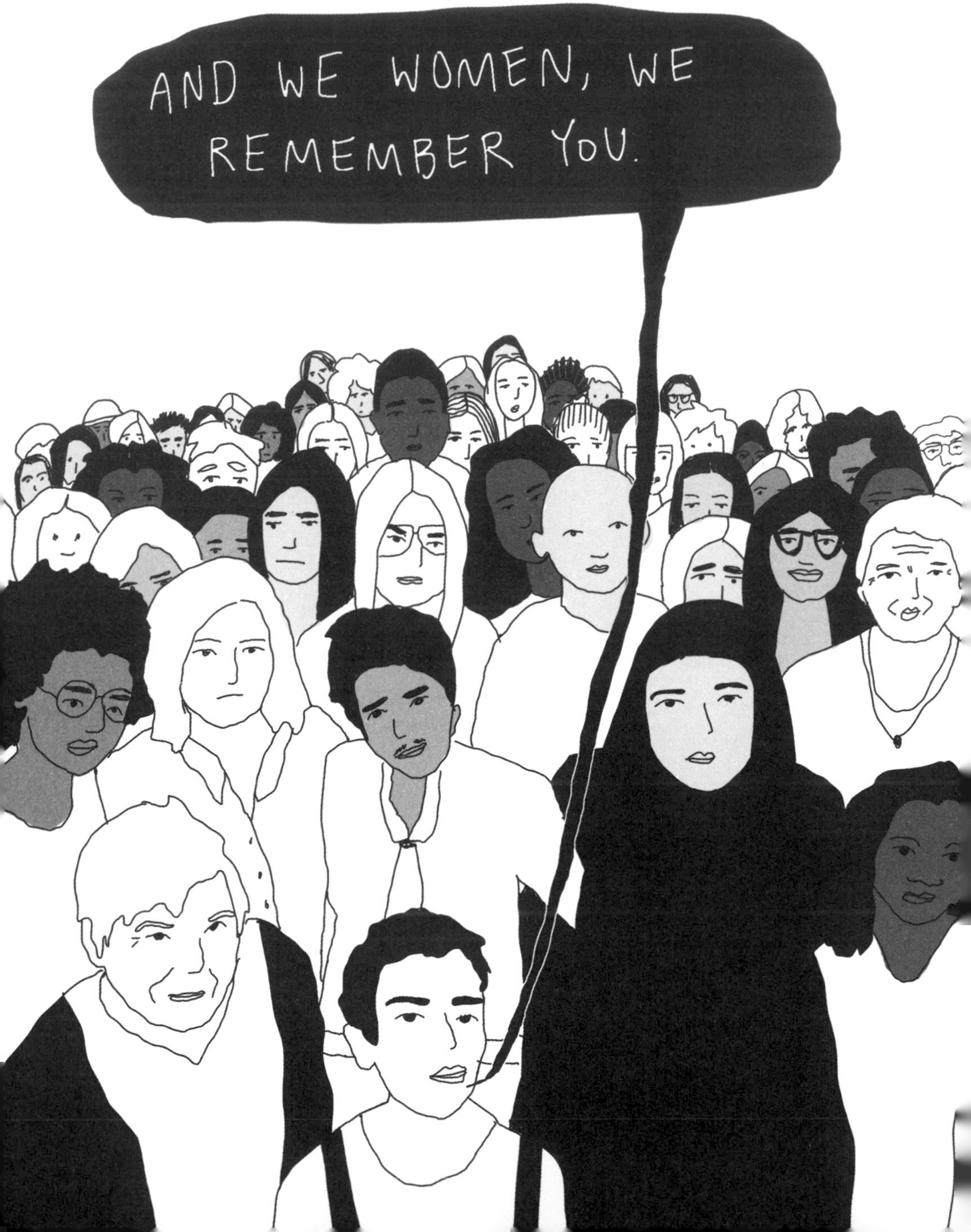
AND WE WOMEN, WE REMEMBER YOU.

HOME

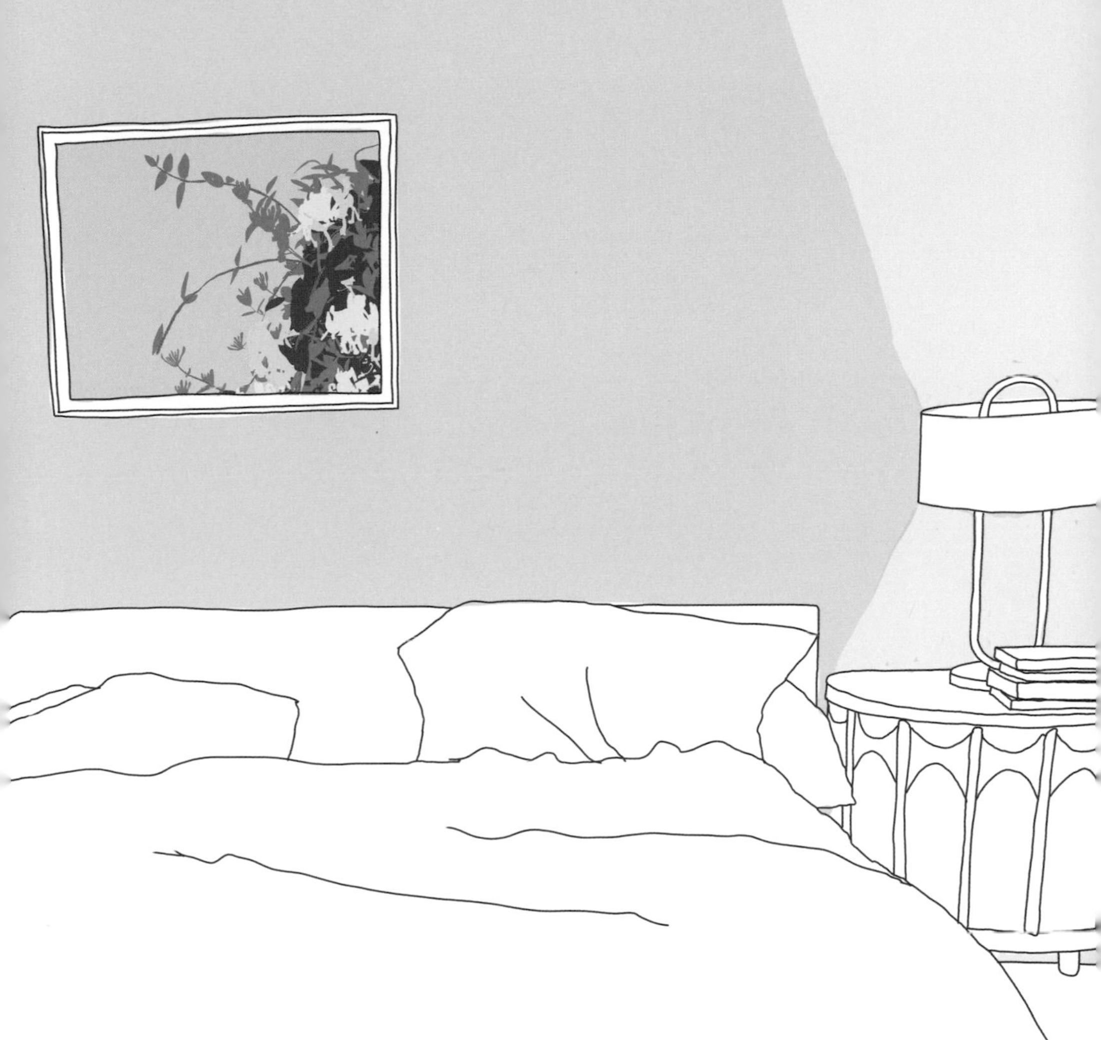

I WALK IN THE DOOR AND PUT MY KEYS
DOWN ON THE BIG TABLE.

INSTEAD OF THE EMOTIONAL WEB OF MY
INTERACTIONS FOLDING INWARD,
MATERIALIZING AS MONSTERS LIKE THEY DO
ON MY MORNING COMMUTE, THEY CURL
OUT LIKE LITTLE FINGERS, LITTLE TOES.
THEY WERE ALL WRAPPED UP IN HER.

SHE SEES ME AND FOAMS WITH
LONGING, SUDSY AS BEER.

EARLY MOTHERHOOD IS ABOUT GRIEVING THE LOSS OF THE SELF AS AN INDIVIDUAL. IT'S HUMAN MITOSIS.

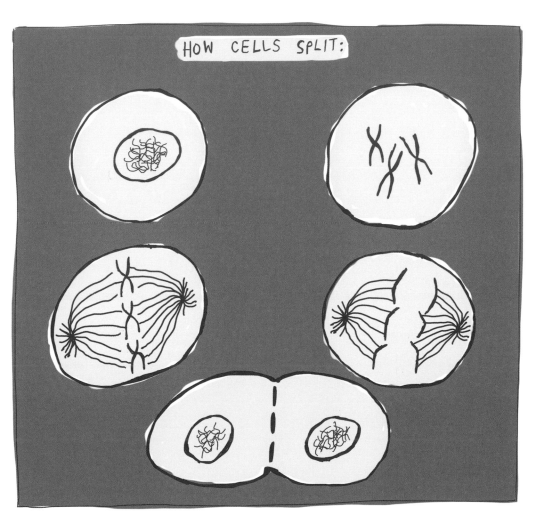

ONE BECOMES TWO.

I QUITE LITERALLY SPLIT RIGHT OPEN.

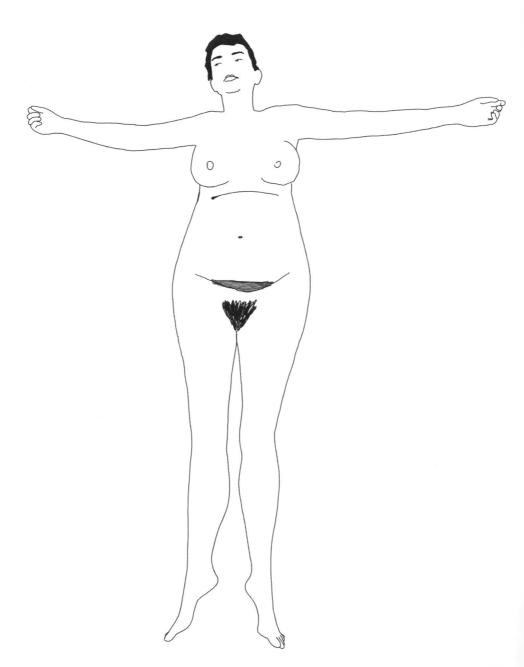

IT'S A DIFFERENT TYPE OF BEING BROKEN.

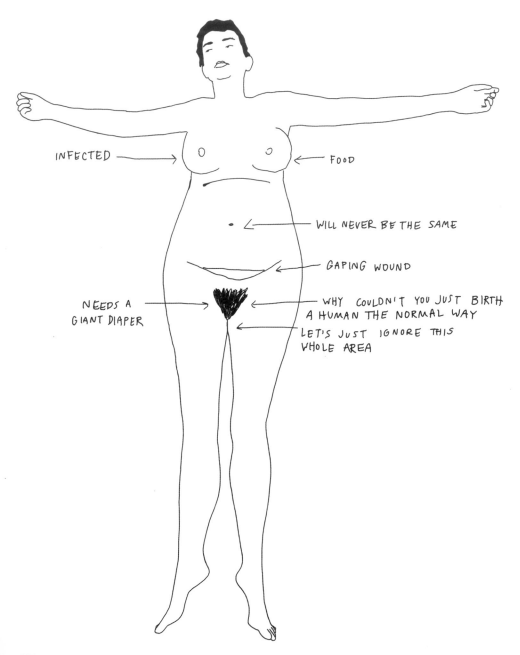

INFECTED

FOOD

WILL NEVER BE THE SAME

GAPING WOUND

NEEDS A
GIANT DIAPER

WHY COULDN'T YOU JUST BIRTH
A HUMAN THE NORMAL WAY

LET'S JUST IGNORE THIS
WHOLE AREA

EARLY MOTHERHOOD IS A CEASELESS, MILITARY-STYLE INDUCTION INTO SELF-SACRIFICE AND DEVOTION TO ANOTHER.

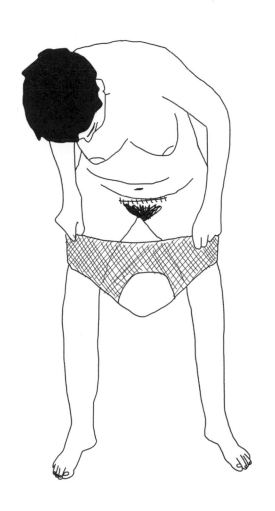

LIFE IS LIVED IN TWO-HOUR INCREMENTS.
IN EACH TWO-HOUR PERIOD WITH A NEW
BABY: SLEEP (NOT YOURS), HUMAN CANNIBALISM
(IF THE LATCH ISN'T RIGHT), HURRICANE-
GALE HORMONES, PHYSICAL PAIN, LITERAL
SHIT EVERYWHERE.

"IT'S 8:46, TIME TO GET SHIT ON."

BUT MORE THAN THAT, IT WAS THE FIRST TIME IN MY LIFE WHEN SIMPLE PLEASURE TURNED TO HORRIFIC PHYSICAL PAIN AND THEN INTO MORE: THE REPLICATION OF MY DNA INTO A SOFT, STICKY CREATURE, PINK AND WARM AND FAT WITH NEED.

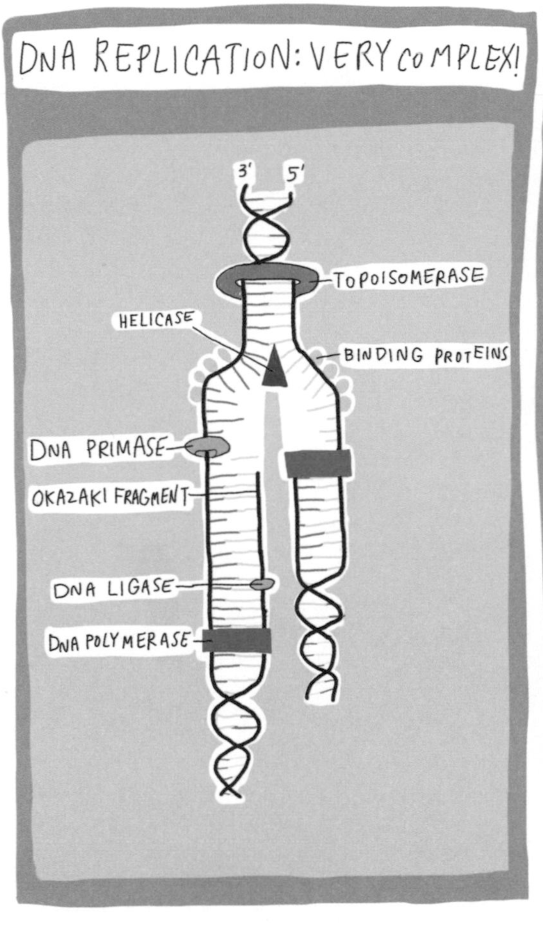
DNA REPLICATION: VERY COMPLEX!
3'
5'
TOPOISOMERASE
HELICASE
BINDING PROTEINS
DNA PRIMASE
OKAZAKI FRAGMENT
DNA LIGASE
DNA POLYMERASE

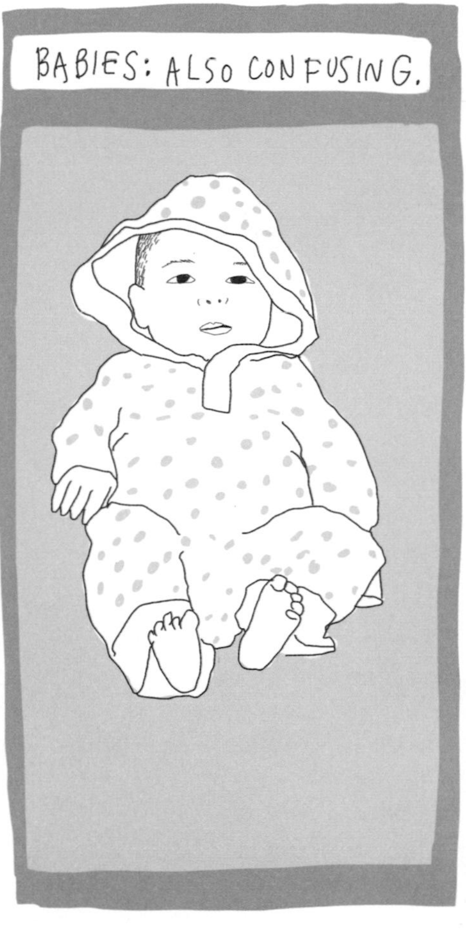
BABIES: ALSO CONFUSING.

WITH NEW MOTHERHOOD YOU ARE BROKEN, AND KEEP BREAKING AND BREAKING UNTIL YOU ARE NEW.

THE NEW PERSON WHO EMERGES IS THE MOTHER.

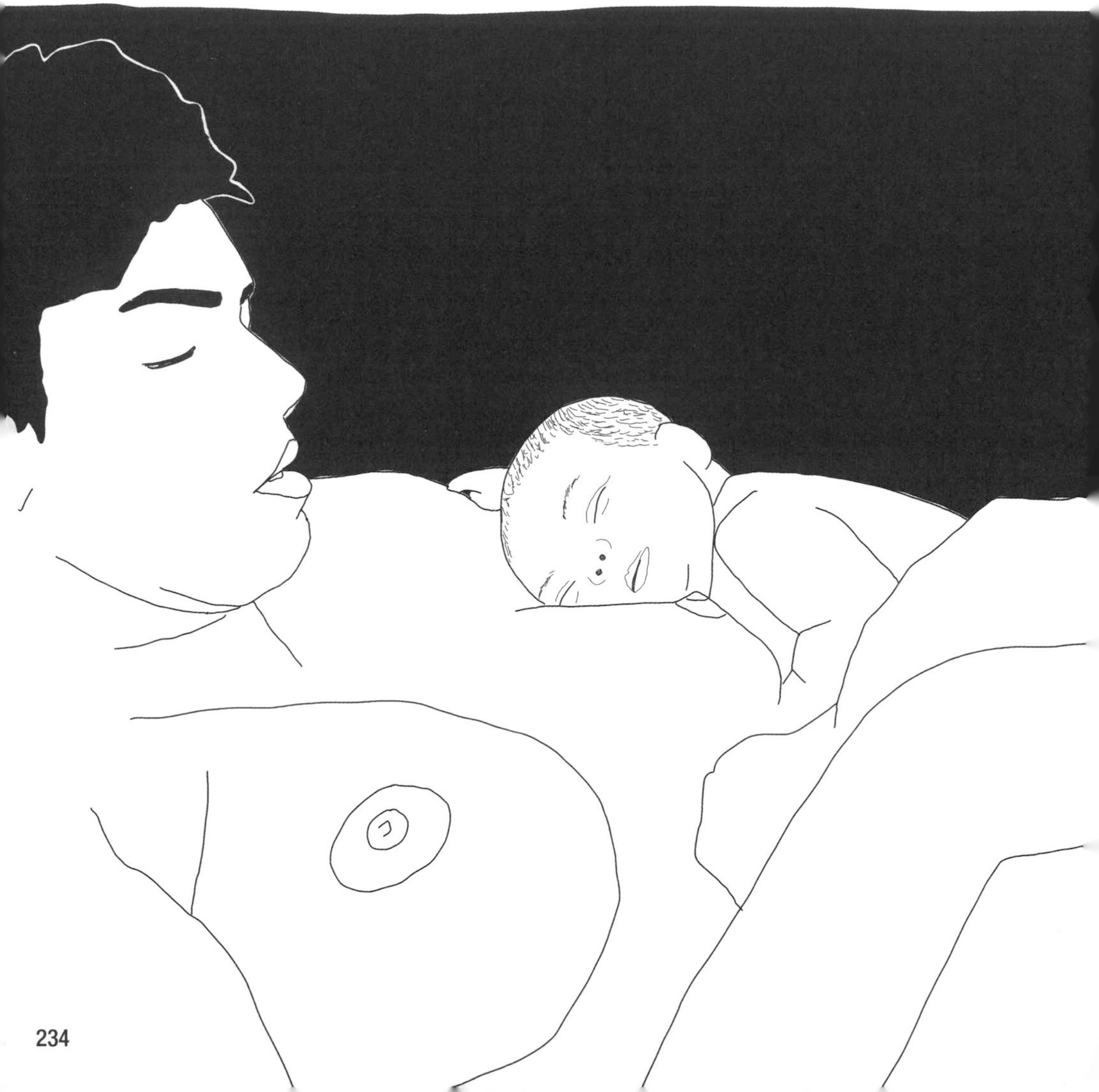

I SET MY ALARM FOR MIDNIGHT, TWO, FOUR, AND SIX TO PUMP FIFTEEN MINUTES ON EACH SIDE WHILE WATCHING RERUNS OF *FRIENDS.*

RACHEL + ROSS

ME

I WAS AWAKE ALL NIGHT LIKE A ZOMBIE OR A DRUNK.

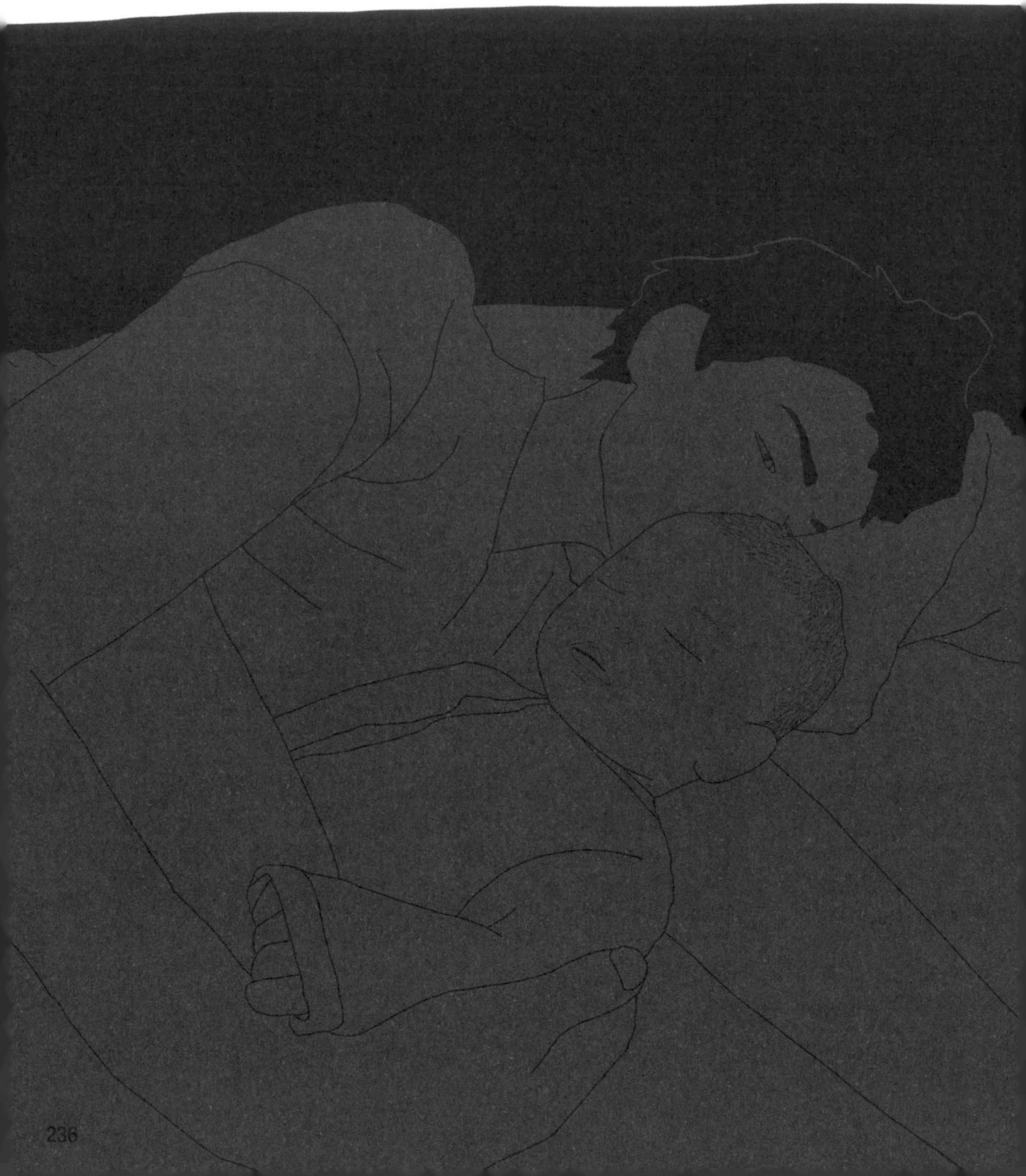

I ATE ALMONDS AND GENERIC GRANOLA BARS FROM MY BEDSIDE TABLE RAVENOUSLY.

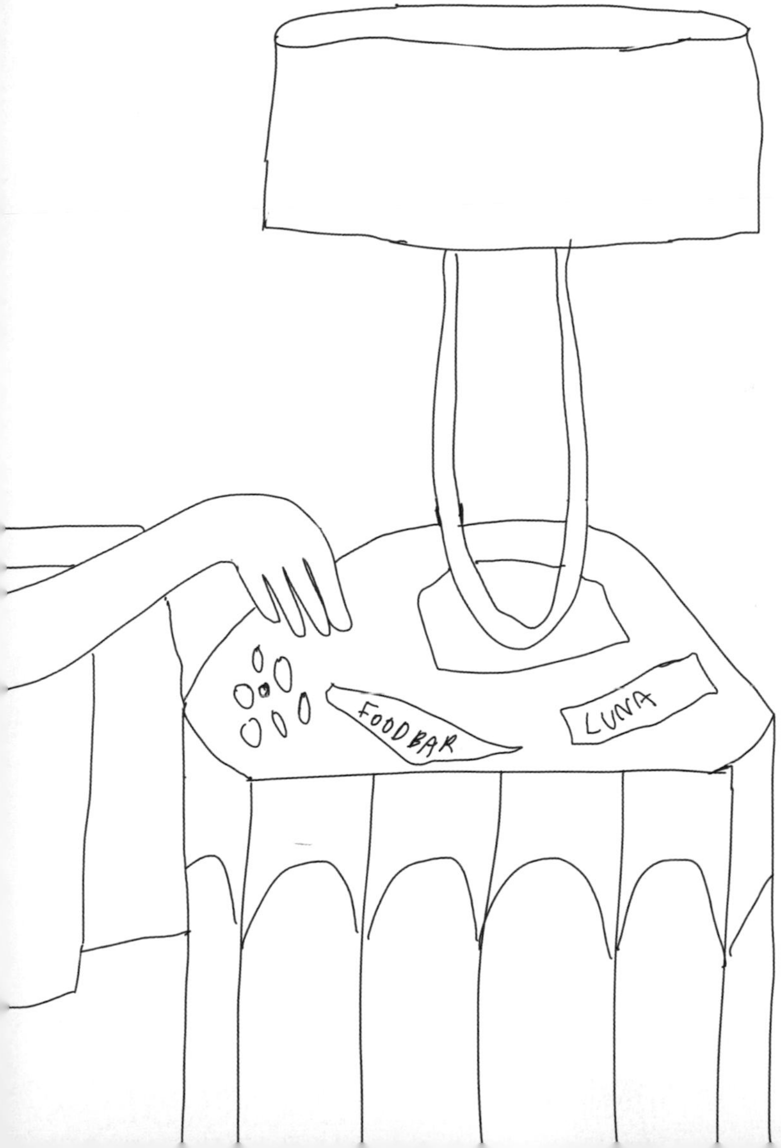
FOODBAR
LUNA

THE BREAST PUMP WHIRRED. IN THE DARK, IT LOOKED LIKE A FACE.

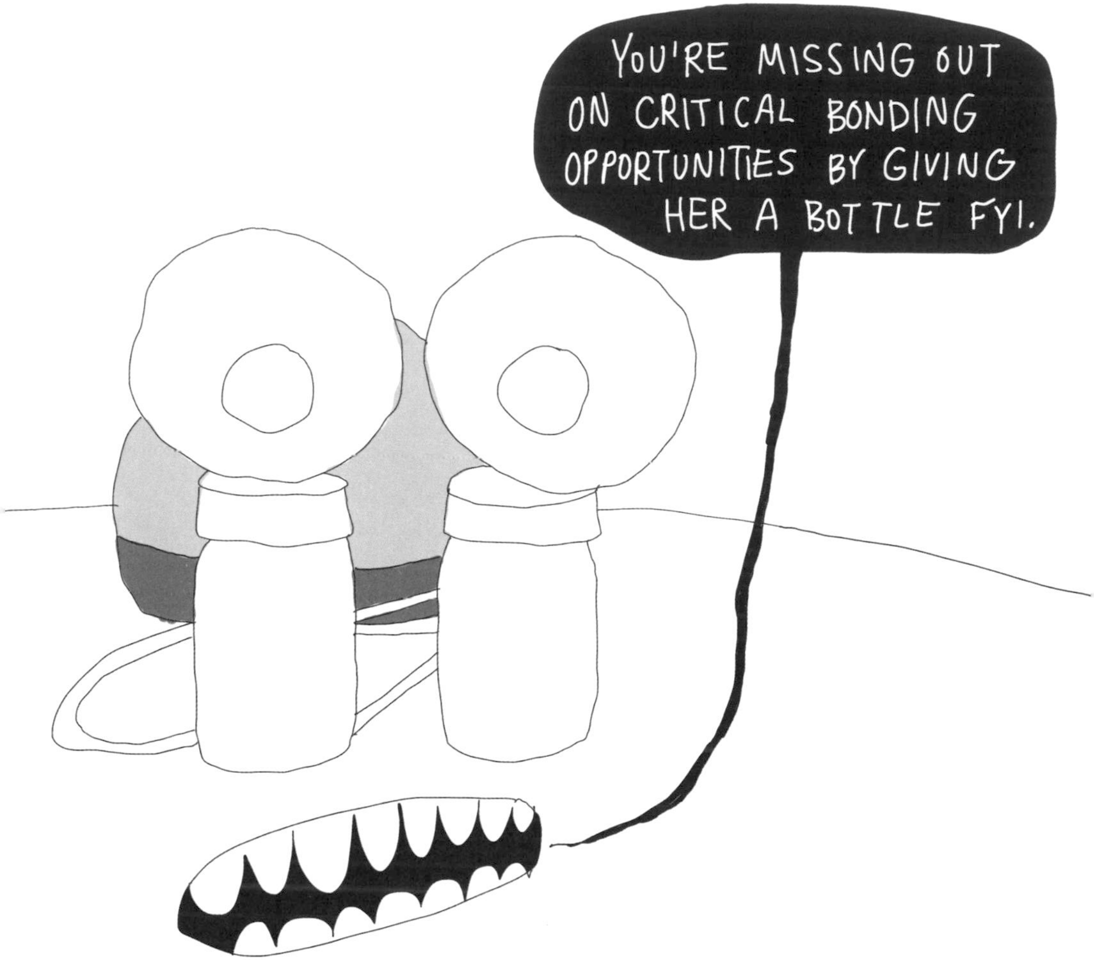
YOU'RE MISSING OUT ON CRITICAL BONDING OPPORTUNITIES BY GIVING HER A BOTTLE FYI.

I NEVER CONSIDERED HAVING A BABY WHEN I DRANK. HOW DOES AN ALCOHOLIC STOP DRINKING FOR NINE ENTIRE MONTHS? DO YOU STOP WHEN YOU'RE "TRYING"?

↑ EN, THIS TERM

JANUARY

M	T	W	T	F	S	S
				1	2	3
4	5	6	7	8	9	10
11	12	13	14	15	16	17
18	19	20	21	22	23	24
25	26	27	28	29	30	

FEBRUARY

M	T	W	T	F	S	S
1	2	3	4	5	6	7
8	9	10	11	12	13	14
15	16	17	18	19	20	21
22	23	24	25	26	27	28

MARCH

M	T	W	T	F	S	S
1	2	3	4	5	6	7
8	9	10	11	12	13	14
15	16	17	18	19	20	21
22	23	24	25	26	27	28
29	30	31				

APRIL

M	T	W	T	F	S	S
		1	2	3	4	
5	6	7	8	9	10	11
12	13	14	15	16	17	18
19	20	21	22	23	24	25
26	27	28	29	30		

MAY

M	T	W	T	F	S	S
				1	2	
3	4	5	6	7	8	9
10	11	12	13	14	15	16
17	18	19	20	21	22	23
24 / 31	25	26	27	28	29	

JUNE

M	T	W	T	F	S	S
1	2	3	4	5	6	
7	8	9	10	11	12	13
14	15	16	17	18	19	20
21	22	23	24	25	26	27
28	29	30				

JULY

M	T	W	T	F	S	S
		1	2	3	4	
5	6	7	8	9	10	11
12	13	14	15	16	17	18
19	20	21	22	23	24	25
26	27	28	29	30	31	

AUGUST

M	T	W	T	F	S	S
					1	
2	3	4	5	6	7	8
9	10	11	12	13	14	15
16	17	18	19	20	21	22
23 / 30	24 / 31	25	26	27	28	

SEPTEMBER

M	T	W	T	F	S	S
	1	2	3	4	5	
6	7	8	9	10	11	12
13	14	15	16	17	18	19
20	21	22	23	24	25	26
27	28	29	30			

OCTOBER

M	T	W	T	F	S	S
			1	2	3	
4	5	6	7	8	9	10
11	12	13	14	15	16	17
18	19	20	21	22	23	24
25	26	27	28	29	30	

I GOT SOBER YEARS BEFORE I HAD MY DAUGHTER. I DIDN'T DO IT TO HAVE BABIES, I DID IT SO I WOULDN'T DIE.

THERE IS NO POSSIBILITY FOR TRANSFORMATION
INSIDE THE INKY, NEBULOUS CAVE OF
ADDICTION.

WHEN I WAS TIRED OF WAKING UP AND
FINGERING MYSELF TO SEE HOW BAD THE
NIGHT BEFORE HAD BEEN, I DRANK FOR
FIVE MORE YEARS.

THEN ONE MORNING I WOKE UP.

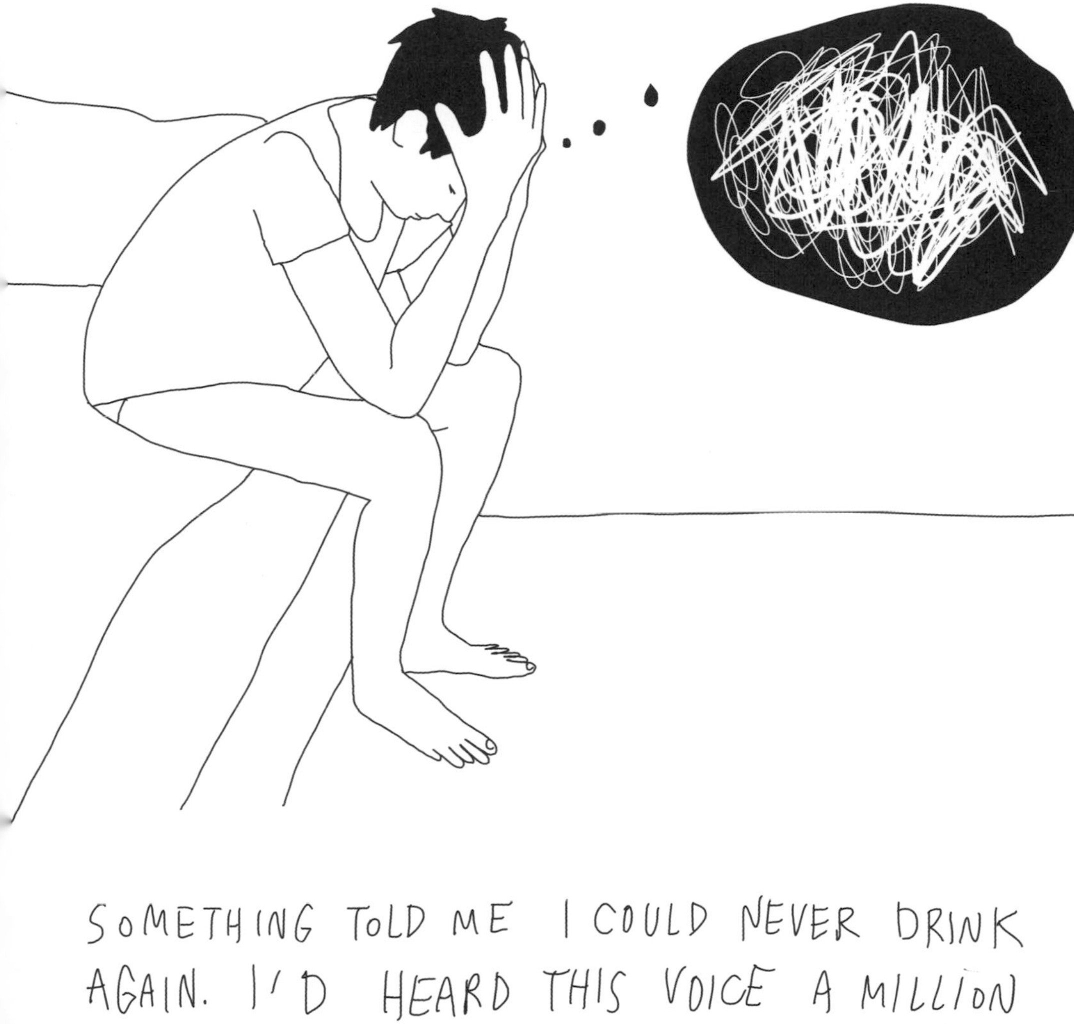

SOMETHING TOLD ME I COULD NEVER DRINK AGAIN. I'D HEARD THIS VOICE A MILLION TIMES BEFORE, BUT COULD NEVER FOLLOW IT. THIS DAY WAS DIFFERENT.

I STOPPED.

HOW: LUCK? GRACE? MEETINGS? ANYTHING
BUT WILL.
TURNS OUT I'M NOT REALLY IN CONTROL
OF THE WORLD.

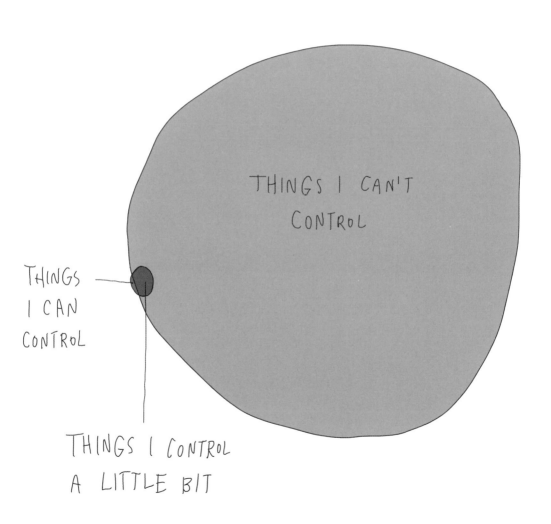

THINGS I CAN'T
CONTROL

THINGS
I CAN
CONTROL

THINGS I CONTROL
A LITTLE BIT

THERE WAS ALWAYS A GOOD REASON TO CONTINUE:

GUILT

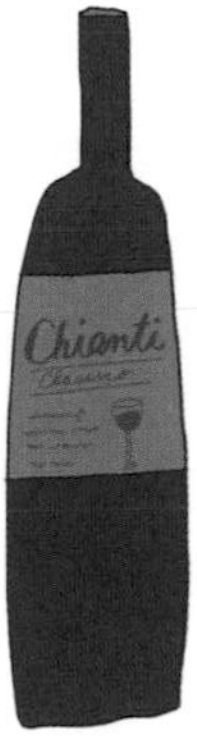
Chianti

CELEBRATION

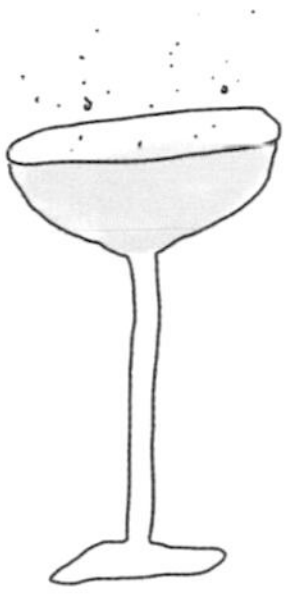

SADNESS

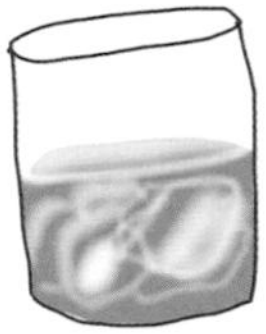

TUESDAY

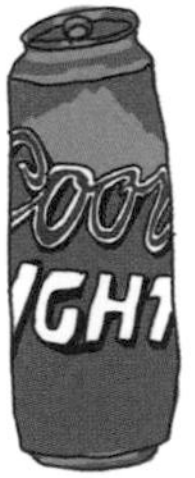

THE **SHAME** OF THE PREVIOUS THREE DECADES FILLED ME TO THE BRIM. THERE THEY WERE:

THE DRINKS

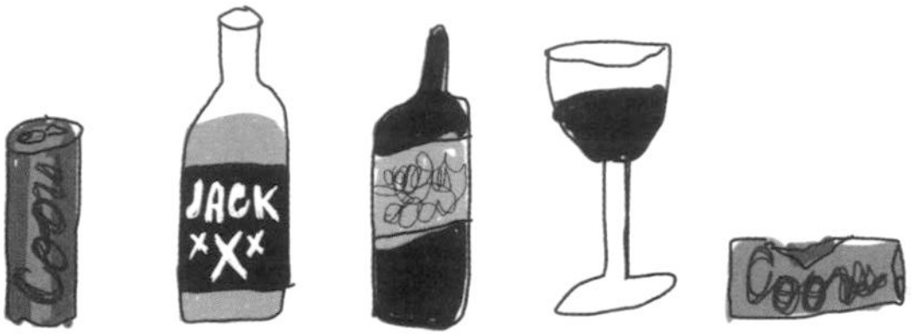
Coors
JACK
Coors

THE MEN

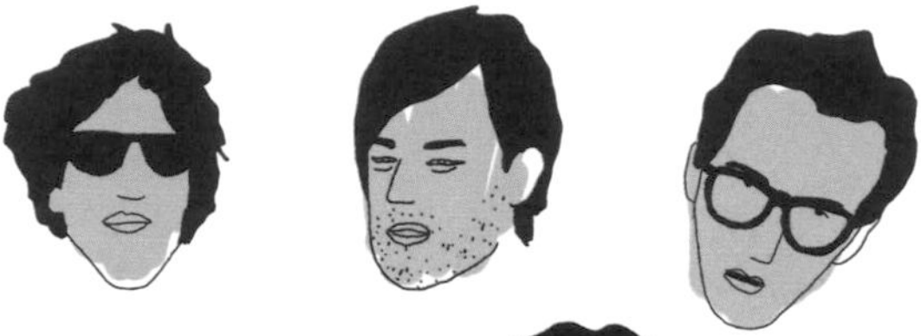

THE ACTOR/COMEDIAN

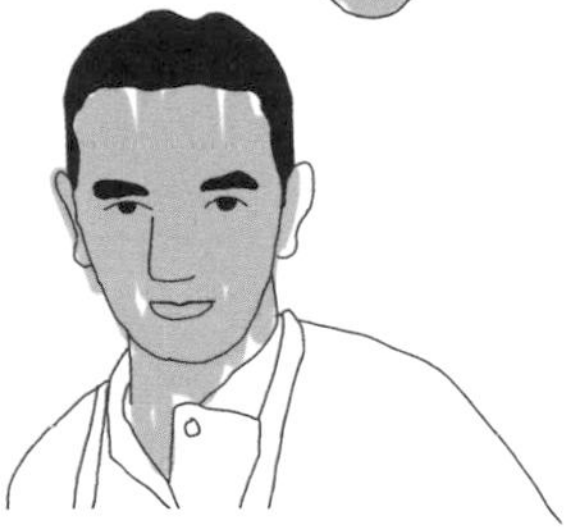

THE FEW ASSAULTS

AND THE MANY, MANY SHADES OF GRAY.

I CRADLED THESE MEMORIES, LET THEM WAIL AND MOAN AND CUT ME. I HADN'T LEARNED HOW TO HAVE EMPATHY FOR MYSELF, ONLY FOR OTHER PEOPLE.

PERSONALLY NOT A FAN OF INSTAGRAM MEMES BEING RIGHT

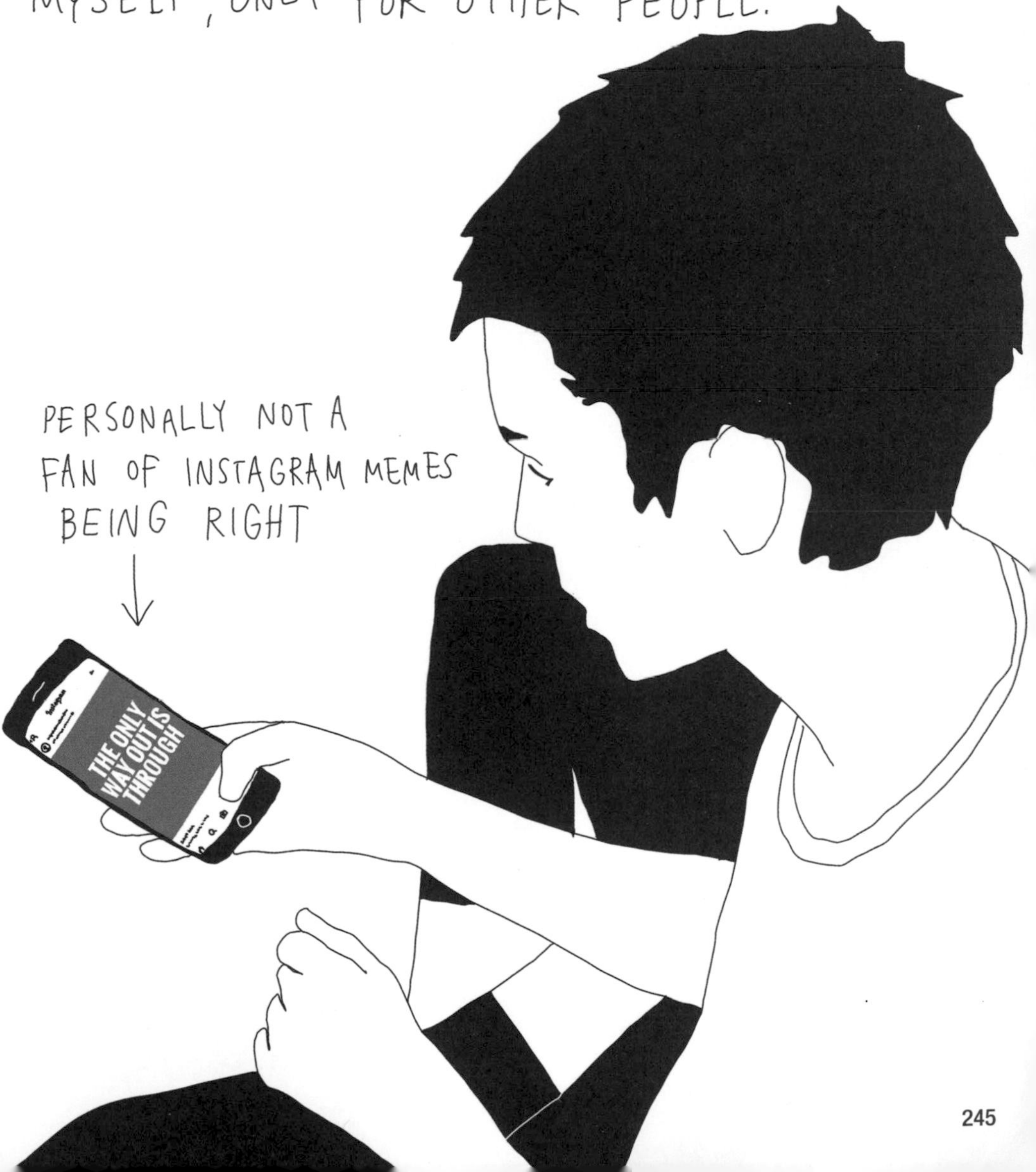
THE ONLY WAY OUT IS THROUGH

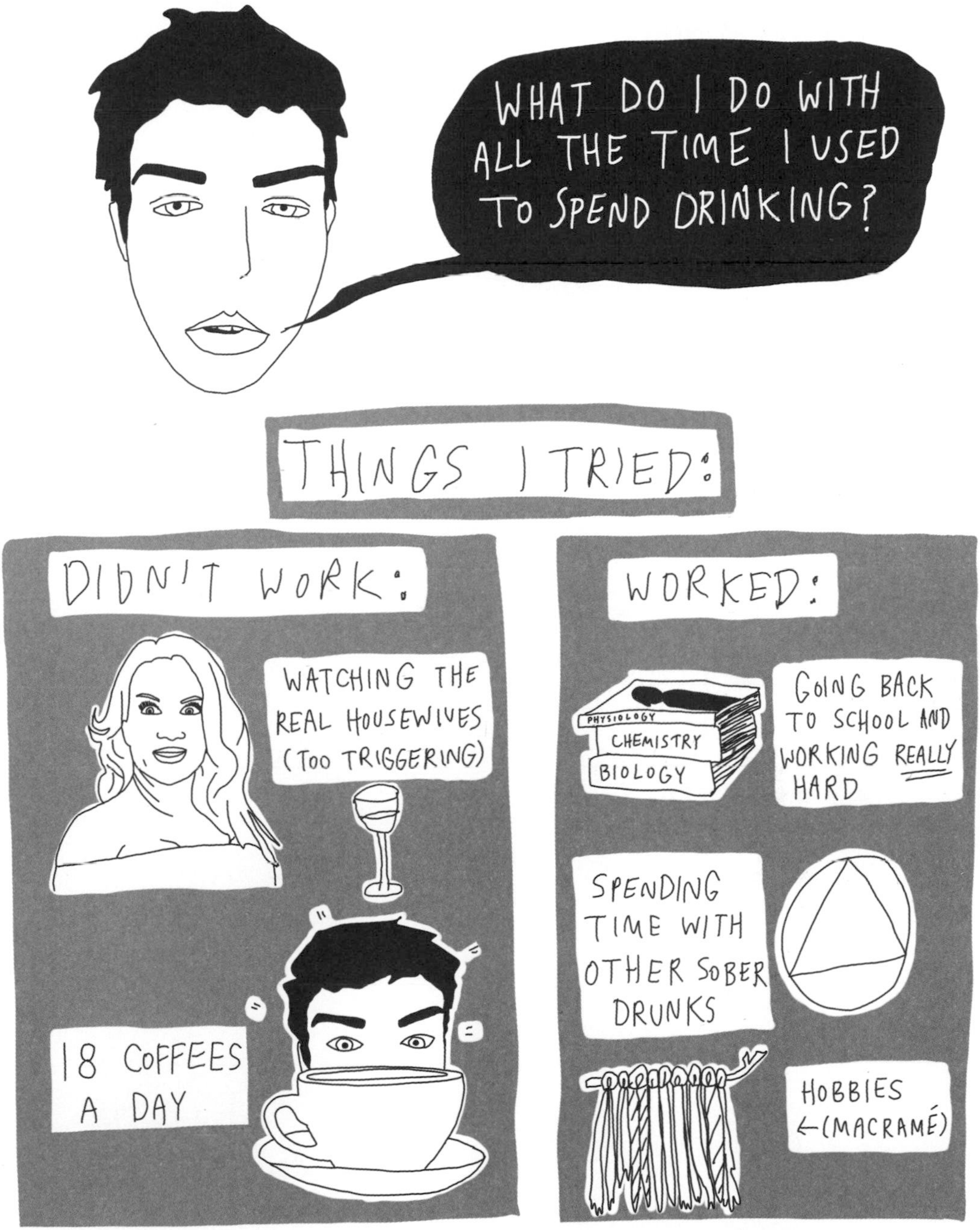
WHAT DO I DO WITH ALL THE TIME I USED TO SPEND DRINKING?
THINGS I TRIED:
DIDN'T WORK:
WATCHING THE REAL HOUSEWIVES (TOO TRIGGERING)
18 COFFEES A DAY
WORKED:
PHYSIOLOGY
CHEMISTRY
BIOLOGY
GOING BACK TO SCHOOL AND WORKING REALLY HARD
SPENDING TIME WITH OTHER SOBER DRUNKS
HOBBIES ←(MACRAMÉ)

I SHAPESHIFTED, REINVENTED MY OUTSIDES.
I LEARNED CHEMISTRY AND BIOLOGY.
THERE IS A WORLD IN WHICH RULES APPLY. I FELT OKAY THERE.

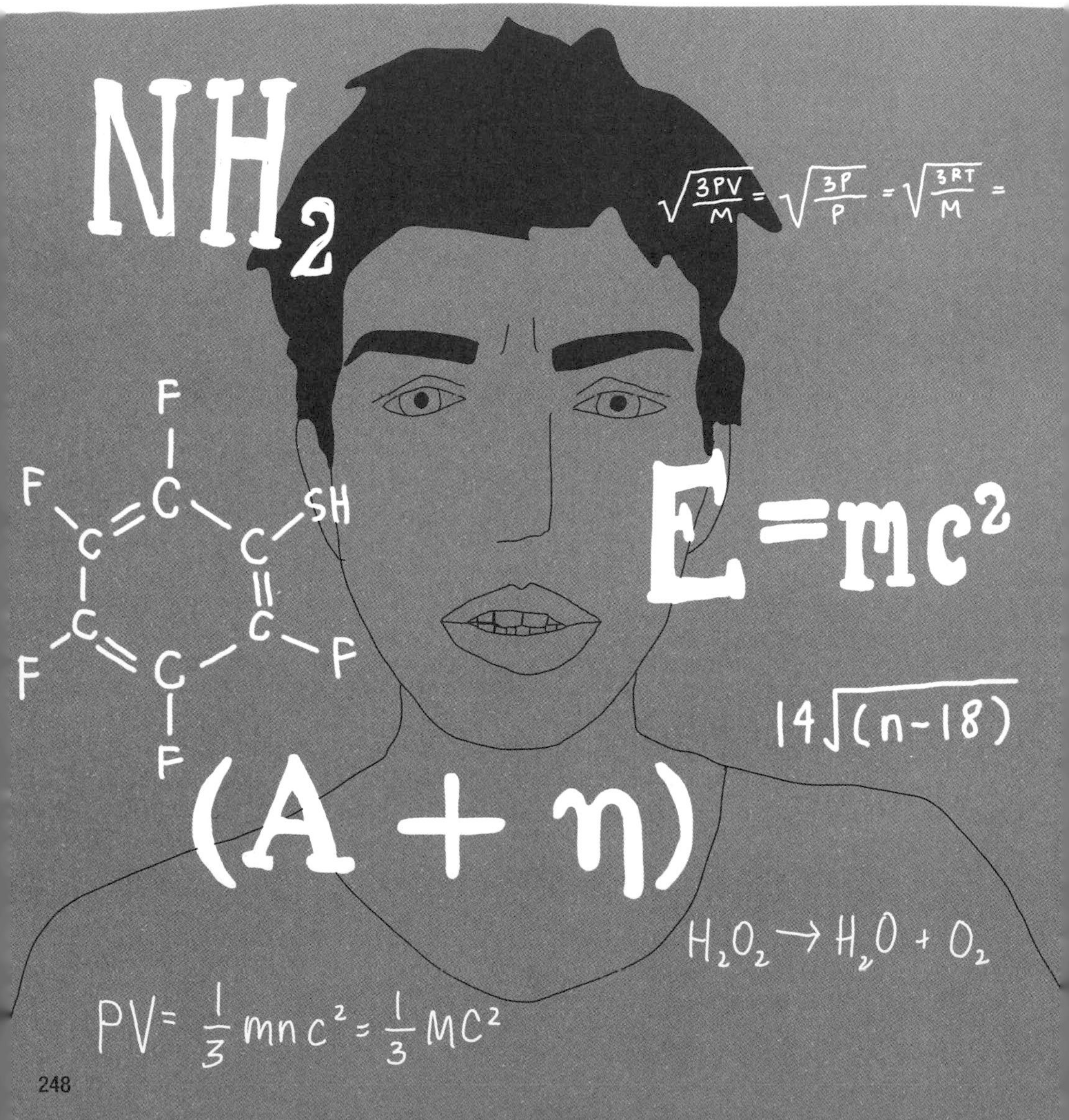
NH_2
$\sqrt{\frac{3PV}{M}} = \sqrt{\frac{3P}{P}} = \sqrt{\frac{3RT}{M}} =$
F, F, SH, F, F, F, C, C, C, C, C, C
$E=mc^2$
$14\sqrt{(n-18)}$
$(A+\eta)$
$H_2O_2 \rightarrow H_2O + O_2$
$PV = \frac{1}{3}mnc^2 = \frac{1}{3}MC^2$

I VOLUNTEERED AT A HOSPITAL, TAKING LUNCH ORDERS FOR CANCER PATIENTS WHO SAT ALL DAY IN BIG CHAIRS WITH NEEDLES IN THEIR ARMS, DRIPPING POISON IN A LITTLE AT A TIME.

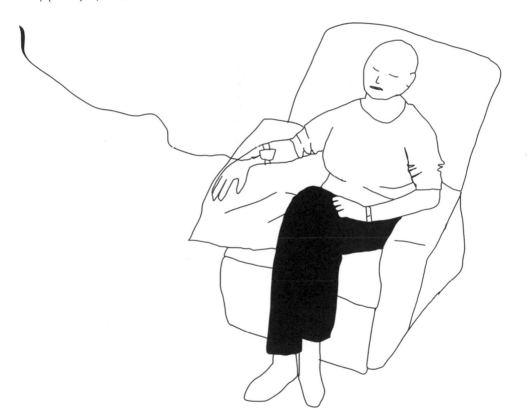

PERSPECTIVE CAN BE HARD TO COME BY WHEN YOU SPEND MOST OF YOUR TIME LICKING YOUR OWN WOUNDS.

THE WOMAN WITH MYELOMA WHO CALLED ME
ANNE HATHAWAY ALWAYS HAD THE TURKEY
SANDWICH.

A BEAUTIFUL BUSINESSWOMAN HAD THE
SALAD, NO CORN, DRESSING ON THE SIDE.

THERE CAN BE COMFORT
IN EASY DECISIONS.

I LEARNED MORE, ANXIOUS TO MAKE UP ALL THE TIME I'D SPENT HOVERING OVER BARROOM TOILETS, MY PANTS AT MY KNEES.

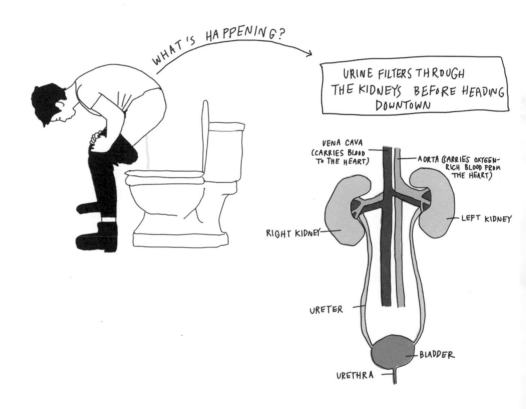

WHAT'S HAPPENING?

URINE FILTERS THROUGH THE KIDNEYS BEFORE HEADING DOWNTOWN

VENA CAVA (CARRIES BLOOD TO THE HEART)

AORTA (CARRIES OXYGEN-RICH BLOOD FROM THE HEART)

RIGHT KIDNEY

LEFT KIDNEY

URETER

BLADDER

URETHRA

I LEARNED TO RELATE TO IDEAS AND TO PEOPLE.

FLAGELLA
PILI
RIBOSOMES
PLASMID
CELL WALL
NUCLEOID
SLIME CAPSULE (ACTUALLY CALLED THAT)
CELL MEMBRANE
A PROKARYOTE CAN SURVIVE THE HARSHEST ENVIRONMENTS. DOUSE IT LIBERALLY WITH ANTI-BIOTICS AND IT WILL LEARN TO GROW DESPITE HUMAN INDUSTRY.
EACH ELEMENT OF THE ARCH-ITECTURE OF A CELL IS THE STUNNING CONSUMMATION OF MILLENIA OF DATA.

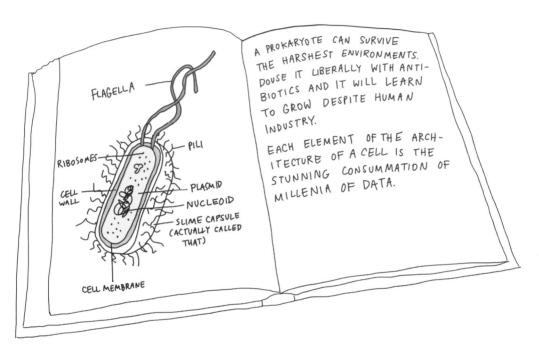

I FELT LIKE THAT, TOO.

I SAT IN CHURCH BASEMENTS. I TALKED ABOUT THE DRINKING. I TALKED ABOUT **THEM**.

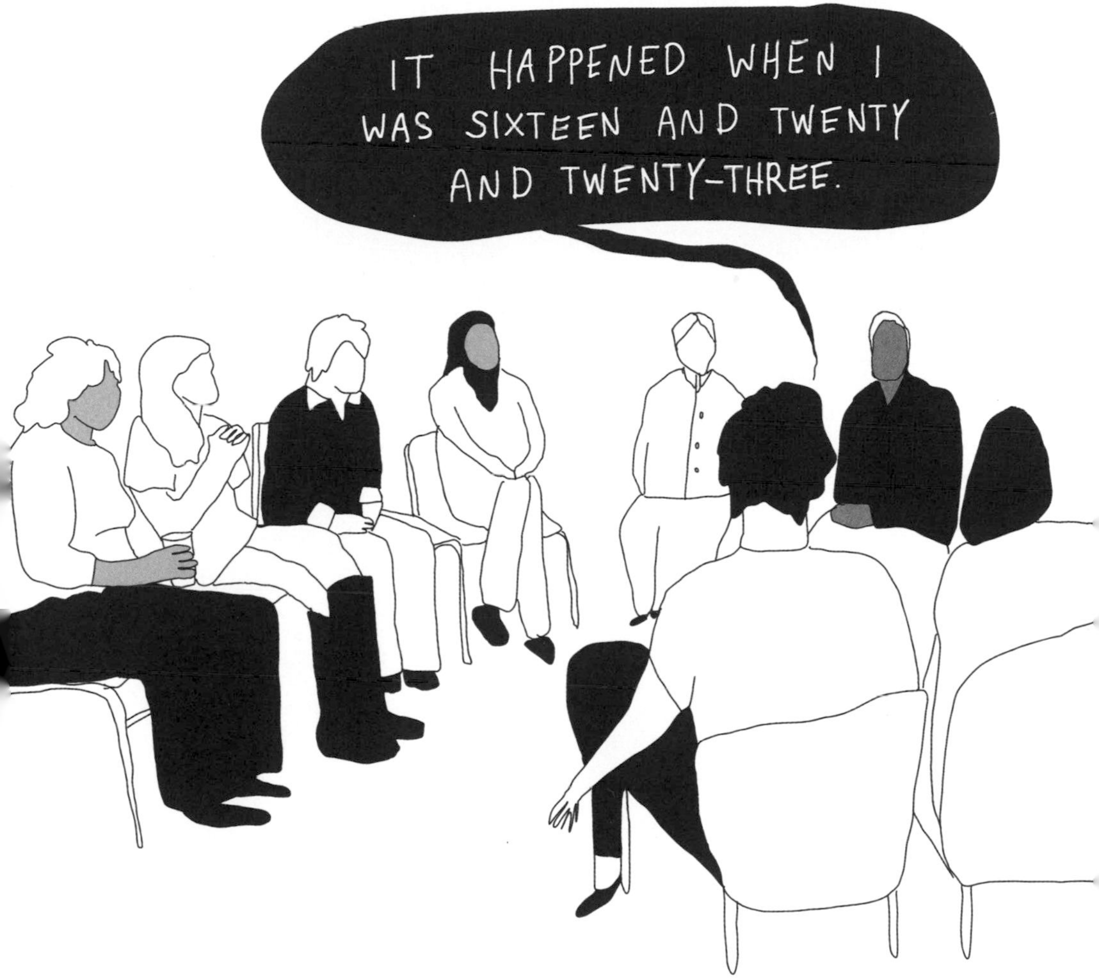
IT HAPPENED WHEN I WAS SIXTEEN AND TWENTY AND TWENTY-THREE.

THE WOMEN NODDED AND NODDED WITH THEIR JELLY NECKS.

THE MEN SKILLFULLY PRACTICED EMPATHY,
SHOCK, OR BOREDOM, AS IF THEIR HANDS
WERE SEPARATE FROM THE ONES THAT
ONCE WRAPPED AROUND MY NECK.

APATHY

INDIFFERENCE

DETACHMENT

DISREGARD

IT'S THE WHOLE STRUCTURE THAT
CHOKES.

I MET A POET. SHE HELPED ME WRITE LONG LISTS OF EVERYONE WHO HURT ME, AND WHO I HAD HURT. THEN I SHARED IT WITH HER. THAT WAS THE FIRST TIME I SAID MOST OF WHAT'S IN THIS BOOK OUT LOUD.

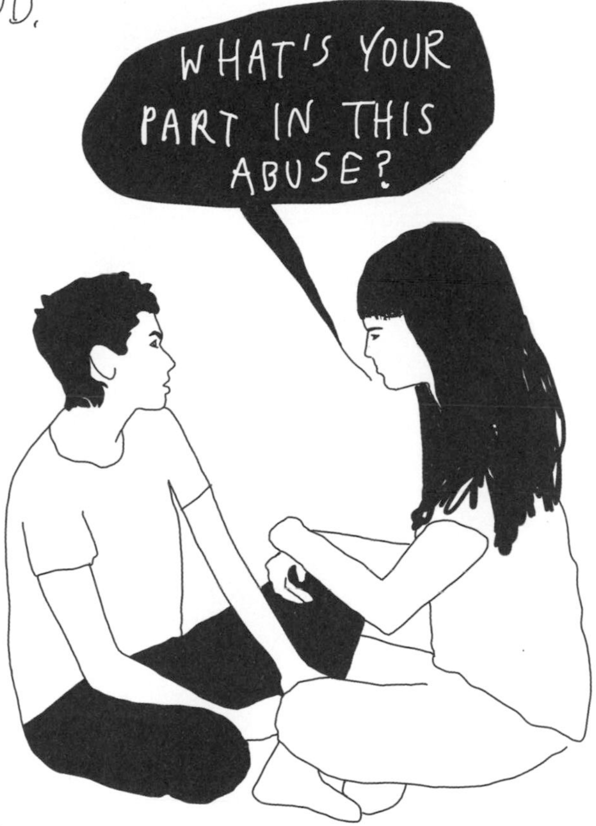
WHAT'S YOUR PART IN THIS ABUSE?

SHE ASKED SO MANY HARD QUESTIONS.

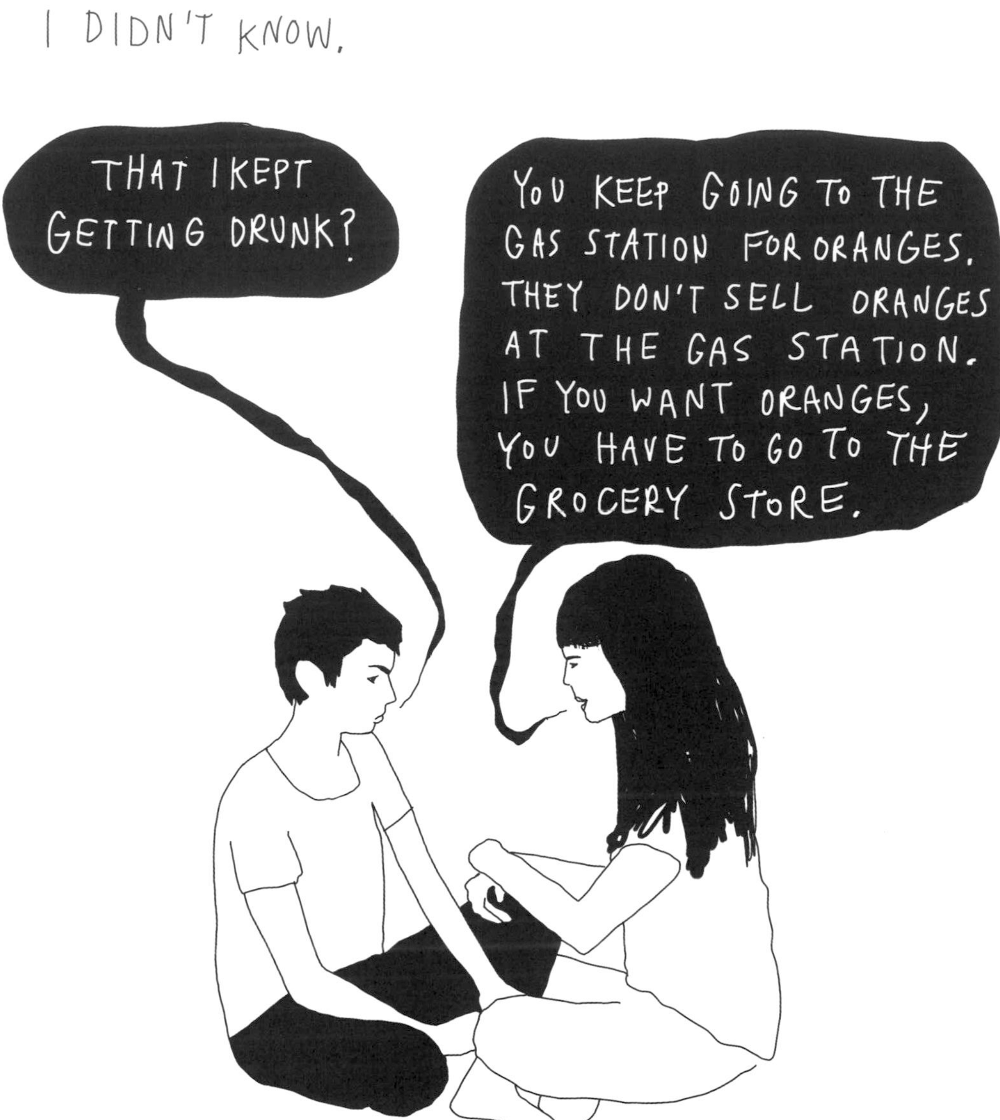
I DIDN'T KNOW.
THAT I KEPT GETTING DRUNK?
YOU KEEP GOING TO THE GAS STATION FOR ORANGES. THEY DON'T SELL ORANGES AT THE GAS STATION. IF YOU WANT ORANGES, YOU HAVE TO GO TO THE GROCERY STORE.

THIS MEANS YOU CAN'T ASK STRANGE MEN
IN BARS TO COME HOME WITH YOU AND
SEE YOU AND FIX YOU AND LOVE YOU.

THESE ARE GAS STATION BOYS, MEANT FOR
PUMPING, SPITTING, CURSING, OVERCHARGING,
STEALING SODA FROM THE COOLERS AND
CIGARETTES FROM THE WALLS.

WE'RE RARELY ALL VICTIM.
FOR A LONG TIME I THOUGHT RAPE
WAS SEX.

WHERE, EXACTLY, DO YOU DRAW THE LINE?

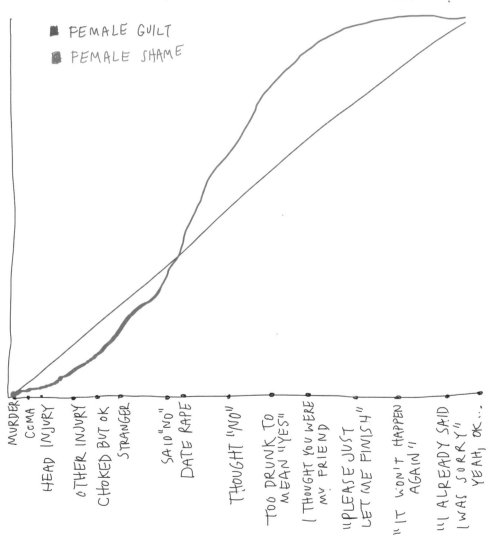

■ FEMALE GUILT
■ FEMALE SHAME

MURDER
COMA
HEAD INJURY
OTHER INJURY
CHOKED BUT OK
STRANGER
SAID "NO"
DATE RAPE
THOUGHT "NO"
TOO DRUNK TO MEAN "YES"
I THOUGHT YOU WERE MY FRIEND
"PLEASE JUST LET ME FINISH"
"IT WON'T HAPPEN AGAIN"
"I ALREADY SAID I WAS SORRY"
YEAH, OK...

ALL THE BAD THINGS CARVE YOUR INSIDES OUT.

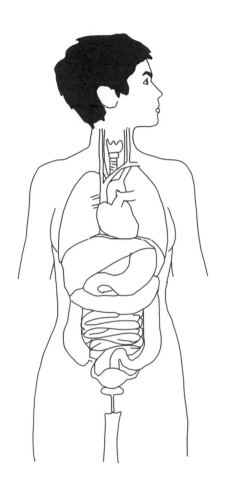

SLOWLY, I FILLED THAT SPACE UP WITH OTHER
THINGS.

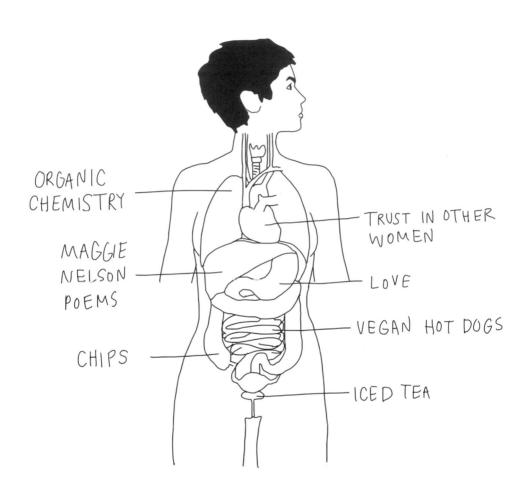

ORGANIC
CHEMISTRY

TRUST IN OTHER
WOMEN

MAGGIE
NELSON
POEMS

LOVE

VEGAN HOT DOGS

CHIPS

ICED TEA

TO ESCAPE THE STEELY VISE OF
ADDICTION IS TO BE REBORN.

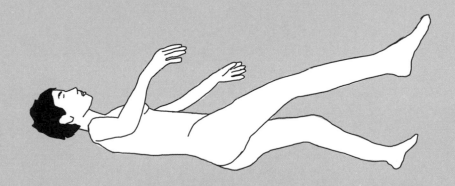

THE FIRST DAYS AND WEEKS ARE IMPOSSIBLY LONG. YOU GO OUTSIDE DURING THE DAY AND THINK:

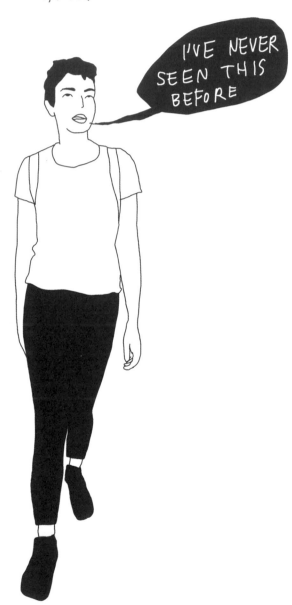

I'VE NEVER SEEN THIS BEFORE

EVERY EXPERIENCE FEELS NEW. YOU ARE NEITHER DRUNK NOR SWADDLED IN HANGOVER SMOG.

THEY CALL IT A PINK CLOUD.

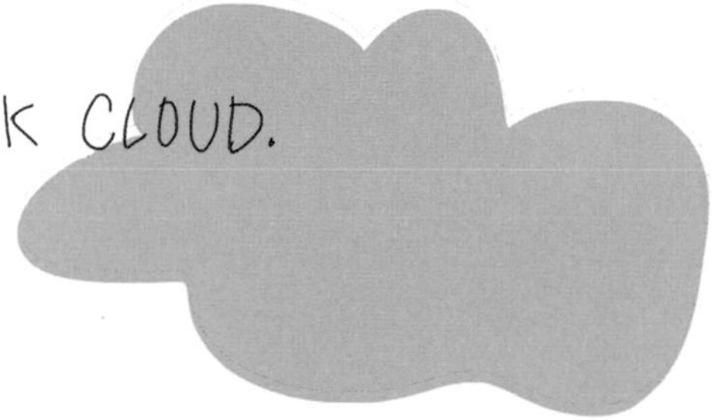

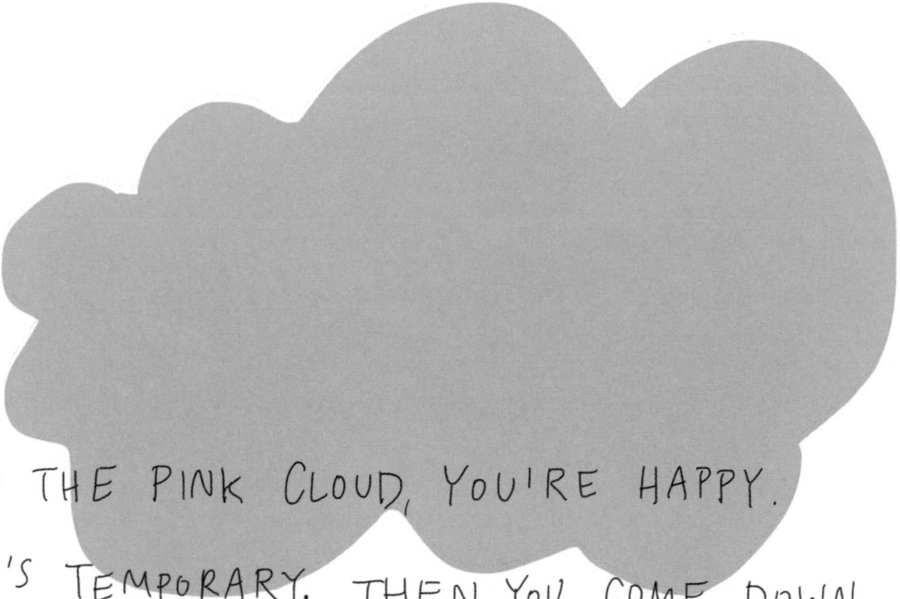

ON THE PINK CLOUD, YOU'RE HAPPY.

IT'S TEMPORARY. THEN YOU COME DOWN AND YOU'RE ANXIOUS AND DEPRESSED LIKE EVERYONE ELSE.

WHEN I FIRST GOT SOBER, I WORKED AS A PREP COOK AT A TACO STAND. I WAS TERRIFIED OF TALKING TO CUSTOMERS.

TURNS OUT IT'S NOT THAT HARD.

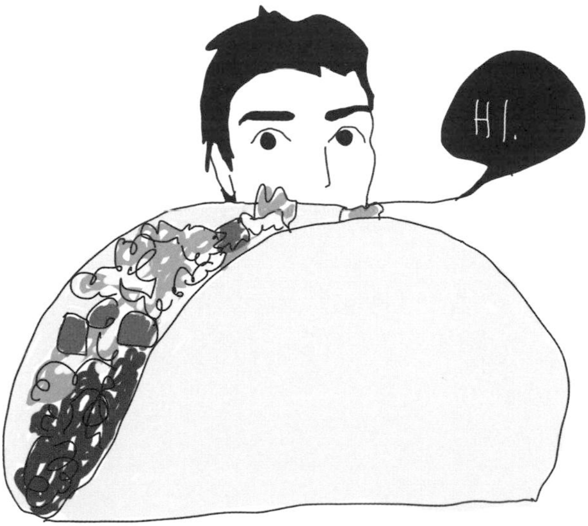
HI.

YOU LEARN HOW TO TALK TO PEOPLE.

I DRANK GALLONS OF DIET COKE A DAY.
I STAYED UP ALL NIGHT WATCHING TV.

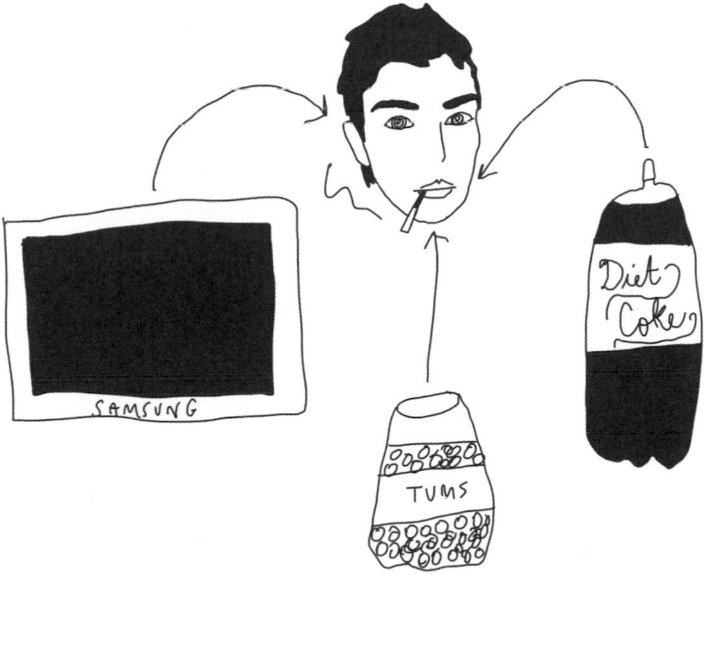
SAMSUNG
TUMS
Diet Coke

WHEN YOU GET SOBER, YOU'RE ALLOWED TO DO ANYTHING ELSE YOU WANT BESIDES DRINK OR DO DRUGS.

AS LONG AS YOU'RE SOBER, NOTHING ELSE MATTERS.

I TRIED TO IMAGINE WHO I COULD BE WHEN
EVERYTHING I'D EVER KNOWN ABOUT MYSELF
WAS STRIPPED AWAY, VOMITED UP, FLUSHED
DOWN, CIRCLING.

ANYTHING, ANYTHING.

THE STAGGERING WEIGHT OF POSSIBILITY
IS ALMOST UNBEARABLE.

MAYBE I'D ENJOY BICYCLING...

OR FEEDBACK...

OR YOGA...

IT WAS WOMEN WHO TRANSFORMED ME.

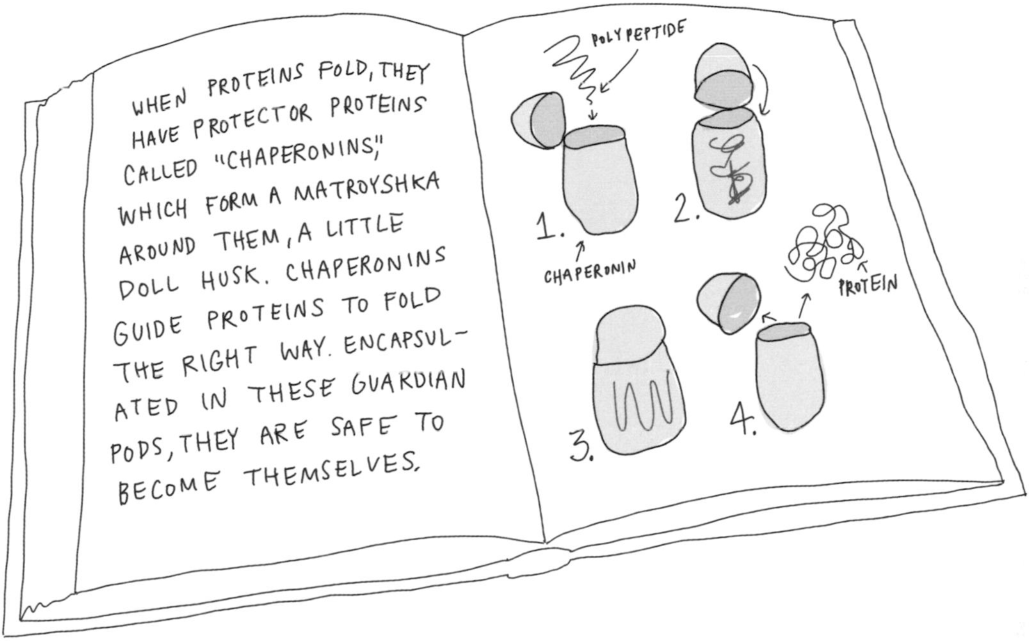
WHEN PROTEINS FOLD, THEY HAVE PROTECTOR PROTEINS CALLED "CHAPERONINS," WHICH FORM A MATROYSHKA AROUND THEM, A LITTLE DOLL HUSK. CHAPERONINS GUIDE PROTEINS TO FOLD THE RIGHT WAY. ENCAPSUL-ATED IN THESE GUARDIAN PODS, THEY ARE SAFE TO BECOME THEMSELVES.
POLYPEPTIDE
1.
CHAPERONIN
2.
PROTEIN
3.
4.

WHAT I LEARNED IN SCHOOL CONTINUED TO MIRROR MY LIFE.

WOMEN PROTECTED ME WHILE I BECAME
SOMETHING ELSE. WHO KNEW WHAT.

CAIT

KATE

JORDAN

KELLEY

AND EMILY AND TIFFANY AND BEX AND
RAFAELA AND DANA AND SARAH
AND ADRIANA AND CATHY AND LIZ...

THEY CRACKED THE SHELL OPEN.
OOZING ERUPTION, HOLY ROT AND
LIQUID GRIEF.

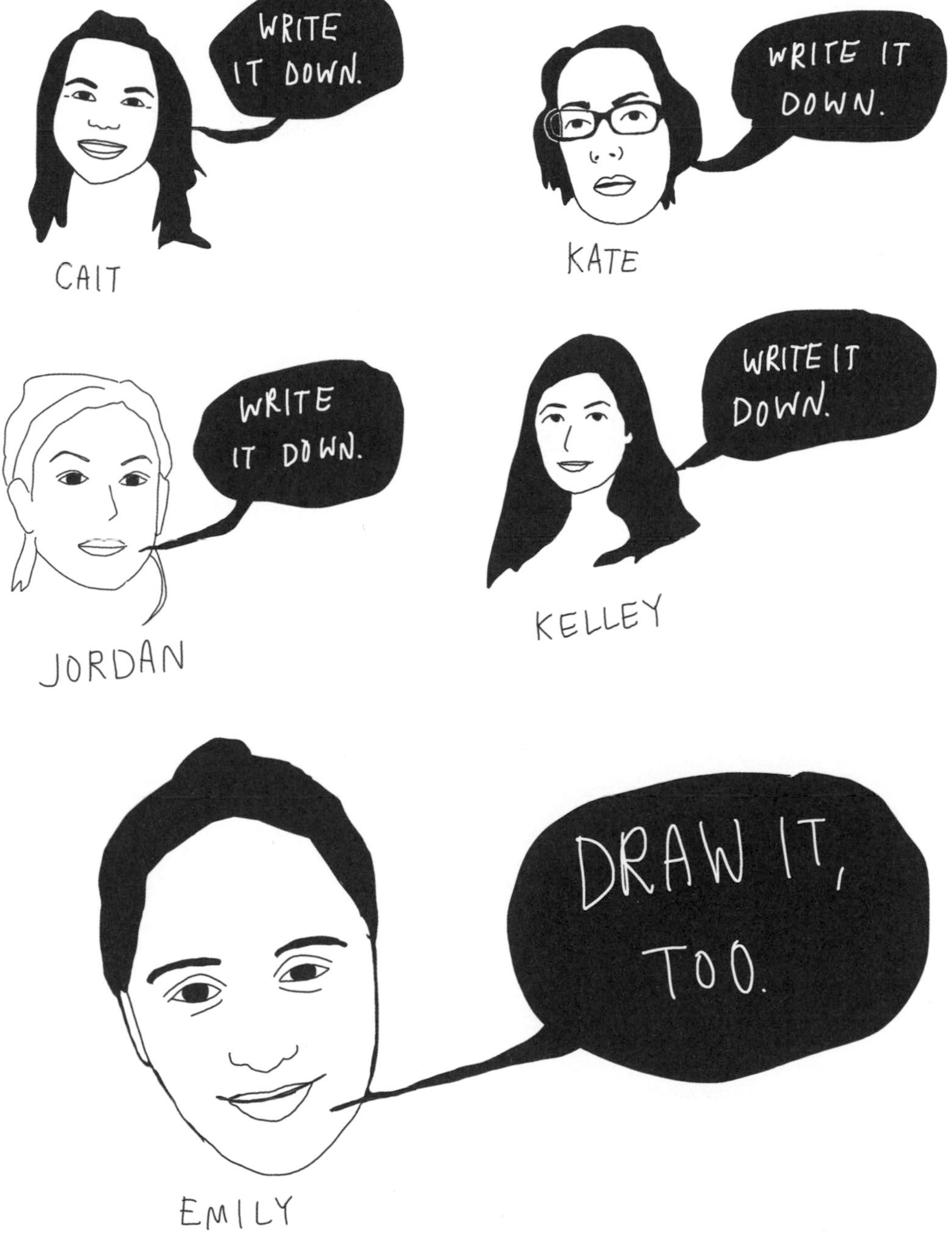
WRITE IT DOWN.
CAIT
WRITE IT DOWN.
KATE
WRITE IT DOWN.
JORDAN
WRITE IT DOWN.
KELLEY
DRAW IT, TOO.
EMILY

THE MONSTERS ARE MINE. THEY SNEAK UP BEHIND ME AND WHISPER THINGS IN MY EAR.

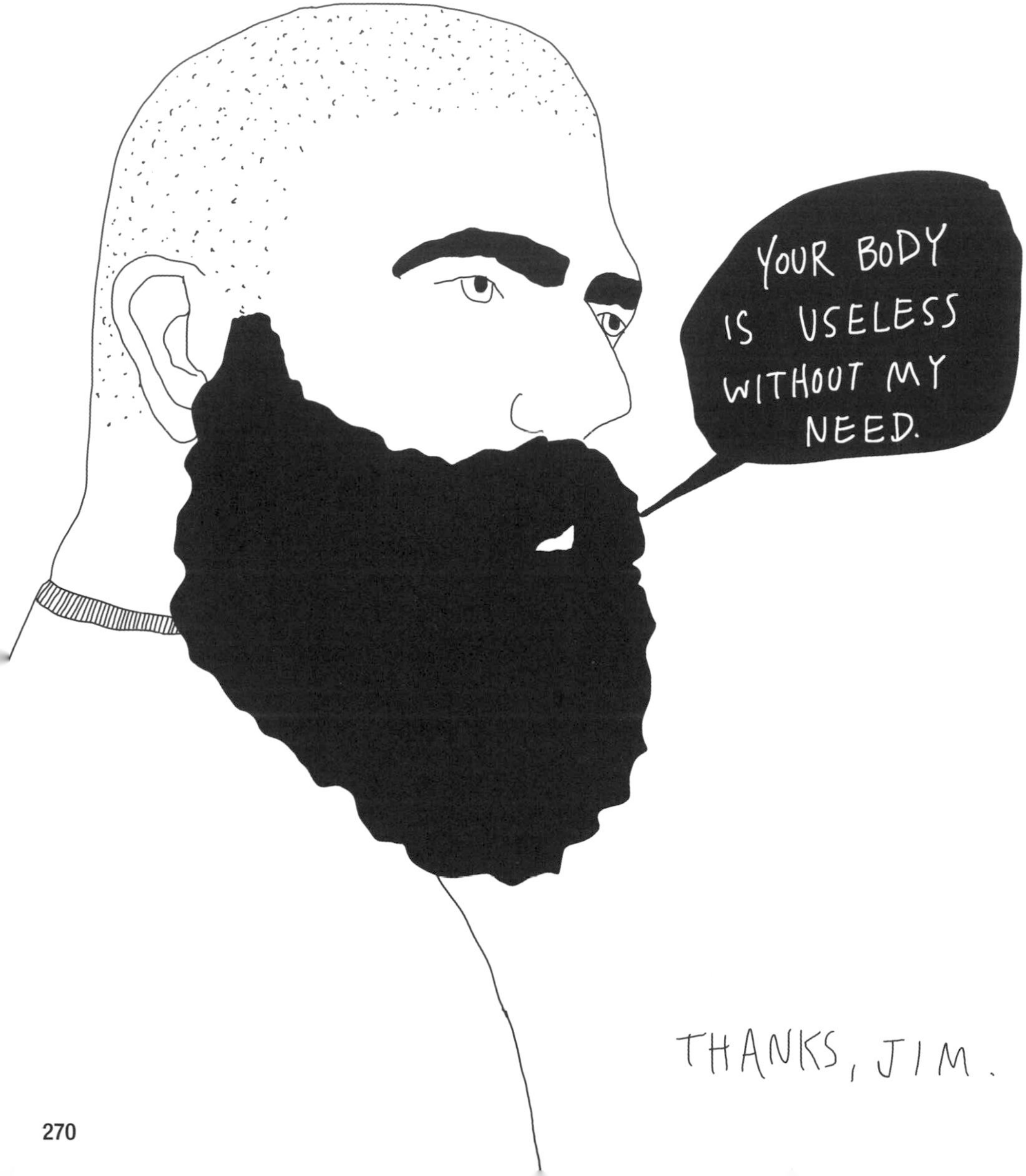
YOUR BODY IS USELESS WITHOUT MY NEED.

THANKS, JIM.

BUT IT'S DIFFERENT NOW...
MY BODY CREATED HER BODY. I GREW
HER FROM SEED TO SPITFIRE INSIDE
A BELLY FURNACE OF SLOW BOILING
RAGE AND A LITTLE BIT OF FORGIVENESS.

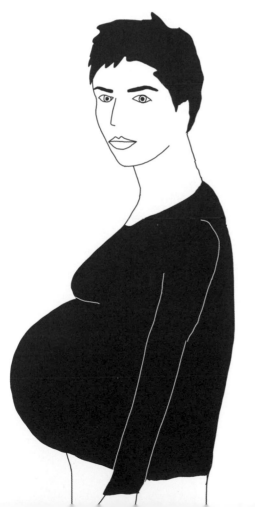

I'M
STILL
WORKING
ON
FORGIVENESS.

IT'S SLOW WORK.

THE REINVENTION OF MY BODY WAS A GIFT.
FINALLY, SOMETHING USEFUL.

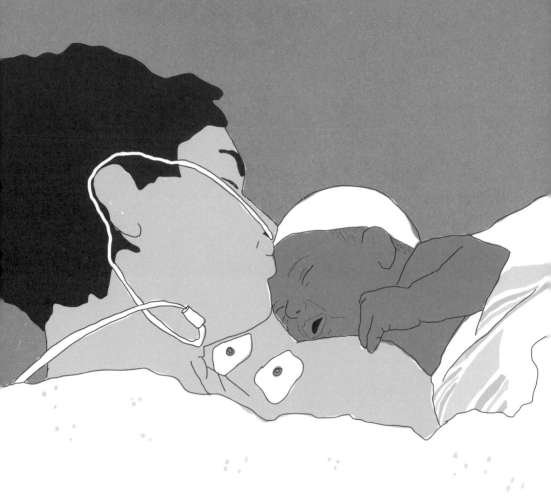

TO FEED SOMETHING, GROW SOMETHING. IT CAN BE INDIRECT.

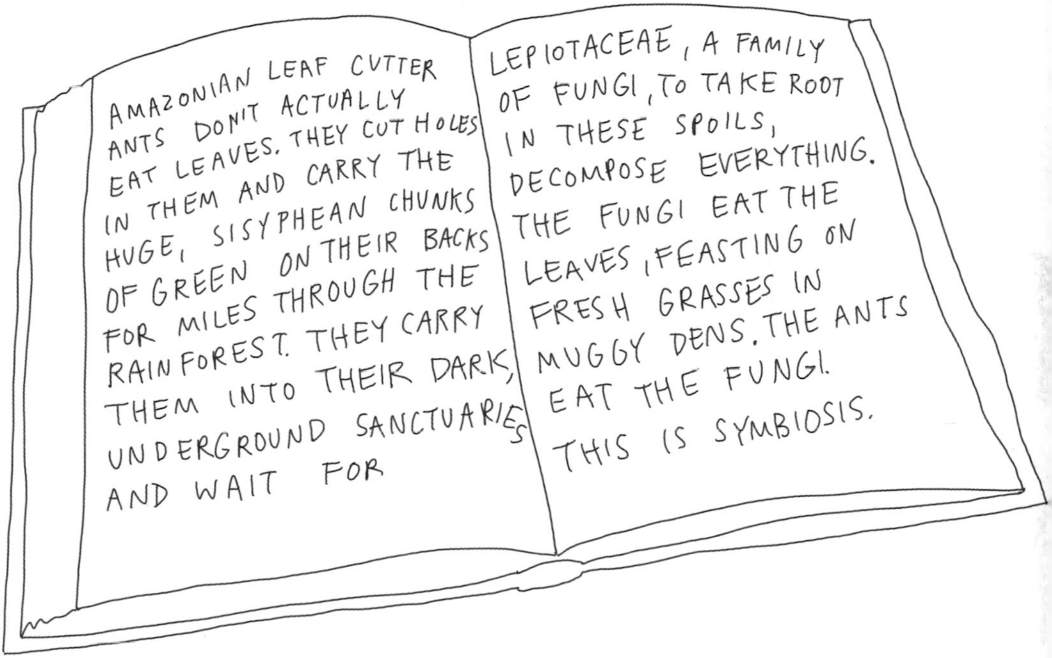
AMAZONIAN LEAF CUTTER
ANTS DON'T ACTUALLY
EAT LEAVES. THEY CUT HOLES
IN THEM AND CARRY THE
HUGE, SISYPHEAN CHUNKS
OF GREEN ON THEIR BACKS
FOR MILES THROUGH THE
RAINFOREST. THEY CARRY
THEM INTO THEIR DARK,
UNDERGROUND SANCTUARIES
AND WAIT FOR
LEPIOTACEAE, A FAMILY
OF FUNGI, TO TAKE ROOT
IN THESE SPOILS,
DECOMPOSE EVERYTHING.
THE FUNGI EAT THE
LEAVES, FEASTING ON
FRESH GRASSES IN
MUGGY DENS. THE ANTS
EAT THE FUNGI.
THIS IS SYMBIOSIS.

SO IT IS WITH MOTHERS AND DAUGHTERS.

THERE IS NO GREATER OBSTACLE
THAN VULNERABILITY, BUT THIS IS
WHAT'S REQUIRED.

THE SHAME OF PREVIOUS
DIGRESSIONS WILL POISON YOU
IF YOU LET IT.

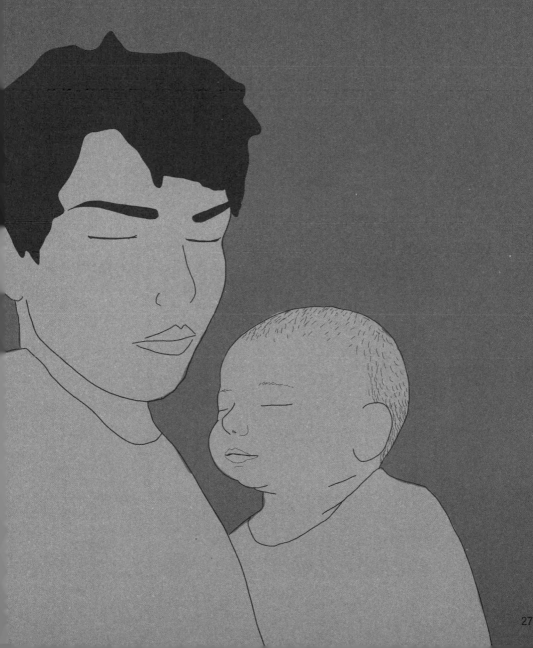

IN ALL OF THESE SEXUAL
TRANSACTIONS, I LOST.

I FORGOT TO TELL YOU ABOUT MARCUS,
WHO TOLD ME ONE MORNING,
LAUGHING, THAT HE LET A DOG LICK
DORITO DUST OFF HIS HAND BEFORE
FINGERING ME.

OR SAM, WHO GRABBED MY CROTCH
REPEATEDLY DURING A MOVIE IN A
ROOM FULL OF CLASSMATES.

OR ROB, WHO KEPT FUCKING ME
AFTER I TOLD HIM HOW MUCH
IT HURT.

DO YOU SEE IT NOW? THESE ARE NOT ISOLATED INCIDENTS.

THE YES OR NO OF CONSENT IS NOT WHAT SEPARATES MUTUAL DESIRE FROM PREDATION.

THE GAME IS RIGGED—ALL THE POWER IS CONCENTRATED ON THE OTHER SIDE.

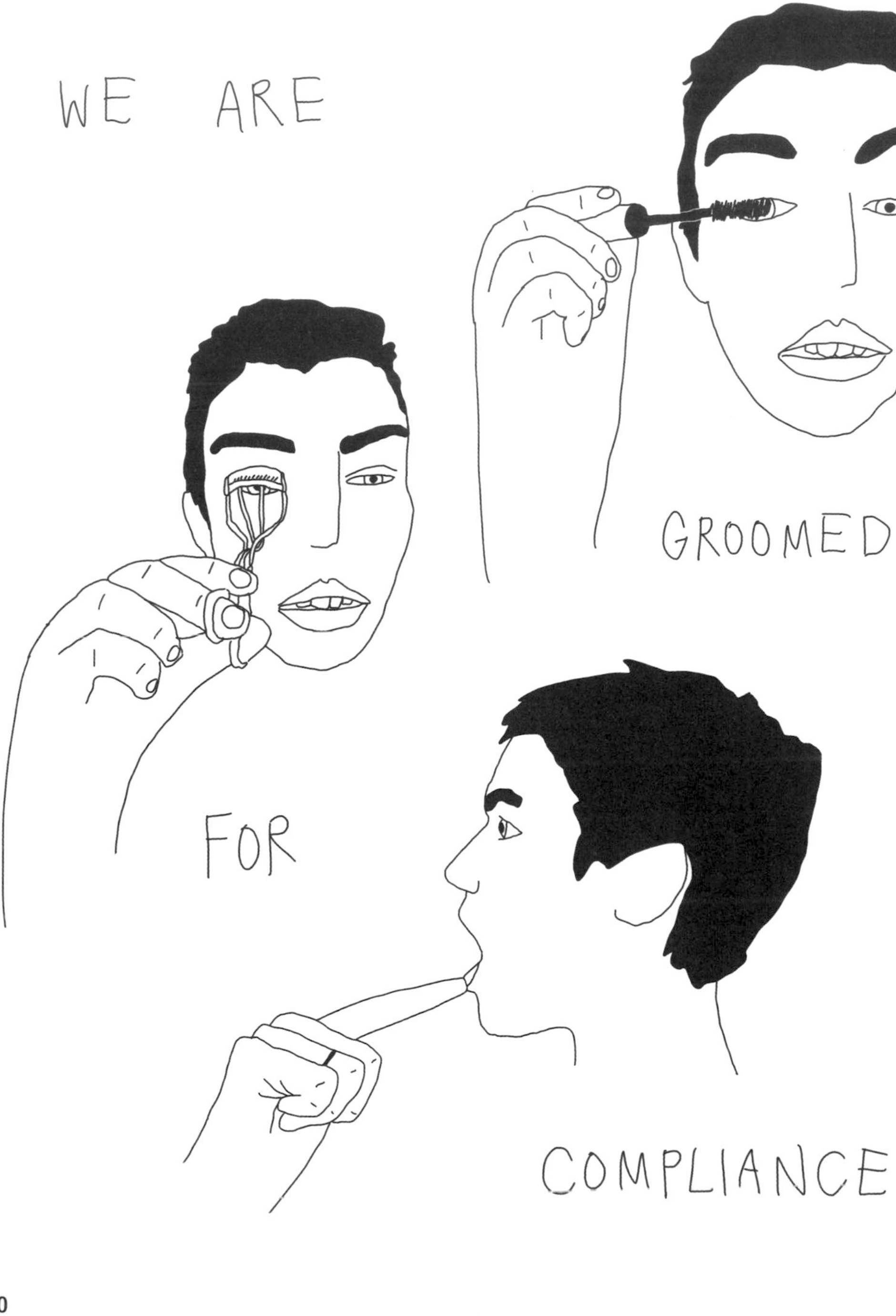
WE ARE
GROOMED
FOR
COMPLIANCE

DEFINING SEXUAL ABUSE AS RAPE AND
RAPE AS LACK OF CONSENT HURTS WOMEN. IT
BELIES MANY OF OUR SEXUAL EXPERIENCES;
THE UGLY, CONFUSING ONES THAT WE DON'T
THINK WE LIKED, BUT COULDN'T QUITE
UNDERSTAND. THE ONES WITH MEN AND
BOYS WE KNEW. THE ONES THAT JUST
FELT BAD. THE ONES THAT TAKE
MONTHS OR YEARS TO UNRAVEL.

NO ONE HAS TO ASK IF WE
WANT TO BE DESIRABLE~WE DO!

FEMALE   DESIRABILITY IS THE
ILLUSION OF POWER.

WHEN JOHN WALKED ME INTO
THAT BACKYARD, I FELT LUCKY
HE CHOSE ME.

WE ARE TOLD, OVER AND OVER AGAIN, EVERY DAY, THAT WE'RE LYING. WE'RE BEING DRAMATIC. WE'RE OVERLY EMOTIONAL, AGGRESSIVE, ATTENTION-SEEKING WHORES. WE HAVE AGENDAS.

WE WOMEN DOUBT THE
REALITY OF OUR OWN
EXPERIENCES.

THE CULTURE THAT DEFINES
US GRABS ONTO THE QUESTION
OF CONSENT SO THAT ALL
OTHER ABUSES OF POWER ARE
STILL AT PLAY.

IT'S OUR STORIES AGAINST
THEIRS.

Our trauma
becomes
our shame

SHAME
IS AN
INSTRUMENT
OF
OPPRESSION.